cries unheard

cries
unheard

Why Children Kill:
The Story of Mary Bell

Gitta
Sereny

Metropolitan Books
Henry Holt and Company
New York

Metropolitan Books
Henry Holt and Company, Inc.
Publishers since 1866
115 West 18th Street
New York, New York 10011

Metropolitan Books is an imprint of
Henry Holt and Company, Inc.

Library of Congress Cataloging-in-Publication Data

Sereny, Gitta.
Cries unheard : why children kill: the story of Mary Bell / Gitta Sereny.
p.   cm.
Originally published: MacMillan Ltd, London, 1998.
ISBN 0-8050-6067-7 (alk. paper)
1. Bell, Mary Flora.   2. Murderers—England—Newcastle upon Tyne—Biography.
3. Juvenile homicide—England—Newcastle upon Tyne.   4. Juvenile delinquents—
England—Newcastle upon Tyne.   I. Title.
HV6535.E53N487   1999
364. 15'23'0942876—dc21   98-33216
                                                                          CIP

Henry Holt books are available for special
promotions and premiums. For details contact:
Director, Special Markets.

First American Edition 1999

Designed by Paula Russell Szafranski

Printed in the United States of America
All first editions are printed on acid-free paper.

1   3   5   7   9   10   8   6   4   2

To Lee Hindley Chadwick,

the teacher every child should have

Pray thee, take care, that tak'st my booke in hand,
To reade it well: that is, to understand.

—Ben Jonson, To the Reader, *Epigrammes*

Contents

Contents

Acknowledgments

I have only a few people I must thank for their help, for only a few knew of this project.

First and foremost, my gratitude and admiration go to my publishers, Macmillan, for their courage in accepting to do this controversial book the way it had to be done. Ian Chapman's and Peter Straus's unfailing enthusiasm, and from the moment she arrived as editor in chief, Claire Alexander's shining intelligence and warmth smoothed my rocky path till the end.

Perhaps I should thank them above all for giving me Liz Jobey to edit *Cries Unheard*. I don't know what to laud most: her understanding of my purposes and principles, her endless willingness to share my problems, or, quite simply, her extraordinary talent—thank you, Liz. For this American edition I was fortunate to have the editorial help of Sara Bershtel and Riva Hocherman, who have made the book more accessible to US readers.

Rachel Calder is my agent and I hardly know how to express my gratitude to her and to Marina Cianfanelli for their unflinching support at all hours of day and night. I feel very lucky to have them at my side.

I have also had throughout this difficult period the advice and counsel of Allan Levy, QC, who knows more about children and the law than almost anyone I know; he too has become a friend.

I think I can say the same about the people whose names I'm not allowed to mention: the two probation officers who speak in the book who, much more than supervising Mary, gave her warmth and encouragement at some of her worst moments; the couple who worked at Red Bank when Mary was there and who shared with me so much of their knowledge; the live-wire prison governor whose sense of humor and passion for human beings made the hours we spent together pass like minutes; and finally "Chammy," whom Mary remembers with love and I thank with affection.

I thank Dan Bar-On and Virginia Wilking for lending me their wisdom, Professor Guy Benoit for giving me so generously of his time, Angela and Mel Marvin in New York and Hannerl and Fritz Molden in Alpbach in the Tyrol for being our dear friends. And thank you to Melani Lewis, who looks after our home—I don't think I could have managed without you.

A special thanks, of course, to my son, Chris, and his wife, Elaine, for their unfailing encouragement and their love.

It seems to me that instead of yet again, in yet another book, thanking my husband, Don, he and I can thank each other that this book is the one coming out in our fifty-first year together.

My last word of thank you is to my daughter, Mandy, who, though several years younger than Mary, was fully aware of her ever since my early research thirty years ago. With this book now, she has immeasurably helped me, with her energy, her intelligence and understanding for what I am trying to do, and last but by no means least, her compassion for Mary.

Preface

M any, perhaps most of you, who first turn to this page will not know what happened in the lovely old northern city of Newcastle upon Tyne in the spring of 1968. You have forgotten, you were too young, perhaps not even born, or lived in other countries that had their own problems in the late sixties.

Briefly then: In the course of nine weeks two small boys, aged three and four, were found dead. Some months later, in December 1968, two children, both girls, were tried for their murder; Norma Bell, age thirteen, was acquitted; Mary Bell (no relation) was found guilty and sentenced to life imprisonment. The case caused an uproar, the trial was widely publicized, and Mary Bell was demonized across the country as the "bad seed," inherently evil. I have already written one book about the tragedy that happened in Newcastle. In *The Case of Mary Bell*, published in 1972, I reported on the facts as the police found them and as they were presented in the Newcastle court in the nine-day trial, which I attended. I told as much as I had found out from family, friends, and teachers about the child who was now detained for life.

The trial I watched then gave me serious misgivings about a judicial system that exposed young children to bewildering adult court proceedings and considered irrelevant their childhood and motivations for their crime. It seemed very obvious to me that there were elements of Mary Bell's story that were either unknown or hidden from the court. And as she grew up in detention and was repeatedly mentioned in the press, I found myself hoping that one day Mary Bell and I could talk. By finding out not from others but from her what happened to and in her during her childhood, I felt we might take a step toward understanding what internal and external pressures can lead young children to commit serious crime and murder. And by talking to her about her years in detention and her life since her release, I thought we might discover what effect imprisonment has on children growing into adulthood and how the way they are dealt with equips them for the future.

So I have been hoping for many years to write the book I am presenting to you here, in which Mary Bell, an exceptionally intelligent child at eleven, released from detention in 1980 when she was twenty-three, and now forty-one years old, speaks to us. She tells us what she did and what she felt, what was done to her and also for her, and what she became. She describes the months leading up to the two killings, her friendship with her neighbour and co-accused, Norma Bell, and their fantasy life together, which was to result in the tragic death of the two toddlers. She recalls the voices of all the learned men at her trial who, for what seemed to her like years, spoke in incomprehensible terms, and she re-creates her horrifying certainty that they would send her to the gallows.

Mary Bell takes us through the twelve years of her detention, the first five (from age eleven to sixteen) in a secure unit* where—for most of that time the only girl with twenty-odd boys—she had no psychiatric care but where she found in the headmaster, a former naval officer, the first honorable adult she could respect and love. At sixteen, however, despite her mentor's pleadings, the system prevailed that demands that juveniles upon reaching sixteen must serve their punishment in prison,

---

*A secure unit is a locked educational establishment for a small number of youngsters held for serious offenses.

and she was removed from the emotional security and academic structure to which she had responded and was sent to a maximum-security women's prison. In our conversations, she talks of battling the institution, rebelling against its rules, using sex to manipulate her environment, in the process losing virtually everything she had gained in the previous five years.

Finally, she speaks about the moment when, like most adolescents sent to adult penal institutions, she emerged into the conditional freedom of a "Schedule One" released prisoner on license (subject to recall on reoffending), as an emotionally and sexually confused twenty-three-year-old in psychological chaos. She recounts then the years since her release, back in the sway of her mother, to whom she has always been tied in a mutual bond of love and hate. In 1984 she had a child, and with the support of her probation officer, Patricia Royston,* fought for the right to keep it. For the first time in her life she felt total love and through the child gained a purpose and a framework for her life. But with her love for her child also came a new and agonizing awareness of conscience that intensified her inner chaos.

In the final section of the book, I return to her early childhood; as we had talked during those many months, the early years had begun to unravel from her mind, which had blocked the confrontation with them for so long. Here she speaks, with excruciating difficulty, about the sexual abuse she was subjected to as a small child upon her mother's direction and in her presence; and in fits and starts over months she searches her memory for the events in her life from the age of eight to the day before she turned eleven, when she killed Martin Brown. She eventually talks haltingly and despairingly about those fifteen minutes on May 25, 1968, at the end of which the four-year-old child was dead, and about the following nine weeks leading up to the killing (I write about both acts only as far as seems necessary to me) of three-year-old Brian Howe.

*All names of people in the public sector who have spoken for this book have been changed.

There are ways and ways of writing about events. One can report on them, describe them, quote the witnesses, the victims, and sometimes the heroes of them. And although, being human, one can never hope to be entirely objective, one must do all this with a large measure of detachment. On another level of the narrative, one must also comment on the events, evaluate their significance, and, if one can, put them into the context of life as we live it, measure them against the rules and principles that by our choice govern our existence.

From all these perspectives, this book has been extraordinarily difficult to write. It is one thing to write, as I have done elsewhere, about men or women who, at least partly as a consequence of unhappy childhoods, became iniquitous adults. It is very different to write about a person who has committed, not once but twice, the worst of iniquities when she was a child but who against all expectations and entirely without the props we have come to take for granted—trauma therapy and psychiatric treatment—appears to have become a morally aware adult.

The difficulty throughout has been to believe. It has demanded on my part a continuous review and renewal of an act of faith in the possibility of metamorphosis; that is, in the integrity of an adult who I knew at one point to have been a pathologically disturbed child, and for years afterwards an alarmingly manipulative adolescent. I was tempted time and again to look at a human being as if she were two people: the child and the adult. And this is, of course, not so: she is one person, as we all are, from the moment we are born to the moment we die. So when I finally realized I must deny myself that consolation, I had to accept that the mystery of transformation starts with the question of what, consciously or unconsciously, can be put *into* a child by another human being to produce actions entirely incompatible with the intrinsic goodness of the human being as born. Is it only a parent who can affect a child in this way, or can it be caused by the behavior of other adults close to the child's life? Would a child, for example, respond as powerfully if he or she were emotionally deprived or abused by foster parents or carers? And in a question brought up not only by this case but by the more recent one of the two ten-year-old boys who killed the toddler James Bulger in Liverpool in 1993 and the spate of child murders in

America, is it possible for children to cause such moral breakdown in one another?

The second question raised by Mary's story is how can a child react in ways that are entirely unthinkable for that same human being as an adult? And therefore what is it, inside the human mind, the nerves, the heart, that first destroys or paralyzes and that can then re-create or reinstate morality and goodness? These are huge questions to seek answers to through the examination of one child's life, but that was and remains my hope.

So the book I am presenting to you here needs to be read with all these matters in mind. There has not been a day in the two years I have worked on it when the families of the two little boys—who would now have been thirty-five and thirty-four years old—have not been in my mind. And there has not been a day, either, when I have not asked myself whether writing this book was the right thing to do: for those who would publish it, for those who would read it, for Mary Bell, from whom, with great difficulty and agonizingly for her, I extracted her life, for the families of the children she killed, and for her own family, above all her child, who now *is* her life.

There is no indiscretion in my mentioning her child, for the media, both British and foreign, who have pursued Mary Bell for years just as assiduously as she has tried to avoid them, have always known of the child's existence. It is indeed to protect the interest of the child that she was made a ward of court almost as of the time when she was born. No one—and this of course includes me—may identify her or write anything that would lead to her being identified.

Consequently, the child, whom Mary loves with every fiber of her being and to whom she is determined to give a happy childhood, does not appear in the book and yet she is, I think, essentially its raison d'être and even its justification. And why this is so, I hope the book will convey.

It is quite rare that a writer can remain with a story for more than half her life, rarer still to be given the opportunity after thirty years to apply it toward a larger purpose. It might seem at first that the story itself, as a critique of the outdated nature of judicial systems in the second half of the twentieth century, *is* the purpose. But while judicial reform as it applies to children is of deep concern to many of us, and Mary Bell's story, with its many tragic elements, can indeed justify a book, my purpose is wider.

It is—and I have no hesitation in saying so—to *use* Mary and her story. The understanding we gain from her memories of her childhood, of her trial, and of her punishment needs to influence the judicial reforms that are essential in countries where growing child criminality is resulting in increasingly punitive measures. But it must also make us look very closely at the nature of the communication we maintain with our children, both within the family and in society as a whole. If I have titled this book *Cries Unheard*, it is because I feel that here lies the explanation for those unknown thousands of children who are in prisons in Europe and America for crimes they committed, not because of what they are, but because of what they were made to be when, early in their childhood, their cries for help remained unheard.

◆ ◆ ◆

This book is about an English child, but Mary Bell could just as easily have been Belgian, French, German, Norwegian, or Japanese—young children of all these nationalities have been hurt as Mary was and have in turn hurt others. Indeed, Mary Bell could just as well have been an American child, one of some 12,300 who are prosecuted each year in US state courts as adults for serious crimes; or more specifically, one of the 910 children between the ages of nine and fifteen who have been tried for murder in America in this last decade of the twentieth century.

In large parts of America, owning a gun or knowing how to use one appears to be a must. This is not, so far, a problem in Europe, where people do hunt animals but strict gun controls are in place; in Britain, as is well known, even the police do not ordinarily carry guns. Nonetheless, in Europe as in the United States, the cases of murder by children over the past thirty years have shown a profoundly troubling degree of desperation, rage, or sexual disturbance, and they are increasing, albeit slowly. When they do occur, antediluvian superstitions are voiced about the children who commit these acts, and almost frenzied demonstrations of anger are displayed against them, whatever their age.

Americans will recognize this reaction from the terrible events of the past few years. Between October 1997 and May 1998, twelve schoolboys in states as far afield as Kentucky, Arkansas, Washington, Mississippi, California, Pennsylvania, and Oregon killed seven adults—their parents and teachers—and sixteen children, wounding forty-nine others, mostly in school-yard shootings. These acts are a minimal part of America's monumental juvenile crime epidemic—1992 figures for delinquency cases, including all categories of offenses, reached a staggering 743,673. By now they will be considerably larger.

However, the sudden surge of fatal acts of violence by and against children and the concern over their easy access to guns has focused public attention on the social phenomenon of children killing children. On the one hand, the killings have resulted in tabloid hysteria identical to that in Britain, in which such children are described as "born to kill" and "natural born killers," and have provoked demands by the Republican majority in the House of Representatives for a Juvenile Crime Control Bill that would require minors who commit violent acts to be tried and in some cases even penalized as adults, irrespective of their age. On the positive side, these cases have renewed the long-smoldering debate on increasing gun controls—good in itself but I fear part of a deceptive and escapist interpretation of child violence.

And indeed, many enlightened Americans are beginning to ask serious questions about why children are becoming so violent. While agreeing that older juveniles should be treated severely if they offend, indeed as adults at the top end of the spectrum, they say the suggestion by some state officials and members of Congress that eleven- to fourteen-year-olds be tried as adults is outrageous. Have we any idea, psychiatrists, lawyers, and social commentators ask, why children kill? Do they even understand that death is final? And to what extent is their exposure to sex and violence in society, to what extent, indeed, are people in their immediate environment such as parents or parent substitutes, to blame?

There are many more questions for us to ask, I think, than even those I outlined earlier: Why do some abused or pressured children reach the "breaking point," as I call it, while others who are similarly traumatized do not? (It seems to me quite simply that some children are stronger and can withstand terrible pressures for longer than others: eleven years in the case of Mary Bell; eleven and thirteen, I suspect, in that of the two boys who killed in Jonesboro. As I have explained, before reaching that breaking point, all these children do cry out for help, not only with their voices but also with their body language and actions. In the case of the boys in Jonesboro, their behavior became ever more conspicuous over the week preceding the crime, and there, just as in Newcastle in 1968, the boys announced their intention loud and clear, even going so far as to write in large letters on the dusty side of a school bus that they were going to kill.) How far do we believe that a person, child or adult, who has committed a crime and been convicted and punished and served his or her time has paid for that crime? Do we believe in rehabilitation? Do we believe a released prisoner—especially one who remains on probation and bound by special regulations for life—has regained his or her rights to a normal working and family life? Above all, do we believe in redemption?

I wrote *Cries Unheard* in a search for the answers to these questions, basing my exploration on the life and the experience of one such child, whom, with her adult consent, I quite deliberately present as an example or symbol of many others. The central account here, the story as Mary Bell told it to me (almost all of which I was able to subsequently check against the knowledge of others), is intended not as biographical literature but as a document that might serve as an incentive to all of us who care about children's well-being. If Mary's painful disclosures of a suffering childhood and an appallingly mismanaged adolescence in detention succeed in prompting us—whether as parents, neighbors, social workers, teachers, judges and lawyers, police, or government officials—to detect children's distress, however well hidden, we might one day be able to prevent them from offending instead of inappropriately prosecuting and punishing them when they do.

cries unheard

Prologue

Today, Newcastle is relatively rich. There are new industries, new factories, new housing. Above all there are jobs. Not enough for everyone but infinitely more than there were in 1968, when it was a decaying city brought to the brink of economic ruin by the dying mining and shipbuilding industries. Newcastle then had the doubtful distinction of the highest crime record, highest rate of alcoholism, and consistently some of the highest unemployment figures of any city in Britain. And nowhere was this more evident than in Scotswood, an area of about half a square mile on a hillside three miles west of the city center, whose streets of run-down council houses, for which the tenants paid £2.4s a week, stretched in long terraces down toward the industrial wasteland along the River Tyne. About 17,000 people lived there then, and the unemployment rate was well over 50 percent.

The people of Newcastle are and always were a friendly lot, even though their reactions can be explosive and their vocabulary, in fun as well as anger, pungent. They speak "Geordie," a dialect that is virtually incomprehensible to outsiders: "home," for instance, is "hyem"; "my wife" is "wor lass"; "pretty" is "canny," but then canny can also mean "many"—as in "a canny few." The language, one might deduce, is intimate rather than logical: when a child thinks it is going to be punished, it speaks of getting "wrong" and the word "me" (he asked me), is always replaced by "us." But however bewildering the dialect, warmth and laughter are innate, and however quick the slap in retribution of naughtiness, there is a lot of love for children now, just as there was in those bad times during the late sixties.

In Scotswood, two long roads, Whitehouse Road and, below it, St. Margaret's Road, curved around the hill with a few small streets and crescents crossing them. Almost everybody in the neighborhood knew everyone else then, and they were tolerant of one another—or so it seemed to strangers. There was one small shop at the end of St. Margaret's Road, variously referred to as "Dixon's" or "Davy's," and nearby the Woodlands Crescent Nursery—a preschool—and its sandpit (sandbox), both of which were to play a part in the terrible events that spring.

The houses on the two main residential streets overlooked the railway lines, an industrial plant belonging to the arms manufacturer Vickers Armstrong, a large and straggly wasteground the children who played there called the "Tin Lizzie," and, beyond it, the main thoroughfare of Scotswood Road, the river, and, in the distance—an excursion away—the city.

Because the inhabitants knew one another and were therefore immediately aware of strangers, children were very free: free, even when quite young, to play in the street, roam the neighborhood, drop in on relatives (extended families were the norm), take the dogs around the corner into the small greenery of Hodkin Park, slip over to the nursery sandpit, or buy chips or a lollipop or an ice on a stick at Davy's. Despite the financial pressures of that period and the resentments they bred against authority—which only appeared either to threaten or, equally resented, to dispense charity—it was a friendly and a sociable life: endless cups of tea, chats over fences, or indeed, an almost southern European effect, from window to window, and, at mealtimes, calls through open doors, very swiftly obeyed, for the children to come in, "John, Ian, Kate, Brian, May, Martin—yer tea."

On May 25, 1968, Martin Brown was four years and two months

old. He was a sturdy little boy, blond and blue-eyed with a round mischievous face. He lived in a two-story red-brick terraced house at 140 St. Margaret's Road with his mother, June, whom he called "Mam," his father, whom he called "Georgie," and his one-year-old sister, Linda, with whom he shared a bedroom. June's older sister, Rita Finlay, lived with her five children a few doors away, at No. 112. June worked, so her mother took care of Linda during the week, and Rita had Martin; he called her "Fita."

That Saturday morning, as always on weekends when his parents slept in, Martin brought up some milk and a piece of bread for the baby, carefully holding the cup while she chewed on the rusk. "He always did that," June told me later. "I'd hear him coax her, 'Come on, Linda, drink yer milk.'" After that he dressed the baby and brought her in to June before having his own breakfast in the kitchen. "Sugar Pops," June said, "them were his favorites. He got his anorak—I was in the scullery—I heard him call, 'I'm away, Mam. Ta-ra, Georgie!' That was the last I saw or heard of him."

It is unimaginable, isn't it? But it really was the last June Brown saw or heard of her Martin. Other people saw him that morning: he stood for a while watching two workmen from the Newcastle Electricity Board disconnecting power cables from derelict houses in St. Margaret's Road—they gave him a cookie. Rita saw him when he woke her up late that morning; he cried when she told him off. "My mam came by while he cried and she gave him an egg on toast. I don't remember seeing him go then—we didn't think to watch when they came and went, you know—all the kids are all over the place; Martin, everybody was his friend."

His father, Georgie, was the next to see him, when Martin shot in just before 3:00 p.m. when Dixon's shop opened to get some money off him for his lollipop. Dixon's son Wilson scolded him because he had his fingers in his mouth and his hands were filthy when he handed him the lollipop. Rita saw him once more when he came in and asked for bread and butter. She told him the butter was for tea, he could have margarine. "He was angry," she told me. "'I'm not coming to your house bloody no more,' he said. 'I won't come again ...' But he couldn't stay mad for long," she said. " 'Oh, don't be like that, Fita,' he said, and then he went and that was the last I saw of him."

At 3:30 P.M., not more than twenty minutes after Wilson Dixon had sold Martin his lollipop, three schoolboys, foraging in the derelict houses for wood to build a pigeon cote, found him in a back bedroom of 85 St. Margaret's Road. He was lying on his back on the rubble-covered floor with his arms outstretched and blood and saliva coming from his mouth. There was no sign of a struggle or a fall, his clothing was not torn or damaged, there were no broken bones, nor, aside from a trivial bruise on his knee, were there any external injuries. Among the rubble there were some empty pill bottles that would briefly make the police think of accidental poisoning. Gordon Collinson, one of the Electricity Board workmen, ran to call an ambulance; John Hall, one of the others, gave Martin the kiss of life. There was shouting all along the street. Rita and June came running, the ambulance arrived in minutes. "They tried to revive him," June told me. "I watched them, but I knew." Martin was dead, they believed for months, because of an inexplicable accident. "All I wanted," June said, "was to lie down and die too . . ."

Nine weeks later, on July 31, 1968, Brian Howe was three years and four months old. He had fine, curly light-blond hair, a pink-and-white complexion, and was not yet grown out of babyhood. He lived at 64 Whitehouse Road with his father, Eric, his seven-year-old brother, Norman, his fourteen-year-old sister, Pat, his older brother, Albert, who was courting a girl called Irene, and his black-and-white dog, Lassie. His mother had left them when he was only a year and a half, but between Albert and Pat, who kept house for the family when she was not at school, Irene, who often stayed with them, and Rita Finlay, whose three-year-old son, John, was his best friend, Brian was well cared for. "I loved little Brian," Rita said, "different like from the way I loved our Martin, but I loved him. I loved Pat too—she was always over here. I used to go and wake her up on my way to taking John to the nursery and then I'd take Brian, too . . ."

That morning, though, it was school holidays and nobody had answered when Rita knocked on the door of number 64. "I said to myself, Pat must be sleeping in. The woman at the nursery asked where Brian was."

By lunchtime, however, Brian and John had met up and were out playing. When Rita went looking for them about 1:30 P.M., she found them sitting on the ground watching workmen pull down one of the old houses in St. Margaret's Road. "I went mad," she told me. "I screamed at the men and said didn't they know better . . . than to let them sit there where they could get hurt? And then I hit the lads so hard, one after the other, my hands were stinging. I put John to bed and I gave Brian some biscuits and . . . told him to tell Pat he'd been to the old buildings but she was not to hit him because I'd already hit them. That's the last I saw him."

We don't know whether Brian went home because Pat, knowing that Irene was in the house, had gone into the city with friends. When she came back at 3:20 and asked after Brian, Irene said he was "playing out the back" and indeed a number of children later said they'd seen him playing in the street off and on in the early afternoon with his brother, Norman, and two little girls on bikes whom they all knew. Lassie, they all said, was with him. Nobody was worried. All the kids were always all over the place, and anyway, Lassie was with him. It wasn't until about 5:00 P.M., when Pat had prepared tea, that she went out into the street calling his name. Mary Bell, who was eleven, the eldest of four children, and lived with her father, Billy, and her mother, Betty, at 70 Whitehouse Road, was sitting on the doorstep of number 66 talking to Maxine Savage—it was Maxine's younger sister, Margaret, whom Pat Howe had been out with that day. Pat asked May, which is what everybody called Mary, whether she'd seen Brian. She said she hadn't but she would go with Pat to look for him. Norma Bell, Mary's best friend, who lived with her parents and ten siblings at number 68, strolled along for a while, too. They looked for Brian at Davy's shop, a magnet for all the kids, and then down the hill at the Vickers Armstrong parking lot, another major attraction. Then they went back up on the railway bridge, from where they could see all over the Tin Lizzie, but they didn't see any children.

Mary Bell suggested Brian could be playing behind or between "the blocks" down there (huge concrete slabs), but Norma, who knew Brian well as she often baby-sat John for Rita, said, "Oh no, he never goes there," and Pat didn't think he would go either, not alone he wouldn't. Pat decided they'd have one more look, in Hodkin Park and along the streets, and if they hadn't found him by seven o'clock, she was going to call the police.

The police, using searchlights, found Brian at 11:10 that night. "We'd all been looking for him for hours," Rita told me. "Hundreds of us, it seemed, till it got dark. It was very hot that night. I think everybody was still up when we heard the police cars rushing down with all the sirens going. People called to each other out of their doors . . . I don't know who knew first—it went from street to street and house to house."

Mary Bell, who was a light sleeper, came downstairs at 11:30 and joined her father, who was standing outside the front door watching the commotion in the street. "What's going on, then?" she asked.

"They've found Brian Howe," Billy Bell said, "over on the Tin Lizzie."

"Oh," said Mary.

Brian was lying on the ground between two concrete blocks on the Tin Lizzie. His left arm was stretched out from his body and his hand was black with dirt. Lying on the grass nearby was a pair of scissors with one blade broken and the other bent back. His body, fully dressed and most of it apparently unharmed, was covered with a carpet of the long grass and purple weeds that grew all over the Tin Lizzie. His lips were blue, however, and there were scratch marks on his nose, traces of bloodstained froth at his mouth, and—no possibility of an accident here—pressure marks and scratches on both sides of his neck. Later they would find other, small, inexplicable injuries. He was dead.

It was strange how these dead toddlers' families—perhaps in a self-protective reaction—remembered them later as so mature. "Lots of people loved Martin," June said a long time afterwards. "He was that kind of lad—grown people could talk to him, like." And, "I miss him," Eric Howe said of little Brian. "I miss him so; he was my life. He was only a bairn, but we used to talk like, you know, really talk. I think of nothing but him. It's destroyed us," he said, tears running down his cheeks, "we're not a family any longer."

"We talk . . . ," said Pat, her face tight. She was sixteen by then, married, with a baby son, but the larger house in a pleasant street the council had moved them to showed no color, was almost sterile in its sadness. "But we don't say anything."

In writing about human beings whose actions have brought havoc into the lives of others, one can never forget the pain that they have caused and the bitterness that inevitably remains in those they have hurt, however long ago it may have been. When writing about such tragedies, writers, searching for explanations for them and for the deficiencies in the system that contributed to them, forget at their peril that there are wounds that can never heal. This is an awesome cloud over an undertaking such as this. Not one word Mary Bell has ever said to me, not one word I have written, can be interpreted as an excuse for what she did.

◆　◆　◆

The first time I saw Mary Bell was on December 5, 1968, in the Moot Hall in Newcastle upon Tyne, where the trial was held and where she, then eleven, and her friend Norma Bell, two years older, stood accused of the murder of the two little boys. She was small then—a lot smaller than the older girl—and exceptionally pretty, with short, dark hair and intensely blue eyes. I had seen her several more times in the following years while she was still a child and in detention. Twenty-five years later, in November 1995, we sat down together in a small room in a probation office in the north of England to discuss the feasibility of this book.

She was very nervous that day. Her hands were ice-cold and a trifle moist, there was a sheen of sweat on her face, and her voice was—not hoarse but husky. She was slim, as I thought she would be, unsuitably dressed for the time of year in something beige, chiffony, in a colored flowery pattern, with dark wool stockings and clunky shoes ("I get everything from Oxfam," she said, almost at once), and her long hair was curly, shiny, and smelled of shampoo. She in fact altogether smelled not of scent but of some quite delicate soap: as I would notice often later and as all kinds of people under whose care she has been over the years confirmed to me, she has constant baths; she is very clean. I put my arms around her and held her for a moment, an entirely impulsive gesture, not at all because it was expected or even appropriate but because I suddenly felt like it.

She had been part of my memory for so long, and the reason for our meeting now was so complex, her motivations so mixed, my feelings about the ethics of this project so ambivalent, that the tension in the small office lent to us by her probation officer, Pat Royston, was tangible, almost electric.

Of course, at the time of her trial in 1968, I couldn't speak to Mary, nor, I know now, was she, traumatized by the events and the formal trial, able to "see" anyone. "It was a blur," she would tell me later. "It was all like a swirl . . . I couldn't understand a lot of the words . . . Someone told me, 'That's the jury,' and I said, 'What's that?' and they said, 'The people who decide what's going to happen to you,' and I said, 'How?' and they said, 'Shh.' And then they said the judge was the man in the big chair in a red robe and that he was the most important man, so I always turned to him to answer when anybody asked me anything. And then my solicitor said that was rude and I must look straight in the face of people who asked me questions—that I had to try and 'make a good impression.' And my mother, who sat right behind me, kept hissing, 'Stop fidgeting!' every time I moved, and she slapped me with her flat hand on the back of my head or right between my shoulders each time I did it again and it hurt, but I couldn't not do it"—she suddenly smiled at me, interrupting her stream of words—"my bum got tired."

It was one of the things I would come to recognize during the months we talked: in her vocabulary, her tone of voice, she sounds entirely like a child when she talks about herself as a child—sometimes discursively, as imaginative children do, but more often intelligently, sometimes with humor but most often with despair. The reason for this, I would come to understand, is not that it was a reaction to searching her memory, nor in any way is it playacting. (Nor, I hasten to add, is it a symptom, as some psychiatrists have conjectured, of a split personality.) It is, I believe, because this is someone who has not had a childhood and who speaks as the child she never was but within herself still is, or needs to be. Her "childness"—not childishness—finally came to be less surprising than those times when she was exactly what she is: a mature and thinking adult in deep conflict with herself.

After the trial, at the end of which Norma was acquitted and Mary found guilty of manslaughter and sentenced to detention for life, I spent months in Newcastle investigating the background of the trial and the disposition of her case and, with the help of some of her family, tracing as far as they could or would assist me in doing so, the events of her childhood—her first ten years with her mother, Betty Bell.

Mary was born on May 26, 1957, when Betty was seventeen. Ten months later, in March 1958, Betty, then two months pregnant with her second child, married twenty-one-year-old Billy Bell, whom she had met a few months earlier. In September 1966, by which time Billy and Betty Bell had had three children together, Mary's birth was re-registered under Billy Bell's name. This is a comparatively rare procedure that can replace formal adoption and provides the child with a birth certificate in the mother's husband's name, canceling out the original certificate in which the father's name would have been blank.

I couldn't know at the time of the trial what Mary's relatives (her aunts and uncles, her "dad," Billy Bell, and her fragile grandmother, Mrs. McC.),* all dazed and bewildered by the tragedy, would eventually

*In order to protect living family members, I do not use last names unless they have already been made public.

bring themselves to tell me about Betty's rejection of Mary. "Take the thing away from me!" Betty Bell had screamed when they had tried to put the newborn baby into her arms. And in the first four years of Mary's life her mother had tried repeatedly to rid herself of this unwanted child. Time and again she attempted to hand her over to relatives and, twice, even to strangers. Four times she tried to kill her. On three occasions her eldest sister, Cath, and Cath's husband, Jack, were so concerned they asked either to adopt Mary or at least to be allowed to care for her until she finished school. What I did not know until, with enormous difficulty, Mary told me last year, was that between the ages of four and eight her mother, then a prostitute, had exposed her to one of the worst cases of child sexual abuse I have ever encountered. Her brother, eighteen months younger than Mary, would have been too young to understand or articulate it, and I am certain that none of her relatives had any awareness of this part of Mary's early life.

In 1968, neither the Newcastle social services, education, or health authorities, the police, nor, most important, any of the psychiatrists who examined the eleven-year-old prior to the trial (and thus eventually no one in the court) knew anything at all about Mary's childhood. This almost total disregard of her background left a large question mark in my mind about the opinion of two court-appointed psychiatrists even before I knew the extent of her troubles. They, no doubt for want of a better explanation, labeled her with that catchall diagnosis (considered highly questionable by most specialists when applied to children) of "a psychopath."

Thus labeled, Mary was easily described by the prosecutor as "vicious," "cruel," "terrifying"; even the judge was to allow the word "wicked" to slip into one of his perorations. Was it surprising that the media, not so much creating as responding to the tone set by the court and to the public outrage and fear, called Mary "a freak of nature," "evil born," and (no doubt after the popular book and the film in the fifties) a "bad seed"?

But I couldn't believe this: even in my first year of research the fact that somehow or other Mary's mother's pathology had to have been the cause of the unbalancing of Mary's mind long before she killed the little boys became clear to me, and this conviction underpinned all my writings about her and about the case. Two long articles in the *Daily Telegraph Magazine* in December 1969 were followed two years later by my book *The Case of Mary Bell*, which recorded the police investigation of the case, parts of the trial verbatim, and as much as I was allowed to disclose about the first years of Mary's detention. Given that the subject of both articles and the book was a child, and her relatives were living, these writings were of course subject to many legal limitations. But the articles and the book would open many doors to me and enable me to follow Mary's life and, when it appeared useful, comment on it throughout the twelve years she was detained.

Mary's case, and her life since her release in 1980, has raised an extreme and, to her, deeply disturbing amount of media interest. Given how interested I have been myself in her for thirty years, I cannot blame my colleagues in the media. She was and is exceptional, with an exceptional life and exceptional gifts for expression. I never wrote about her after her release and never passed on, to colleagues or even to friends, information I had about her whereabouts and circumstances. I thought she would need years of readjustment and felt she should be enabled to live in anonymity for a long time. But I also believed for many years that if anyone could ever help us one day to understand, firstly, what can bring a young child to the point of murder, and second, what needs to or can be done with and for such children, then with that strange intelligence of hers which I assumed would endure, Mary would be able to. I always thought the day would come when she herself, without outside pressure, would want to tell her story.

It began to happen, oddly enough, in the autumn of 1995, on the night of the launch party in London for my book about Albert Speer, when Hilary Rubinstein, who had been my agent for *The Case of Mary Bell*, asked me quietly whether I might still be interested in writing about Mary. The next morning he told me that Mary's mother had died the previous January and that this might be the time for Mary to find a way of telling her story. Since her release she had received several offers of grotesque sums of money from both British and foreign magazines for her story (a German magazine offered £250,000), all of which she had refused. Rubinstein had first been asked to represent her interests in 1983, when her then partner, who could see his future paved with gold, had persuaded her to have a stab at writing herself about her life. But though she has a distinct gift for words and had produced a draft of a hundred pages that a publisher thought with professional help could be made into a book, the project was abandoned because the conditions could not be agreed.

Rubinstein believed that Mary might now be ready to try again. He had spoken at length with her probation officer and her solicitor, who together, he said, had rescued her from many setbacks, helped her to cut loose from that first relationship, and shielded her from the media for the past fourteen years. He had suggested to them, and subsequently to Mary herself, that if what she was thinking of now was a serious book, she should meet with me. After some persuasion she had agreed to do so. "She is quite extraordinarily distrustful," he said, "oddly enough, particularly of you." I did not think that odd. No one had exposed Mary or, of course, her mother, as I had done. If anything surprised me, it was her willingness now, comparatively soon after her mother's death, to meet me at all.

"For my mother you were the devil, you know," Mary said almost the moment we sat down in that small room in the probation office. "She said you'd written that book full of lies; that you went through rubbish bins to find the dirt on people; that you had accosted my five-year-old cousin, my Auntie Cath's boy, for information about her; that you'd called her a prostitute. She said she went to all the bookstores in Newcastle and turned your book around so people wouldn't look at it. Oh, she hated you, I think to the day she died. And, well, I was just a kid, wasn't I? So for years I believed her."

When had her mother first warned her against me? I asked.

"Oh, I remember that very well," she said. "That was long before she told me about the book. It was at that inquiry . . . you know . . . about that housemaster. Do you remember? You came over to talk to me."

We had, in fact, met face to face twice before the day she mentioned, but she had forgotten. Early in 1970, shortly after the *Daily Telegraph Magazine* had published my articles, and again a few months later, the Home Office had allowed me to go to Red Bank, the special unit where Mary had been sent after being sentenced, to see her and meet the unit's staff. Both times I chatted briefly with her, as one does with children, about her artwork, her writing, and what sports she liked most (swimming).

She had been at Red Bank for sixteen months when, in June 1970, then just thirteen, she accused a housemaster of sexually molesting her. The inquiry she was now referring to was held to determine whether there was a case to answer. I had stepped over to chat with her that day during a break—we talked about a young woman teacher I had been told she particularly liked—not because I wanted to know anything (that would have been unthinkable) but because, incomprehensibly, she had been left sitting on her own and looked lost. I will write more later of the housemaster episode, but in 1995, when we met again, I was surprised to hear that she could recall our chat of so many years earlier. She told me, in fact, that she had only put all the pieces together after her release, when she had seen a photograph of me on the jacket of my book.

"That day I had no idea who you were," she said. "But my mother was there and saw you talk to me. And she ran over and screamed at me: I was not to, not to, *not to talk to you, ever.* She was always angry, but that time she was . . . just manic. I was so frightened."

Mary talked a great deal about her mother in the next few hours without actually saying anything that made her seem real. Betty was like a shadow weaving in and out of the background of her memory: a figure repeatedly referred to as "smart" but equally frequently as "sick" and "sad." She kept appearing without becoming even momentarily a *person.* She came and went amid the torrent of words that gushed out of Mary as if this were—as if this had to be—the occasion when she would tell me everything: about Red Bank, where she stayed for five years, and about the headmaster there, Mr. Dixon, who implanted in her a first inkling of the difference between right and wrong—"You couldn't *not* learn to understand that, with Mr. Dixon as your headmaster. I loved him," she said. "I will love him till I die." She was unstoppable about Mr. Dixon, unstoppable, too, about her mutinous prison years—"I wasn't going to give in to them. I wasn't going to become their creature." So she learned about power games and corruption, and during those years, virtually unmanageable for the prison staff, she used sex (with fellow inmates) and her manipulative gifts (on inmates and staff) in her attempts to dominate her environment. She talked about her life after her release and about her child: again and again about the child, but never, not with one word, about her own childhood.

Had she actually read *The Case of Mary Bell* (in which there was so much about her childhood)? I finally asked her. In 1981, a year after her release from prison, she said, by now living under a different name, she had signed up for courses at a College of Higher Education in West Yorkshire—she refers to it as "the uni"—and it was in the library there that a student she knew, walking by with a book, had asked her whether she'd read it. "It's so sad," the girl had said, "so sad what they did to that little girl Mary Bell." After that, Mary had read "not all of it, just bits," she said. "It just wasn't a bit like my mother had said. I couldn't believe that there had been somebody who'd felt compassion for me. My mother had always said nobody did, nobody could, because I was so bad . . . such a shaming thing in her life. When I was released she said I was never to tell anybody that she was my mother, that she couldn't live with the shame of it, and she introduced me to her pub pals as her sister, and at other times her cousin." She wanted now to talk about it all, she said, but even more, she wanted help in thinking about it all: she called it "setting the record straight."

I asked her what there was to set straight. Was she claiming that she had been unjustly convicted? She shook her head. Not that, she said, manifestly unable to go into it any further then. It was almost five hours later by now. We had had sandwiches for lunch and unending cups of coffee and tea and she looked pale and very tired. "It wasn't that . . . simple," she said. "I want to talk about the way it happened . . . the way it was done . . . and . . . and . . . you know, go over the record of it, for myself. How could it have happened? How did I become such a child?"

Did she realize, I asked her, that such a book was bound to be controversial? That people were bound to think she did it for money? That both of us would be accused of insensitivity toward the two little victims' families by bringing their dreadful tragedy back into the limelight and, almost inevitably, of sensationalism, because of some of the material the book would have to contain? Above all, did she understand that readers would not stand for any suggestion of possible mitigation for her crimes? And had she faced the reality that if she did collaborate in such a book, it would expose her to renewed onslaughts by the media if they found her?

In the months to come her ability to ponder for long moments over questions she was asked would become very familiar. On such occasions she would sit very still, her hands slightly curled, almost in a meditative position, with a curious inward look on her face. I would never get tired of observing this effort at concentration, this obvious seeking inside herself, not for a "proper" answer, as one might suspect—and I did at first that day—but for something that was meaningful, both to herself and to me.

It was the question about Martin Brown's and Brian Howe's families she replied to first. She had hurt them so much, she said, she really didn't want to hurt them more . . . and suddenly she was crying, "But . . . but . . . there are things they don't know . . . it won't change anything for them, I know, but still . . ."

What sort of things? I asked.

"Oh, I don't know. Just things . . ." It was clear that helping her to organize her thoughts and bringing out whatever it was she wanted to say would, as I always suspected, require the right environment, carefully structured conversations, and, above all, time.

The continuous media interest, she said a little later, was one of the many reasons she had come to her decision. She thought that once she had told me all her story, answered all my questions as honestly as she could, perhaps they would leave her alone. "After all"—she smiled a little crookedly—"once you get through with me, there won't be much left for anybody to ask, will there?"

I tried to disabuse her of this optimism. Newspapers, I told her, particularly the tabloids that had pursued her for so long, were a very different medium from a book, with a different readership, and reporters would always find questions to ask. And the money I myself would propose she receive if she decided to go ahead (hopefully to put in trust for her child), because I thought it was right as without her such a book could not be written, would be a real moral problem, not only for the media but for the families of the dead boys and for many sensitive people.

Discussing money would later always be difficult for her. Even though she wanted it quite desperately in order to change her family's unsettled way of life, she was very aware of the possible moral objections, and when she spoke of money, her voice stiff as she repeated arguments that were not her own, she would, unusually, sound defensive, stubborn, and not quite true.

She and her partner, who has by now been her principal emotional support for thirteen years, had suffered long periods of living a hand-to-mouth existence. With Mary a notorious lifer released on parole, hunted by the media, they have rarely been able to hold on to jobs for any length of time and have frequently resorted to living on the state. Except for one period of several years when, living in the more prosperous south of England, both of them were regularly employed, Mary's partner has had long stretches of being out of work, and Mary herself, who has had many jobs since her release, has had to give them up after a few months or even weeks, either because the Probation Service considered the job inappropriate for her or because she had been, or was afraid of being, recognized.

Her partner, Jim, is an interesting man. When I first met him I found myself faintly irritated by some of his rather esoteric New Age philosophies. But there are other aspects of his personality, such as his total rejection of racism of any kind, his opposition to hard drugs and alcohol, and his deep belief in tolerance and family values, that are admirable. Above all, one has to recognize his steadfastness to Mary, whose neediness, lack of self-confidence, and profound feelings of guilt are no doubt exhausting to live with. He is, too, I'm told by those who know, an excellent father.

But there was from the start a radical difference in their attitudes toward the money she would receive. He felt that, notwithstanding the crimes she had committed as a child, she was now, and had been for years, quite a "different person." Given what she had suffered at the hand of "this crappy system," whatever money she could get was neither a gift nor charity: he felt she "deserved" it. Mary did not feel that (nor, of course, did I) and for a long time Jim was very skeptical when she or I tried to explain the priorities for the book project that had nothing to do with money. In the course of time, though, Jim came to understand entirely the real importance of this undertaking.

When we talked on this first occasion, what she said about the money did not seem unreasonable to me. "I'm not going to say that I don't want money," she said. "That would be dishonest: everybody wants money. But what I want most of all is a normal life. I want to get off the treadmill of social security and do work I enjoy. I want roots and a normal settled life for my child," she repeated.

Much more than money, she said, she had come to feel she needed to talk. Yes, about what she had done, but also (she shook her head slowly, another gesture of bewilderment and often despair that would become very familiar to me) about what had happened to her. When I suggested, and I was to repeat this suggestion many times over the subsequent months, that a psychiatrist might be a better solution for this than talking to me, I was taken aback by the vehemence of her reaction. "No," she said. "No. I won't talk to psychiatrists, I won't. I won't, *ever.*" Her voice had grown almost strident with tension. "If you don't want to do it, I'll find somebody else." She got up brusquely. "I'm going out to have a cigarette," she said, and walked out of the room.

Earlier that morning, I had talked at length with Pat Royston. Rather surprisingly, she had been in favor of the book project from the start.

Given that her own experiences with the media on Mary's behalf had been largely unfavorable, what was it, I asked, that made her agree with Mary's decision to cooperate with me on this book?

"It is because I think somebody needs to find out and explain how terrible crimes such as Mary's, the two ten-year-olds who killed James Bulger, and quite a number of other young children's serious offenses come about," she said. There could not be any question of excusing, or through understanding them, legitimizing such acts, she said. "But in the public's justified horror about these events and their ready acceptance of 'evil' as an explanation [for them]," she continued, "people tend to forget that these are, or were, children. They were children who," she emphasized, "prior to what one might call their 'explosion' into such acts of violence, carried around a baggage of childhood experiences unknown to or ignored by any responsible adult."

She said her experience had taught her that if such children were as young as Mary, and indeed as the two boys who killed James Bulger, the reason for such a baggage of childhood experiences—"If one can use the word reason," she said bitterly—will have been entirely incomprehensible to the children themselves.

"Maybe we have progressed since 1968," she said. "Maybe, though I have my doubts, those two young boys [now serving life sentences, as did Mary] are being helped to understand what brought them to the point of killing little James. But as far as Mary is concerned, the childhood experiences she suffered prior to committing the crimes are still undigested, still neither really understood nor accepted. She would have needed continuous psychiatric help throughout her detention. But basically, except for the human kindness shown to her as a child by the headmaster and staff of Red Bank, and a short stretch of once-a-week group therapy in prison—a privilege she had to fight for—she had no professional attention or guidance whatever for the twelve years of 'growing up.'"

Probation officers in Britain are not usually trained therapists; it is not their function. "I happen to be very interested in it," Pat Royston said, "and have developed this style of working with the help of further training. And because of this, I was able to help Mary begin the long process of untangling her confused emotions, which then made it possible for her to create a family and thereby begin to have something of a life." There were four reasons, she said, why, after long soul-searching, she had supported Mary's decision to cooperate on a book. Two applied specifically to Mary, and two to the many other children in trouble.

"The first is that if Mary is ever to become a normally functioning human being, she must be helped to understand not what she *did*—for even though she can't bear to face it in detail, she knows inside what she has done and feels a grinding guilt for it—but what was done *to* her as a child. And this means that she must take issue and be helped to come to terms with what her mother was and did to her, and with her own feelings about this mother." Secondly, she said, she also hoped, as Mary does, though with less optimism, that once her whole story is on record, the media will leave her alone and she can at last begin to lead a normal life.

Her third reason arose from her concern about the grave deficiencies in the training of social workers, primary-school teachers, and also probation officers, which result in a lack of awareness about and care for seriously troubled children. Without any doubt, she said, this contributes to the catastrophic rise in serious crimes committed by children.

"Finally," she said, "my fourth reason is my own distress, and that of most people of my service, with the way children and young adolescents who commit serious crimes are dealt with by the judicial system. I've come to feel that, although very unconventional—and normally neither welcome nor even acceptable to professionals like myself—perhaps to have Mary, who is very articulate, take issue with herself, so to speak, in public is a legitimate means of demonstrating, firstly, the degree to which society fails in the care of children, and secondly, how we doubly fail in our dealings with the resultant tragedies. I've come to the conclusion that such a book may be the only way to alert people to the crying need for changes in public attitudes and in the law."

When Mary returned, with a mumbled "Sorry"—apologies were never to come easily to her—I tried to explain why I was, in a way, playing devil's advocate against my own wish to do this book by questioning whether she should really go in for such a difficult undertaking. But it would still take considerable time to get across to her what a book like this would have to be, what she would have to give of herself to make it possible for me to produce it. And until we actually worked together, I warned, we couldn't be sure that it *could* work and that we wouldn't eventually have to abandon the attempt. I couldn't know, I said, how she would respond to questioning, how honest she could *bear*, let alone want, to be with herself or with me about things that almost certainly were unbearable to speak about. I couldn't even be sure, I said, that I was the right person to do this with her, that it was *right* for me to do it, which was the reason why, earlier on, I had suggested that it might be preferable for her to see a psychiatrist.

Throughout our time together over the next year, she would fight this idea. About a month after we began to talk she told me of her mother's efforts to frighten her into silence. "I think I was six or seven," she said. "We, my mother and I, were going to see my dad's parents, who lived on the other side of the Tyne Bridge. I remember it was dark, because there were lights on the bridge and on the cars. We were walking along the bridge. My mother was angry, I don't remember why. She grabbed my arm and she pointed ahead at a sentry box, you know, one of those concrete things, and she said, if I told anybody stories, that's where I was going to be put. 'That's what they do with children,' she said, 'who don't keep their mouths shut as they are told.' And she shook me."

In any event, that day it would have been impossible—and wrong—to bring up her childhood. I had always been convinced that it had been even worse than her family had admitted to me, and I suspected that full knowledge of it could lead to an explanation for her terrible acts in 1968. We would need time and patience. As for the acts themselves, it would, of course, be essential for her to confront what she had done. She had always denied the true circumstances under which she had killed Martin Brown; in fact, she mostly denied having killed him at all. I believed she had also always understated the extent of her responsibility in the death of Brian Howe. Before one could search with her for the reason, it would be necessary for her to fully face the fact that she had committed these acts, whether someone else was present or not. All these were matters I needed to approach with great care, leaving the initiative of when and how to talk about them largely to her and, if and when she was able to approach them, protecting her from the shock that was almost bound to follow such disclosures.

As I would often notice in the future, her attention had wandered soon after I began this long and difficult discussion, and her thoughts were so deeply elsewhere, she probably hadn't heard half of what I said.

"Norma," she said, as if answering a question. "I don't want to say anything against her ... but ..." She stopped and then started again. "Poor Norma ..."

There were many thoughts that remained unspoken between us that first day, but a number of points she felt relentlessly bitter about were to come up time and again over the next two years. The fact that the Newcastle court had declared Norma innocent and acquitted her is probably Mary's single most bitter memory of that December day in 1968 when the trial ended, even though she no longer feels any personal animosity toward her childhood friend. "I can remember quite clearly the feeling of knowing that would happen," she said. "I don't know how I knew. It must have been from what they said ... About her? To her? I don't know." (I could have told her, though I didn't that day, that, yes, it was entirely clear days before the trial ended that that court with that jury would never bring themselves to convict both girls and that Norma would go free.) "How could they?" she would later ask time and again, and then often add, as on that first day, "Poor Norma ..." And months into our talks she said, not once but several times, "Perhaps what happened to her was finally worse for her than what happened to me was for me."

Another source of Mary's bitterness is the media, and the image they created of her in 1968 as a monster. To her mind this "myth," as she always refers to it, has endured ever since, irrespective of the fact that since then there have been a number of "similarly dreadful" (her words) and even higher-profile cases both in Britain and elsewhere. This myth has kept her estranged from her aunts, uncles, and siblings, whom she loved, and from their children, whom she longed to know. As for the public, which she feels, with some justification, has not forgotten her, the myth of her own unique and innate evil continues unabated, confirmed by Norma's acquittal.

The third point of bitterness is that she was, and by extension still is and always will be, she thinks, remembered as a liar and manipulator. "But for God's sake," she said. "I was a kid; what else could I do but lie?" The fourth, not unconnected to the above, is her resentment at being considered exceptionally intelligent. In her memory of the trial, every mention of her "intelligence" is bracketed with the suggestion of manipulation. "And that means that people think I can never be honest. But I am, I *am* . . . " she would say over and over, and she would cry.

Did I believe her tears, that day and later? Did I think when she left me late that afternoon that I would be able to trust her, that her motivations were as she described them, and that her story, whatever it turned out to be, would be true? I am not given to illusions. I thought her motivations were mixed and her descriptions of them disingenuous, but this was a result of insecurity and inexperience rather than manipulation. She didn't know me, and she had never known anyone like me or anything like the world in which I live. And what she was proposing to do, even if she didn't yet understand the dimensions of it, was a huge step outside the very specific boundaries of her life, and it demanded courage.

But yes, I thought she would try to manipulate me, as others, far more sophisticated than she, have tried. Equally I knew there would be lies—how can there not be when human beings agree to lay open to another the worst within themselves? But I felt certain by the end of that day that any *deliberate* lies she might tell would be about small things in the present rather than important things in the past. For—and this was decisive for me—I believed her unhappiness about what she had done. I believed her sadness for the families whom she had robbed of their children, and I believed her need to know herself.

Even on that first day, however, I knew that working with Mary would never be easy. I had told her at the end of it how I envisaged our time together: that although eventually I would arrange to work with her in places within close reach of her family, I believed the best thing would be if for the first week she would agree to come and stay with me in London, where we could begin to work and get to know each other better.

I realized that, except for her supervision by the Probation Service, which was a condition of her release on license, or parole, her past life had made her almost obsessively resistant to being tied down. I had warned her that from the moment publishing contracts were signed, we—both of us—would be bound by their conditions, both to the dates they specified and the absolute discretion they would require of us. For I had known in advance—Pat Royston had warned me, and Mary's solicitor had confirmed it—that the court responsible for Mary's child's welfare, even if they did not object to this project, would demand absolute secrecy in order to protect the child.*

This need for secrecy was emphasized, even while we waited the six months it took lawyers, agents, and publishers to reach agreement. Pat Royston received a request for an interview with Mary from one of her most persistent press pursuers, and twice there was evidence that a strange car was cruising the streets near where Mary lived and that questions were being asked of people in the neighborhood. It was clear, as on numerous previous occasions, that she would have to move. Although she did and a legal letter was sent to remind the editor of the paper concerned of the court order, our awareness of our obligation to the court intensified.

The secrecy not only about Mary's whereabouts but about the whole project was to become a heavy load for both Mary and me. On her side, no one knew of our arrangement except her partner, Jim; two close relatives of his; Mary's stepfather, George; her lawyers; four former teachers

---

*Mary's child will be a ward of court until eighteen. In 1985, because of the media's continued pursuit of Mary, an injunction was issued forbidding any publicity that could lead to the identification of the child.

at Red Bank who agreed to talk with me; the Official Solicitor; and a top official of the Home Office responsible for released life prisoners. Pat Royston and another of Mary's former probation officers, Samantha Connolly, worked with me throughout and essentially corroborated most of her story. For Mary the secrecy meant virtually total separation for almost three years from the few friends she had made.

On my side, in addition to my family and my editor, only one friend (a former social worker) who assisted me with some of the paperwork, and a barrister friend who advised me (an expert in crimes by and against children) knew from the start. Later I would consult a few others, psychiatrists in Britain and abroad, social workers, and two of my closest friends, both fellow writers, both abroad. All this forced me into a strange and quite disturbing isolation, even from my closest friends and colleagues.

The extent to which the prospect of the book and the conditions it laid down worried Mary would become apparent the very first time we arranged to work together. I had not known what time she would arrive in London, but she had telephoned from the station in the early evening and said that she had money on her and rather than wait to be picked up would take a taxi. That was the last I heard from her until she arrived the next morning at 11:00 A.M. in a state of collapse, carrying a bulging suitcase and four plastic bags stuffed with papers and photographs. "I'm sorry," she said, repeating it again and again, "really sorry, but I had to be alone."

But where were you? What did you do? I asked.

"I walked," she said.

All night? I said unbelievingly, and she nodded.

Later I found out she had had endless cups of tea and, in the manner of bag ladies, rested in doorways until morning. Finally, not wanting to ring my bell too early, and also by then horribly reluctant about the whole project, she had sat in a nearby snack bar drinking one coffee after another while gearing up her courage to approach the residential street where I live.

That morning all I could do was run a bath for her and put her to bed and, when she woke up six hours later, give her a telephone to ring home. By the evening—an indication, I thought, of the chaos within her—she had covered every available clear space in my study, where she slept, with papers, toiletries, makeup, and a litter of ill-assorted, obviously haphazardly packed clothes.

But, far more indicative of her state of mind, all that she wanted to speak about that first evening and the next day was her child—almost as if before saying anything about the past she wanted to establish for me her identity in the present. And to herself Mary is, above all other things, the mother of her child. It was to be several days before I understood that there are two entirely distinct parts to her. One is the attractive, warm, and unconditionally loving young mother who with talent, imagination, and intelligence is dedicating a large part of her mind and personality to creating something of an ideal childhood for her daughter. In this part of her life she is calm, organized, disciplined, and happy. The other part— the one I would inevitably become more familiar with (even though there wasn't a day in those months when the subject of her child wouldn't arise)—is chaotic, almost incapable of organization and discipline, and, despite a lurking, roguish sense of humor, often very sad.

One of the things I would only discover many weeks after we began to talk is that she had developed a partial dependency on painkillers, which were first given to her in prison and are still prescribed to her for frequent migraines. When she had one of these attacks during the week she stayed with me and I remarked upon the obvious severity of the pain, she said that she was so frightened of it coming that she sometimes took the pills, which also had a calming, indeed soporific effect, before the attacks came, and took a larger dose than was prescribed. It was later that I realized—and, clearly hoping for help, she admitted to me—that the slurred speech I had occasionally noticed was due to her taking such a preemptive dose of this medicine. She would tell me then about the number of drugs that had been prescribed to her in prison. (One of the positive consequences of our discussing this problem was that she admitted it to her doctor and is being helped to reduce her intake of this medication.)

27

The months we talked, the length of time extended by her quite fre-quent failure to appear—I once spent two weeks expecting her in vain at 9:15 every morning—were dominated by the necessity, which would become almost immediately obvious, not only to give her an incredible amount of time to get to the point of many of her recollections, but also to recheck the authenticity of her memories by repeating my questions time and time again. But over the months her replies, if per-haps differently worded, were basically indentical, and I was to become entirely convinced of her essential truthfulness and the reality of her pain.

"How did I become such a child?" These are the words that stayed in my mind during the sleepless night that followed that first meeting in November 1995. And they would remain with me as we worked together when, day after day, she brought up the ever-present specter of her mother, Betty, who having almost succeeded many times in killing—and certainly succeeded in emotionally damaging—her daughter, only nominally freed her when she died in January 1995.

PART ONE

THE TRIAL

December 1968

The Court

The age of criminal responsibility in England and Wales is ten years old (eight in Scotland). Children between ten and thirteen, however, until the passage of the Law and Disorder Act in 1998, were presumed in law to be *doli incapax*, incapable of criminal intent, and this presumption had to be rebutted before a child could be convicted. The prosecution had to prove that the child not only had carried out the alleged acts but knew at the time that what he or she was doing was seriously wrong. The 1998 act has abolished even this safeguard, and anyone ten or over is considered to have the same moral awareness of right and wrong as his or her elders.* The trial of Regina v. Mary Flora Bell and Norma Joyce Bell uniquely highlighted the problems of *doli incapax* and of trying young children in adult courts, but there was never any doubt that it would take place.

Judicial procedure in any country is bound by its own firmly established rules, but however and wherever a trial finally takes place, it is

---

*In the United States the age of criminal responsibility varies from state to state, ranging from eight years up; the venue for trial—adult or juvenile court—varies as well. With recent rises in juvenile crime, a number of states are now waiving delinquency cases to adult criminal courts.

preceded by a police investigation and the arrest of a suspect, who, except in cases of murder, in Britain at least, is either granted bail or held in detention. In Britain the decision as to whether a case goes to trial has traditionally been made by the Director of Public Prosecutions, the government's chief legal executive. Cases of murder, however, almost invariably end up before a judge and jury, and, until 1972, this meant that cases outside London would be heard at a session of the Assizes—the courts to which High Court judges made their "circuits" several times a year, traveling across the country in closed-off railway carriages and living in virtual seclusion in judges' residences in all the major cities where they dispensed justice.

The purpose of any criminal trial, whether conducted under the accusatorial system (as in the UK and US, where the prosecution must prove guilt beyond reasonable doubt) or by the inquisitorial Napoleonic Code (as in most European countries, where the judge plays a much more active role), is to establish guilt or innocence. In theory, facts alone determine this end, although judges can affect the outcome both by their questions and by their interpolations, which more often than not indicate their own position and without doubt influence juries. Equally, the judge's summing up will weigh heavily on any juror's mind and, as this case would so classically prove, judges, too, are only human, are subject to emotion, and can be swayed by appearances.

The circumstances in which a trial is conducted, however, can be predetermined, and in Newcastle in 1968 provision had been made for frequent breaks in the proceedings and for the children's relative comfort. The police officers and court staff on duty had received special instructions to keep the atmosphere quiet and treat both the children and their families gently. Nonetheless, a jury trial for murder is a fearful matter, deliberately grave in its procedure and awesome in its effect.

The Newcastle Assizes were held in the Moot Hall, an early-nineteenth-century stone building on the south side of the city where, until a new building was recently constructed, all court proceedings were conducted. The public gallery in the center of the court, and the two side galleries, reserved on this occasion for the press, were only full on four days of the nine-day trial: day one, when the prosecutor, Rudolph Lyons, presented his case; day six, for Mary's examination-in-chief; day eight, for the judge's summary to the jury; and day nine, for the verdict. On those four days—the next day's schedule was posted in the press room at the end of each day's proceedings—there were reporters from all the main papers and many foreign ones, and there were lines from early morning for the public seats. On the other days, however, much of the public gallery was almost empty and most of the reporters stayed away.

This obvious aversion to the case, in Newcastle and in the country as a whole, indicative of the difference in public attitudes between the sixties and the nineties, was also reflected in the conduct of the trial and the atmosphere in the court throughout it. The court—the judge and the lawyers—and the psychiatrists, a number of whom attended in specially assigned seats from which they could observe the children, were of course intrigued, but the members of the public (who, twenty-five years later, would line up at dawn on every one of the seventeen days of the so-called Bulger trial) and the national press backed away from the case: in 1968 troubled children were not yet in vogue, and "evil" was best ignored lest it might infect. Although the trial's progress was briefly reported on news programs, and commentaries appeared in the quality papers after the verdict, the BBC, in consideration of young viewers, prohibited any mention of it during the six o'clock news, and, more surprisingly still, the Sunday tabloids, all of which a quarter of a century later would dwell for weeks on the Bulger case and pay large sums to members of the Bulger family for their stories, rejected it altogether. During the trial, one tabloid, the *Sun*, specifically refused the story of Mary Bell's life as offered for sale by her parents.*

*Sidney Foxcroft was Newcastle reporter for the *People* and the *Sun*. "A man phoned me one day," he told me. "He said he was a friend of the Bells and they wanted to come and talk to me about something. I got a friend of mine to sit in on this meeting. You know, I could hardly believe it myself. They came along, Betty and Billy Bell and their pal, and they said they wanted

Major trials were usually assigned to Court One, the largest in the Moot Hall, but in this case the trial had been transferred to Court Two, a comparatively small room paneled in dark oak. It was considered less forbidding and had an adjacent waiting room and lavatory, which would make it easier to take care of the two children. It had no dock and thus allowed them to be seated in a row between their legal advisers in front and their families behind them, which made them feel and seem less isolated, and it had excellent acoustics, which would permit them to be heard even when—as frequently happened—they whispered.

Despite the careful provisions made for the two girls, neither of them had been prepared for the solemnity of the court proceedings. For nine days two mutually incomprehensible languages would be spoken in that ancient chamber. One was the language of adults, and formal language at that; the other was the language of two highly disturbed children, the workings of whose minds were a mystery to virtually everybody present. ("Nobody told us anything," Mary would tell me later. "Not about people coming in to watch, either.") Nor had they expected the crowds who attended the opening day of the trial, and both girls—Norma reacting just an instant after Mary—laughed with excitement when three knocks preceded the usher's "Be upstanding in court!" ("We didn't talk . . . hardly at all during the trial even when we could have," Mary said. "But, yes, I remember: we laughed. I can't think why and what about, but whenever we looked at each other, we laughed." And twenty-five years later, in another courtroom, I noticed the two boys in the Bulger trial doing exactly the same almost every time their eyes met.)

I was sitting in the gallery above but just across from the two girls and noted how the difference between them—Norma's terror against Mary's apparent fascination—showed up almost immediately. As the judge in his red coat entered in slow and measured steps, the bewigged

---

to sell us the story of Mary's life. Their kid was on trial for murder over there in Moot Hall and they sat here and said, 'We tried to teach her right but we couldn't do a thing with her . . .' Well, it was my job to listen to them, but I've never been so sickened in my life. I rang through to the office in London afterwards and told them. They said they wouldn't touch it with a ten-foot pole."

barristers and court officials bowed deeply, and the many police officers spread throughout the court stood stiffly to attention, Mary could hardly contain her pleasure at the spectacle. Norma, however, her whole body expressing bewilderment, turned round to her parents, her face reflecting the mixture of nervous smile and incipient tears that would become as familiar to the spectators as her mother's shake of her head and gentle movement of her hand, which propelled the child back to face the court.

Norma, too, was a pretty girl, her hair also dark brown and as shiny as Mary's. Every day both of them wore immaculately clean and ironed cotton dresses, white socks, and polished shoes. Taller and physically more developed, Norma had a round face that looked perpetually puzzled and large, soft brown eyes. One felt worried about Norma almost all the time, sorry for her often visible distress and concerned for her obviously caring parents and numerous relatives, who, sitting behind her, attended every session, stroking and petting the desperate child the many times she burst into tears. Her ten brothers and sisters, ranging in age from her handicapped sixteen-year-old brother down to a baby in arms, waited outside the court every day of the trial, waving to her enthusiastically whenever the door opened. And at every recess they rushed in and down the steps to what Mary, years later, would describe to me as "the dungeon," the arched vault in the basement of the court building where, until the fifth day, when the judge ordered the girls to be kept in separate rooms, the two groups huddled at opposite corners of the huge chamber during breaks in the proceedings. There was love and determined gaiety around Norma from the beginning to the end of the trial. And nobody in court could have thought for a single moment that anyone in her family believed that little girl capable of murder.

Mary, much smaller, with her heart-shaped face and those remarkable bright-blue eyes, was not alone either, though the members of her extended family who attended appeared unable to hide their anxiety and distress. Her grandmother Mrs. McC., Betty's thin, fine-boned mother, was there every day, with a white, tired face, straight-backed and silent. And her aunts, Betty's sisters, Cath and Isa, and Billy's sister,

Audrey, came, and so did Audrey's husband, Peter, and Cath's husband, Jack; all of them respectable and quiet, avoiding contact with anyone around and, during the breaks, directing (what one Newcastle police-woman described to me as) "forced-like cheer" and "desperate affection" toward Mary.

The person who was most conspicuous, however, and impossible to ignore, was Betty. Anything but silent, she exclaimed volubly, sobbed wildly, and time and again, the straggly blond wig that incompletely covered her jet-black hair askew, demonstrated her indignation at what was being said about her child by stalking furiously out of the court on her high clicking heels, only to return, just as ostentatiously, shortly afterwards.

Billy Bell, tall and handsome, with black hair and red-blond side-burns, sat hunched over with his elbows on his knees and his hands supporting his head, for much of the time hiding his face. I never saw him speak to anybody, though the policewomen who guarded Mary would tell me that he was gentle with her during breaks and, while so taciturn in the courtroom, worked quite hard downstairs to make Mary laugh. Except for an almost obligatory kiss on leaving, her mother never comforted her unless she noticed someone watching. But Billy hugged and kissed her every time he came and went, and she, who several of her relatives said had never allowed herself to be kissed by any of them and "always turned her head away" when they tried, clung to him.

Mary told me later she was very frightened of her mother during the trial. "She became more and more . . ." More what? I asked. ". . . Angry with me," she said.

It was a long time after the trial that three social workers told me about their first experience with Betty Bell. Before the case finally arrived at the Assizes, the two children had appeared in court four times for the extension of their detention. Billy Bell and Audrey, with Mary's grandmother, had attended the first remand hearing in Juvenile Court on August 8, the day after the arrest. But to the fury of the Newcastle Children's

Department, Betty was absent. The social workers were disgusted, they said, and on the late afternoon of the day before the second remand hearing on August 14, three of them, signing themselves out on a half-day holiday for the purpose, drove up to Glasgow. "Officially, of course, we weren't allowed to do this. But it was bad enough that we knew so little about that child, we weren't going to have her be unsupported by her mother for one more day." They found out Betty's pub and her "stand," as they put it, in a Glasgow street. "We just went and grabbed ahold of her and bundled her into the car and drove back to Newcastle in the night. She screamed and yelled, effing us, the department, and the court, but she was going to be there to support that child in the morning if it was the last thing we did."

It was an interesting act, less of compassion than of principle, for all three admitted to me at the time that they didn't "like" Mary and that in fact she gave them "the willies." (And all these years later, Mary, searching her memory, would add what she remembered about seeing her mother the first time after her arrest. "She came to see me, I think it was in the cells at West End police, and she went totally hysterical, shouting at me, what had I done to her this time, having people track her down . . . It was my fault and what a shameful thing I was in her life.")

As the two children sat through the proceedings in court, Norma's attention span, we would see very quickly, was short: she would listen carefully for a few minutes, then begin to squirm, look around the court, and turn to speak to her mother, who invariably turned her head back to face the judge. One would then see her obvious effort to listen until, seconds rather than minutes later, her eyes would again begin to swivel up and down the room and the galleries and yet again she would turn her head back to her mother, who, with infinite though one felt weary patience, repeated the process of directing Norma's attention to whoever was speaking.

Mary, on the contrary, was astonishingly attentive. She hardly appeared to notice her mother's dramatics, nor did she seem puzzled or particularly distressed. The general impression she gave was one of intense interest. Her face, intellectually alive when she spoke either in whispers to her solicitor, David Bryson, who sat next to her, or later when she testified, had a perpetual listening quality though it was, except in anger, emotionally blank. Mary's body was almost completely still; her nerves were in her hands. Disproportionately broad, they moved constantly, as if a separate part of her. Apparently absentmindedly she stroked her dress, her hair, herself, and constantly had a finger, though never a thumb, in her mouth. Every few minutes she took it out, wiped her lips with the back of her hand, and then rubbed first the back of the hand, then the finger lengthwise dry on her skirt only to immediately put it, or another one, back in her mouth. (And twenty-five years later, under almost identical circumstances, I would see a repetition of this extraordinary manifestation of disturbance, when one of the two ten-year-olds who murdered James Bulger demonstrated similar, sometimes identical mannerisms. He too sat much of the time of the trial with a finger, or in his case usually his thumb, in his mouth or in his ear, and he too, off and on, absentmindedly wiped it dry on his trousers only to immediately reinsert and move it around or to and fro in his mouth.)

Mary appeared to listen to every word, even when she quite clearly could not comprehend the formal language. But in marked contrast to the other child, she seemed isolated from her surroundings. Except for her young solicitor, who three or four times during the nine days responded to questions from her, no one talked to her. And except for the few times when, obviously tired, she fidgeted and received a sharp tap on the back of the head from her mother, and for the day of the verdict, when she began to cry and David Bryson for a moment held her, no one touched her.

By the time of the trial, the two children had been in custody for four months. Court-appointed solicitors prepared the case for each child and instructed barristers who would represent them at the trial, all paid by legal aid. Norma was represented from the start by a highly reputed barrister, R. P. Smith, QC, one of the youngest and (so I was told) brightest silks* in the country, who within days of her arrest had persuaded a judge in chambers in London that she should spend the period of the remand as a patient at a nearby mental hospital being "observed" by nurses and doctors.

Mary was represented by a distinguished older barrister, Mr. Harvey Robson, whose long legal career had included several terms as Attorney General in the Southern Cameroons, and after that many criminal cases in the northeast of England, though none for murder. Mr. Harvey Robson, I was later reliably told, had not tried to obtain a hospital order for Mary's remand. (Her solicitor would later tell me that was because he considered it a hopeless endeavor.) She was sent first to an assessment center in Croydon, near London, and then to a local remand home in Seaham, closer to home in County Durham, run by the prison department for girls between fourteen and eighteen, among whom, because of both her age and her alleged offense, she immediately figured as a star.

In cases of children accused of serious crime in Britain, it is very unusual for psychiatrists to be involved before a trial except to establish that the accused minor is capable of distinguishing right from serious wrong and that the child was mentally responsible for his or her acts at the time they were committed. To this day, any other kind of psychiatric attention before a trial is held to risk adulterating the evidence. It was astonishing, therefore, that permission was given for Norma to spend the months of remand in the children's wing of Prudhoe Monkton hospital under the supervision of a psychiatrist, Dr. Ian Frazer.

While both Norma's hospital and Mary's remand home were benign places, and neither of the children appeared unhappy, the difference in the arrangements that had been made for them—a medical environment for Norma, a quasi-punitive one for Mary—became known very soon.

---

*Queen's (or King's) Counsels. Barristers appointed annually by the Crown on the basis of ability, experience, and seniority.

It is almost impossible nowadays for people, however disciplined or determined, not to be affected by what they read in our aggressively intrusive press or see on the ever-present screen. Considering the amount of public interest cases such as this are bound to attract, there is a measure of hypocrisy in continuing to rely on the objectivity of juries or even of the courts. And thirty years ago, too, the inevitable publicity—at the death of the two toddlers, the arrest of two (at that point unnamed) little girls on suspicion of murder, the conditions of their remand (first rumored but then disclosed at the trial), and finally on the occasion of the trial itself—all no doubt considerably influenced the eventual attitude of the court and, arguably, the outcome of the trial.

It was before the jury was seated and the children were brought into court that the judge, Sir Ralph Cusack, asked the defense lawyers whether they wished him to prohibit the girls' names from being published. Both barristers replied they had no objection to the publication of the names. Their reason, unconvincing to me at the time, was that the identity of the children was already known in Scotswood and that, unless the two girls were named, a slur could conceivably remain on other children whose names would come up in the course of the trial. Twenty-five years later, it was the precedent set by the Mary Bell case that persuaded the court in Preston to allow publication of the names of the two ten-year-old boys accused of killing James Bulger. That decision has caused the same damage to the boys' families and will reverberate in their own lives as has the one taken by Mr. Justice Cusack in 1968 in Mary's and in Norma's lives.

Mary—Reflections I

When we talked so many years later, Mary spoke a lot about Norma, but her memory of her is only of the child and when she tries to transpose this into adult terms she speaks of her purely with sympathy. The resentment she bears, although associated with Norma, is not against her but against the system that she now thinks used Norma to make herself appear worse.

"Norma's family moved in next door to us in Whitehouse Road a week after we arrived [in the spring of 1967]," she said. "When I heard they were called Bell, too, I asked my dad whether they were related to us. He said, 'Not a chance.'

"I was fascinated by their having eleven children. I was terribly curious how they lived, how they managed. You know, their house was just like ours: a kitchen, a scullery, a bathroom, and a living room downstairs and three bedrooms and a lavatory upstairs. How did they put thirteen people in there? Later I found out that they ate in shifts.

"They were good people, you know. I got to like her mother a lot. I can't imagine how she managed. She must have worked her fingers to the bone. And she was nice, you know. She used to sing. I could hear her . . .

"My best friend was a girl called Dot who had lived near us in

Westmoreland Road [a then notoriously run-down section of New-castle where the Bells lived before they moved to Whitehouse Road], but she moved to a different area just about when we did and so our friend-ship sort of dwindled off. I very quickly became friends with Norma's sister Susan, who was my age, but she turned out to be a whinger, a goody-goody, so I started playing with Norma. She was a couple of years older and they said later she was young in her mind, but I never thought so. I was always caught red-handed when I did anything, but she could always get out of anything by being sort of 'glaicky'—that means glassy, not quite with it. She was very good at making herself look like that, and her appearance—those eyes, you know—helped that along. But she was pretty canny. And she was witty, quite funny. She used to make me laugh and I made her laugh."

Looking back now, I asked, did she think she had been an angry child at the time?

"I was a 'dare me' child," she said. And as she thought about it her voice became dreamy and she jumped from memory to memory, rarely completing a sentence. "I wanted to . . . You see, when you are a child . . . I used to think I could be in a sort of Jesse James gang, you know, ride a horse and break someone out of prison by wrapping a rope round the bars and getting the horse to run off, dragging the bars like I saw in Westerns I watched with my dad on TV . . ."

Quite aside from Westerns, did she think that as a child she fanta-sized about crime and prison?

It was one of the questions that made her ponder for a long time—the pondering, I soon came to understand, was hardly ever because she was afraid of "incriminating" herself but rather when she knew that her answer would be revealing something private, something she considered her own. "Well, you know, my dad . . . Well, nobody told me anything, you know, but I used to hear bits and bobs and I was aware of the police and that he was sort of like a gangster person. Well, in a very small way, you know. He was just robbing, wasn't he? He never hurt anybody, he never would have, but he was often, you know, on the run, sort of. And though I didn't know it then, I know now that our way of life . . .

my family's, you know . . . was anti-authority. The police, the social services, the government, laws, all of it was treated with contempt and derision. And so was work, I think.

"My mother never referred to anybody in authority without the
f-word. Apart from my Uncle Philip—my mother's brother in Scotland who'd been in the army—and my Auntie Audrey's husband, my
Uncle Peter, who was a long-distance lorry driver, and Auntie Cath's
husband, Jack, who'd worked in the mines till he got ill, I didn't know
anybody who worked. Of course graft was 'work,' and you know what
my mother was doing, and *it* was called being away 'on business.' I didn't
know that then, but the words 'work' and 'business' were totally dis-
torted. If people went out to burgle a shop or nick things off lorries, it
was called going to work or, again, 'doing business.' The police would
come to the door and my dad would be out the back like a flash, and I'd
say he was away or that he didn't live there. I loved him and he was a hero
to me because he was always good to us. But now I know that if families
live like that, then it's not only the police who are the enemy, anyone in
authority is.

"I liked school, you know, but I stayed off a lot. Now I think that,
perhaps without understanding it, I did that out of some confused sense
of solidarity with my dad—you know, 'teachers are enemies too.' So
perhaps I thought if I played at despising them, I'd be admired for it.

"It was confusing, because actually if my mother found out, either
that I'd missed school or been rude there, never mind how rude *she* was
about the teachers or the school system, I'd get beaten for it. But it didn't
matter. I went right on or right back to 'daring' people."

And was Norma that sort of "dare me" child too?

"Not in the same way, no, not at all. Her family was actually very
straight, you know, poor of course, but honest. But she was a fighter. She
picked fights—colored kids—I don't know where she got it from but
she didn't like them."

After that Mary talked for a long time how passionately she and
her partner feel about bigotry, and how her own child would never feel
intolerant of, or superior to, anyone because of the color of their skin

or their religion. "Children are what you make them to be," she said finally.

"Anyway, she was in lots of fights," she said, returning to Norma. "Now I think it was only to get attention—like me, though not like me. I—as I know now—needed attention from some adult to . . . to get me away from my family. With her I think it was probably the opposite. She just wanted her family to notice her. It must have been hard in that family, with so many children, to be an older and as they later said a slower child. Perhaps you got forgotten. But she really loved her brother who was handicapped, and when children made fun of him, you know, as children do, she'd stand in front of him, her fists balled, and shout, 'Put your dukes up!' and she'd look savage."

Did they fight her then?

She laughed dismissively. "No, of course not. She'd scare them off, and I admired that. And then, I was terribly impressed because she was a runner . . ."

A runner?

"She'd run away from home several times . . ."

But why had she run away? Did she speak of being unhappy at home?

"Yes, she kept saying she hated home, she wanted to be away from them. Much later I wondered whether they ever noticed when she ran away . . . Now that I think of it, she was also often . . . I don't know . . . just sad. I think we were both, in our own way, very sad little girls."

"The first time I saw Norma since the remand was the first day of the trial," Mary said. "They said we weren't to speak to each other, but of course we did. And she was different . . . She just seemed a completely different person to the girl I knew. I became very quickly aware that she was being . . . oh, given a lot of sympathy. I saw her as playing on this and on being simple and everything. She may have been educationally subnormal as they said, but simple, that's a load of rubbish. I thought then that she was conniving, but looking back I don't really think that anymore. I think she did what she was told to do, by her family, by the lawyers . . ."

Did she think her own behavior in court was dictated by her lawyers and her family?

"Well, I never really had anything to do with my barrister. Mr. Bryson [her solicitor] told me right away that anything I wanted to say to the barrister had to be through him. I remember thinking how could my barrister talk about me when he didn't know me? And then, when I heard them say things in court which weren't true, I wanted to tell Mr. Bryson, but he told me off for whispering to him. He also told me off for smiling at Norma and for laughing a couple of times when they said something I thought was funny. He said what I had to do was sit quietly and listen."

What had she thought was funny?

"It was when somebody—I don't know who—called me a 'monstrosity of nature' or something like that. I thought those were really funny words, nothing to do with me. You know, it made me think of a TV program I'd seen, *Lost in Space*. A lot of the time, anyway, I thought all of it had nothing to do with me, as if I wasn't there, you know, or there but standing outside looking in."

Had her parents or others in her family talked to her about what was happening and told her how to behave?

"Never," she said at once. "Nobody ever mentioned the reason for the trial, except my dad once, when he came to see me during a break, and suddenly hugged me and whispered, 'You'll be all right. I know you'll be all right.' " (Billy believed for years that Mary was innocent and—so somebody in her family told me—when it became obvious that she would be convicted, conceived a cockeyed plan with some of his chums to kidnap and hide her.) "My mother never said anything, though she brought me dresses. She made the dress I wore on the day of my cross-examination, or at least she said she'd made it."

Her mother did come every day to the trial, I reminded her.

"Well, my gran came, and my aunts, so she wouldn't have dared *not* come. But . . . it was a performance for her, a show. My dad, my aunts, my uncles too, I think now they were desperate for me and probably about me, too. She was desperate about herself, and after a few days she started hurting me when she came to see me whenever nobody was looking."

Hurting her how?

"Nipping and pinching me, on my arms and the skin of my back. I knew all the time, all the days of the remand and the trial, that when I got home—part of me thought they'd have to let me go home—she would beat me to death."

The Investigation

In the two key cases in Britain since World War II—the case of Mary Bell, as it became known, and the murder of "Jamie" Bulger (whose picture, caught by a shopping mall security camera and showing him holding the hand of one of his child abductors, dominated TV screens and front pages in Britain for weeks in 1993)—there was no doubt from the start that children had been involved in the killings. I have in front of me as I write a copy of the report Detective Chief Inspector James Dobson wrote out on August 15, 1968, which would form the basis of the evidence for the trial.

It is strange to read it now, so many years later, for its official phrasing makes it sound nothing like the deeply human man I came to know. Tall, with bright-blue eyes and an incisive mind, he soon told me that his trenchant manner was a necessary cover for a "soppy" heart where children were concerned. Of all the people involved in the investigation, James Dobson was the only one who suspected quite soon that there was more to this case than an "evil child," a "freak of nature," as the press called her. "Let us say I sensed there was something terribly wrong," he told me soon after the trial. "But my function was to determine who had perpetrated the crime and how it was committed. In our system, it is not the business of the police to find out why crimes are committed. But as we have seen here, sadly, when the perpetrators are children, it doesn't appear that it is anyone's business."

He had been asleep at home when a phone call came at one o'clock in the morning of Thursday, August 1, 1968, to tell him that three-year-old Brian Howe had been found dead, believed stabbed. He'd pulled trousers and a sweater on over his pajamas, put shoes on his bare feet, and "belted over" to Scotswood. "I'd parked up on the road," he said, "and as I walked down to the Tin Lizzie, I suddenly thought of Martin Brown. I'd had nothing to do with that case and I had no idea what I would find on the Tin Lizzie. But I had stopped the car just across from the house where Martin had been found and somehow he stayed in the back of my mind throughout the next days."

By the time he reached the Tin Lizzie, arc lights had been put up. "The whole area was brightly lit. There were a lot of people around," he recalled, "but somehow it was very quiet." It was, he felt, a first indication of the shock that would soon pervade Scotswood, New-castle, and the whole country. "Murder is always special, whoever the victim; but there is something very different for us, something very personal, when it's a child," he said. "What I heard most was the clank-ing of the railway. It's very loud at night. Our chaps," he repeated, "were quiet."

After examining little Brian's body in situ, the pathologist, Mr. Bernard Tomlinson, had concluded that he had been strangled, not stabbed, and had probably died between 3:30 and 4:30 the previous afternoon. The first assumption, immediately after the body had been found, was that a pervert was on the loose. But the pale pressure marks on Brian's neck and nose and the lightness of the stab wounds—there were six tiny puncture wounds on his thighs and legs and a small area of skin loss in the middle of the scrotum—were all much more tentative than such injuries would be had they been caused by an adult, and clearly indicated the actions of a child or children. "There was no anger, none one could see, none one could feel," said Mr. Dobson. "There was a ter-rible playfulness about it, a terrible gentleness if you like, and somehow the playfulness of it made it more, rather than less, terrifying. It was incomprehensible. How could it have happened? And why?"

A hundred Criminal Investigation Department officers had been called in and were assembled into teams. "I told them we'd be working around the clock until we solved it," said Mr. Dobson. "We took preliminary statements during the night from family and neighbors, and we produced thousands of mimeographed questionnaires to distribute the next morning. We started in Scotswood at 8:00 A.M. and except for snatches of sleep we didn't stop for eight days."

During the first twenty-four hours, a thousand homes in Scotswood were visited and 1,200 children between the ages of three and fifteen, and their parents, were given the questionnaires to fill out. There would be many incomplete replies and about twelve children were asked for additional statements, among them Norma Bell and Mary Bell.

The differences between the two girls' families were remarked on from the first day of the investigation, when Detective Constable Kerr arrived at Norma's house to ask for clarification of part of the questionnaire. There were ten questions on the sheet and in Norma's case, her answer to question 8—"Do you know anyone who played with Brian? If so: name and address"—was not legible.

"This was a family where at least seven of the eleven children fell into the age three-to-fifteen category," Detective Constable Kerr would tell me later. "Of course they were overcrowded. But they gave me the impression of a close family. I talked to the mother and several of the children; they were nice polite kids, and clean, too, which I thought was an achievement when there were so many.

"I did think Norma was peculiar," he added. "I mean, I was inquiring into something pretty awful and little Brian was a child they had all known well, but there she was continually smiling as if it was all a huge joke. Her mother—and I thought that was odd, too, under the circumstances—was quite sharp with her: 'Didn't you hear what he asked? Answer the question!' "

Norma eventually gave DC Kerr the first of several statements she would make over the next few days (and which would eventually form part of the evidence the jury would be able to see in court). Examined in retrospect, for a child who was considered educationally subnormal and was scheduled in the coming term to attend a special secondary school, it turned out to be a remarkably intelligent mixture of truth and invention.

> The Howe family moved into our street about one year ago and little Brian Howe started to play with my brothers John Henry and Hugh Bell . . . I have never seen any of them playing near the railway lines, behind the Delaval Arms public house. I have only been down there about 2 or 3 times, and the last time was months ago.
>
> The last time I saw Brian Howe was about 12:45 P.M., Wednesday, July 31, 1968, when he was playing with his brother and two little girls on the corner of Whitehouse Road and Crosshill Road . . . Between 1:00 P.M. and 5:00 P.M. that day I played in my street with Gillian and Linda Routledge, 59 Whitehouse Road. We were making pom-poms. [Next to this last sentence appears the police remark "verified."]

At this point the police had made no connection between Norma and Mary. When Detective Constable Kerr went next door, to 70 Whitehouse Road, it was only to clarify Mary's replies to question 6—"When did you last see Brian?"—and question 9—"Were you playing behind the Delaval Arms public house near to the railway lines between 1:00 P.M. and 5:00 P.M., Wednesday, July 31?"

"It was a very different atmosphere in there," DC Kerr told me. "No feeling of a home whatever, just a shell: very peculiar, no sound, beat-up furniture and very little of it, and airless, stuffy, dark, you know, on a brilliant summer afternoon. The only life one felt was the barking of a big dog, a ferocious-looking Alsatian.

"Mary was the most evasive child I'd ever come across," he said. "And her father was very odd. I asked him: 'You be her father?' And he said, 'No, I'm her uncle.' 'Where are her parents?' I asked. And he answered: 'She's only got a mother and she's away on business.'" (It seems that when the Bells had moved to Whitehouse Road a year and a half before, Betty Bell had notified the council that her husband had abandoned her. She proceeded to claim the relevant social security benefits and the children were instructed to call their father "uncle" when any stranger was within hearing.)

"All the questions I asked Mary," DC Kerr continued, "she was continually looking at Billy Bell for guidance." He finally wrote to Mary's dictation, her statement shorter but parallel to Norma's:

> I last saw Brian Howe in Whitehouse Road about 12:30 P.M., Wednesday, July 31 . . . when he was playing with his brother. I did not go near the Railway Lines or the wasteground near there at all on Wednesday . . . I have been down there before, but it was at least two months ago.

DC Kerr returned to Norma's house several hours later that first day, after the two girls' statements had been studied by Mr. Dobson at the West End police station. The evasive and too-perfect replies of these "best friends" were suspicious. Norma now amended her statement to add that she had "met" and "played" with "Mary Flora Bell" that Wednesday morning until 1:30 P.M. in their back gardens; that she had picked her up again at 2:30 P.M., and that both of them had gone to play for half an hour with "Elaine the daughter of the owner of Davy's shop [at the corner of their street]." Returning to their respective houses "for about 10 minutes," she said, they joined up again about 3:15 P.M. and "played in the street [Whitehouse Road] until about 5:00 P.M." This was of course a lie: as I would find out during my talks with Mary in 1996, Norma was still at this point keeping faith with a "pact" the two girls had made. "I then went over to Gillian and Linda Routledge's house and we sat on their front step making pom-poms. As far as I know Mary Flora Bell just went into her house. I didn't see her again until 7:00 P.M. in the back lane behind our house, when she was on her own. I don't know where she had been."

The making of the pom-poms—which had really happened off and on that afternoon—would remain until the end Norma's security blanket, her proof that she had been in the presence of someone else. As it had been in her first statement, though, most of the timing was untrue.

The next day, Friday, August 2, another officer, Detective Sergeant Docherty, saw Mary again about further inconsistencies in her answers. She had remembered something else now, she told him. On the day Brian Howe was killed, she saw a little boy (whom the police called boy "A") standing by himself in Delaval Road and "he was covered with grass and little purply flowers." She had seen him often playing with Brian and also seen him hit Brian for no reason at all around the face and neck. And, digging a deep hole for herself in her attempt to lie herself and Norma out of trouble, she added: "I've seen ["A"] play with a pair of scissors like silver-coloured and something wrong with [them] like one leg was either broken or bent. And I saw him trying to cut a cat's tail off with those scissors."

"Those scissors Mary Bell mentioned, which we had found lying in the grass near Brian Howe's body," Mr. Dobson said, "had not been photographed or described in any of the newspapers. 'A' was eight years old; he was the first child I saw myself, and we spent two days on him. His story, as he told it clearly enough over and over, was confirmed not only by his parents, who one might of course expect to cover up for him, but by a whole lot of other people." "A" had in fact played with Brian Howe in the morning but had gone on a family outing in the afternoon and not come back to Scotswood until 10:00 P.M.

"Everything 'A' had said had proved true," Mr. Dobson continued. "But Mary Bell had said that she saw 'A' with those scissors. How did she know about those scissors, which could have been used to make the puncture marks on Brian's body? How could she know enough to describe exactly what they were like? Those two girls, Mary Bell and Norma Bell, had already changed their statements twice. By that time we had pretty well eliminated everybody else. I had not seen them yet but they had remained in a pocket of my mind: it had to be them, or one of them."

On Sunday, August 4, a third police officer, Detective Constable Thompson, questioned Norma again at home. He confronted her with having been seen by others with Mary Bell and her dog that Wednesday at times other than those she had stated. At this point Norma broke down and burst into tears. It was clear that she was by now under great pressure from her family to tell the truth. They were sure that Norma could not have done anything bad but they did suspect Mary. She asked to speak to the officer without her father being present and her father left the room before DC Thompson could stop him (police are not allowed to interview a child except in the presence of another adult). "I was down Delaval Road with Mary and the dog," she said quickly. "Mary took me to see Brian ..." Constable Thompson stopped her, called her father back in, and said he was taking Norma to the police station. Norma said again she didn't want her father along and again Mr. Bell agreed but was taken there shortly afterwards in another police car.

When Mr. Dobson saw Norma at 8:10 that night, she was pale and nervous. "Her eyes darted from one of us to the other and there was this nervous smile that turned to tears at the drop of a hat," he said. "I knew it wasn't quite the moment of truth, but almost ..."

After he had cautioned her, she told him that she had gone down to the "blocks"—by which she meant the concrete blocks on the Tin Lizzie—with Mary Bell, "and I tripped over his head." Brian was dead, she said, and claimed that Mary had told her she had "squeezed his neck and pushed up his lungs," and that she had told her, "Keep your nose dry and don't tell anybody." She then described how little Brian had looked and lain, and that Mary, after showing her a "razor," and where she had "cut his belly," had hidden the razor under a block and told Norma not to tell her dad or she would get into trouble. Asked whether she could show Mr. Dobson where the razor was hidden, she replied yes, and fifteen minutes later, taken to the place on the Tin Lizzie where Brian had been found, she pointed to a concrete block, under which the police found a razor blade. When Mr. Dobson then told her to show him the position Brian's body had been in, Norma lay down on the ground in the exact position Brian had been found.

Less than half an hour later, back at the police station, Mr. Dobson asked Norma in her father's presence whether she wanted to make another written statement. "She'd been given tea and a sandwich," Mr. Dobson told me. "She was very tired by then. But there was nothing for it. We had to have it." Norma had begun to give her statement nervously but then stopped, looking anxiously at her father. Mr. Dobson had asked her whether she wanted him to go out. She said yes, and he had a policewoman come in to sit with her.

According to this, her third statement, Norma had known nothing of Brian's death until, walking with Mary, she had come upon his dead body, after which, she says, Mary had told her she had killed him. In her second statement she had already established a series of times and names aside from Mary's that could show her as being anywhere except the Tin Lizzie that afternoon. In this third statement now she admits to a "walk" with Mary and her dog and a stay of "ten minutes" at the blocks before she was back making "pom-poms" at 4:00 P.M.: precise times and the "pom-poms" would keep reappearing. After that, she says, she "didn't see [Mary] for a long time." At a quarter to seven, she said now, she joined up with Pat Howe, Brian's fourteen-year-old sister, and Mary, to look for Brian, but she left them, she says, by 7:00 P.M. and went back to play with Linda until half-past eight, when she went home and stayed in.

Very little in this statement was true except her joining in the search for Brian (though much earlier than she stated) and the making of pom-poms. But now too tired to keep up the logical sequence she had managed so far, she ended up with what James Dobson called "a whopper." She hadn't told anybody about what she had seen, she said, " 'cause I was frightened and if I had snitched, May could have taken anyone else's bairn. The last time I saw Brian," she lied, "was about dinner time [noon] when he was playing with Norman [his brother]. I forgot to say when we left Brian, May put some purple flowers on top of the grass that was over Brian." It was the first time she admitted some involvement.

At 10:30 P.M., with her father's agreement, Norma was taken to stay at Fernwood, the county council children's reception home, where four months later Mary would spend the two weeks of the trial in an attic on the top floor, guarded round the clock by a rota of fourteen police-women. ("I never knew till long afterwards," she told me, "that my two little sisters and [her brother] P. were there all the time* while I was locked in, upstairs.")

Detective Constable Kerr, meanwhile, was once again knocking on the door of number 70. "Mary came to the door," he said. "I asked whether I could come in. She said, 'No.' I asked her why not and she said, 'My uncle's not in.' I asked her where he was, and when she said at the pub, I told her to get him. Billy Bell was very hostile when they got back and Mary was again continually looking at him. Of course, I believed he was her uncle. I had no reason not to. And I had the feeling that this uncle was only passing through, you know, not living there. I got no further information from them that evening." DC Kerr was correct in his impressions: Billy and Betty Bell at this point no longer lived together: she exercised her profession almost entirely in Glasgow and, as Mary quite rightly said, was "away" much of the time. Whenever she went, Billy came. If he was away, too, in prison or exercising his own trade of small-time burglaries and petty crime, his sister Audrey, who lived virtually across the street, took the children or at least the two youngest, leaving Mary and her brother to perambulate between her house and their own.

At 12:15 A.M. on Monday, August 5, just under two hours after Norma had given her third statement, Mr. Dobson went to Mary's home with two police constables. The house was in darkness except for a blazing fire in the living room, and the television, which was going full blast. "In a murder inquiry," Mr. Dobson said, "you have to ignore the

*The three other Bell children had been taken into care temporarily and would be released to their father after the trial.

time of day or night." Billy Bell had been watching television. His wife, he said, forgetting the "uncle" fable when he answered their knock and stood across the door preventing them from coming in, was away. The four children were asleep upstairs. "I told him I wanted to question Mary at the police station. When he refused to wake her up I told him we were quite prepared to go up and get her but that it would be easier on her if he did." Billy Bell then told them to wait outside and went across the street to get his sister. Audrey came quickly, got Mary dressed, and went with her in the car to the police station. "The aunt had talked to her very sensibly in the back of the car, telling her to speak the truth. I took them straight up to my room and got somebody to bring tea and biscuits," Mr. Dobson said. "But Mary didn't seem very bothered. She was fresh-faced, chirpy and confident. She was completely alert in spite of being woken up like that."

For the next three hours, Mr. Dobson said, Mary gave an extraordinary performance. Yes, she said, she knew about Brian being dead, because she had helped look for him when he was missing. Where was she the afternoon of Wednesday, July 31? Playing with Norma. No, she never went down to the railway near the concrete blocks. "I never go there." She'd been there once, a long time ago. And she'd gone down to the car park with Pat Howe and Norma "when we were looking for Brian." Had she seen Brian that day? "Yes, about half past twelve. He was playing with his brother in Whitehouse Road."

Mr. Dobson said he had reason to believe that she had gone to the concrete blocks about 3:45 P.M. that day with Norma and seen Brian Howe there. "I never," she said. She'd gone to the park with her dog, by herself. Was she sure she had been by herself? She gave in a little: "No, I remember, I was with Norma." They'd come back at 4:30.

Forensic tests had turned up gray fibers on Brian's clothes and brown ones on his shoes. "What were you wearing that day?" Mr. Dobson asked. Her black dress, the one she was wearing now, she said, and her white blouse. Another of the officers present, Detective Inspector Laggan, said he had reason to believe she had been wearing her gray dress. "No, I wasn't. I haven't worn it for weeks." And no, she never played with Brian: "He's only little."

"I have reason to believe that when you were near the blocks with Norma a man shouted at some children and you both ran away from where Brian was lying in the grass. This man will probably know you," DI Laggan said.

"He would have to have good eyesight," she replied.

"Why would he need good eyesight?" Mr. Dobson asked quickly, and she caught hold of herself at once: "Because he was . . ."—she paused for a few seconds—". . . clever to see me when I wasn't there."

She got up. "I'm going home."

Mr. Dobson said she couldn't go home yet. "Then I'll phone for some solicitors," she said. "They'll get me out. This is being brainwashed."

"I have reason to believe," Mr. Dobson continued, "that when you were in the blocks with Norma, you showed her something which you said you had done something to Brian with. Then you hid it."

"I never," she said.

"Norma showed me where this thing was. I now have it," Mr. Dobson said.

"What was it?" Mary said. "I'll kill her."

Mr. Dobson asked her if she wanted to make a written statement saying where she was that day. "I'm making no statements," Mary answered. "I have made lots of statements. It's always me you come for. Norma's a liar. She always tried to get me into trouble."

All this had gone very slowly, Mr. Dobson told me. She had frequently sat silent for long moments and questions had to be repeated to her. "Or else she fidgeted, jumped up saying she was going, she wasn't staying there. At one stage I received a telephone call and she said, 'Is this place bugged?' She appeared to see herself in a sort of cliché scenario of a cops-and-robbers film: nothing surprised her and she admitted nothing. I had her there for three hours and she just stuck to her story: she didn't know a thing.

"Of course, it could have been true. I was not at all sure it wasn't.

Certainly these two girls had been involved, had been there. But who did what? I had no idea. At that time we had not yet made the connection with Martin Brown and frankly, even when we did, we weren't that much wiser."

At 3:30 A.M. they sent Mary back home. "It was extremely worrying," Mr. Dobson said. "Whichever child had done this was very, very disturbed, and very dangerous at that point of disturbance."

The next afternoon, Norma, who had been with the police all day, said she wanted to make another statement. She said it was to tell Mr. Dobson what she had left out the night before. She was cautioned again, and once more said she didn't want her father there: "I only want you."

"Detective Constable Thompson will have to be here," Mr. Dobson said.

"All right," she answered. "He is one of your men."

"It should have been funny," Mr. Dobson said to me later. "Except it wasn't." Had he felt that she was trying to get round him? "With her head, no. Instinctively, perhaps," he answered. Did he know why she didn't want her father present? Did she seem afraid of him? Dobson said he wasn't sure, but what was certain was that she had told and probably intended to continue to tell lies and didn't want her father to hear them. "I think specifically it was her father she was frightened of," he said. "But it was more complicated than that. She was very, very excited, and I've never been sure that it wasn't this curious excitement she didn't want her father to see." Excited because she had done something? "I didn't know whether she had or hadn't, but excited, above all, because she felt important." Had his feeling been that Norma lied and Mary didn't or that both of them lied but one more than the other? "I didn't know. We couldn't tell. Norma was much, much more childlike than Mary. Mary was lying, too, of course. But to tell the truth, she was a mystery to me. What preoccupied me a great deal was that there was, about both of them, a curious fantasy feeling I could never quite get a grip on. I always knew I should have, but of course there was the dead little boy and we couldn't really be doing with thinking 'fantasy.' It wasn't our job. And whichever way one looked at it, Mary's conduct was exceptionally and disturbingly sophisticated for an eleven-year-old Scotswood child. We didn't know then what to make of her, and, as you know, nobody ever did later, either."

Norma had been very nervous that Monday, Mr. Dobson said, "twitchy, wriggling in her seat, looking around the room even though there was nobody there and nothing to look at. I don't know what had gone on in her head, but she was falling over herself wanting to be helpful."

Norma's fourth and longest statement, though some of the details were wrong and her description certainly specifically accused Mary of killing Brian, was by no means a complete exculpation of herself. For in it she not only admits to being present when the act was committed but makes no claim that she herself was either forced or frightened and admits that she voluntarily returned twice to the scene of the crime after the toddler was dead.

At about one o'clock that Wednesday she had been playing with May, she said, and about three o'clock they had seen Brian Howe playing with his brother and his brother had given Brian a pair of scissors. "We both went with Brian. May said we would take him . . . We went over the railway lines. I had taken the scissors off Brian in the street and I carried them." They went down the bank and over two fences—"I climbed over first and May bunked the bairn over"—and walked alongside the concrete blocks until they came to an old tank. "There was a hole in the side of the tank," Norma said. "May got in first, I bunked Brian up to May, then I got in. It had a stinky smell so we all got out again. May then said, 'The blocks Norma howay,' and we went along to the blocks. Then May said to Brian, 'Lift up your neck.' "

It was at this point that some boys appeared and Brian Howe's dog, Lassie, which had followed them, started to bark, and Mary said,

'Get away or I will set the dog on you.' The boys went away. May said to Brian again, 'Lift up your neck.' She put her two hands on his neck, she said there was two lumps you had to squeeze right up. She said she meant to harm him. She got him down on the grass and she seemed to go all funny, you could tell there was something the matter with her. She kept on struggling with him and he was struggling and trying to get her hands away. She left go of him and I could hear him gasping. She squeezed his neck again and I said, 'May, leave the baby alone,' but she wouldn't. She said to me, 'My hands are getting thick, take over.' Then I ran away.

Norma had gone back to Whitehouse Road, she said, where she played for about twenty minutes until Mary appeared and asked her to come back down. "I forgot to tell you," Norma said, "that when I ran away and left Brian and May, I left the scissors on the grass. We went round by the car park. We didn't take the dog that time. That was when I tripped over Brian's head like I told you in the other statement. On the way down May found a razor blade on the path."

This was untrue: the razor blade came from one of the girls' homes, though as each of them accused the other, it was never quite clear whose. "I didn't tell you before," Norma added, "that when I lifted Brian's head and shoulders up a bit and patted his back but his hand fell on one side and I laid him down again, I felt his pulse but it wasn't going up and down. May pressed the razor blade down on Brian's belly a few times in the same place. She lifted his jersey and that's when she did it. I didn't see any blood. That was when she hid the razor blade and said, 'Don't tell your dad or I'll get wrong.' "

It was as a consequence of this statement by Norma, who could not have known that there is no bleeding after death, that the child's body was re-examined and the pathologist found on his stomach the faint outlines of the letter N, to which a fourth vertical line had been added, the pathologist thought in another hand, changing the letter to an M.

Norma said she had left the scissors "in the corner near the blocks beside Brian's feet," and that they had then both gone back to their homes. About five o'clock she saw Mary again after her tea and they took the dog and went down to the car park "to see the bairn again. May said she would make him baldy," Norma explained, "and she cut a lump of hair off his head near the front, she put it on the grass above his head. She pressed the scissors onto his belly a few times but not hard." It was at this point that the man who had seen them had shouted, and Mary, said Norma, "hadn't time to cut any more hair off before we ran away. The hair she put on the grass was separated a bit. She put the scissors on the grass somewhere beside him on the side where his hand was." Then they had gone back up to Whitehouse Road. "I saw May again about a quarter to seven when we looked for Brian with Pat."

An hour later, Mr. Dobson confronted Norma with eight pairs of scissors and asked her if she recognized the ones Brian had on Wednesday when they took him to the blocks. She immediately picked up the correct ones, threw them on the desk, and said: "That's them."

"I saw her again several times the next day, August 6," he told me. "I asked the same questions over and over. She never backtracked an inch. Either she was a masterful liar or she was speaking the truth."

The day of Brian Howe's funeral, on the morning of August 7, came in the middle of the investigation. "It was a brilliant hot summer day. There were masses of flowers," Mr. Dobson said. "There were at least two hundred people there. A lot of them who had nothing to do with the Howe family cried. It was very sad."

He said Mary was standing close to the house when the coffin was brought out and he was watching her. "It was when I saw her there that I knew I did not dare risk another day. She stood there, laughing. Laughing and rubbing her hands. I thought, 'My God, I've got to bring her in, she'll do another one.'" A woman police sergeant was sent to get Mary at 4:30 P.M.

("Oh my God," Mary said to me when I read Mr. Dobson's comment to her. "That sounds so awful, so hard, so *callous*...," she cried. "It's true," she then said, "I do tend to laugh when I'm nervous, even now. But I couldn't have ... you know ... laughed the way he said. Could I?")

. . .

Mary was very apprehensive when she was brought to Mr. Dobson's office that afternoon on August 7. "She was pale and tense," he said. "She gave me the impression she knew the time of reckoning had come." He had asked her first about her dress on July 31 and she said she had the gray one on part of the day but changed into her black one in the afternoon. "I want to tell you the truth, but I'll get wrong," she added.

Did she mean because it wasn't true that she had changed her dress? he asked.

"No," she said. "I mean about when I was there when Brian died."

She dictated her statement immediately after the nurse Mr. Dobson had requested to sit with her arrived from nearby Newcastle General Hospital.

Brian was in his front street and me and Norma were walking along towards him. We walked past him and Norma says, 'are you coming to the shop Brian' and I says, 'Norma, you've got no money, how can you go to the shop. Where are you getting it from?' She says, 'nebby' [keep your nose clean]. Little Brian followed and Norma says, 'walk up in front.' I wanted Brian to go home, but Norma kept coughing so Brian wouldn't hear us. We went down Crosshill Road with Brian still in front of us. There was this coloured boy and Norma tried to start a fight with him. She said, 'Darkie, whitewash, it's time you got washed.' The big brother came out and hit her. She shouted: 'Howay, put your dukes up.' The lad walked away and looked at her as though she was daft. We went beside Dixon's shop and climbed over the railings, I mean through a hole and over the railway. Then I said, 'Norma, where are you going?' and Norma said, 'Do you know that little pool where the tadpoles are?' When we got there, there was a big, long tank with a big, round hole with little holes round it. Norma says to Brian, 'Are you coming in here because there's a lady coming on the Number 82 and she's got boxes of sweets and that.' We all got inside, then Brian started to cry and Norma asked him if he had a sore throat. She started to squeeze his throat and he started to cry. She said, 'This isn't where the lady comes, it's over there, by them big blocks.' We went over to the blocks and she says, 'Ar—you'll have to lie down' and he lay down beside the blocks where he was found. Norma says, 'Put your neck up' and he did. Then she got hold of his neck and said 'Put it down.' She started to feel up and down his neck. She squeezed it hard, you could tell it was hard because her finger tips were going white. Brian was struggling, and I was pulling her shoulders but she went mad. I was pulling her chin up but she screamed at me. By this time she had banged Brian's head on some wood or corner of wood and Brian was lying senseless. [The postmortem would prove this was untrue.] His face was all white and bluey and his eyes were open. His lips were purplish and had all like slaver on, it turned into something like fluff. Norma covered him up and I said, 'Norma, I've got nothing to do with this, I should tell on you, but I'll not.' Little Lassie was there and it was crying and she said, 'Don't you start or I'll do the same to you.' It still cried and she went to get hold of its throat but it growled at her. She said, 'now, now, don't be hasty.'

Then, Mary said, they went back home and took Brian's dog, Lassie, with them.

Norma was acting kind of funny and making twitchy faces and spreading her fingers out. She said, 'This is the first but it'll not be the last.' I was frightened then. I carried Lassie and put her down over the railway and we went up Crosswood Road way. Norma went into the house and she got a pair of scissors and she put them down her pants. She says, 'go and get a pen.' I said 'No, what for.' She says, 'To write a note on his stomach,' and I wouldn't get the pen. She had a Gillette razor blade. It had

Gillette on. We went back to the blocks and Norma cut his hair. She tried to cut his leg and his ear with the blade. She tried to show me it was sharp, she took the top of her dress where it was raggie and cut it, it made a slit. [Examination of the dress, however, would later disprove this claim.] A man come down the railway bank with a little girl with long, blonde hair, he had a red checked shirt on and blue denim jeans. I walked away. She hid the razor blade under a big, square concrete block. She left the scissors beside him. She got out before me over the grass on to Scotswood Road. I couldn't run on the grass cos I just had my black slippers on. When we got along a bit she says, 'May, you shouldn't have done it cos you'll get into trouble,' and I hadn't done nothing I haven't got the guts. [This was so manifestly absurd that when she later repeated it at the trial, it would cause a ripple of nervous laughter in the court.] I couldn't kill a bird by the neck or throat or anything, it's horrible that. We went up the steps and went home, I was nearly crying. I said, if Pat finds out she'll kill you, never mind killing Brian, cos Pat's more like a tomboy. She's always climbing in the old buildings and that. Later on I was helping to look for Brian and I was trying to let on to Pat that I knew where he was on the blocks, but Norma said, 'he'll not be over there, he never goes there,' and she convinced Pat he wasn't there. I got shouted in about half past seven and I stayed in. I got woke up about half past eleven and we stood at the door as Brian had been found. The other day Norma wanted to get put in a home. She says will you run away with us and I said no. She said if you get put in a home and you feed the little ones and murder them then run away again.

The court would not realize, when this was read out later, that Mary's reference to "feeding the little ones" and murdering them was a clear allusion to a story in *Grimm's Fairy Tales*, pages of which Mary's mother, Betty, had glued into the "book" that she carried around at all times and that Mary read in secret.

"Do you know it's wrong to squeeze a little boy's throat?" Mr. Dobson asked her.

"Yes," she replied. "It's worse than Harry Roberts. He only did train jobs."

It was not only that she had mixed up Harry Roberts, who in fact killed three policemen in London in 1966, with the Great Train Robbery in 1963, which netted the criminals (most of whom were caught) several millions of pounds. What was more remarkable was that both these children appeared unaware of the nature or the gravity of the crime—the finality of death. Norma, who had shown above all "excitement" before and during her principal statement, was mainly concerned with the razor blade and scissors, and her desperate rejection of those items, or what had been done with them, would continue throughout the trial. But in Mary's statement, too, the child's killing and his death barely figure.

"She felt nothing," the nurse who had sat in on her statement told me later. "I've never seen anything like it. She said all those awful things they had done, but she didn't feel a thing. I thought she was a very intelligent child. But she didn't seem like a child at all. I have a boy of eleven, but he couldn't use words the way she used them. All that evening I repeated to myself what I'd heard. And even so, I couldn't believe it . . ."

Both Mary and Norma were charged on the evening of August 7 with the murder of Brian Howe. Mary answered, "That's all right with me." Norma said, "I never. I'll pay you back for this," and she cried.

Mary—Reflections 2

I was upstairs at my Aunt Audrey's when they came for me," Mary told me, thinking back to August 7, 1968. "My mother was in Glasgow. My dad wasn't there either. He had to go to the police in Durham about something he'd done, I can't remember what, and my Auntie Audrey'd gone with him. So Uncle Peter was baby-sitting all of us, their kids and our lot. There was such a kerfuffle you know, policewomen, policemen, and all of them so big . . ." She suddenly laughed. "P. had seen them arrive and he'd been in some mischief, I don't know what, and he thought they'd come for him and he ran off. He was *quick!*" she said with pride.

Had she been surprised when the police came?

"Not really. They had been several times—their house-to-house, you know—and I knew Norma had seen them even more than I had, they sort of went from one to the other and back. Then they told me Norma and Brian and I had been seen together and I told them I don't know what lies. But then they went back to her and she turned around and said, 'It wasn't me, it was May . . .' " She said Norma cried when, talking over the fence, she told Mary what she had said.

"I knew it was . . . different for her," Mary said. "I think her family had been talking to her, and in order to get out of it, they wanted . . ."

The truth? I asked.

"Yes, yes, but . . . um, they wanted her to be the first to say something, or to admit that, you know, she had anything to do with it."

And what about you? Did your parents talk to you about it?

"My mother wasn't there. She was away."

And what about your dad? Did he ask you whether you had anything to do with it? Do you think he knew?

"He did, sort of," she said slowly. "It was late at night and Brian had been found and my dad called me and we were sitting on the doorstep, and . . . um . . . he turned around and looked at me and said, 'They've found him, he's dead.' And he just looked at me and I just . . . put my head down."

Did she feel now that he knew or guessed something?

"I think the fact that I didn't ask where they'd found him . . . I don't know what he thought. I only remember us sitting there and there was a lot of noise from over down the Tin Lizzie, and a lot of lights, and my dad saying nothing, just looking at me . . ."

Her Uncle Peter had gone with her to the police station. "I was sitting on one of those swivel chairs they had and I was fooling around on it, you know, and Uncle Peter came up to me and slapped me across the face and he told me I was in big trouble, and I was to keep my mouth shut, to admit to nothing."

I asked her whether it had felt to her then as if her uncle expected her to be guilty. She shook her head. "I don't remember now what I felt, but of course I knew I'd done wrong and I would have expected to be slapped and whatever. I knew my mother wouldn't even have asked any questions, she would just have nearly beaten me to death. But thinking of it from the perspective of today, much more than believing me guilty of such a terrible thing, he may have thought that I would blabber something or other to the police that I'd made up, to show off, you know. My mother always told everybody that I fantasized and that one couldn't believe anything I said. It was years and years, a lifetime really for me, before I understood why she did that, and that it was to protect herself.

So the reason he slapped me was probably less for what I had really done—which he couldn't really know, could he?—than because what I might say was going to get my dad, his brother-in-law, into trouble. He wanted his family to have no association with this."

She remembered that slap when she talked to me, but she didn't remember that first trip to the police station in the middle of the night, two days earlier, when her Aunt Audrey had sat in the back of the car with her arm around her, talking to her quietly, urging her to tell the truth.

Earlier she had told me repeatedly that both she and Norma *wanted* to be caught. Well, I said, now you were.

"Well, that wasn't the way we had imagined it," she said.

Was there any sort of agreement to take responsibility together? I asked.

"There was no . . . um . . . we hadn't got that far really . . . We never thought . . . we thought we would be on the run, in Scotland, like big-time criminals, you know."

But big-time criminals are on the run, I said, because they know they've done wrong. Did they never realize that the police were clever and that they would find themselves arrested?

"Yes, we did, but . . . how shall I put it? That was what we *wanted*. It was all part of it. But we weren't thinking logically . . . rationally," she said. "And even while we wanted to be caught, to get away from where we were . . ."

From your families? "Yes. But we also had contingencies of how we would get away. Our horses would come with a rope and the horse would pull down the jail. That's how we imagined it, for hours, days, weeks . . ."

Of course, "jail" in their childish imagination was the sort of thing they had both seen in the innumerable Westerns they watched on TV and had nothing to do with the reality of juvenile cells in the West End police station—two small rooms at the end of a little passageway that led from the washroom to the main office. Lighter than the ordinary detention cells, they were used, with the doors open and a police officer (in this case a woman officer) sitting in the corridor within sight, if minors had to be kept overnight.

Pauline J. and Lilian H. were the policewomen on duty there that first night and when I talked to them a year later they, like all the other officers I would speak to, were still full of what they had seen and felt. "When we started our shift at ten," Pauline said, "they were lying together on a cot in one of the rooms chatting away. First thing they told us was that they'd had fish and chips for supper: 'Mr. Dobson bought them for us,' Mary said, sort of proudly, you know."

("Yes, I remember two police ladies," Mary said. "But chatting? We were arguing. I was terribly frightened I would wet the bed.")

"It was such a hot night," Pauline went on, "and they were that wrought up they couldn't sleep. We had them in different cells after a while. I sat with Mary and Lil sat with Norma. At one moment Mary shouted, 'I'll kill my mother!' . . . I'm not sure she said that," she added after a second, pondering her own memory. "It may have been, 'I'll kick my mother.' "

("I can't remember saying that," Mary said. "I wouldn't even say, 'I'll kick my mother,' not in front of a policewoman.")

"She was more concerned about her torn shoes than anything else," Pauline went on. " 'I told my mum I needed new ones,' she said. 'What will people think if they see me like this?' I tried to calm her, you know, talked to her quietly, and after a while she said that she was frightened she'd wet the bed. 'I usually do,' she said."

("That's what I remember most," Mary said. "I thought of it all the time. I always thought of it later, too, wherever they took me.")

"I told her not to worry about it," Pauline said, "but she did. She kept going to the bathroom. She didn't wet the bed, but she didn't sleep, either."

When had Mary first seen her mother after her arrest? I asked her.

"Auntie Isa was the first I saw," she said. "She came that first morning. She put her arms around me and she smelled of fresh air. I didn't see my mother till I think a week later or whatever. That's when she shouted at me as I told you, what had I done to her this time and all that."

Another officer, Lynn D., took Mary to the Croydon assessment center after that second remand hearing on August 14. "She was cheeky, you know. It was easy to dislike her with what they thought she'd done and all. But on the train to Croydon she suddenly went very still and I looked at her and thought, why, she's nothing but a little kid. She suddenly looked all pale and tired and I put my arm around her, even though her head was full of nits, and she went all limp ... soft, you know. 'I hope me mum won't have to pay a fine,' she said. I couldn't believe it, but that's what she said, that's what she was worried about. And then she talked about having to go into court again next week— they had to appear every week until the trial—and she said, 'Me mum will be there. I hope me mum won't be too upset.'

"I said her mum was upset that morning, she was crying," said Lynn D. " 'I know she was,' she said, 'but she didn't mean it. I think she doesn't like me, I'm sure she doesn't. She hates me.'

"I said, 'She's your own mum, she must love you.' 'If she loves me, why did she leave?' she said then, and I didn't know what she meant."

It is questionable whether Mary herself, at this point of confusion and despair, knew what she was trying to say, though someone trained in the minds of children would have realized how much she was revealing and might have helped her, even then, to reveal more. We can see that even at this terrifying stage of half awareness that she had done something dreadful and that dreadful things were about to happen to her, she cried out for help, and she would continue to do so in many of her remarks to the carers and policewomen who guarded her during the four months of remand and nine days of the trial. But nobody heard; nobody was equipped to understand.

The policewomen who guarded her told me they had to report every word she said, and I'm sure they did conscientiously. But this information was only required to provide the police and the lawyers with possible further evidence, not to enlighten them about the personality and problems of the accused child.

The whole problem of trying children in adult courts is that the entire judicial process is based solely on evidence. Motivation is marginal in British murder trials: it is neither the duty of the police—as Mr. Dobson said—nor that of the prosecution to seek an answer to the question why children commit crimes such as this. Under the system as it stands, there is no built-in mechanism that requires knowledge about and from a child as part of an inquiry into the crime he or she might have committed. There is no automatic investigation into the family background and circumstances of the child, which would be admissible as evidence in consideration of the case. Above all there is no sense that children are any different from adults in their understanding of the proceedings and function of the court and in their understanding of right and wrong. In fact, they are tried as small adults.

For adults, who in theory can be expected to be equipped with the same sense of right and wrong as those sitting in judgment over them, this system is justifiable: they have to be held responsible under the law for what they do; anything else would lead to chaos. But for children, for whom there is a wide separation between what they should know or are believed to know and what they do feel and understand, the evidence that proves their crimes, once obtained, should become almost irrelevant. The only thing that should count is human evidence—the answer to the question "Why?"

The Prosecution

When the trial opened in Newcastle in December 1968, the prosecutor, Rudolph Lyons, took all of the first day and half the morning of the second to make his presentation. These two very young girls, he said, were charged with the murder, within the space of little more than two months, of two little boys; but though the similarities in the choice of victim and the method of killing—strangulation—tended to indicate that both boys were killed by the same person or persons, this did not absolve the jury from considering each charge separately.

Following Mr. Dobson's hunch, the investigation of Martin Brown's death had been reopened. Mr. Lyons spent more than two-thirds of his presentation on the murder of Martin Brown, basing the Crown's case, as he explained, not on the original police findings in May, when the conclusion had been accidental death, but on those following Brian Howe's murder in July. This second investigation, he said, had produced new testimony involving the two accused girls in events that both preceded and followed Martin's death on May 25, and he went on to describe the evidence that, he said, suggested that one or both of the girls were responsible for Martin's murder.

First, he said, on the afternoon of Martin Brown's death, these two girls, Norma Bell and Mary Bell, had appeared on the scene at 85 Whitehouse Road within minutes of the discovery of the body and before any other member of the public. Only minutes later, they had eagerly informed Martin's aunt, Rita Finlay, of the child's death. On the following day these same two girls had broken into a local nursery and left four vulgarly worded notes beginning "We murder . . .", which the police had found the next day. And four days later, he said, Mary Bell (he emphasized) had rung the Browns' doorbell and, smilingly, asked Martin's shocked mother to let her see the little boy in his coffin. Then, in late July, Mary Bell had visited the house of Brian Howe, whose fourteen-year-old sister, Pat, she knew well, and told her and a friend that "Norma got hold of little Martin by the throat." She had then showed these girls how Norma allegedly throttled Martin— this before anyone suspected that Martin had died of anything but an accident.

In September, after Brian Howe's death and the girls' arrest, Mr. Lyons said, a teacher had found a drawing in one of Mary Bell's old exercise books that until then had been mislaid. Under the heading "My Newsbook" she had drawn the figure of a child in exactly the position Martin Brown's body had been found, with the word "Tablet" next to the little figure and a workman wearing a cap and carrying some sort of tool. The significance of this, Mr. Lyons said, was that Mary Bell had made the drawing within two days of the child's death as part of a school assignment to write a news story—it was dated 27/5/68*— before there had been any mention by the police or in the press that an empty pill bottle had been found near Martin's body. But when questioned after the murder of Brian Howe, she said that the first time she had seen Martin Brown's body was in a workman's arms shortly after he was found. And furthermore, two weeks before Martin Brown's death, on Sunday, May 12, Mary Bell, coming to the local nursery sand-pit (once again he conveyed the impression that Mary had been on

*See the facsimile in the Appendix.

her own), had attacked and squeezed the throats of three little girls four years younger than herself. The jury might feel, he said, that this indicated an abnormal propensity in one of these girls to squeeze the throats of young children. "A propensity of this kind," he said, "could be valuable as a means of identification when there was no motive besides pleasure and excitement, or possibly the feeling of superiority and a child showing herself cleverer than the police."

In his comparatively brief description of the death of Brian Howe that followed, he said that in statements taken by the police, each of the two girls had told lie after lie. But while both denied they had anything to do with the death of Martin Brown, they had both admitted to being there when Brian was killed, though each said the other had committed the act. Fibers exactly matching those from a gray wool dress worn by Mary had been found on the clothing of both Martin Brown and Brian Howe. (Mr. Lyons neglected to mention at this point that fibers matching Norma's brown dress had been found on Brian's shoes.) Mary, however, he said, had tried to involve a totally innocent small boy in the killing of little Brian.

We know now, of course, much more about what Mary did and cannot go into great detail about Norma. Certainly, one cannot fault Mr. Lyons's facts, which were supplied to him by an exceptional police team, and there is no argument whatsoever about Mary's guilt. But the effect of evidence, as we shall see, depends not only on what is said, and the tone in which information is conveyed, but also on what, either deliberately or by default, is not said; and it was impossible not to see how the prosecutor's interpretation of the facts in this case, and the use he made of them, inevitably had to affect the court, the jury, the public, and the lives of all concerned.

A trial does not happen in a void: it is necessary to consider the circumstances that bring it about, the circumstances under which it is conducted, and the circumstances it creates for future lives. As I have said, the first question that should have been asked is how children could have gotten to this point of disturbance without anyone in their families or among those in charge of them being aware. The second is by what yardstick guilt was apportioned. And the third, which should apply to all cases involving serious crimes committed by children, is how guilt is interpreted—firstly by the court, then by the various authorities to whom the child's case, or punishment, is delegated, and finally by the public.

Mr. Lyons had listed seven incidents that pointed to the involvement of one or both of the girls in Martin Brown's death. I would later discover that there had been other, equally serious incidents that the prosecution either hadn't known about or hadn't mentioned. In order to gain some understanding of how the fantasizing minds of Mary and Norma developed in the three months of May, June, and July, here is a list of thirteen dates from May 11, two weeks before Martin Brown's death, to July 31, the day Brian Howe died, when both girls—or, on three of these occasions, Mary alone—either behaved conspicuously or actually offended against the law: May 11, May 12, May 25 (the day of Martin Brown's murder), May 26, May 27, May 29, May 31, June 1, June 8, June 14–16, June 17, approximately July 27, and a date in either June or July that Mary cannot recall and of which there is no record. On five of these thirteen days, both girls (and on a sixth, Mary on her own) came to the attention of authorities.

In the early afternoon of Saturday, May 11, two weeks before the murder of Martin Brown, police were called to the Delaval Arms pub in Scotswood, where a three-year-old boy, Mary's cousin John Best, had been brought in by two girls, Mary Bell and Norma Bell, with a minor head wound. Sobbing bitterly, he said he had been "pushed down" a nearby embankment but adamantly refused to say who had pushed him. As it had been Mary and Norma who had found him, they were questioned the following morning.

Their statements were virtually identical. They had been playing in the street late Saturday morning when they met little John and took him to Davy's shop to buy him some sweets. They then told him to go home. After collecting wood in some of the condemned houses nearby and taking it home to their mothers, they went to play in the parking lot next to the Delaval Arms. When they heard a child shouting "May! Norma!" (they both said) they ran to the nearby embankment and saw that John, lying at the bottom, was "bleeding from the head." They shouted to a passerby, "but he wouldn't help," so they jumped down and with some difficulty got him out. Then another man who came by carried little John to the pub and an ambulance was called.

"I have never seen John playing down there before and I have never taken him down there," Norma ended her statement.

Mary said, "I don't know how John got down behind the sheds. I have never taken him there to play before."

Even though the police were aware that little John had said he had been "pushed," it never occurred to the three officers who questioned the girls to wonder why the boy had so specifically called out "May! Norma!" (as any small child will beg for help from those who hurt him). And as the child's young mother thought he had fallen while playing in a forbidden place, they logged it—not surprisingly perhaps—as an accident. They had, after all, more serious cases to worry about in Scotswood. Nonetheless, when I later checked the date of this "accident" with the police, I found that it and the girls' names had been quite properly recorded. The prosecutor, however, did not mention this first recorded incident in the chain of events involving both girls.

He did, however, mention the "sandpit incident," as it became known later, which occurred the next day, May 12, and was reported to the police at 9:30 P.M. that Sunday night by the mother of seven-year-old Pauline Watson—one of the three little girls Mary was accused of attacking. Pauline told two policewomen the next morning that they had been playing in the sandpit when "two big girls came in. The smallest one of the two girls told me to get out of the sandpit. I said no. She put her hands around my neck and squeezed hard. The bigger girl was behind the hut, playing. The girl took her hands off my neck and she did the same to Susan . . . The girl who squeezed my neck had short dark hair. I don't know this girl and had not seen her before." But older girls who had been playing around the sandpit identified Norma and Mary as the "two big girls" and Mary as the one who had caused trouble. So on Monday afternoon, May 13, Norma and Mary once again gave virtually identical statements to two policewomen who came to see them, except that this time each of the girls, in almost the same words, accused the other, a pattern that would become very familiar in the coming months. The only deviation was that Norma, after telling how Mary had attacked the little girls, ended her statement on what I found a convincingly childlike note. She said that after squeezing Pauline's and Cindy's necks, Mary had done the same to Susan Cornish. "Susan had some rock," she continued, "and Mary took this off her. I said to Mary, 'There'll be trouble,' and then Mary asked me if I wanted some rock. I said, 'Yes,' and had a little piece from her. I then ran off and left Mary. I'm not friends with her now." (Twenty-eight years later Mary, though with some corrections, would essentially confirm the little girls' story, though she would quite strenuously avoid using the word "throat": "Cindy had thrown sand at me," she told me, "and she and the two others were going to hit me, so I put my hands around their ears or hair or something . . .")

This case, too, I would find in police records. A Sergeant Lindgren wrote that he had seen the three little girls on Sunday but that "they had no marks or injuries to substantiate the complaints" and that the parents, informed that they could take out a private summons for common assault, had declined. Sergeant Lindgren added, "In view of the home circumstances of the two older girls, the [social services] Children's Department has been notified" and "the girls BELL have been warned as to their future conduct."

I would discover later that Newcastle social services had been aware of the two Bell families all along. Norma's because, with eleven children, there was a fairly constant need for material help; Mary's because of her father's repeated troubles with the police and her mother's frequent absences. And a social worker tried to explain to me why there was no record of any social workers visiting the families following the police notification after the sandpit incident. "Children are always squabbling around here," she said. "And you saw that the police didn't actually find any damage on the little girls. We have to be very careful not to intrude too much on families. It is easily resented and then we can do nothing with them. We need their trust." The children of both Bell families, she said, appeared to be properly fed and clothed and were attending school, so they were not considered at risk. Social workers are on the whole strongly protective of their clients' privacy. One can appreciate why, but the practice puts children at risk, for it means that unless parents are conspicuously negligent or abusive, the priority for social workers is to keep families together, at almost any cost.

On May 25, the day three schoolboys found Martin Brown dead inside 85 St. Margaret's Road at about 3:30 P.M., one of them, Walter Long, feeling sick minutes later and getting some air at a window, saw two dark-haired girls (the smaller of whom, Mary Bell, he knew) climb through a basement window into the condemned house next door, from which, by climbing up a flight of stairs that was still intact, it was possible to get through a broken wall into the boarded-up ground floor of number 85. He would testify at the trial that he told the girls to go away when they came up the stairs and that Mary replied (in her usual show-off way), "It's all right. The police know I'm here." Only a few minutes later, as Mr. Lyons had told the court, these same two girls were knocking at Mrs. Finlay's house to tell her that her nephew had had an accident.

Rita Finlay talked to me about that day some weeks after the trial. "There was a knock on the door . . . and it was them two, Norma and Mary," she said. "And I said, 'What do yous want?' and . . . that Mary . . . she said, 'One of your bairns has had an accident . . . No, I think it's your June's. But there's blood all over . . .' " When Mrs. Finlay, running all the way, arrived at the derelict house, Mary was there again and told her she could show her where the body was. "I was going hysterical," she said. "I told her to get out of my way and followed a man up some stairs into a small bedroom where I saw Martin in the arms of another man. He looked asleep."

And from that point on, if only it had been understood, the two girls' behavior became ever more indicative of profound disturbance.

Mrs. Finlay also told me that the next day, Sunday, May 26 (Mary's eleventh birthday), "those two girls, Norma and Mary, came and asked to take [her] John out." She knew the girls well, particularly Norma, who had baby-sat John often and whom she liked a lot. "I thought it was very good of them," she said, ". . . with me so upset. They came every day after that to play with him or to take him to the shops. But then they kept asking me, 'Do you miss Martin?' and 'Do you cry for him?' and 'Does June miss him?' and they were always grinning. In the end I could stand it no more and told them to get out and not to come back . . ." Mr. Lyons appeared unaware of this development.

June Brown, too, told me about this curious grinning. She said that Mary had knocked on her door four days after Martin had been found and, smiling, asked to see Martin. June remembered that there was another girl, or maybe several girls, standing giggling down the garden path. "I said, 'No, pet. Martin's dead.' And she said, 'Oh, I know he's dead. I wanted to see him in his coffin.' And she was still grinning . . ."

It was, however, the dreadful notes the girls left when they broke into the Woodlands Crescent Nursery on that same Sunday, May 26, that Mr. Lyons particularly emphasized. Several members of the jury had felt visibly unwell earlier when shown photographs of the dead boys and looked reluctant when they were handed photostats of the notes and specimens of the girls' handwriting for comparison.

The police had found the notes among the wreckage of smeared paints and torn school and cleaning materials when they were called in on Monday morning (the same morning when, in school a few streets away, Mary made her drawing of a little body on the floor). There were four pieces of paper with words scribbled on them in childish writing. The letters looked as if they had been formed alternately by two different hands (as did the letter N, altered by another hand to M, on Brian Howe's stomach, the pathologist said, two months later). One note said: "I murder SO That I may come back." The second, after the capital letters "BAS" at the top, read: "fuch of we murder watch out Fanny and FAggot." The third note said: "WE did murder Martain brown, fuckof you BAstArd." The fourth: "YOU ArE micey y BecuaSe we murderd

Martain GO Brown you BEttER Look out THErE arE MurdErs aBout By FANNYAND and auld Faggot you srcews." (Mary would later say she was "auld Faggot.")*

But the young policemen who had come in answer to the nursery teachers' telephone call decided that the mess and the notes were a nasty prank, and the notes were filed away in the station sergeant's drawer. The nursery, however, was a valuable property so it was decided to install a beeper alarm system in the loft. On May 27 Mary drew the picture of Martin in her school notebook, and on May 29 she asked to see Martin in his coffin.

What Mr. Lyons did not tell the court was that the new alarm went off on the afternoon of May 31, and when the police got there they found Mary and Norma. Questioned at the station, they swore they'd never broken in before and would never do it again, and as the police never took the "We murder" notes seriously and didn't for a minute associate the two break-ins, the girls were charged with breaking and entering and released into their parents' custody until the case could be heard in Juvenile Court, which (they were told) would be months later.

What Mr. Lyons also didn't tell the court—under the judicial system as it stands it wouldn't have been part of the evidence—was that the very next day, on Saturday, June 1, Mary and Norma ran away from home. They were picked up the following day by the police in South Shields, about ten miles away, and brought back.

The Woodlands Crescent Nursery sandpit was evidently a social center for Scotswood children. On June 8, a week after the second break-in—two weeks after Martin Brown was killed—twelve-year-old David McCready witnessed a fight there between Norma and Mary. This, too, Mr. Lyons did not tell the jury, though they would hear about it later in the trial.

Mary had thrown Norma to the ground, David said, and was hitting and scratching her. And then he heard her scream, "I am a murderer!" She had then, he said in court, pointed in the direction of the house

*See the facsimiles in the Appendix.

where little Martin had been found and called out to him, "That house over there, that's where I killed ... Brown." David said he'd just laughed because Mary Bell was such a show-off. Everybody knew she was, he said.

Then on June 14, the two girls ran away again. This time they were on their way to Scotland and were on the loose for two days before being turned off a bus at Alnwick, forty miles north of Newcastle, because they were trying to travel with used tickets.

Mary would tell me a great deal about her absconding with Norma, but although she remembers being brought back both times in police cars (and remembers getting beatings from her mother), she has no memory of being questioned on June 17 either by police or by social workers about it. "Social workers came to the house to see my mother but she threw them out, and they didn't come back," she told me. "And if they had questioned us, what could we have said? That our dream was to live with horses in the wilds of Scotland? That we planned to eat carrots, dig a hole if it rained? That the only practicalities we'd thought of was to steal enough money to buy the first bus tickets and to take some matches to light fires? We were just two nut cases, and it wouldn't have meant anything to them. I knew that then and I know it now."

She also remembered—"It wasn't long after that, though it's all a bit of a blur now, you know, like images going into each other"—telling that awful tale to Pat Howe about Norma killing Martin. "I had had that awful fight with Norma. We were fighting and threatening each other all the time and this was just part of it."

Pat and her friend Irene, of course, hadn't believed a word of it: everybody knew that Martin had died in an accident in the condemned houses two months earlier. All Scotswood had mourned with June and George Brown and hundreds of people had gone and demonstrated in the Newcastle streets to protest because the houses should have been pulled down long ago and were a danger to their kids. But Pat and Irene had warned Mary that Norma's dad would find out she was telling such tales and she'd be in awful trouble. "I went and apologized to Norma's mother," Mary told me. Did she know, I asked her, what made them take three-year-old Brian, Pat's brother, just four days later and she shook her head.

But, unconsciously, the eleven-year-old girl knew more than the forty-one-year-old woman now remembers. What is important about the drawing Mary did only forty-eight hours after killing Martin, about the writings left at the nursery, about her shouts of "I am a murderer," and about all the bizarre behavior described by Mr. Lyons to the jury as that of a vicious and monstrous child, is not what she was trying to hide but what she tried to disclose. Under a different system, a different kind of "court"—though just as certain of Mary's guilt—would have known what these disclosures meant. Informed about the child's circumstances before coming to decisions about her life, they would have realized how unlikely it was that a girl as intelligent as Mary would have deliberately drawn attention to herself, as she did over and over after Martin's murder, for any other purpose than the unconscious one of wanting to be stopped and helped.

By the end of that first day, there could be no doubt in anybody's mind where the prosecutor stood. Already he had planted the seeds in the jury's mind that, two weeks later, would lead to a verdict of not guilty for Norma and guilty of manslaughter because of diminished responsibility for Mary. Norma, Mr. Lyons concluded his argument, would be shown to be an immature, backward girl who, but for the fact that she and Mary lived next door to each other, would never have been in the terrible position in which she was now placed. Mary, however, as witnesses would testify, had this propensity for putting her hands on the throats of smaller children. Although two years and two months younger than Norma, she was the cleverer and more dominating personality. And it was Mary, he said, who in one of her statements had tried with cunning to involve a totally innocent small boy in the murder of Brian Howe. He then told the court how Mary had told the police long before anything had been published about the scissors that had been found next to Brian's body, about eight-year-old "A," who had often played with Brian and that she had seen this little boy attempt to "cut a cat's tail off" with a pair of scissors "like silver-colored and something wrong . . . like one leg . . . either broken or bent."

Mr. Lyons's last words that first day of the trial would somehow establish Mary not as a disturbed or sick child but as an evil being, irrespective of age—a monster. Magnifying Mary's rather pathetic, childish effort to get herself and Norma out of trouble by putting it all on an innocent eight-year-old boy made it take on a significance out of all proportion to the real tragedy, the death of the two small boys, and become a reprehensible deed against which everything else had to be measured. "This gives you some indication of the sort of girl she is," he said, finishing his presentation.

And late that night, in the locked little top-floor flat at the Fernwood reception center where Mary was kept isolated under police guard for the nine days and two weekends of the trial, she asked policewoman Barbara F. the meaning of the word "immature." Each of the policewomen had their own feelings and reactions to Mary, and Barbara F. told me frankly that she hadn't liked her and felt "creepy" about her. "But of course, if she asked about something, I tried to answer."

"Would that mean if I was the more intelligent I'd get all the blame?" Mary asked.

"I just shrugged," the policewoman said. "What could you say?"

Mary—Reflections 3

Mary had talked again and again about "a pact" she and Norma had made and she tried many times to explain it to me but, apparently never sure herself just how and when it came about, never quite succeeded. However, while the timing changed again and again, the fact that it was "an agreement to do everything together" remained constant.

This "pact" or "agreement" had two aspects, both of which appeared and reappeared throughout Mary's many attempts to recall the events that reached a first tragic peak with the killing of Martin Brown. The first was, as stated, to do everything together; the second element remained constant too: there was never a "plan" to kill a child, only increasingly terrible fantasies that these two unhappy children shared.

"You see, what we did, more and more as time went on, was to 'dare' each other," Mary said. "I was 'Miss Dare Me' and Norma ... well ... she'd dare me to do things and I did and then I dared her to do it too and of course she would; she wasn't going to be chicken. She'd say, 'I dare you to walk on the pipes over the Tyne Bridge,' and I'd do it. And then she'd do it too, never mind if we might have fallen down into the Tyne. We'd do more and more dangerously naughty things ... we kept hoping we'd be arrested and sent away. It was all I wanted and [all] she said she wanted too . . ."

That first date in May, when the two girls came to the attention of the police after pushing little John down the embankment, was already part of this increasing drive to do "bad" things. "We were going to get into the factory [the Vickers Armstrong plant] down by the Delaval Arms," Mary said. What were they going to do there? I asked, and she shrugged, "I haven't got a clue, but certainly mischief. He was pestering us and he wouldn't leave us alone, so I pushed him and said go away and he fell down a bit of an incline where there was like a little workman's hut type of thing . . ."

Was he hurt?

"No . . . he got up and came back and I says . . . I says [wrong grammar or repeating words is invariably a sign of stress in Mary, who now usually speaks middle-class English], 'Go away,' and he was a stocky little thing, and I said, 'I'll push you again, I'll push you off there.' He sat down, the little bugger, so I grabbed him by the leg and hurled him over the edge; he could practically touch the bottom, you know. I just dropped him. I says, 'Now go away and stay away.' I didn't want to hurt him; it was like, Bugger off, you nuisance . . ."

What did she remember about the sandpit incident? I asked. Did she touch those three little girls as was said in the trial?

"There were loads of us children there," she said. "And Cindy Hepple threw sand at me. But I didn't put my hands around her throat like they said. I put my hands around her ears or her hair or something like that . . . I don't even remember the other two they said, but two big girls came— they were about fourteen—and throttled me. Somebody had her hands around my throat and I passed out or felt like it and they threw me into a bed of nettles. It was because I had hit Cindy, they said, but you know, that was the way it was, no matter how old anyone was, that was the way we used to be. Those older girls, they were massive as far as I was concerned, but I remember . . . I got so angry I just . . . jumped up and I pulled them down and bashed their heads off the floor. And then I just felt unstoppable [but] then other big girls came and I got kicked all over . . . I was battered all over, had black eyes and was blue all over, but that wasn't ever reported . . ."

Had Norma come and helped her?

"She was just in the background there. [Norma would tell the court that she was playing "behind a shed" and the small girls confirmed this.] My father said something like, you know, 'It's always the same, someone else loads the gun and fires a bullet but you are the bullet that comes out. You are the idiot that comes out.' You see that's why Norma . . . It's another thing that requires a certain amount of intelligence, doesn't it, to stay in the background? And that was her way of coping and who can blame her? I don't. Not *her*."

In several of her versions of the death of Martin Brown, Mary claims she told Norma that she had killed Martin the moment she went to get her at her house that Saturday afternoon, where Norma had been watching her mother ironing (and Norma confirmed this at the trial). And she quotes Norma saying, "You didn't, you didn't? *Show* me." But when they went back to St. Margaret's Road after the murder, Mary and Norma both said at the trial, Norma never came with her "all the way up" to the first-floor bedroom where John Hall, the electrician, was holding the little boy in his arms after trying to give him the kiss of life. "She turned around before we got there," Mary told me, "and ran down. And later she kept saying . . . for weeks she did . . . 'You didn't really do it. It was an accident. He had an accident, everybody says so.' And I kept having to tell her that, yes, I *did*, and that although we had agreed to do everything together, she hadn't been there, she was a traitor, she hadn't helped." Nonetheless it is clear from all the testimonies during the trial, and confirmed by Mary's memories now, that both girls were feverishly excited by what Mary had done. (The fact that it took her several months and four different versions of the terrible fifteen or twenty minutes during which she killed Martin before what she said made any sense at all might tempt one to dismiss it all as lies: certainly I knew that her first three versions were in part, though never altogether, escapes from an unbearable reality into gentler fantasies. What was true, however, from the very start, was that she never claimed once that Norma was aware in advance that she was really going to kill a child.)

Why had she gone to Martin's house four days after he died? I asked her. When she had been asked that question at the trial, she said that she and Norma were daring each other, that neither of them wanted to be "chicken." Her answer to me, weeks after she had begun to try to recall her state of mind during those days, was more searching—"To see if he was yet alive."

Her inability, when she killed Martin, to understand the finality of death, permeates every one of her attempts to account, to me as well as to herself, for what she did. "I didn't understand the concept of death [being] forever . . . It was unreal, incomprehensible. I had nothing against Martin or him against me. I didn't mean to kill him forever. I just thought I'd get taken away . . . I strangled him, but I thought of, you know, 'Play dead.'"

Was it a game? I asked.

"No, I didn't think it was a game . . . I just thought, I'm not really hurting you . . . I told him to put his hands on my throat and I put my hands on his . . . Obviously, I must have been messed up inside, but I never associated it with the afterwards . . . I think to me it was: 'You'll come around in time for tea.'" (And during another attempt to talk about Martin's death, she talked as she thought she must have spoken in her mind that awful afternoon. "I must have done, I must have known, I must have [thought] that he'll come round, it's all right, you'll come round, you know. You go to sleep and you'll come round, come round, come round in time for tea . . ."—all of this interspersed with hacking sobs.)

The first break-in at the nursery was obviously a signal point in both girls' disturbance. Mary's recollection of it now, however, shows how deliberate the action of writing was and how aware she was of the dangers. "I was doing it with my right hand," she said, "because they were able to tell, you know, if one was left-handed [Mary is left-handed]. I'd never seen Norma's writing before, really. I hadn't seen work that she'd done. She was two years older than me and in a different class. In the note where it says, 'There are murders about,' she put 'murder' and I says, 'No, it's "murders" [i.e., murderers],' so she added the 's' and that's when she said, 'You should kill one of your little ones,' and I said, 'No, I won't, why don't you kill one of yours, there's so many of you it wouldn't even be noticed.' "

Running away on those two occasions in June was another stage in the development of their relationship, and according to Mary—and the description of the place they went to appears to prove it—at least the first of these two trips was made not on Mary's but on Norma's initiative. "I hadn't run away before," Mary said. "But Norma had, and she said it was easy. She said, 'We'll go to South Shields. I've been there before,' and she told me about a man there who liked her and we stole money from home for the bus. I was really excited at the thought of running away, we both were. Norma came by and before going I peed on the floor [this is one of the classic symptoms of aggression in children] and I laughed and laughed and Norma laughed too . . ."

Did you wipe it up? I asked her.

"Oh no," she said. "I left it right there. If I could have opened my bowels, I'm sure I would have done that, too."

And then she digressed to talk about her bed in Whitehouse Road. "I didn't have any sheets or blankets, just bits and pieces like an old coat on top of me. There was just a mattress which had a dip in the middle where the urine collected and I was always up very early and my bed was always wet and when my mother was there she would rub my face in it and I had to haul the mattress out onto the window[sill] so that everyone could see, because she said I was just doing it to spite her." They had taken the bus to South Shields, she then said, about an hour away, and Norma took them straight to a house she obviously knew well. "I know Norma's parents thought later I led her astray," Mary said when I put it to her, "but it was she who took me to South Shields. She'd run away there before and wound up at the house of this man who sexually abused her."

Norma told you this?

"Yes. She told me the house had a lot of rooms and a nice kitchen and we could cook if we wanted to . . . The man would let us do anything we wanted. She told me he'd done things to her and that she had liked it."

How old was the man? I asked.

"Oh, I don't know," she said. "To an eleven-year-old anybody is old. I said I just wanted to make toffee cakes and he said OK, but we should have a bath first. So we got into the bathtub and when I got out he tried to put butter on me, you know, down below, and I said I didn't want to and I pushed him off onto Norma and he did it to her . . ."

He did what?

"He penetrated her."

How did you know the man was doing that?

"I watched, and later Norma said again that she liked it."

Did the man live alone in the house?

"We didn't see anybody else, and at about five o'clock in the morning he got us up and took us in a car to some backstreets and left us there. That's where the police picked us up."

Had they told the police about the man?

"God no, we were in enough trouble as it was."

It was after this running away that they confirmed their "pact," she said. "We were taken back to Newcastle in a police car and the police got Norma's father and my mother to pick us up at the station. I got beaten for it by my mother and I'm sure Norma was in trouble, too, but in a funny way we were proud of ourselves. You see, my dad was always in trouble with the police, and now I'd been taken to the police station as well. After that we said we were criminals together and we promised each other that everything we did from then on we would do together . . ."

But had they actually said they would kill someone together?

She looked at me helplessly. "How can one explain this now? No, I don't think so, not in that way, but yes, we probably said words like that . . . You know how people—not just children, adults too—say 'I'll kill her' or 'I could kill them.' But when you ask me like that I don't know what to say. I think now we *were* fantasizing, dreadfully, grotesquely. I remember asking my dad what the worst thing was that someone could do and he answered, 'Kill a policeman.' And after that, yes, we kept talking about killing . . . someone . . ."

A child?

"No, it wasn't . . . No, no, it wasn't . . . It was just . . . to do the worst thing that could be done . . ."

And obviously, you couldn't kill a policeman. But why did you want to do the worst thing that could be done?

"I don't know. We talked all the time about running away, being on the run to somewhere in the wilds of Scotland, living with horses. It was . . . It was . . ." She was stammering. "Don't you understand? . . ." Her voice was beginning to sound strained. "It was fantasy. But I think we didn't know it was fantasy and we built it up and up until—it now seems—we never talked about anything except doing terrible things and being taken away. But we agreed we wouldn't ever . . . Not our brothers and sisters or cousins . . ."

So in fact by then "killing" and "children" were on your minds?

She shook her head. "It wasn't like that. It wasn't . . . real . . . like that."

What she remembers very vividly (and given the lack of communication between different Newcastle authorities, Mr. Lyons almost certainly didn't know about this) was the other significant event in her life, toward the end of June or the beginning of July, which she associates with the running-away episodes. Although she cannot remember dates and mixes up the times of some of her most momentous experiences, she thinks it was just about after the second running away, on June 14, when they had two days on the road to Scotland before they were caught, that she was sent again to a convalescent home for enuretic children in Rothbury, about fifty miles north of Newcastle. She had been a bed wetter, she thinks, since she was four years old and had been there several times. "I loved it," she told me. "A young couple ran it and they were really nice. I can't remember their name. We did physical things all day long, all kinds of sports, and the place was so clean and pretty. It was such a contrast, so tidy and friendly, you know, while our house in Whitehouse Road was always dirty and angry and loud when my mother was there. So when they told me one evening I had to go home the next day, I said that I didn't want to go back home and asked them to let me stay there. Couldn't I just live with them? And they . . . they asked me questions I couldn't answer. But then they went and told on me. And when they took me back to Newcastle, I got taken to some office, magistrates' or some children's service or what have you, and the woman there . . . I had to stand across from her, on the other side of a table . . . She said did I really not want to go home? And I didn't answer because my mother was standing behind me, and the woman said, 'What is it? Do you want to be sent away?' and I could hear my mother breathing back of me so I took a jug of water that stood on the table and chucked the water in the lady's face and my mother slapped my face and we went home.

"It was so stupid," she said to me. "You know, to ask me in front of my mother whether I *really* wanted to leave home." The moment they got back to the house, "My mother grabbed me by the hair and shook me, and her midriff was bare, and she had a checkered skirt on, and there was that female smell, period kind of smell, disgusting, and I was crying. And I tore myself loose screaming, 'I don't want to be here!' And I ran outside and bounced up and down on the fence between Norma's house and mine, showing off, I suppose, and I was being 'Puppet on a String,' which was number one in the charts at the time, and Norma's mum came out and sang along with us and then she asked me to sing 'Congratulations,' the Cliff Richard one, and then she said how well I sang and that perhaps I'd be a singer one day. It made me feel so much better."

Had she ever wondered why Norma kept saying she hated home and wanted to be away from her parents when her mum was so nice?

"No, I was too small to think about that," she said. "I thought of me."

When Mary went to the house of Brian Howe on or around July 27 and told fourteen-year-old Pat the lie that Norma had killed Martin Brown, it was, one might say, her last cry for help. It was grotesquely tragic that it should have been to the sister of the little boy who was to die four days later.

The Verdict

As the trial progressed, Norma's frequent tears and Mary's controlled stillness created an almost tangible atmosphere of compassion toward one and animosity toward the other. The tone of newspaper reports and of remarks in the lobbies during breaks, and indeed the reactions of the court, clearly showed that the smaller girl was increasingly seen as a dangerous and frightening freak whom no one could think what to do with.

From Friday afternoon, December 6, to Tuesday afternoon, December 10, the court heard the prosecution witnesses: Martin's mother, June Brown, and his aunt, Rita Finlay; Brian's sister, Pat Howe, and their friend, Irene Frazer; Roland Page, a handwriting expert; the two forensic pathologists, Dr. Bernard Knight (for Martin) and Dr. Bernard Tomlinson (for Brian); the forensic scientist Norman Lee; Mary's teacher, Mr. Eric Foster; Detective Chief Inspector Dobson and several officers of his team; eight-year-old Pauline Watson (unsworn), who was questioned about the sandpit incident; ten-year-old Susan Bell, Norma's sister, who claimed that Mary had tried to throttle her too when she was angry; and Norma's parents, who confirmed the story. "I gave her a clip on the shoulder," Mr. Bell told me later, describing how he had separated Mary from Susan. And Mrs. Bell said she tried to stop Norma from seeing Mary: "But I couldn't pry them apart." Twelve-year-old David McCready, who was the thirty-ninth prosecution witness, gave his account of Mary's fight with Norma in the nursery sandpit two weeks after Martin's death, which is when he said, yes, he'd laughed, because everybody knew what a show-off May Bell was.

The judge would later point out to the jury that several of these testimonies, taken individually, were questionable. Pauline was considered too young to be sworn. Susan was Norma's sister and her parents, of course, were Norma's parents and therefore interested parties. But, the judge suggested, if the jury accepted the evidence as presented, that is, as capable of corroborating Pauline Watson's testimony about the sandpit incident, then Norma's own testimony in the matter, though to be treated with care, was (if accepted by them) capable of corroborating it as well. The judge said: "She [Norma] was actually there, she says, and in substance, though not in detail, gives the same account as Pauline. If, having given due weight to my warnings, [you think that] it did occur, well then it is something which is relied upon by the prosecution and by those defending Norma as indicating the identity of the killer of the two little boys because, they say, here was a little girl in the neighborhood with access to those two little boys, and she was doing to other children the very thing which caused the death of those boys."

More than at any other time it was when the accused children were on the witness stand that one became desperately concerned about the failings of a judicial system in which children are tried in adult courts. Juries, unfamiliar with traumatized children, are required to evaluate their tortuous thought process and muddled words, and the current system neither requires nor provides mechanisms for communicating or teaching such understanding to them. The court was totally unaware of the fantasies that fed and ruled Norma's and Mary's lives together, and at times when the truth, as we shall see, accidentally emerged, the court would invariably ignore, reject, or flee from it.

Norma was called for her examination-in-chief at the beginning of the afternoon session on December 10, the fourth day of the trial. It would take a day and a half and be followed, on the morning of December 12, by Mary's. Mr. Justice Cusack always made a point of addressing the children, whether the accused girls or child witnesses, in a special and personal way. Rather than speak more slowly or raise his voice, he would move in his big red chair until his whole body was turned toward them, thereby forcing their concentration upon him. However, there was a clear difference in his demeanor toward each of the two girls, and when he spoke to Norma it would have been impossible for anyone in the court not to notice his gentleness and protectiveness toward her.

"Norma," he said very quietly. Very pale and already crying, she was standing in the witness box with a policewoman next to her (to whom—a touchingly childish gesture not lost on the public—after being handed a clean handkerchief each time she cried, she would always return it, balled up and wet, after blowing her nose). "I want to say something to you before you start telling us what you have to say. When you went to school, were you taught about God?"

"School and church," she whispered.

"You were taught about God. Do you know what the Bible is?"

"Yes."

"And if you take the Bible and say that you will promise before God to tell the truth, what does that mean?"

"I must tell the truth."

"Yes, you must tell the truth. She may be sworn . . ."

For children, it is not the formality of the oath that decides whether they will lie or tell the truth but, a far more elusive quality, the degree to which they feel bad about telling a lie. And this degree is first of all determined by whether the environment in which they grow up is a truthful environment. In the case of Norma and Mary, Norma's parents, though under permanent economic stress and—perhaps like anyone else—ill-equipped to deal with the psychological and social needs of eleven children, basically provided for them (as the police officers taking statements from Norma would notice) a "truth-orientated" environment. Mary's, as she would so clearly describe to me twenty-eight years later, was the opposite. Whatever the environment, though, children will lie if they have done something they know or sense was wrong and are scared of the consequences.

Norma's capacity for thinking ahead was limited. But she knew three things: one, that her parents were absolutely convinced Mary alone was responsible; two, that as a consequence of this certainty, they wanted her to "tell the truth." ("We told her from the start," Norma's mother explained to me a few months after the trial, "tell the truth about everything: tell them everything.") But three, she knew that, whatever she had done, they were her safe haven. ("The difference between Norma and I," Mary said to me, "was that she could always return home and be safe, while I never knew what I was walking into.")

By the time Mr. Justice Cusack called on her, there had been almost four days during which, with increasing horror, Norma had been forced to remember those months between May and August when she and Mary had so tragically been friends. During the therapeutic months in the hospital, away from the anxiety of her parents, her involvement in the terrible events of the summer had quite simply become an impossibility; and she had, in fact, been supported by the staff to suppress it. But now, when she could not avoid hearing with at least some part of her mind the endless repetitions of the events that resulted in the deaths of the two boys, her involvement became an enormity that she could hardly face. Her worst moments during her examination-in-chief were when she was confronted with matters in which, because the factual evidence proved it, she had to admit that she had been involved, not in Martin's death but in the "We murder" notes and the excited visits to Martin's relatives.

Brian Howe's death, however, was a different matter: the jury had a so-called bundle of evidence containing, among other things, all the girls' police statements, which were frequently referred to during testimony. Though Norma will have understood very little of the discussions between the learned men in wigs and the many directions the judge gave to the jury throughout the case, she knew they had the statements and therefore knew of the lies she had told and that she was there both when Brian "was hurt" and, time and again, when he was dead.

There were two things she could bear to speak of only as related to Mary, never to herself: the razor blade that, in her inability to think ahead, *she* had brought to the attention of the police and then led them to, and the scissors, which in her final statement she admitted to having taken from Brian's brother Norman and carried to the Tin Lizzie when she and Mary (or Mary and she—both claimed it was the other's initiative) took Brian there. The fact that Brian had been cut with the razor blade and made "baldy" with the scissors seemed more horrible to her than his death. And, whether true or not, it was essential to her, not from the point of innocence or guilt, but to her as a person—a little girl who could not hurt a child— to separate herself from anything that had been done with these two objects.

Her replies about Martin, however, were fairly straightforward, except when the questions put to her either dealt with what Mary had told her about his death or appeared to force her mind into proximity with it. She had been watching her mother ironing for about five minutes, she told her counsel, Mr. R. P. Smith, when Mary called her through a hole in the fence between their houses.

"Did she want something?" he asked.

"She wanted me to go down to number 85."

"Do you remember what she said?"

"There's been an accident."

"Did she say anything more about it at the time?" Norma did not reply and Mr. Smith did not press for an answer. (It was at this point in our conversations that Mary said, "I told Norma right away that I had killed Martin," and Norma said, "You didn't, you didn't? *Show* me.' ")

"Well, we went down," Norma continued. "She took us down 85 . . . There's a hole in the toilet [she meant of 83 St. Margaret's Road, next door]. We went through there . . . and up the steps." The excellent shorthand writer carefully noted the children's reactions and wrote here, "the witness became excited."

"Did Mary say anything more to you about the accident before you went through and out into the back and through the hole in the wall?"

"No, but she knew the name 'cos she said Martin Black ... 'It's Martin Black who has had the accident.' But I don't know who she really meant ... I don't know Martin Black."

The fact was that Norma knew little Martin (Brown) very well because she had frequently seen him when she dropped in on his aunt, Rita Finlay, whose little son John she often baby-sat. But oddly enough, Mary, who didn't particularly care for small children, didn't know Martin well at all and may not have known his surname.

Norma said she had only gone a little way up the steps of number 85.

"Did you ever get up to the room upstairs in number 85?" Mr. Smith asked.

"I never went in. There was a crowd ... they wanted to know whose little boy it was and Mary went up—but I never went up. She went up into the room and she named the boy."

"How do you know she went up, Norma?"

"I saw her going through the wall and she told me ... ["the witness became excited and upset   "]."

"Did you see Mary come out?"

"No." But she obviously saw her shortly afterwards, for she said they went to Rita Finlay's house: "May wanted to tell Rita that there had been an accident, 'cos she said there's been an accident and Martin and something about blood all over ... ["witness became excited"]."

Time and again over the two days of her testimony, the judge interrupted proceedings to give Norma a rest, even when it meant that a question remained unanswered or remained unchallenged if it had been answered but required clarification. This was the case first of all when she was questioned about the girls' outrageous calling on Martin's mother, June Brown, four days after her little boy was found dead.

"Norma, did you ever want to see little Martin Brown lying in his coffin?" asked Mr. Smith. ("The witness nodded head, 'no,'" the stenographer wrote, confusingly, for she had in fact nodded yes.)

"Were you there when May went to see Martin's mother to ask if she could see Martin in his coffin? Were you there?"

"Yes," Norma whispered.

"Yes or no?"

"Yes."

This admission of Norma's that she was present at the call on June Brown would be discounted. The assumption that it was yet another appalling initiative of Mary's fitted more comfortably into the pattern that by now ruled the trial.

There is no doubt that to the court and jury the most bewildering aspect of the two girls' conduct that weekend of May 25 was the notes they wrote, first in the scullery of Mary's home and then in the nursery after breaking into it. It was the prosecution's contention that these notes amounted to a confession that the two girls had killed Martin Brown. The defense for both girls held that, however vulgar and unpleasant the wording, they belonged to childish fantasy. As it turns out, both sides were wrong.

The two girls admitted, as handwriting expert Roland Page had concluded, that the notes had been written by both of them. Norma, although she volunteered the information that she had written "a first letter," which Mary had "put inside her shoe"—she didn't say what the letter had been about and why Mary put it in her shoe, and she wasn't questioned further about it—said that the notes had been Mary's idea. Mary said and maintains to this day that it was "a joint idea."

Still questioned by Mr. Smith, Norma said that she and Mary had been at Mary's house, first playing Mary's recorder and then "drawing."

"And then when you had finished drawing, what did you do next?"

"Wrote some notes."

"What with?"

"A red Biro pen."

"Whose was it?"

"Mary Bell's."

"I want you to look, Norma, please, at four notes, exhibits 12 to 15. You have got the notes there, Norma, have you?"

"Yes."

"Do you see the one which reads. 'I murder so that I may come back'? Exhibit 12?"

"Yes, I wrote that one."

"You just hold it up. The original is written in red. Why did you write that, Norma?"

"Just for me and Mary."

"Whose idea was it?"

"Mary, 'cos she wanted to get some papers to write some notes but she wrote a few and put something . . . ["the witness became inaudible and excited"]."

"Would you say that again, Norma?"

"May wanted some notes to be written . . . to put in her shoe . . ."

After a long discussion about another note, exhibit 15, which Norma said Mary had written and also put "in her shoe," Mr. Smith asked again whose idea it had been to write these notes.

". . . Mary's, 'cos she first got scrap paper and I was writing a different letter on it and I wrote that and she put that in her shoe. I don't know why. I didn't know what she was going to do . . ." It went on for hours and ended in Norma's total confusion when she first claimed that they had done nothing else in the nursery (they had in fact totally trashed it) and that the police caught them in the yard (this was in fact a week later).

Norma's parents, too, could have had no idea about the fantasies these two girls developed between them and, as was obvious from her reluctance to have her father present while she made her statements to the police, Norma was deeply afraid of his discovering what Mr. Dobson had described as her "curious excitement." We cannot know whether for Norma, who had perhaps craved for years to be noticed, this "excitement" was simply about the attention suddenly focused on her or whether it was a response to something deeper within her recent experience. Her behavior after the deaths of both Martin Brown and Brian Howe would point to the latter. But judging from the report Dr. Ian

Frazer, chief of psychiatry of Prudhoe Monkton Hospital, gave to the court about Norma, this behavior had changed quite radically during the months of remand in the sympathetic care and calm of the hospital, where (the crime itself probably not being discussed as that would have been totally illegal) she was helped, at least for that healing period, to put the crime out of her mind.

Dr. Frazer was the only medical expert called by the prosecution or the defense to testify about Norma and, very unusually, the judge would quote the report word for word in his summation. In Dr. Frazer's testimony, which he gave to the court as the psychiatrist who had studied her case ever since she had come into his care on August 28, 1968 (three weeks after her arrest and three months and a week before the trial), he said that her behavior was good and that she gave no trouble. When she had first arrived, he said, she had found it difficult to show her feelings, but as she got used to the surroundings, she expressed them fairly well. She had not tried to run away and got on well with the other children and the staff. She had not shown any physical aggression. She had attended lessons and done her work well. Intelligence tests administered to her indicated that although she was thirteen years old she had the mental age of a child between eight and nine. Her comprehension and reasoning powers were limited. She could cope with concrete thought much better than with anything abstract or involved, by which he meant that she could give a physical description of things but had great difficulty with abstract terms necessary to describe feelings, motives, and reasoning.

"Physically," Dr. Frazer testified, "Norma was small for her age," and that included her strength. This was a curious assertion, unwarranted, I felt at the time, either by fact or by his function, and the notes I made then express my surprise: "Is he telling us that she didn't have the strength to hold a boy of three, or to press his neck?" I wrote. Like everyone else in court, I had been observing the thirteen-year-old girl for hours every day and, like them, had been touched by the contrast between her physical sturdiness and her obvious emotional fragility. I had been repeatedly moved by her tenderness toward her young siblings, whom, when they ran up to her, she picked up and swung playfully, sometimes two at a time, holding them in a tight embrace, their feet off the ground.

Not surprisingly, however, Dr. Frazer also found Norma emotionally immature. She was, he said, "an insecure little girl" who did not have the capacity "to be a leader," "to express herself readily," or "to reason . . . Almost anybody of subnormal intelligence," he said, "is more easily influenced than a person who is of normal, or above normal intelligence, and that is true in the case of Norma. She has more suggestibility. If someone . . . present with her showed influence, she will tend to be influenced by that person rather than by what she was told half an hour before by somebody else. And if you ask her the reason 'why?' in relation to something, she had difficulty in finding words to express herself, although her powers of concentration are quite good for her intelligence."

Cross-examined by Mr. Lyons, Dr. Frazer said that Norma's capacity to know that some things are gravely wrong was limited. "Is she capable of knowing it is wrong to kill?" he was asked. "I think the probability is," he said, "that she would not know that pressing on the throat hard would kill. I don't think she has the capacity to appreciate that people are sometimes killed by strangulation. Under nonstressful conditions," he concluded his testimony, "Norma asked and replied to questions quickly and relevantly, but under stress, of course, the situation is different."

There is no doubt that in a friendly hospital environment, in the company of sick children, many of them younger than she, Norma presented exactly as Dr. Frazer described her. However, the fact that he was convinced Norma was blameless in the deaths of the little boys and incapable of harming children, as he told a number of colleagues whom I later spoke to, must have meant that Norma had not fully confided in him. If he had known of her fantasy life with Mary, it would have had to affect his judgment. He might still, and perhaps quite correctly, have considered her incapable of actually harming a child, but he would have known of the frightening dreams the two girls shared and might have weighed his words—which he would have known would greatly influence the jury—accordingly.

Mary's state of mind was different from Norma's and yet in some ways the same: different, because she was immeasurably more disturbed, morally damaged, and alone than Norma; the same, because the acts she had committed were not real to her, not something she had done, but rather—had she been able to express it this way—something that had happened in her, or to her, she doesn't even now know which. The essential contradiction of the trial was that "killing" had a fantasy connotation for both these children, and neither of them, though of course familiar with the word, understood "death" in the sense either of "forever" or of "loss," though Norma, oddly enough, knew the symptoms of death and recognized it when she saw it. Mary, incapable of connecting her compulsive need to "act out" with the consequences of her actions, simply could not conceive that every action has a consequence, and it would take her many years to recognize this.

The most important development in Mary's mind during the months of remand and the weeks of the trial was that she began to dissociate herself from her own acts. In the beginning she did this deliberately, and consciously, with quite remarkable dexterity, as Chief Inspector Dobson would describe, noting her clever lies. Eventually, however, the psychological blocking mechanism that protects the mind from the unbearable took over and made this dissociation "real."

Mary would deny for twenty-seven years having been the one to kill Brian Howe and only acknowledged the details when she talked with me in 1996. About Martin Brown, she denied for the first six years of her detention having had any part whatsoever in his death, although at fourteen she jotted down bits of her life for a teacher whose approval she craved, and spoke there of his death, still representing it, however, as an accident. In 1975, at eighteen, during a brief period of group therapy in Styal Prison, she had her only positive contact with a psychiatrist and invented a first fantasy of how Martin might have died as a result of an innocent game. She told the group that she had picked Martin up by "his ears, and he slipped. It was an accident" (this same evasion she still used when talking to me about the sandpit incident). In 1983, three years after her release, talking to her probation officer, Pat Royston, the story changed: she and Norma, she said, had strangled both boys. In 1985, in the draft of her "life story," she wrote yet another obviously false and simplistic description of killing Martin "in anger." (When I challenged her on this, she said she had thought if she described it as "an ordinary murder," people would "find it easier to cope with.") After that, she said, she never spoke of it except to her current partner of thirteen years, until our talks in 1996, when she almost immediately admitted to having killed Martin on her own. But it would take months, and several different versions, all related with enormous difficulty, until the last one in which she finally convinced me she was telling the nearest she would probably ever get to truth. Even then, however, she would never be able to tell me why she thought she had done it.

"Mary," the judge said at 10:30 A.M. on December 12. "I want to ask you some questions." Unusually pale, wearing the yellow dress she had told the policewoman the night before her mother had made for her, she stood very straight facing him. "Have you been taught about God?"

"Yes, sir," Mary answered in her singsong Geordie accent, which put the "sir" two tones higher than the "yes." She would never forget to add this respectful "sir" during the hours of testimony that followed unless it was to show anger, or even contempt for the questioner.

"Do you go to church at all?"

"Sometimes, sir, to the Mission."

"Sometimes to the Mission. Do you know what the Bible is?"

"Yes, sir."

"And if you take the Bible and promise before God to tell the truth, what do you think that means?"

"You must tell the truth, sir."

"You must tell the truth. Very well, she may be sworn."

As I write this now, I have no difficulty recalling the atmosphere in court that day. Unlike any of the other sessions, it had a sense of breathless expectation to it, a kind of hunger, with the undercurrent of morbid curiosity that in particularly lurid murder trials makes voyeurs of the spectators. I don't know whether others had the same reactions, but I remember a sharp feeling of unease. I hadn't felt this listening to Norma's whispers and watching her sob. It was the younger child's straight back, the blankness in her face, and that awful self-control which could so readily be interpreted as an incapacity to feel that aroused in me a curious resistance to being part of it, a reluctance to watch, almost an embarrassment at being there.

In recalling my distress at the proceedings, particularly the instinctive partiality of all those present in favor of the unhappy childlike Norma and their almost passionate rejection of the apparently unfeeling, self-possessed Mary, I'm anxious not to mislead anyone now. Like everyone at the time I was quite sure that Mary had killed and that, whatever part the older child might have played, Mary had to have been the dominating figure in this unhappy alliance. Where I differed (leaving aside here my opinions about Norma's role) was that, although I was deeply aware that what had happened to the little boys and their families was monstrous, I did not for a moment see this eleven-year-old child as a monster, and I was appalled that others did. This was not because I knew more about her background than they did—I didn't until much later—but because I had, in the aftermath of World War II, worked with many children who had been traumatized by their experiences in the camps or working as forced laborers in Germany. The majority were between the ages of four and twelve. Some were silent to the point of being catatonic. Others were hyperactive, talking not only all day but through the night in their sleep. Some wanted to be held, others trembled at the least touch and pulled away. But one thing almost all of them had in common on arrival, and for many weeks afterwards, was an absolute rejection of anything that smacked of moral concepts. The words "good" and "bad" had no meaning for them; their faces went stiff, their eyes blank at any attempt to explain the necessity, for their own safety, of a few rules.

There was a minimum of imposed discipline, but at the slightest indication by an adult of disapproval or impatience, many of them exploded, forcing us to watch them acting (for acting it was) wilder, "badder," more knowing in every way than they essentially were.

The resemblance between these seriously damaged children and their rejection of conventional morality in 1945, and Mary in that English courtroom in 1968, totally at sea with the moral concepts she was asked to swear an oath to, was quite striking for me. From day one, with her so obvious lies and fantasies, her puzzling but indicative movements with her hands and fingers, her strange intelligence, her stillness and isolation, she appeared to me nothing so much as a horribly confused child to whom something dreadful had at some time been done.

She was first questioned about Martin Brown's death, as Norma had been. Both girls had admitted to having seen him in the street the day before his death, but neither had admitted to any guilt surrounding his death or blamed the other. Mary had initially told the police quite truthfully that she had never played with him. Four months later in court, however, in one of several demonstrations of exceptional mental agility, which had the effect of confusing not just the public but the barristers and the judge as well, she carefully adapted her reply to the evidence she had heard.

After a forensic expert testified that fibers found on Martin's clothes matched those taken from the dress she had worn that day, she affirmed that, no, she had never played with Martin, but added, emphasizing the difference between the two acts, that while she hadn't played with him, she had "given him a swing before dinner" shortly before 1:00 P.M. on the day he was found dead. ("I made it up," she told me now, "after the police told me they had found the fibers.")

Asked about her ringing the Browns' doorbell four days after he died, Mary answered honestly enough. "I asked his mother if I could see Martin," she said, questioned by her counsel, Harvey Robson. "Me and Norma were daring each other . . ."

"You were daring each other?" Mr. Robson repeated. "What did you want to see Martin for?"

"I don't know, sir, because we . . . er . . . were daring each other and one of us did not want to be chicken or something."

It was yet another example of the different reactions the two girls elicited from the court—not because of what they said (though in their eagerness to accuse each other their replies were frequently diametrically opposed) but because of how they said it. Norma, answering unwillingly and with distress, constantly provoked sympathy and compassion. Mary, speaking succinctly with aplomb, often embedding her answers in a mass of extraneous information designed with extraordinary dexterity to give her time for reflection, both confused—and irritated—the court.

"I want to ask you, first of all, about the notes," Mr. Robson said to Mary. "Do you understand what I am referring to?"

"Yes, sir."

"Do you remember how the notes came to be written?"

"Well, we wrote—it was a joint idea."

"Yes, where were you?"

"In our house. We only wrote—er—er . . . two in our house, I think."

"How did it begin? Norma, I think, has said something about you were playing a recorder?"

"Oh well . . ."

"Is that right?" Unwittingly, Mr. Robson had opened the door to one of her frequent diversions.

"Yes," she began, "I can play a recorder. I was playing a recorder. I was playing, 'Go to Sleep, Little Brother Peter'; I was playing that or 'Three Blind Mice.' I was playing one of those tunes and I just put it back in the box because too much playing it makes the inside go rusty or something . . . We went into the back scullery, I think—no, I had a cat upstairs which was a stray cat and it was a black one and me and Norma were trying to think of a name for it, and we were thinking of names for it and it was a black cat . . ."

"Did you go upstairs?" Mr. Robson tried in vain to get her onto the subject of the notes—the paper Norma had said Mary got from her bedroom.

"Yes."

"Into what room?"

"My bedroom."

"And what did you do in your bedroom?"

"We were thinking of a name for the cat."

"Yes?"

"But the dog, it was coming up and sniffing under the door because it could smell the cat."

"And how did you come to make the notes?"

"Well, the doll's pram was at the side of my bed and Norma went over to it and looked under. It has . . . has got I think it is a red hood, I'm not sure what color hood, but it has got like a thing to cover it and it has got the two studs at one end, and Norma went in because she saw, she was looking at the doll . . . and she saw there was a red Biro pen and she got it out, and she was doing some drawings and it was a joint idea to write the notes, so we both wrote them, but we never wrote them in the bedroom, we wrote them in the scullery."

"Do you remember how many notes altogether you wrote in the bedroom?" asked Harvey Robson, quite obviously lost.

"We never wrote notes at all in the bedroom," she repeated patiently. "We only wrote them in the scullery because you cannot do none in the bedroom because if you rest it on the bed the pen would go straight through it because the bed is soft, and there is like a sideboard thing and it has got a round thing which has a frilly thing on it."

"You did not make any of the notes in the bedroom. How many notes did you make in the scullery?"

". . . Two."

"And when you had made the notes, did you stay in or did you go somewhere?"

"We went—er—Norma says, 'Are you coming to the nursery?' I said, 'Yes, howay then,' because we had broken into it before." (Now it is Mary who confuses the two break-ins, but everyone was so tired of the notes, nobody appeared to notice.)

"Yes?"

"We had been in a week and all—the week before that."

Again, the discussion of the notes went on for mind-numbing hours. By the end of it, it seemed to me that the notes, though certainly part of the morbid game they were both playing, had clearly been part of a classic cry for help and that both children were very nearly telling the truth.

On the previous evening, after Norma's examination-in-chief, Mary had shown to the policewoman guarding her how frightened she was becoming. "They won't be able to do anything to one of us without the other . . . ," she had said that night to Pauline J., whom she particularly liked. "After all, we were both . . ."—she hesitated—"in it. It would be unfair to punish one without the other." And a little later that sleepless night she said, "They are going to blame it all on me, because they'll say Norma's daft . . ."

And toward the end of her first morning of cross-examination, questioned once more by Norma's counsel about the notes, Mary gave way to her anger about the court's obvious partiality and her fear about what would happen to her. Her answer was certainly partly true and gave some indication of the turmoil in the relationship between her and Norma and the increasing frenzy of their fantasies.

"What does a 'joint idea' mean?" Mr. Smith asked her.

"It was both of us."

"Both of you what?"

"That wrote the notes."

"Yes, but who decided the notes should be written?"

"Her."

"She did?"

"Yes."

"What did she say?"

"She says, 'We will do it for a giggle.' . . . I says it to Mr. Robson [she means Dobson] and all, it was both of us."

"Did you ask why she thought this would be a giggle?"

"She wanted to get put away," Mary said, sounding very angry now.

"Is this true, what you are telling the court?"

"Yes, because after that she asked me to run away with her . . ."

"Where to?"

"She just says, 'Run away with us.' . . ."

"What for?"

"I don't know. I have run away with her before."

The judge now intervened. "But did she say why she wanted to get put away?" he asked.

"Because she could kill the little ones, that's why."

"Because *what?*" the judge asked, startled.

"And run away from the police," Mary continued, unasked, her voice now shrill with suppressed hysteria. "She was going to go . . ."

Mr. Justice Cusack firmly shut his notebook and stood up, bringing everyone immediately to their feet with him. "I think we will adjourn now until 2:15," he said.

"I'll kick her mouth in," Mary shouted, but everyone had begun to talk as if to shut out her voice. For the first time she had tried to bring up the dreadful fantasies that bound her and Norma together but it was, of course, incomprehensible to this assembly of good and decent men and women who were neither qualified nor required to deal with the pathology of disturbed children.

"I think it's all a dream," she said that night to policewoman Susan L. "It's never happened. Do you think I'll ever go home again? I wish I was going to sleep in my own bed. Do you think I'll get thirty years? I think he is a horrible judge if he gives me thirty years. If I was a judge and I had an eleven-year-old who'd done this . . ."

"I realized she'd said 'done this,'" Susan told me later. "But I didn't report it. I felt I shouldn't."

"I'd give her . . . eighteen months. Murder isn't that bad," Mary went on. "We all die sometime anyway," and then, an apparent non sequitur, "My mam gives me sweets every day . . ."

All of it meant something, the memory of daily sweets from her mother right after the mention of death and of murder, and above all her outburst in court about Norma, about planning to "run away from the police," "running away from home," and "killing the little ones." It was all quite true: the running away from home was a fact; the rest was part of a terrible fantasy that had become real. But no one looked, no one asked, and no one therefore was in a position to associate one event with another. If the girls' behavior had been recognized early on, perhaps someone would have realized that serious trouble was brewing in the two girls' minds and—the most devastating thought of all—perhaps both little boys would have lived. But even if, in the months leading up to the trial, when some of the social workers realized the deficiency in their knowledge—as we know they did—efforts had been made to gain some understanding of the dynamics of these families' lives and to discover what Mary's childhood had been, the resulting picture would have proved how wrong adult assumptions can be and perhaps could have led to different decisions being made.

A few minutes after Mary's three-hour examination-in-chief was concluded, the defense called the two psychiatrists it had requested to examine Mary. Under British law as it stands, accused children can only be seen by psychiatrists for the defense in order to show that the child is "incapable of criminal intent," and for the prosecution to rebut that presumption.

Dr. Robert Orton had seen Mary twice, in August and November. In his opinion, he said, she was a "psychopathic personality," which he defined as having "a persistent disorder or disability of the mind . . . the primary symptoms [being]: 1), a lack of feeling quality to other humans; 2), a liability to act on impulse and without forethought . . . ; 3), . . . aggression; 4), a lack of shame or remorse for what has been done; 5), an inability to profit by or use experience which includes the lack of response to punishment; and 6), . . . the presence of viciousness or wish to do damage to things or persons."

From the moment Betty Bell had started visiting Mary, before the trial and shortly afterwards, she had told her, "Never, never talk to psychiatrists." Betty herself was no stranger to psychiatrists; she had been in and out of hospitals for years with nervous breakdowns, real and imagined illnesses, and on at least one occasion had been committed at her older sister's request. Her fear of psychiatrists appears to have been above all what Mary might be brought to disclose.

"There was just one time she and my dad came together," Mary told me. "And she said that I must just say I wouldn't talk to psychiatrists: these doctors could put things in my head and send me to outer space, 'into a twilight zone,' she said. My dad told her not to say something so stupid, but it terrified me." Up to this point she had mainly rejected all questions about her family and childhood, but after this she virtually refused to cooperate at all.

Dr. David Westbury had visited Mary four times, but could only talk to her twice—in October and early November—when she was, he said, "sulky and only partly cooperative." Though he expressed himself less radically than Dr. Orton, Dr. Westbury concurred that Mary showed "no evidence of mental illness or severe subnormality, or subnormality of intelligence," but had a "serious disorder of person-ality ... [which] required medical treatment." He added that Mary's abnormality of mind arose from a condition of retarded development of mind "caused partly by genetic [i.e., inherited] factors and partly by environmental factors." Replying to questions from Norma's counsel Mr. Smith, he agreed that Mary was "violent" and "very dangerous." (Three years later, in 1971, reassessing Mary on behalf of the Home Office, he would write an entirely positive opinion of her and recom-mend that she be considered for release by 1975.)

By the time the court recessed after all the testimony had been heard, neither the public nor the media had any doubts: they had all heard the judge impress upon the jury at the very start that it was not only what the accused said that counted but their demeanor while they said it. All of them had seen Norma's despair and been witness to her family's affection and faith in her. And all of them had watched that blank face of the smaller girl and finally found her to be exactly as the prosecutor,

Mr. Lyons, was to describe her the next day: "a most abnormal child: aggressive, vicious, cruel, incapable of remorse . . . a dominating personality with a somewhat unusual intelligence and a degree of fiendish cunning that is almost terrifying . . ." She had had, he said, "an evil and compelling influence over Norma, almost like that of the fictional Svengali . . ." By this time there wasn't anyone who could have doubted that Mary had killed Martin Brown and that Norma was innocent of that crime. I too thought that this was the case, and indeed it was.

When it came to Brian Howe, there was never any doubt that one or both of the girls had killed him, but on the evidence alone it could have been either of them or both. They had been questioned about it for hours. Fibers from both children's clothes were found on Brian, though in Norma's case only on his shoes. Both of them, questioned first by the police and then at the trial, blamed every piece of evidence on the other: the use of the scissors and the razor blade, the cuts on Brian's body, the pressure marks on his nose and neck. The only thing both girls accepted having had a hand in was the carpet of wildflowers that covered him. Except for the fact that Mary's lies, a number of them based on the evidence she was hearing, were more cleverly composed and thus of course more blatant, the only thing the court could be certain of was that both girls were on the Tin Lizzie with Brian that afternoon, once while he was still alive and twice more when he was dead.

Of all the official people in the court, Mary probably had only one ally, her solicitor, David Bryson, who was a modest man and desolated afterwards because he felt that he had failed her. "I think he's thick," Mary told one of the policewomen. "He doesn't know what he's doing." But she was wrong.

Her analysis of him almost thirty years later is nearer the truth: "He was young," she told me now, "probably too young for such a case." I think that is correct, but it was because he was young that he felt compassion for her. "I simply couldn't see her as the monster, the 'evil seed' she was described as," he told me. "She was a sick child. I didn't know what was the matter with her but I knew that what was happening in that court was wrong." Mr. Harvey Robson, he said, had been convinced from the start (as it turned out, rightly) that she would be found guilty. "That's why he went for diminished responsibility," he said. "He thought it would give her a better chance." In principle, it would have, but as it turned out, it made no difference.

The next day, Friday, December 13, Mr. Smith concluded his defense of Norma, saying that she had been "an innocent bystander" who had told childish lies to get herself out of trouble. Mary's lies, on the other hand, trying to get an innocent little boy into trouble, he said, had been "wicked; one was tempted to describe her as evil . . . [But]," he continued, "it is not part of my duty to blackguard Mary . . . Although this is a ghastly case, and . . . some of the evidence may have made you ill, it is possible to feel sorry for Mary . . . Her illness—psychopathic personality—is said to be the result of genetic and environmental factors. It's not her fault she grew up this way; it's not her fault she was born . . ."

"She never slept the nights of that weekend," policewoman Valerie M. told me. "Four of us guarded her those three shifts and she asked every one of us: 'What's a psychopath?' What could one tell her?"

Another of the policewomen had pondered deeply about it all by the time we talked in 1970. "I took courses in criminology in college and read quite a bit about psychopathy and serial murderers," she said. "I was astonished when the psychiatrists called her a psychopath, which is a condition extremely hard to treat, not to speak of curing it. I know—I have read that some people have tried to apply the term to children, but I felt it was nonsense, gobbledegook, and should surely never be used by psychiatrists about a child they barely knew, had barely examined. I was disgusted by it," she said, and asked me not to name her.

By comparison with the others, Mr. Harvey Robson's final speech to the jury was not long. "What was there to say?" David Bryson said sadly a few months later. Mr. Robson sounded resigned to the inevitable, but oddly enough his conclusion contained the one grain of wisdom every-one had studiously ignored. "It is ... very easy to revile a little girl," he said, "to liken her to Svengali without pausing even for a moment to ponder how the whole sorry situation has come about. Although you may think that this last is the most disturbing thought of all, I believe that in the course of your deliberations you, as a jury of this city, will be able to discover some measure of pity ..."

The judge's summing up was to last four hours, and although his legal arguments were perfectly correct, few people present could have fol-lowed their logic, or indeed detected logic in them. He made very clear, however, what he expected the jury to do about each child.

In the course of laying out the evidence, he very properly reminded them that even if Norma had said that when Brian was being conducted along to the Tin Lizzie she did not know why or for what purpose, "she does admit, and it is an important factor in the case, that at the time she did think that Mary had killed Martin Brown because [she said] Mary told her she had.

"If, as Norma claimed, two boys died at the hands of Mary," he said, "then Mary having told Norma about killing Martin meant that Norma had done nothing to protect Brian Howe ..."

For a few moments it had sounded as if the jury would be directed to let facts rather than emotions rule their decisions. "If any unlawful killing occurs and two people participate in it," the judge continued, "it does not matter whose hand actually does the deed. If one person com-mits the act which causes the death, and the other is present and knows what is intended and what is happening, and is either helping or ready to help, that person is equally guilty."

Shortly afterwards, however, it became clear what he intended: "If, however, the person is there as a mere spectator and not there to help and not giving any help, that person cannot be held responsible. It may be wrong ... but it is not a criminal offense."

This was difficult to understand: for while we had all heard Norma state that she had "never touched Brian," we also heard her admit that she had lifted Brian's "head and shoulders up a bit and patted his back but his hand fell on one side and I laid him down again." We had heard her say that she had "felt his pulse but it wasn't going up and down"; and we had heard the experts tell the court—reminding us of the alternate writing of the nursery notes—that the little cuts on the toddler's stomach were "in the shape of an N with a vertical stroke added in another hand making it an M." ("How can she then be described as a 'mere spectator,'" I noted at the time.)

But the judge went even further: "Secondly, and much more importantly, if you find that one girl did kill, or participate in the killing, but that at the time she may have been so under the domination of the other girl that she had no will or mind of her own, then she would not be acting 'voluntarily' and you ought not to convict her."

This made it crystal clear: even if Norma not only had been there but had actually, however marginally, participated in the killing (possibly just by the encouragement of her presence), the fact that Mary was manifestly the leader meant that Norma was innocent of the killing.

The judge then told them it was evident that his instructions referred only to Mary—which was as good as telling the jury to acquit the other child—and that there was an alternative to murder open to them on each charge, which was manslaughter, and, moreover, there was manslaughter with "diminished responsibility."

After explaining again the meaning of the term, he reminded them that they had heard two doctors testify that Mary was suffering from a "psychopathic personality disorder, such as substantially impaired her mental responsibility for her acts or omissions" but which was susceptible to medical treatment and came within the statutory definition of diminished responsibility. "Murder," he concluded, "requires an intent to kill or to do serious bodily injury knowing that death may result. Manslaughter does not require that intent at all. It is sufficient if there is a voluntary, unlawful and dangerous act which results in death ... The degree of understanding required to make a child of this age responsible in law is sometimes referred to as having 'a guilty mind' . . . but . . . the mere fact that a child commits an act which in an adult would be a criminal offense is not evidence in itself that that child had a guilty mind. You have to look outside the act itself to see if that child had an understanding of right and wrong, an appreciation of what is good and what is bad, so as to make that child responsible in the eyes of the law . . ."

In his summation, the judge had made his feelings very clear. In the corridors that afternoon, those who had attended all of the trial had no doubts: we all knew, I think, that the following day Mary would be found guilty of manslaughter with diminished responsibility, and most of those I spoke with thought and hoped that Norma would be acquitted. I, too, was certain that whatever else had happened before and during the actual killings, Mary had been the leading figure in this tragedy. Nevertheless, I was disturbed by the legal point the judge had made: "If . . . the person is there as a mere spectator and not there to help and not giving any help, that person cannot be held responsible."

I thought it not only possible but probable that, whatever Norma's mental capacities were, she had demonstrated during her testimony that she *had*, in fact, a moral sense, as did her parents, and that she would end up extremely disturbed by her part in these children's deaths, however passive that part might have been. I thought therefore that her total acquittal—which appeared almost certain—would not only be wrong toward Mary but, in the final analysis, be damaging to Norma, too.

But there was another point that puzzled me: How had the psychiatrists reached the conclusion that Mary was suffering from a "psychopathic personality disorder"? What was it? What had caused it?

"Does it mean she is mentally ill?" I had asked Dr. Westbury after he had testified, and he had shaken his head. "It's not a mental disease," he'd said. "It's a condition."

"Is it curable?" I had asked, and again he had shaken his head.

"It is treatable," he said.

I was, I admit, momentarily reassured. The trial had seemed disastrous, but in the end, I told myself, they would do the right thing. Rather than punish this unhappy child, who was not mentally ill but had somehow become subject to a condition of profound disturbance and as a consequence caused such awful suffering to the families of her victims, they would send her to a hospital where she could be treated and cared for. Dr. Westbury told me that he had already been making inquiries as to where Mary, or both children if they were both convicted, could be sent.

That night of December 16, Mary knew that the next day the jury would decide her fate. "What would be the worst that could happen to me?" she asked Pauline J. "Would they hang me?" Pauline had felt sick, she told me. "I wasn't supposed to talk to her about the case but . . . you couldn't not answer a question like that, could you? I said no, they didn't hang little girls. A bit later she asked me again, would they send her to prison for thirty years like Harry Roberts? I said that they didn't send little girls to prison, either. But then she started talking of going home as if, you know, they just had to let her go home, so I told her they'd send her somewhere where she'd be . . . looked after . . . It was better to tell her, prepare her sort of, you know."

It was quite clear: Mary, an avid watcher of Westerns, had seen men being chased, caught, and hanged. And she knew about "Harry Roberts" who got "thirty years"—he was a sort of hero in her family. But for her there was no connection between these mental images of pursuit, murder, and violent death and what she had done. As she told Pauline, they just had to let her go home. Why not? What had she done that was so bad?

It was 2:15 P.M. the next day when the jury came back with their verdict. The judge had warned he would tolerate no outbursts or demonstrations in the court, and there was silence as the clerk of the Assize, Mr. Peter Robinson, asked for the decision. "Do you find Norma Bell guilty or not guilty of the murder of Martin Brown?"

"Not guilty."

"Do you find her guilty or not guilty of the murder of Brian Howe?"

"Not guilty."

The only sound was Norma's momentary clapping of her hands, which ceased just as suddenly as, with the same gentle motion we had seen so often, Norma's mother turned the beaming child back toward the court.

The row of faces of Mary's family: her mother; her grandmother, Mrs. McC.; Billy; the three aunts, Cath, Isa, and Audrey; and some of the uncles were all stiffly facing the front as the clerk then read on: "Do you find Mary Flora Bell guilty or not guilty of the murder of Martin Brown?"

"Guilty of manslaughter because of diminished responsibility," the foreman replied. And again, moments later, about Brian Howe, "Guilty of manslaughter because of diminished responsibility."

Betty's immediate screaming sob was so expected it hardly moved one; Billy, as he had done time and again during the trial, leaned forward covering his face with his hands; Mrs. McC. sat rigid, unmoving. Mary, who had listened with that strange immobility we had noticed before, only reacted—I saw it plainly—as she looked at her family, from face to face: *then* she began to cry and Mr. Bryson put his arm around her.

Ten minutes later, the judge pronounced sentence on Mary.

The child need not stand and I shall address myself to the matters without specifically addressing myself to her.

On the verdict of the jury in this case, Mary Bell has been found guilty on two counts of manslaughter. The verdict is one of manslaughter because the jury found that at the material time she had diminished responsibility. Otherwise their verdict would have been one of murder. In the result it means that this child, now aged only eleven, has in fact been found to have killed two other children.

My difficulty is to know what order should now be made by the court.

Having regard to the medical evidence put before me, I should have been willing to make . . . a hospital order, so that she could have been taken to a mental institution to receive the appropriate treatment ... accompanied ... by a restriction order ... which would have meant that she could not have been released from a hospital without ... special ... authority.

Unhappily, I am not able to make such an order because one of the requirements of the Mental Health Act is that I must be satisfied, firstly, that there is a hospital to which she could go; secondly, that she could be admitted to that institution within twenty-eight days.

Evidence has been given to me by Dr. Westbury ... that it has been impossible to find any institution to which she can be admitted for treatment under the Mental Health Act ... The responsible Government Department requires time to consider what they wish to do ...

I make no criticism of that Department. But it is a most unhappy thing that, with all the resources of this country, whether it be the Ministry of Social Security, or the Home Office, it appears that no hospital is available which is suitable for the accommodation of this girl and to which she could be admitted.

All the requirements, apart from the one I have mentioned, of the Mental Health Act have been satisfied, and I am merely precluded from doing what I would otherwise do by the fact that no such hospital is available. No evidence has been put before me which would enable me, therefore, to make an order of the kind I would wish to make.

I must, therefore, turn to other matters.

If this had been the case of an adult, having regard to the evidence put before me, which I fully accept, that this is a child who is dangerous, I should have felt obliged to impose a life sentence for the reason that, not only did the gravity of the offences warrant it, but that there was evidence of mental disease or abnormality which made it impossible to determine the date when the person concerned could be safely released.

It is an appalling thing that, in a child as young as this, one has to determine such matters, but I am entirely satisfied that, anxious as I am to do everything for her benefit, my primary duty is to protect other people for the reasons that I have indicated.

I take the view that there is a very grave risk to other children if ... she is not closely watched and every conceivable step taken to see that she does not do again what it has been found that she did do.

In the case of a child of this age no question of imprisonment arises, but I have the power to order a sentence of detention, and it seems to me that no other method of dealing with her, in the circumstances, is suitable.

I therefore have to turn to what length of detention should be imposed. I say at once that, if an undeterminate period is imposed, as in the case of a life sentence of imprisonment, that does not mean that the person concerned is kept in custody indefinitely, or for the rest of their natural lives. It means that the position can be considered from time to time and, if it becomes safe to release that person, that person can be released.

For that reason the sentence of the court concurrently in respect of these two matters upon Mary Bell is a sentence of detention and the detention will be for life.

The child Mary Bell may be taken out of court.

Mary—Reflections 4

It is very rare in Britain, because it is essentially illegal, that a juror comments on a trial for which he has sat on the jury. But on May 13, 1995, a year and a half after the trial of the two ten-year-old boys who had killed James Bulger in February 1993, Vincent Moss, a retired university lecturer and a juror on that case, sharply condemned the use of jury trials for children on a BBC Radio program, *Tales of the Jury*. The case had remained in the news because of a controversy that arose soon after the two boys were found guilty of murder and sentenced to a detention. The judge, Mr. Justice Morland, had suggested a minimum sentence of eight years for "retribution and deterrence" (after this their case would be reconsidered), which the Lord Chief Justice two days later increased to ten years.

A campaign by James Bulger's parents, strongly supported by the *Sun* newspaper, resulted in 250,000 signatures calling for the two young murderers to be jailed for life. The Home Secretary at the time, Mr. Michael Howard, then announced in July 1994 that, in consideration of "the special circumstances and the need to maintain confidence in the justice system," he would impose a "tariff," i.e., a minimum sentence, of fifteen years. This meant that the two ten-year-olds—eleven by the time of the trial—would spend four years in a special unit, three years in a secure youth facility (i.e., a maximum security prison for juveniles), and as of age eighteen a further eight years in adult prison, until their first possible parole at the age of twenty-six. The boys' lawyers initiated an appeal to the Commission on Human Rights in Strasbourg on the basis that the trial process involved breaches of various articles of the European Convention on Human Rights relating to a fair trial and the involvement of a politician in the sentencing procedure.

On March 6, 1998, the commission ruled the application admissible and the European Court will hear it in early 1999. By this time, Mr. Howard's decision had been judicially reviewed in the English High Court and ultimately, on appeal to the House of Lords, was found to be flawed. Britain is a signatory to the European Convention on Human Rights and if, as expected, the European Court pronounces against British procedure as it stands, radical changes will have to be made. In the meantime, the present Home Secretary, Mr. Jack Straw, is reconsidering the tariff for the two boys, who are now sixteen years old.

Juror Vincent Moss, however, discussed what he clearly considered an even more pivotal point than the length of sentence: did these ten-year-olds know right from wrong, and could they be considered responsible for their actions? In his opinion they could not be considered responsible in the same sense as a mentally competent adult. The extent to which the boys were morally aware and understood the concept of morality was, he said, very questionable. He felt that a jury's possibilities in an adult trial—their choice being only between guilty or not guilty, murder or manslaughter—were far too restrictive for such a case. "We should have gone back into court," he said, "and we should have said, 'Yes, we do have a verdict: these boys are in urgent need of social and psychiatric help.'

"These two children," he said, "had sat there for a month [in fact seventeen days], bored, uncomprehending, and appallingly distressed when, at full volume, the court heard recordings as they cried and screamed for their mothers." He confessed that he had been horrified at the judge's description of the boys as "vicious and hardened criminals." He and his fellow jurors, he said, had no genuine freedom to decide on the boys' guilt or innocence and had not even been offered the option of a verdict of guilty with diminished responsibility. "We were there simply to rubber-stamp a verdict," he said.

While considering what an intelligent juror felt in 1993, and before hearing more of how a child felt during and after a jury trial in adult court in 1968, it is perhaps worth considering a *Times* editorial written a hundred years before, on August 10, 1861, about an almost identical trial in an adult court of two eight-year-old boys who, on April 11, 1861, in Stockport, Cheshire, beat to death a child they also did not know, two-and-a-half-year-old George Burgess.

> Children of that age [wrote the *Times*] cannot be held legally accountable in the same way as adults . . . Why should it have been absurd and monstrous that these two children should have been treated like murderers? . . . As far as it went, their conscience was as sound and as genuine a conscience as that of a grown man: it told them that what they were doing was wrong . . . [But] conscience, like other natural faculties, admits of degrees: it is weak, and has not arrived at its proper growth in children; though it has a real existence and a voice within them, it does not speak with that force and seriousness which justifies us in treating the child as a legally responsible being.

What was the principal feeling she recalled about the trial? I asked Mary. "Unreality," she said. "You see, they talked all the time about the dead little boys. But it was this that was unreal to me. Of course I knew I had done something wrong, but, you know, nobody ever talked to me . . . *me* . . . about the little boys in ways I could . . . respond to."

Did the fact of their being dead mean anything to you?

"No, nothing, because I hadn't intended . . . Well—how can I say this now?" she said right away. "But . . . I didn't *know* I had intended for them to be dead . . . dead forever. Dead for me then wasn't forever."

This is hard to understand, or even to believe. Most of us who have been parents of eleven-year-old children think they know what death is. But perhaps we are wrong. Perhaps they only know when the person who dies is someone who has been close to them and they sense the finality of it, not as a result of knowledge or understanding, but in reaction to the pain they see in others they love around them. It is a persuasive and a tempting thought, for it is no doubt the gentlest and most healing way to learn about death.

It would also go some way to explaining why Mary might not have had a concept of the finality of death. No human being she loved had died by the time she was eleven. And unable even now, returning in her memory to that time, to understand herself and thereby to explain, she reaches for childlike illustrations. "You know, my dog, my Alsatian, he had died, two or three times I think, but I can't really remember because each time my dad brought me the same . . . well, to me the same dog the next day. I know that doesn't explain anything to anybody else, but it's one of the things I've found for myself.

"In the court, while they were talking and talking, I remember thinking of what I would say when it was my turn. I'd tell them I wanted my dog. I wanted him with me when they sent me to be hanged. That's what I thought would happen: I'd be sent to the gallows and they might just as well have said that right away because it was just as meaningless as life imprisonment or . . . well . . . death. None of it meant a damned thing, not a thing . . ."

But you were frightened just the same?

"I think probably more of the whole thing, the kind of hushed atmosphere, the reaction from adults . . . adults . . ." She repeated her words as always in moments of stress, losing all structure, rhythm, and patterns of speech " . . . adults, you know, literally avoiding me . . . looking at me like . . . like . . . like a specimen."

But that isn't a word you would have known then, is it?

"No, I wouldn't have," she said, the search for an intelligent reply reordering her mind. "It's one of the things I worry about now. I think that what I felt then and remember, and what I've been told since, is mixed in my head and I wonder whether that is what is meant by 'selective memory.' How can one know this? What *is* memory? I'm trying to tell you and to find in myself the truth, about . . . about . . . about a hundred things. But what is truth, if it is mixed with truths about fantasies?"

I said, during the time the trial went on and you heard the things that were said, was it in your mind that you had done something because of things which had been done to you? Because you had been hurt?

"No, never," she said at once. "But, you know, we are talking about this as if it had been the dawn of civilization. Where . . . where were all the professionals?"

I reminded her that at least some psychiatrists had tried but couldn't get anything out of her. Does she think now that with greater effort they could have?

"Of course," she said. "Before my mother scared me to death with what they could do to me, anyone with a bit of kindness could have found out . . . not . . . not all of it, no, because I now think it was buried in my own mind, but . . . enough."

Enough for what?

"I'm not sure. And perhaps nothing would have helped. But when I think of it now, it's really funny to think that nobody, nobody at all, ever talked to me in a way that could have made what I did real to me."

But all these doctors—Westbury, Orton, Gibbens, Rowbotham*— they all spoke to you about the dead children, didn't they?

"All that remains in my mind is questions," she said, "just impossible questions. You see, now I realize of course that what they must have hoped or waited for is that I would burst into tears and show remorse, shame, regret. But how could I if none of it was real to me? That I remember perfectly well. All that mattered was to lie well. After

---

*Professor Terence Gibbens saw Mary after the trial at the assessment center at Cumberlow Lodge, Monica Rowbotham earlier, during her remand in Newcastle.

all, I was saying I had done none of it, that it was all Norma. For a child of my age then, it must have been quite difficult to keep all the lies going."

But why did you put it all on Norma?

"Because she put it all on me. I was very angry. She had betrayed me."

Of all the psychiatrists who were briefly unleashed on Mary, it was Dr. Monica Rowbotham—the only woman who saw her and the only psychiatrist to mention in her report the "closeness" of her relationship with Norma—who came nearest to making contact with her. But because Mary's one aim by then was, as she now confirms, to "put it all" on Norma, the reason for her anger—their fantasies and Norma's "betrayal" of their pact to be criminals together—never emerged. And the haphazard fragments of indications the psychiatrists' reports provided appeared entirely out of context when quoted during the trial and did nothing except confuse the court, the jury, and the public.

The most meaningful of these, in the sense of the potential for providing a host of answers if the questions had been properly asked and the replies properly evaluated, were always those that touched on the bizarre bond between the two girls and its origin. Despite the hopeless entanglement of her lies and truths, Mary's attempts to communicate some of the essence of these events remained consistent. Thus in every statement, description, and finally in the cross-examination about Brian's death, she mentioned, always in the same words, Norma's screaming. "She just went mad, she just screamed . . ."

"Did she say or shout or scream anything particular or just make a screaming noise?" asked her counsel, Mr. Harvey Robson.

"Just made a screaming noise."

Whether it was true that Norma had wordlessly screamed at the sight of the little boy on the ground in shock or had screamed words of blame and fear at Mary, the screaming, we can be sure, happened and has remained in the forefront of Mary's mind to this day. And on one occasion, when her defenses were down, while she talked with Dr.

Rowbotham, the memory, complemented by another image, surfaced in part. And this part, alone, without the screaming that might have suggested the manic aspect of the scene, was heard some months later in court, when Mary, talking about Brian's death, had said: "I was full of laughter that day."

There was an audible gasp in the chamber, followed by outraged whispers, quickly silenced by the judge. It would be many years before Mary, as an adult seeking understanding of herself as a child, was able completely to articulate the story of the day of Brian's killing. And it was only then, when there was no longer any need for lies or embellishment, that she added—thus explaining what she had meant when talking to Monica Rowbotham before the trial—that Norma had suddenly stopped screaming and "started laughing, hysterically laughing, and I started laughing, too."

So you were very angry with Norma, I said.

"Then, yes, with her. Later I learned to understand it wasn't really her at all, and it wasn't even her family. It was those clever lawyers who told her what to say and how to say it."

But that isn't really so, I said. Norma had already said all that in her statements to the police, before lawyers had anything to do with it. Her story didn't change much.

"Not her story but the way she told it," Mary said. "They will have been at her like mine were at me, and hers were much cleverer. I do remember that after Mr. Bryson said over and over I was to be quiet . . . I just sat you know . . . maybe I was listening . . . understanding, I don't know . . . I think there were words or expressions, just bits of it I took in because they were untrue or mean to me; that meant something. I was bored, you know, because I couldn't understand a lot of the words they used. Mr. Bryson had told me that the judge was the most important person and I remember calling him something like Your Honor or Your Worship or Your Kingdom . . . Oh, I don't know what I called him, but I tried only to speak to him because the jury . . . the jury . . ."

What about the jury?

"They looked at me with those eyes, so I never wanted to look at them. You know, all the time it was going on, what I was most frightened of was that they [the lawyers] were going to say . . . tell everybody . . . that at Seaham, where I had been for most of the time of the remand, I had had a fight with a girl and called her a prostitute. I was taken aback myself, even as I said it, because she wasn't, you know, and I was frightened even there in case that became known. Miss Alexander, who was the head there, had said she had to write reports on everything I did . . . so I was frightened that they would ask me how I knew what a prostitute was. That was the most frightening thing of all to me . . . that meant something to me, you see, everything else really didn't."

You were more frightened of that than the idea of their hanging you?

"That was all part of the unreal . . . you know, the other side. The prostitute thing was real. It was something I knew I had said and how could I explain that I knew what it was? I'd never used that word before, though I'd used the other word on girls when I had fights or arguments . . . 'whore.' I called my mother a whore once, no, twice. I knew that a prostitute charged money, a whore didn't."

So your fear was that they would ask you whether you knew the word "prostitute" because of your mother?

"I don't remember now at all whether I ever put it into words for myself. I only remember being frightened of that all the time. I kept thinking, 'Now it'll come up, now it'll come up.' I never stopped thinking about that coming up till the end."

Her memory of Fernwood, the children's remand home in Newcastle where she was kept in a locked attic room under twenty-four-hour police supervision during the time of the trial, is particularly unhappy. "I felt bored, really bored. I think now it was because of Fernwood that I thought the trial went on for much longer than it did. I was a Category A prisoner [a prisoner accused of a serious crime]. I know now what it means but of course didn't then . . . and that meant the light had to be kept on all the time with somebody watching me. On weekends, there was no point in waking up because I could just as well just lie there and do nothing as there was nothing *to* do. I asked for a bath. I remember asking for a bath quite often. ["She wanted baths all the time," one of the policewomen told me. "Some of us stayed in the bathroom with her; a few of us just left the door open but left her alone—to give her some space."] Once I turned the light off and just lay in the bath and the next minute all hell broke loose. I don't know what they thought I was doing. I was just . . . well, I had my head under the water, just a different kind of being alone . . ."

Perhaps they thought you wanted to drown yourself?

"I think that would have been impossible and they should have known that. It's funny, you know, that's the only bath I remember. I mean remember in the sense of feeling it, feeling the water, the quiet . . . you know what I mean? It was so long, so damned long. I couldn't go out, couldn't even lean out the window; there was something about a cat [outside the window], I don't remember what, I actually thought it was a bantam, and after that I was told I couldn't even *look* out the window."

"It happened the first weekend," policewoman Mary S. told me. She had allowed Mary to pick up a cat that was on the roof outside the window. "I was looking at a magazine or something and then . . . I realized she was holding the cat so tight it could not breathe and its tongue was lolling. I . . . tore her hands away and said, 'You mustn't do that. You'll hurt her,' and she answered, 'Oh, she doesn't feel that, and anyway I like hurting little things that can't fight back.'"

Mary said she couldn't recall this incident with the cat. "I remember feeling irritable a lot. I must have been exasperating for them. I felt so cooped, I wanted to run. I'm surprised I didn't have any real outbursts, scream and shout, you know . . . I must have contained an awful lot, I was so physical."

I know they were aware that it was a long, tiring day for you, I said, and they gave you your tea as soon as you got back from court, and I was told you had a TV.

"Yes, I remember there was, but in that attic room it was sort of around a corner and it depended on the policewoman whether I could watch. I remember having a lot of headaches and I didn't tell anybody and I don't sleep much anyway but it was very hard to sleep with the light on and the policewoman sitting there. It was all . . . all nothingness, you know. I remember being glad when the weekends were over. Going to the trial was a relief, like, a break, you know, something . . . not to amuse but to distract me. I didn't like being alone. I didn't like not being *physical*. The police in court . . . they were nice to me. They'd ask me, 'Would you like this or that? Would you like something to eat, something special?' There was one of them, I can't remember his name, but he was really nice. When I was in the dumps a bit he asked me was there anything at all I wanted . . . and I said I wanted to see my dog. He always called me blue eyes and he used to sing funny bits of songs to me at the end of the day and ruffle my hair. I loved that . . ."

But your family came to see you, didn't they?

"I saw them in the court. And sometimes, for a few minutes during breaks, in a back room there."

You don't remember their bringing you things, chocolates, toys? Because they did, you know.

"Did they? No, I don't remember it. Only at the very beginning, and at the end, too, I remember Auntie Cath coming and telling me it would be all right. And Auntie Isa, she took me in her arms, I remember that. She was the only one who did . . ."

Did what?

"Oh, hold me. The day before . . . something was said about a summary, and I thought that was something to do with a holiday. I remember thinking, Hum, holiday, some sort of convalescence place like Rothbury, you know."

Did you listen to the summing up with care?

"I don't think so. It was just more of the same, you know. And then I . . . I don't remember very well but it seems to me after the jury was sent out I was driven . . . no, I can't remember . . ."

What *do* you remember?

"I just remember sort of . . . I think Norma's name was called out and it was, like, not guilty, not guilty, and then it was me and a whole lot of commotion . . . my mother started screaming and I was just thinking, now what happens next? Like, so this has happened today, what happens tomorrow, you know? I was still waiting for something to happen. I was still waiting for handcuffs to be put on me, you know, to be physically hurt. I think I was expecting . . . I had expected all the time to be beaten to death.

"The longest chat I remember with my family was after the sentence had been passed when they took me to that great big room and it was just me. Norma wasn't there and everyone was crying. My dad cried, Auntie Cath was there, she was crying, and I didn't know what was going on. I was waiting to go back . . ."

But you had heard the judge?

"It didn't mean anything . . . I still thought something physical would happen. When they'd all gone, I asked the policeman—you know, the nice one—and he started to cry, too . . . A man, yes, he had sort of tears in his eyes, and when I said, 'What's happening?' he just said, 'You are going to somewhere nicer.' And then they came and threw a horse blanket over my head and led me out and put me into . . . well, I presume it was a car. I thought it was the gallows. I was being sat on because I obviously panicked. I heard somebody say things . . . obviously they were trying to reassure me. But I couldn't take it in and they only took the blanket off me inside Low Newton [in County Durham], which is a prison for adults.

"The first thing I remember when the blanket came off was the smell of urine and cabbage. Now I know that it is a prison smell, but then I didn't. There were reception officers with a prison officer in charge and I went through the procedure all prisoners go through. I was stripped and searched. No, there wasn't a doctor, no medical. I'd had lots of medicals before. There was a concrete slab. Standing around after being hosed down . . . was sort of like . . . I don't know: not me, not May, not real, not happening . . . You know, that strange echo of gates slamming and keys turning, one off, one on, one off, one on, and the shouting, it was something . . . sounds . . . I knew of, but . . ."

Knew of perhaps from TV films?

"Perhaps. I can't remember what I felt."

You must have been very tired?

"I don't remember. My clothes were taken away and I stood around in some kind of green prison apron-type wraparound thing, which of course would fit most people but which on me was twice my size, and it trailed on the floor, so they had to give me my own clothes back."

And your underclothes?

"I'm not sure. I seem to remember wearing a nightgown. They kept mentioning the governor. There were quite a few people there, I remember being surrounded by people. I think they were curious. I asked what the governor was and they said she was the head of the place and was deciding what was happening with me. I was sent to the hospital wing, which was just a cell with a bed, and I couldn't get on it because it was too high up. It was just a bare cell and someone came and looked through the spy hole and I jumped up, or rather down, bumping my head on the rim of the bed, and I spat through the spy hole. Everything was green: the walls, the corridor had been, too; the cell had nothing except the bed and a plastic floormat . . ."

Was there a toilet?

"No, a plastic chamber pot."

No sink?

"No. They'd take me out for ablutions twice a day. There was a very old, old-fashioned shower and little soap tablets, Windsor soap, it was called, two inches long, like hotel soap. But I'd never had a shower in my life. It felt sort of clean, nice.

"The governor came to see me, I don't remember when, but I think the first morning, and she was a very kind lady with a kind face and wasn't in uniform. She seemed very old to me—I now think she was probably under fifty, but that was old to me. She told me that I had to drink a pint of milk a day, that it was the rule for young offenders, and that I had to be sure to drink it and did I like milk? So I said I quite liked it and I told her about my dog and she came back just a little later and gave me a photograph of her dog, also an Alsatian, but I can't remember her name . . ."

The dog's?

She laughed. "No, the lady's. She also said I was entitled to write two letters a week but that I wouldn't be allowed to mix with other prisoners. I asked her how long I would be there and she said she didn't know, but not long."

Did you tell her that you thought you were going to be hanged?

"I can't remember how I put it, but I remember she told me I wouldn't be hanged. There wasn't any arrangement for school, you know, and she said the regulations were I had to have schooling. So she . . . the governor . . . was lumbered with me for about an hour a day. She would sort of read and write with me. I'd read to her. I remember that she brought me a book, *Black Beauty*, and except for when I stole my mother's book and was beaten black and blue when she found out, that was the first whole book I'd ever read. I loved it. She tried to find out what parts interested me and I read it out loud to her. I could read quite well and she said so, too. She apologized because I had to stay locked in my cell."

Her mother's "book" was very vivid in Mary's mind throughout our talks. She had always thought of it, she told me, as "Mam's book," and it was her mother's most precious and carefully guarded possession. "She could sit for hours with it on her lap, sort of hugging it," Mary said. "I was so curious about it when I was small, I hurt." By the age of eleven she had, of course, succeeded repeatedly in satisfying her curiosity and had read it from cover to cover. At the trial it was rumored that the "book" was a Bible and that Mary was fascinated by the list of dead family members glued to the inside cover. But in fact—neither the Bible nor a real book—it was a folder, about the dimensions of a legal-size page but a foot or more thick, which Betty's father had won in a raffle. As Mary had put it to me about her mother: "It contained her life. It was all kinds of things she cut out but also things she wrote, letters and poems. It was full of pictures, too, of Jesus and the Virgin Mary, crucifixes, and people leaning over graves. It also had pop-up pictures . . . I think it was a Grimm's fairy tale her father had given her and when she started that book, she put it in that thick folder . . . She always had this huge thing with her wherever she went or lived . . . I don't even know how she managed to lift it or hold it, it was so heavy," Mary said. "And at home she hid it. Of course, I always found it and used to look at it when she went out. I was fascinated with the pop-up pictures and read the fairy tale and other bits of it, poems to her father ... you wouldn't believe it ... love poems—to her *father*?—and obituaries, and locks of hair ..." (The rumors about the record of dead relatives were apparently true: I was told by one of Betty's sisters in 1970 that she kept a list on the inside cover of people in the family who had died. "The book had lots of Betty's drawings in it from when we were children," said her sister Isa. "They were always of religious things," she said. "She always drew nuns, and altars, and graves and cemeteries." "Betty was that religious and good," her mother, Mrs. McC., added, "always with the saints' pictures and rosaries all over the place. We all thought she was going to be a nun.")

What kind of hair was it, I asked Mary. Children's hair?

"Oh no ... I'm sure they were my grandad's. I think now he was the only person she ever loved ... Anyway, when she caught me looking at it that first time, she picked me up by my hair and shook me and shook me. I thought my head would come off. And then, eight years ago [1988], when I briefly stayed with her, I saw the book again. And now it was even more massively thick and she had countless cuttings in it, about me. It was ... it was so sad. And then, when she died, the book just wasn't there. Everybody looked for it—I think we thought her will would be in there, too. Anyway, it had gone. Perhaps she burned it before she died."

Even during the stressful period of remand and trial Mary quite easily took a liking to people, but certainly the one she spoke of with real pleasure was this governor at Low Newton whose name she never knew.

"Yes, I really did like her," she said, "but I can't remember what she looked like ... I just have a vague image in my mind, quite blurred, I don't know why."

So Low Newton is not such a bad memory?

"That's true," she said. "Funny, isn't it? Because of her, I think. But also, even though I was locked in and couldn't be with other people, it felt . . . I don't know how to say it . . . like as if there was a purpose to it, as if I was going somewhere."

The being alone was like a purpose? Or the potential going somewhere?

"Both, perhaps? The governor, and the prison officers, kept talking about my being transferred, moved on, and being moved on didn't mean to me like moving house or sideways . . . it meant something forward. And I got used to the sounds . . . the keys, the orders . . . and in the night, the light was out and I was alone but not frightened. I felt more free in Low Newton than perhaps ever, I don't know why. I'd shout a lot, sing, kick the doors, generally be a damned nuisance. They'd tell me off but not roughly, you know—well, they didn't have any other children there, did they? And now, thinking about it in retrospect, specially the governor, you know, I think they were . . . how can one say it . . . *uncomfortable* with it? Well, wouldn't you be? I would, if I were a prison governor or officer. I used to do handstands in the cell. There was an exercise square and they'd take me out there for about fifteen minutes every day, and I had to walk around it by myself, just walk, not run. I don't know how long I was there. I don't think I know how long I was anywhere. But it was before Christmas when I was moved on to Cumberlow Lodge, so it couldn't have been that long, less than two weeks, I suppose."

Cumberlow Lodge, a short-term remand home with high-security provisions in outer London, was used as an assessment and classifying center where young female offenders could be observed by a large qualified staff and psychiatrists before being sent to suitable institutions. When Mary arrived there about a week before Christmas 1968, the youngest detainee by four years—as she would be practically everywhere she was sent—the Home Office still had no idea what to do with her, and the problem would continue after Christmas. "There was conference after conference about her," one of the people who attended many of these meetings told me at the time. "Nobody could think what to do."

Again Mary retained some memories of her stay there. "The couple who ran it were Mr. and Mrs. Hart," she said. "Mr. Hart reminded me of David Niven . . . but I only remember bits about that time . . . four, five weeks, wasn't it? It's very blurred in my mind. I was put in a separate unit with four girls, which meant that much of our time was spent together in a fairly small room. They were all a lot older than me and they could all smoke after each meal. I thought that was brilliant. And there was greenery outside, you know, not walls. I remember, my first morning there, I looked out of the window—they were locked and had security glass, but there were no bars like in prison—I saw squirrels, and there was a tennis court; I tried once to play. We were very supervised and at night we were locked in separate rooms and I hated that, I don't know why. I remember I behaved apallingly. One other girl was fourteen or fifteen, I think, and she and I had to have a tutor who would be there from about ten to about four trying to teach us, all in that one room. I can't remember what or how she taught. I think I wasn't taking much notice. I wouldn't sit down. I was like a monkey. I think now that part of it was that there were no restraints, no lines to cross, nobody was punished or disciplined. Now I know, of course, that that was the method, how they were observing us. But I don't think it can have been right. I only know for myself that it was . . . I don't know, it put my back up. I remember Mr. Hart, who was nice, you know, trying to speak to me a couple of times, but of course it was useless. I was like . . . I don't know . . . frantic, I suppose. I'm sure I needed nothing so much as boundaries, and there weren't any."

Though she was exceptionally provocative and difficult throughout her six weeks or so in Cumberlow Lodge, she was met—as I was told later by one of the girls who had been there at the same time—"with nothing but compassion from the other girls. We all knew who she was," this girl told me, "but we hadn't somehow realized how young she was, how small. Most of the girls there were, you know, between late fifteen and seventeen, with all kinds of quite serious problems—more family and personality conflicts than criminality, really. And the ethos of the place was to treat us as far as possible as grown-ups. It was a good way for us, but not for her. She really didn't fit in there at all. She was not . . .

oh . . . personally aggressive, you know. I honestly don't think she would have dared, we were all so big by comparison. She was just dreadfully *naughty*, somehow as if she was bursting with need or needs or whatever. I remember one girl in my unit—she was very clever and did A-level psychology later—saying once to Mr. Hart, 'Why don't you just give her a spanking? She just wants to be stopped, that's all, and no talking to her will do it.' And Mr. Hart saying that that was quite true, but as we knew perfectly well, talking was all he could do. To be honest, even though we had been horrified about the killing of the little boys, I think most of us got to be sorry for her."

In retrospect Mary seemed to agree with the older girls' description. "I think the teacher we had was a psychiatrist, and I wonder what she can have learned about me, or anybody, under those conditions. Nothing, I bet," she said. "But they made a big effort about Christmas. Everybody joined up, it seemed like hundreds of girls, and after Christmas dinner with paper hats on, they had presents for everybody. I remember feeling all right that day. I was one of many and nobody was bothered."

Did you get a present?

"Yes, I think I got a doll."

Any presents from home?

"I can't remember. I don't know if everything that arrived was just sort of pooled. I really don't know. I got taken back upstairs after dinner and locked in, but I felt better.

"It wasn't long after Christmas, my mother came to see me. Her face was all swollen. She said she had a toothache. It was her pattern. She always had something, or said she had something, that would make me be sorry for her or guilty about her."

Were you glad to see her?

"I can't really remember. Mr. Hart was there all the time and she said to him—and to me, angry, you know—that here she had come all that way and she felt she was being observed and she told him she didn't like it. She didn't stay long at all." As often happened when Mary was speaking about the past, she had fallen back into Geordie, and her voice sounded oddly sad.

Did she tell you again not to talk to psychiatrists? I asked.

"I don't think so. I don't think now she would have said that with any-body there, you know. She'd said it again when I saw her that last day in Newcastle, you know, something about their getting into my head, like she did before, but I only remembered that much later . . . I didn't really hear anything anybody said that day."

And when psychiatrists like Professor Gibbens saw you at Cumberlow Lodge, did you remember that then?

She nodded. "I don't think I talked to any of them—said anything really—after that. I didn't have nothing to say, you know. It was years before I said anything . . . even in Red Bank, even to Mr. Dixon."

Mr. Hart told her about Red Bank a few days before she was moved. "He told me that I was 'going back up to the smoky mills.' I asked what did he mean and he said, 'Oop north'—sort of taking the mickey out of my accent, you know. It was only then I realized I had an accent for [peo-ple who lived] down south. He told me about Red Bank, but he didn't say where it was . . ." She laughed. "Or that it was going to be all boys."

PART TWO

RED BANK

February 1969 to November 1973

Forgetting

It was on February 4, 1969, that James Dixon and his wife, Jean, traveled south to pick up what was to become their most challenging and also their most taxing charge.

Mary always spoke of Mr. Dixon in touchingly proprietary terms. "He had on his checked tweed jacket with his fawn trousers and his brogues," she said. "Mrs. Dixon was like a little butterball, small, cuddly, jolly, with a soft round face and what I think is called an English complexion. She was in a flowery print dress. Mr. Dixon was tall, about six feet two, I think. I had to look up at him. He had a weatherworn sort of face, a handlebar moustache that made one smile and kind, twinkly eyes. My introduction to them was very formal. He was very military; all his analogies were very military but, you know, you looked at Mr. Dixon and you knew he wouldn't tell a lie. The world should be full of Mr. Dixons."

The leaving formalities, she remembered, took quite some time. "Mr. and Mrs. Dixon arrived [at Cumberlow Lodge] around ten in the morning, I think, and there was a lot of palaver, hours of it, before we left. Mr. Dixon spent a long time with Mr. Hart—at least, it seemed very long to me."

The seven-hour "or so" car journey to Lancashire, she said, was at first very exciting. "Everything—you know, the houses, people in the streets, the traffic, it was like . . . oh, I don't know . . . freedom . . . no, not freedom—I think I knew I wasn't going to be free, like *free*, you know. But it was . . . seeing ordinary life. You know, it made me feel more . . . ordinary."

Did you stop for food on the way?

"They stopped at service stations on the motorway for petrol and I suppose bought things to eat, but I don't remember it. Mrs. Dixon came to the toilets with me. Of course, I was an unknown quantity for them. I suppose they could have been afraid I'd run away, and Mr. Dixon—well, he wasn't a young man. I mean if I'd run, I don't know that he could have caught me."

Did it occur to you to run?

"Oh no, not at all. I liked Mr. Dixon right away. I wouldn't have run away from him." She thinks she slept in the car for quite a while. "When I woke up it was dark outside and when they said we were nearly there, I felt real excited."

Did the Dixons tell you anything about Red Bank?

"As we got closer, Mr. Dixon said that I'd find it was 'a tightly run ship' and that there was no preferential treatment. 'By that,' he said, 'I mean we are all equal, staff and children: we all eat together, the same food, and we work together.' He said I would find that people talked a lot to each other and made decisions together. But he never told me that it was all boys until just as we were going round a corner before arriving. Then he turned around, with a laugh and I suspect a look of glee in his eyes, and said: 'By the way, do you know it's all boys? And they are expecting a big blond with a thirty-six-inch chest. They've got a surprise coming, haven't they?' I saw Mrs. Dixon nudging him and shaking her head. I didn't know how to feel."

Red Bank Special Unit is the secure part of what was, in 1969, still referred to as an "approved school"—a reform school. In an assessment center and vocational school, Red Bank provided considerable space, comfort, and a fair degree of training or education for about five hundred boys. The special unit, in those earlier years deliberately situated in the very center of the approved school complex so that it looked out on daily life and thus avoided visual isolation, was planned for twenty-six boys requiring a high degree of security and was locked at all times. Once inside, it was a pleasant environment, full of light, with vivid colors on the walls and modern furniture. There were lots of long narrow windows that could be opened to let in the fresh air, and in winter the whole building was centrally heated. On the ground floor were the library, sitting rooms with comfortable armchairs, an airy dining room with many small tables, and a number of classrooms with blond-wood desks where the children were tutored in groups of three to six according to age ("May's probably getting better schooling than ours ever will," her Aunt Cath said to me in 1971). There was also a well-equipped art room with long tables, exhibitions of paintings and drawings (Mary pointed out one of hers when I was there in 1970), and a pottery kiln.

Within the perimeter walls of the unit was a garden, a greenhouse, and a shed for pets. Outside it, on the school grounds, was a swimming pool that the boys from the approved school had built and that the children from the special unit had the use of every day in the summer.

On the second floor were two dormitories, each for four senior boys, and individual bedrooms for the others. "I was told later, by the deputy head, Mr. P.," Mary said, "that when it was decided to send me to Red Bank they sectioned off seven rooms for girls. But in the nearly five years I was there, only five girls came, all a lot older than I was, and only one of them stayed as long as three months; the others left after a few weeks."

At the time of Mary's arrival and when I visited in 1970, there were eighteen teaching staff, predominantly men, but later a few young women came, and the domestic staff of twelve were all female. Among the teaching staff were Ben and Carole G., who met and fell in love while working there. For both of them, Red Bank was their first job. Ben started in August 1970, a year and a half after Mary arrived, and Carole in 1972. Both of them now hold responsible administrative positions working with troubled children. "We've both been on countless courses since then," Ben said, "but—and I think this goes for both of us—when we came to Red Bank, just after completing our teachers' training, we really knew nothing about the needs of such children. And to be honest, while many of the other staff had, of course, vastly more experience, none of them had, well, formal training, either in special education or psychology, and that includes Mr. Dixon, who really was the most exceptional and inspiring man."

"Yes, I'm not surprised that May remembers him with so much love," Carole said. "Many of the boys loved him too." She smiled. "But he was . . . well, perhaps a little naïve. He knew that many of these kids were very disturbed . . . some of the boys probably quite as badly as Mary. But he thought that love conquers all and, of course, it can do a lot. Or let's say that without the atmosphere he created at Red Bank, nothing can be done. But all the love in the world can't give people like us the skill to help children unlock their troubled minds. For that you need teaching and training."

"We didn't realize that then," Ben said, "but we know it now. But, let's be fair," he added, "even as it was, the place did benefit quite a number of boys: it *was* structured, and there *were* very precise rules to support that structure."

Red Bank remains very clear in Carole and Ben G.'s minds, not only because it is where they began their life together but because it is essentially where they decided what to do with their professional lives. After leaving Red Bank, both of them worked in other schools for children with problems, but they are now established in a large local authority in the west of England, each heading different departments, one dealing with special schools and personnel, the other with the specific problems of particular children. Once they had a child of their own, they both said, they could no longer work day in, day out in places such as Red Bank. "I did it from the age of twenty for seven years," Carole said, "and Ben from when he was twenty-one. But having a child changes you. You are more vulnerable, and you become aware that your child needs protection from that, too. You think more deeply about yourself, your actions and your reactions."

James Dixon selected all the personnel for Red Bank himself, they said. "And it seemed as if he very deliberately chose people of different ages, backgrounds, and very different personalities," said Ben. "Almost as if he was trying to supply the children with a microcosm of society. Of course, almost everything at Red Bank was due to Mr. Dixon's own personality. And because such men, or women, are very rare, as an individual you can try to emulate what they try to do, but such a setup can't just be copied."

"It had a kind of 'purity' about it in terms of what it offered the kids," Carole said. "It was untainted, if you like, by anything they might have experienced before."

"Because he was such a good man, it made one feel that bad things couldn't happen," Ben said. "Of course, they did happen, as we see from May's experience with that housemaster, but in an environment such as the one Dixon created, the effect of such a shock on the community as a whole would have been minimal rather than, as one might have expected, major and enduring."

Even when they were there, they said, there were other children at Red Bank who they realize now were as damaged as Mary and who, because of the deficiencies in staff training and lack of specialist knowledge, were not helped in the ways they should have been. "But you have to look at the other side of the coin, too," Ben said. "Whatever was lacking, they *did* have this period of sanctuary, of affection and warmth in a carefully structured environment. And they had the strong moral influence James Dixon doubtlessly exerted. May's search for self-knowledge now is the proof of it. It did help them to grow."

"Mr. Dixon always explained everything very openly," Mary said, "specially if he felt resentment of the rules. Except when I was locked into my room, at night and for half an hour or an hour's rest after lunch, I was never allowed to be alone, even to go to the toilet." She shrugged. "It bothered me a lot at first, but then Mr. Dixon explained, and I accepted it. After a while I hardly noticed. In retrospect now, I think perhaps it even made me feel safe . . . looked-after, you know."

What struck her most when she arrived was the smell of polish. "It was so clean and pretty, so different from everywhere else I'd been, and of course anywhere I had lived." The Dixons took her into the common room, "And I could see what he'd meant by 'surprise,'" she said. "Even the staff looked amazed seeing this little scrap he'd brought in. He said: 'This is May—that's what she likes to be called.'" After that, Mr. Dixon took her to the library and Mrs. Dixon brought in some scrambled eggs. "I couldn't eat. I felt sick after that long drive, the petrol fumes, and the smell of polish. He said, 'All right, but you won't get anything else.' They took me upstairs, and I was really surprised how they unlocked and locked every door behind them as we went through."

Surprised? I interrupted. Why was that surprising?

She was startled by my question. "Well," she said, "it *was* a school, wasn't it? They took me to my room and Mr. Dixon told me I'd be locked in, everybody was. 'No preferential treatment,' he said again. And he said Mrs. Dixon would introduce me to the housemother, Miss Hemmings, and I was to go get a shower and settle down for the night. I asked him how long I was going to be there for and he said, 'We'll see. A lot depends on you,' and that, anyway, he was tired and didn't have all the answers."

Miss Hemmings had told her the schedule: up at 7:00 A.M., shower, bed making, go downstairs, and before breakfast at eight line up for shoe parade and fingernail inspection. "It was all very shipshape," Mary said. "Of course, Mr. Dixon was ex-navy and it showed."

Did she still wet her bed?

"Oh yes, that went on for years. Miss Hemmings already knew about it when I arrived and they'd put one of those rubber sheets with a bell on the bed and she said to ring if I woke up wet in the night and somebody would bring me a clean sheet, like. Throughout the time I was there, nobody ever said a word about it if the bed was wet. I or Miss Hemmings would strip it in the morning and she'd take the sheets away.

'Don't worry about it,' she said once. 'I'm used to it: lots of the boys have that problem.' It was ... like in Rothbury ... [it] made me feel easier, you know."

"Miss Hemmings, the 'housemother,' was a special type of person," Carole G. said. "On the outside, the unsmiling battle-ax, but she had a heart of gold underneath and was a tower of strength for the kids."

Did she like Mary? I asked.

"Much more than like, she adored her—she became the child she'd never had. What one is apt to forget," she said, "is just *how* young and how ... well ... small ... May was. For Miss Hemmings, who'd of course never had a little girl to care for there, it must have been a real shock when she saw her first."

If most of Mary's memories of her years in Red Bank have a decidedly rosy glow, she becomes almost poetic when she speaks about James Dixon, quoting him—almost verbatim, she claims—as addressing these children in his care with deliberate formality and largely in naval officer's terms. "It is how he talked," she said. "I couldn't forget, ever."

That first day, at the morning assembly after breakfast and the daily PT, or physical training—"After a couple of years," she said, laughing, "when I ... you know ... developed, I was excused from PT"—he had formally introduced her to the boys. "He said: 'As you can see, we have a new member among us, of the more delicate sort of species. I know you'll treat her with respect as she will you. Her name's May and that's all you need to know.'"

Had the boys known why she was there? I asked.

"Oh yes," she answered. "Everybody always somehow knew everything about everybody who came. The teachers talked to us ..."

They told you about the other children?

Again she was taken aback at the question, which implied criticism. "Well, yes," she said defensively, "they trusted us ... well, some of us. But also, boys came and went, you know, so people came in knowing things. But nobody said anything, not to my face anyway, not until much later."

147

Classes were from 9:00 A.M. to 12:45 and 2:00 P.M. to 4:00 P.M. "The older boys did a lot more practical woodwork and metalwork. I was given some tests and put into a group of four that was mainly academic. I had a brilliant teacher for English language and literature, Mr. Shaw, but we did all subjects. And we took exams under the supervision of the local authority."

"May was very bright, incredibly bright really," said Ben G. "But not so much academically: she learned through people rather than books. In books she only dipped. She is a big dipper, you know, pages here and there but rarely chapters, not to speak of whole books. What she did— we experienced it ourselves and saw her do it with others—is borrow people's lives to develop her dream of what life should be. When she did it with you, it was very tiring—'Tell me some more. Talk to me. What then? What did you do? What was it like? Describe it.' It was draining, but in a way we thought there was something wonderful about her always wanting to fill in the gaps."

"Dinner—that is, lunch," Mary continued, "was at 1:00 P.M., then we were locked into our rooms for a rest. Between four and five we could choose to play draughts or chess. At five was tea, the last cooked meal of the day. At six, no matter what the weather ["in summer only," said Ben G.] we had half an hour of swimming in the open pool belonging to the approved school. On weekends it was an hour twice a day. After swimming there was football, athletics, or whatever, all organized in groups, a very tight schedule, no time for brooding. At eight it was showers, then supper of cocoa and sandwiches."

Did they have to dress again after showers?

She laughed. "After I came they did. Before then, I think they could come down in pajamas. And from eight-thirty to nine, which was bed-time ... lights out was at nine-thirty ... we could see TV if there was something suitable, a documentary or sport. If there was a good film the member of staff on duty could decide we could stay up longer. I remember the landing on the moon: we were allowed to see all of that. The staff watched it with us. Mr. Dixon said it was history in the making."

How long was it before she knew that she'd be in Red Bank for years?

"I don't think I ever knew," she replied. "Years were nothing, you know, time ran into time. The average for a boy there was five months. There was a system of reward points through which people could get all kinds of privileges, outings, home leave, and earlier release. Not me, of course, at least not for a while."

Did Mr. Dixon encourage her to talk about the crime, about the little boys she had killed?

"No. Oh no. For years I said I'd never done it, so how could he have talked about it?"

But there was a psychiatrist who came to the unit once a week, wasn't there? I reminded her. I met him at the time; he was a nice man, wasn't he?

"I don't know whether he was nice or not," Mary said stiffly. "I didn't like any psychiatrists, but him I didn't like at all because he used to sit there and wouldn't say anything . . ."

And that made you feel uncomfortable?

"I didn't know what he was about . . . I like to know where I am with people . . ."

What hadn't she liked about him? I asked, and she became evasive. "It wasn't really that I didn't like him, I just couldn't relate to him. I didn't know how I was supposed to relate to him with him just sitting there scrutinizing me. I mean, if he had asked questions, like others had done, you know, I could just have told him to fuck off, but with him not saying anything, there wasn't really anything I could say."

Was bad language allowed at Red Bank? I asked, and she laughed, suddenly happy. She enjoyed describing Red Bank. "Oh no," she said. "Not at all. You really got into trouble if you swore. You got a talking to and, of course, you could lose points. After a while I didn't swear at all."

To most of the boys—all except for two, she said, who were in for life like she was—these reward points were very important, because after they got forty of them they got released. "So they had something to aim for. I didn't really, except . . . you know . . . what I came to feel for Mr. Dixon. And he did try to make the reward system work for me, too, within the limits of the circumstances. If I did well, I'd be allowed to pick fun classes to go to, you know, rather than my scheduled program; and for a day or two I didn't have to get out of bed early; and once Mr. P. took me out with his family, to see the film *Wuthering Heights*, and Mr. Roberts and his wife took me to see *Godspell*. Then there was Mr. G.—he was courting Miss Jeffries—they were both very young and they took me for an outing by a lake and they had a bottle of wine and they put it in the lake to cool and that was fun."

In their essentials, Ben G. and Carole confirmed most of Mary's Red Bank stories. It is only in the details—dates, and who was who in some of her stories—that her memory sometimes fails her. "By the time I came," Carole said, "May was fifteen and I was just twenty. It must have been quite strange for her to suddenly have somebody there . . . well, quite feminine and close to her age, who was so obviously new to all the things that go on in such a place. She is quite right if she says we were close: it really was a fact, we were more like sisters than teacher and pupil. I let her call me by my first name, not in class, of course, but when we were alone—I think perhaps it wouldn't have been allowed had it become known. Mr. Dixon was quite strict on maintaining distance. But it seemed to be important to her and I saw no harm in it.

"After I had been there for a while I was given permission to take her out. My parents had a pub nearby and I took her . . . well . . . out into my world, to meet them, and sometimes for a haircut, or just to sit and talk. And yes, Ben and I took her out once for a day, a picnic by the lake and later to dinner at a restaurant. She used to write to us quite often after she left and, yes, she always mentioned that picnic; it was a special day for her."

"But the bottle of wine she remembers cooling," said Ben, "that was at the restaurant. It probably came in one of those coolers. I would never have taken alcohol to a picnic with a kid, but in a restaurant, yes, that was all right." He couldn't think, he said, how she had come to imagine that bottle of wine she had so precisely described to me cooling in the lake held by a string. He shook his head. "It just never happened."

"But she loved that evening's outing." Carole said. "She was wearing one of my dresses: we'd gone through my cupboard together and she had chosen it. It was the first time she had been in a restaurant like that, with a formally laid table, with flowers and all the cutlery and glasses. She just loved it. She asked about everything . . . you know . . . what is this spoon for or that fork and how do you open a bottle? She soaked up information like a sponge." And that, they said, was also the experience of other teachers who took her out.

"One day, Mr. and Mrs. Dixon and Miss Hemmings took me . . . just me . . . to Blackpool," Mary continued. "Though I think the other two . . . lifers, you know . . . also got taken out. But there were very happy times and I really thought I was going to be all right, and I know Mr. Dixon thought so, too."

He became a sort of grandfather figure for you, didn't he?

"No, not family . . . more than that," she said. "When you meet someone you like, you can say you like them, but finally it isn't that I *liked* him: I loved him. You don't love anyone right away, I mean like falling in love or loving your own child. Getting to love someone the way I loved Mr. Dixon takes time, a long time . . ."

But given that you came to love him, didn't you ever want to talk to him . . . about that "inkling," that feeling you told me you had more and more as time went on, that you had done something very wrong?

She nodded. But then, as if there were two simultaneous thoughts in her, she said, "No, no. I didn't want to, because I didn't want him to be disappointed . . ."

In what?

"In me."

The two times I visited Red Bank, I had been astonished to see that Mary's room—unlike the others I was shown, most of which, aside from the odd photograph, poster, and toilet articles, were comparatively bare of possessions—was chockablock. "She is so showered with presents from her relatives," said Mr. Dixon, who was showing me around, "that we can't give her all of them, we hold some of them back." There were dolls, soaps of every shape and color, tins of talcum powder and packets of bath salts, bottles of toilet water and scent, diaries and greeting cards; they filled every inch of every surface of the room and were stacked up in the corners against the wall. Three-quarters of these presents, carefully arranged as if for a window display, hadn't even been opened but were in their original cellophane or plastic wrapping. "It's like an exhibition, isn't it?" said Dr. Dewi Jones, the psychiatrist Mary now told me she hadn't been able to relate to. And another member of the staff I met said, "She doesn't use any of them, she just looks at them."

"When I first met May," Carole said, "she had more 'stuff' than I'd ever had, and she loved her things and they were very important to her. She cared for them meticulously and she was very clean and tidy."

"She was always having baths," Ben said. "She'd often go up for bed with the early group so she'd have time for a bath. I can hear [Miss] Hemmings now, banging on the door, saying, 'Come on out, come out *now!*'"

"She'd say: 'I'm intent on having a bath tonight and I've got all my smellies and my bubble bath,'" Carole added. "But you see, if there was some deep psychological reason behind that business of having baths . . . and I don't know that there was . . . but anyway, we wouldn't have known and there wasn't anybody around there who would have."

Dr. Dewi Jones, a young, rather thoughtful consultant from Liverpool Children's Hospital, was convinced, even before I related to him what Mary's family had told me, that she was blocking experiences and feelings from her childhood and needed to be helped to take issue with them if she was ever to develop into a normal adult. He didn't think this could be done except in a kind of psychiatrically oriented environment that, he admitted, didn't exist in Britain.

He felt that Red Bank, with its well-intentioned staff, although pleasant and even reassuring for Mary, was quite wrong for her. He confirmed that, apart from special short courses in the treatment of maladjusted children, the teachers were untrained in any kind of psychological discipline. He pointed out that before Mary arrived the staff were given a written directive on how to deal with her but were told that her background was unimportant for them to know about. He wished he could believe, he said, that this suggestion was only made in the realization that it was pointless to give them knowledge they wouldn't know what to do with. But he suspected it wasn't so. The writers of the directive actually believed that a negative memory of the past—which they, like so many others, no doubt conveniently reduced to a childhood of poverty and neglect, that is, a class question—was best overcome by a positive approach to the present. This rejection of the significance of early childhood experiences, that is, of the basic tenets of psychiatry, was, he felt (in 1970), part of the establishment dogma and deeply harmful to the care of troubled children.

Dr. Jones said his own role at the unit proved the point. He was not there to see individual children but to attend a weekly case conference to advise the staff on problems. This meant, of course, that he was dependent on their assessments. Most of them were devoted to the children, he said, and in some instances were passionate about their jobs, but because they had little or no training in any of the therapeutic disciplines, their observations were at best those of the intelligent layman, which was simply not enough when dealing with severely disturbed children.

(It is fair to say that in this particular respect there have been improvements over the past twenty-five years. There are now four special secure units in Britain dealing with severely disturbed children, of which Red Bank is one. If a child agrees to treatment, therapists are now made available to them on an individual basis.)

Dr. Jones had realized in 1970, very soon after Mary's mother had begun to visit her, that these meetings were having an adverse effect on Mary. "But I must admit, I sensed this from reports on her behavior *after* the visits, rather than understanding it from my own observation," he told me. As a result, however, he recommended stringent control on which members of her family should be allowed to see her. "I suggested the mother should be excluded, at least for a period, but I was told one couldn't forbid a mother to see her child." (This was the identical response I had received when, after discovering from her family some of the things Betty Bell had done to Mary, I made this same suggestion to the relevant department at the Home Office.)

Dr. Jones had insisted at that point that he should be allowed to see Mary regularly and on her own, and permission had been granted. But when they talked, he admitted, it had turned out to be useless. He couldn't help her by seeing her for half an hour or an hour once a week in the environment of Red Bank. His subsequent suggestion, that she be brought instead to see him at the hospital two or three times a week, was rejected. "I don't think it was because of the bother of bringing her or because of money," he said. "Just as the powers that be quite honestly thought, months earlier, that knowledge of her background was irrelevant for the unit's staff, so they now, just as honestly, believed she didn't need psychiatric attention. You can't do part-time therapy with a child as disturbed as Mary in what, however organized and benign, is a lay environment," he said. "There are increasingly large numbers of children quite as disturbed as Mary everywhere in the world, even if they haven't committed the ultimate crime. As long as we do not have long-term medically or therapeutically orientated educational units—basically like Red Bank but staffed with specialized educators—children such as Mary will not get what they must have. They are likely to remain a burden on society as long as they live, and they themselves will pay in unhappiness for these deficiencies in our system."

In the course of my involvement with Mary's case, which has lasted— at various degrees of intensity—for almost thirty years now, I have talked to many leading psychiatrists and social workers about her life specifically and about the treatment of damaged or unstable children in general. In 1995 I talked to Professor Guy Benoit, a leading French child psychiatrist, both about Mary Bell and about the boys who killed James Bulger. What he said echoes what the Oxford child psychiatrist Christopher Ounstead, director of the Park Hospital for Children, who guided me during my earlier research, told me in 1969. In both these cases, Benoit said, insufficient connection was made between the crimes these children committed and their mental or emotional conditions. "Sibling violence is comparatively frequent," he said. "But the kind of explosion that leads to a child committing a motiveless murder of a smaller and unknown child is very rare." What is not at all rare in such cases, he said, is the condition of long-pent-up anger and suppressed emotional pressure that the child has suffered and that becomes obvious to trained observers (Dr. Benoit—I think wisely—avoids the term "psychopathy," replacing it with "intolerable pressure"). "My files, and I am sure those of any child psychiatrist working in this field, are full of children who border on this 'explosion' or 'breaking point' and, if not helped, must reach it, if not sooner then later. This 'explosion' will inevitably become increasingly violent, whether towards animals or humans, towards others or towards the child itself." Child suicide, which has become so horrifyingly frequent and which more often than not follows a final cry for help in the form of repeated attempts at self-mutilation, is the ultimate manifestation of this explosion point.

Last year, however, Mary only remembered the positive side of Red Bank. Had she ever felt angry about the unit and about being there? I asked. "Oh no, no, no. I was a tomboy, really, you know, and . . . well, maybe it was wrong for me to be virtually only with boys for years. I suppose it must have been. But I really liked being the only girl. I made some really, really good friends there, fast and firm friends I'll never forget. And teachers I'll never forget. A lot of them are never more than a thought away . . ."

If that is so, I said, why haven't you tried to see any of them since your release?

She shrugged. "They'd be too busy," she said.

It hadn't all been so rosy, I reminded her. I said I knew that she'd had quite a bit of trouble and that some of the staff didn't like her or she them. Several teachers, though asking me not to name them, had spoken to me very frankly in 1970 after I told them, as I told Dr. Jones, what I had found out in Newcastle about Mary's childhood. "In all relations with adults," one of them said, "it is Mary who decides events. She even persuades them into believing that they feel no differently about her than they do about the other children."

Another teacher explained to me that the children chose their own counselors. By mid-1970, he said, Mary had had four. "In the case of most boys, if they request a change of counselor, the staff just shrug it off. But every time Mary has asked to change, people have become worried, introspective about it. They feel it is a reflection on themselves. They feel guilty. They feel they have failed." There was also the problem, he said, with teachers failing to maintain their detachment toward Mary. Two members of staff, he said, had left, solely because they felt themselves becoming too involved with her. "The third still sometimes broods on why Mary didn't stay with him. And the fourth—who has also now left—became convinced that Mary was innocent of killing those little boys."

It was this particularly intelligent teacher who first explained to me how exhausting many of the staff found dealing with Mary. His remarks were prophetic. It wasn't just what I found when I worked with her so many years later, but two of her probation officers, who between them have had charge of her for seventeen years, would both tell me how draining they found her. "There is in her," this teacher said, "an extraordinary inner intensity . . . a neediness one can neither really understand nor handle. And most of us feel we fail with her because, not understanding what it is she so desperately needs, we can't give it to her. That's where the sense of failure comes in."

Carole G. told me of an occasion when she experienced that sense of failure. "It was only a few months after I came to Red Bank. I was playing ball with a group of kids, May among them, and a big boy called Ross kicked the ball to me, shouting, 'Here you go, Carole!' and May absolutely flipped. 'She is not Carole to *you!*' she screamed at him. 'Miss Jeffries, *Miss* Jeffries to you!'

"Well, I managed to calm her down that day, but two days later I was giving guitar lessons in an upstairs sitting room when this boy Ross started it again, and May flew across the room and started hitting him for all she was worth, calling him every name under the sun. The guitar went—not quite around his neck, but something like that—and she was gone, completely gone. When, with another boy helping me, I finally managed to pull her off Ross, she was trembling all over and her body was almost stiff with tension. I took her down to the duty officer then and he sent me home, I was so upset.

"Of course, it wasn't unique—the lads often had physical outbursts—but usually, the way the place was set up, there would be several staff around and it was quickly contained. In this case I was alone with them and it upset me terribly, firstly that she had got so angry obviously because of . . . well, in defense, she thought, of me. And secondly that I hadn't prevented it or stopped it quicker. The boy Ross was black and blue all over the next day."

Was Mary sorry afterwards?

"She was very apologetic the next day—to *me*, not to the boy, and not because she fought him, I think, but because she swore at him. Mr. Dixon really didn't allow swearing. I was really upset. I walked home and shook like a leaf for an hour. I cried and cried. She . . . she really did get one too involved with her. I think—and this applies to almost everybody there—if we had had proper training for dealing with such needy children, it would have protected us—not entirely, but at least better—from our emotional responses."

The only person who somehow managed with her, Ben said, using almost exactly the same words another teacher had used twenty-five years earlier, was Mr. Dixon: "He had a kind of genius for dealing with young people, not because he was better trained—because he really wasn't—but simply because of what he was as a human being."

When Ben and Carole were with her, I asked, had they often, or ever, thought of her as a child who had murdered?

They both thought about this for a long time and then Ben said: "Well, no. You dealt with the here and now. We did know she was a danger, perhaps to herself, perhaps in moments of stress to others, because, particularly in the early days, we'd seen her at moments of furious anger. But in terms of day to day, we didn't really think of her as a child murderess, no. Not only because nobody ever talked or was supposed to talk about it, but also because we knew that she had never disclosed—had never said that she had done that, and actually there was always that element of doubt. There were quite a number of staff in the end, including, I have to say, Jim Dixon, who thought she was innocent, that there had been a misjudgment. I know now, of course, that that wasn't good for her. She lived in denial and we supported that instead of helping her to understand herself and then to come to terms with it."

"Months later," Carole said, "she suddenly said to me: 'Don't you worry about being in the room on your own with me?' It quite shook me—the inference being, of course, who she was—and I said at once, 'Of course not.' And it didn't. But I have to say, the day of that outburst in the music room, the thought did cross my mind—'My God, there it is . . .' Of course, I was wrong. That wasn't it at all. There was tension between her and this boy anyway, but this outburst was primarily because of her possessiveness of me; had I been more experienced or better trained, I would probably never have allowed it to arise. I understand all that now but then all our reactions were instinctive rather than imposed and immediate rather than sustained."

"She was just May to us," Ben said, "a little girl I knew was growing up, who was a right little beggar, pushing the boundaries all the time. But did we think of her as a child who had murdered? No, in the sense of your question, no, we didn't."

Mary seemed unconcerned at my knowing about her difficulties at Red Bank. She shrugged. "It's true, I was a little horror at times. I fought and was abusive, you know, used bad language, and yes, there were the odd one or two staff who disliked me. Mr. Dixon would say it was all down to jealousy and my manipulation of people, how I played one off against the other. You know, it took time for me to . . . to calm down. I had to grow up, you see, and if I did . . . well, more or less," she laughed deprecatingly, "it was at least partly because nobody treated me as if I was a freak. I was always talked to, things were explained to me, even after I'd been atrocious . . ."

For the first ten months of Mary's time at Red Bank, Billy Bell was her regular visitor. "And once he brought his mother, my Granny Bell," Mary said. "He used to get there practically at dawn. Mr. Dixon would come into my room at six in the morning and say, 'You have a visitor,' and I'd jump out of bed and there would be my dad."

But why did he come so early?

"I don't know; I never asked him. I was just so glad to see him. He and Mr. Dixon got on really well; they had great respect for each other. They weren't so different, you know, except one was educated and the other wasn't."

Well, Mr. Dixon's life principle was surely discipline and order, wasn't it? I asked. In what way did you find him and your father similar?

"I think it was my father's as well," she said. "My dad had his own values, funny though that may sound. I remember once as a youngster having a fight. I came in and he asked me who had started it and said if it was me, I'd damned well better not come in crying. He said if I went out looking for trouble and bullying people it was the wrong thing to do, and I wasn't to go round telling the world that my dad would show them, would beat up on everybody. Of course, if it wasn't me who had started the fight, that was a different matter. You see what I mean? Mr. Dixon could have said all that."

What did she and her father do when he came to see her?

"I wasn't allowed to be alone with visitors. Mr. Dixon was usually there, or else we sat in the sitting room, where there was always a supervisor, you know, and just chatted. He could never stay long anyway. I think he came so early because he took a night train, but then he had to get back the same day, so it was never more than a couple of hours."

All Billy would say to me at the time about Mary at Red Bank was that she liked the school. "She has a nice room," he said and claimed (wrongly) that it was "that place in London [Cumberlow Lodge]" Mary had liked best. "That's where she had the most freedom, like," he said.

But at the end of 1969 his visits stopped for quite a while. On December 10, he and the woman with whom he was living at the time were tried at the Moot Hall in Newcastle for robbery with force. Rudolph Lyons, who had prosecuted the case against Mary a year earlier, sitting as a judge, sentenced the woman, who was eight years younger than Billy Bell, to thirty months but gave Billy the comparatively light sentence of fifteen months in prison. "I am reducing the sentence I would normally have passed," he said, "because of the tragedy surrounding this man's family life." Billy eventually served nine months of his sentence. His sister Audrey took the three children, Mary's ten-year-old brother, P., and the two little girls, aged seven and three, whom their mother, after one short visit in early 1969, had never asked to see again.

But at the end of that year, on Saturday, December 20, ten days after Billy was sent to prison, Brian Roycroft, the children's officer at Newcastle social services (later the director), happened to come upon Betty Bell sitting on a bench in the corridor outside his office. "She didn't know who I was and asked me whether I knew where she could find the railway tickets and money [that the Children's Department provided] for the trip to Lancashire," Mr. Roycroft told me at the time. "We had been trying to get her to go and see Mary for some time and she had always refused. I told her, yes, I knew where it was and that I'd get it for her." When he came back, he sat down next to Betty and asked whether she knew what train to catch and about a place to stay. "She said that she'd heard there was a train at noon and that she didn't want to stay overnight but would come back on the night train. I asked her how she now felt about Mary and whether she was looking forward to seeing her and the unit," he said. And then, he said, Betty Bell burst into tears and told him about being "on the game." Then, "crying even more, she said she sometimes wondered whether she had harmed Mary, whether she was to blame. She was particularly disturbed about 'the speciality she was known for' as she put it, saying that the police had picked her up many times and warned her. This 'got around,' she said and a lot more people came to her for 'it.'" After she had referred to this "speciality" several times, Mr. Roycroft finally asked her what it was. " 'I whip them,' she said, and added quickly, 'I always hid the whips from the kids.' "

Betrayals

The unit's staff, who knew nothing about Betty's background, were apparently quite curious to see Mary's mother. "Mary was to await her mother in her room but got impatient and came downstairs," one of the counselors told me. "When her mother arrived, Mary ran towards her and embraced and kissed her. Later they sat in the library, with Mary on Betty's lap, and they both cried."

Other family members came to see her: "My Auntie Cath came about six times over the years," Mary told me. "And she brought my little cousin. I have photos showing me teaching him to swim in the pool. He remembers it, too. My Auntie Audrey never came, but Uncle Peter [her husband] came once. My dad's mum came once, and my gran [Betty's mother], whom I loved most of all, came as well, once with my mother and once on her own, all the way from Glasgow though she was so old and frail by then. She stayed overnight that time and I was so happy to see her. But my Uncle Philip [Betty's brother] never came, never a card, not even for my birthday. And Auntie Isa never came either. Her baby died of leukemia not long after I was sent away and my mother told me Isa blamed me, that it was God's vengeance on the family for my being such a bad person. When I was, oh, I don't know, maybe eight or nine, Auntie

Isa was expecting her first baby and she let me feel it move in her tummy. I never forgot about that. It was special. She was special for me. So I was just devastated to think she blamed me for the second baby's dying. And then much later I heard it wasn't true. She had never blamed me."

For several years Betty would now be Mary's most regular visitor. Until the middle of April 1970 she came once or twice a month, and one of Mary's teachers would confirm what Dr. Dewi Jones had told me. "May looked forward to the visits but she was always unsettled afterwards," the teacher said. "She'd become surly to adults and aggressive to the other children, in a way regressing to the way she had behaved—towards children, never to adults—in the beginning months: fighting, using bad language, lying, biting, scratching. And she cheated at games and when told one didn't do that replied that *she* could." With Betty, too, Mary was never left alone. The staff felt that Betty was putting on an act. "She 'played' at being a mother," another teacher said. "May once said she didn't think Betty was her mother—'She just isn't like a mother,' she said."

"I remember the first time she came to see me," Mary told me, "she brought me a lamp, a sort of lantern, you know, the little brass kind of thing with a torch in it you get in gift shops? Because of course I wouldn't have been allowed to have a candle. But I chucked it back at her. Practically from the moment she came she'd been telling me about her aches and pains and how terrible her life was—I knew she meant by comparison to mine. She was sitting there and I knew, I really knew she was trying to make me feel sorry for her. She did it at the trial, and now she was doing it again, you know, a year later. I really resented her then, probably because I believed her. I thought it had to be all my fault. The visit was stopped very quickly. She told Mr. Dixon that day not ever to leave me alone with her, that she was frightened she was going to kill me."

How did you know Betty had said that to Mr. Dixon?

"She said it, right there, in front of the duty staff, she'd rather kill me than see me in there. I don't think that was the point. I mean, she knew she couldn't kill me: we were never left alone. Much later I understood that seeing how I was surrounded with ... you know, middle-class adults, educated people, she must have been terrified of what I was going to come out with. More often than not when she was with me, she talked to the duty staff rather than me. Anyway, she was always very aware of their presence and she didn't really have anything to say to me, did she? She couldn't talk to me about my dad, because they'd split up. She couldn't tell me about my brother and sisters, whom I really wanted to hear about and see, because she'd left them and never saw them anymore. She did bring her boyfriend, whom I made myself dislike, though later—she was married to him by then—we became really good friends. He was twelve years younger than she was, a really good guy, hardworking, honest as the day is long, and incredibly loyal to her for years, even after they got divorced and he remarried." (This positive description of Betty's last husband was confirmed by Pat Royston, and he himself in a way proved his enduring loyalty when he told Mary, who asked him to talk to me about the years he had known Betty, that he would never speak about her to anyone.)

Quite a few of her mother's visits to see her at Red Bank were stopped, Mary told me, because both of them became upset.

"I used to get knots in my stomach, you know ...," Mary said. "She started to get upset and I thought it was me and I thought it would be better ..."

Were you always upset after she left? I asked.

"Yes, because she would tell me how sad she was, about how she was always writing to the prime minister, and not to worry, she'd get me out. And I would ask about S. and K. [Mary's sisters] and she would say I'm the only one that matters, 'I've got enough on my plate because of what happened to you. I can't look after the others.' So I thought that was my fault too—that the kids had no mum!"

Did Billy ever talk to you about her giving up the other children? I asked her.

"No," she said. "He just said they'd split up."

Did he ever talk about her?

"No, my father never involved me in the ... he tried to make it as simple and clear-cut as he could, as people just splitting up, you know. And he said that my mother was a very nervous person, not very strong, and that she had a breakdown and so, you know, it was better for her to be away from us so she could go off on her fancy trips ... He never questioned me, you know, he never sort of asked me ... things like my mother did ... 'Who do you love most?' "

Did he talk to you about the other children?

"Yes, he would just say different things, you know, how they were doing, how they were getting on."

I told her that when I'd spoken to Billy back in 1969 he'd not been very forthcoming.

"Well," she said, slightly defensively, "he spoke to Mr. G., he spoke to Mr. Dixon. I don't know, with you he was probably gob-smacked, not knowing what to say."

"I think what annoyed Mr. Dixon," said Ben G., "I mean what he was really very concerned about was that there was a very obvious controlling factor in the relationship between May and her mother. She used May. I remember one visit when, after her mum had gone, I asked May whether she had enjoyed the visit, and she said, 'Yes, I've been writing her some poems.' And I said, 'That's nice,' and she said, 'Not really. She'll only use them on gravestones and greeting cards.' I asked her what she meant and she said, 'Oh, she sells them,' and implied that her mother had directed her in what to write." From her arrival at Red Bank, and throughout her detention, Betty would offer information and stories about Mary to tabloid newspapers.

Ben's memory here, of Mary at twelve and her bitterness about the use her mother made of her and her notoriety, was in sharp contrast to Carole's impression of Mary's feelings two years later. I had asked whether Mary spoke to her about her family and Carole said yes, but mostly about her grandmother. "She loved her gran. About her mother," she said, "I think in some respects she may have fabricated a relationship for my benefit which didn't exist. Her mum used to come and it was like a fantasy of an entourage, you know, a *big* visit. There were never any negative stories about her mother like what Ben just quoted her saying.

It was like a romantic illusion—mum this and mum that, and that she loved, just loved her mum. And all this time we knew that Mr. Dixon was very worried about her visiting . . ."

From what these two young teachers had observed then, though differently at different ages, it seemed that while James Dixon's intuition told him to cut off the visits altogether (as Dr. Dewi Jones had recommended from the start), his lack of knowledge about her background and therefore his inability really to evaluate the dangers, combined with his strong conventional sense of fairness, made anything more than occasional intervention impossible.

How would you have felt, I asked Mary, if Mr. Dixon had stopped your mother's visits altogether? She pondered for a long time. "I don't know," she finally said. "I was always very confused about my feelings for her. You see, she was very pretty . . . even Mrs. R. [one of her teachers] always said how pretty she was and what lovely legs she had and all that, and it pleased me, made me feel proud, you know. At the same time . . ." She stopped. "I want to be careful," she said then, "because perhaps I'm saying this *now*, with my feelings now, which are so different. Still, no, I think it's true that even then I always had a slight . . . a vague sense of discomfort about her after a while, something I couldn't and didn't even think to identify, you know, in the pit of my stomach. But often, often when she sat there, I felt, 'Oh no, I don't want her here. She isn't . . . like . . . a mother . . .' "

Did you ever try to talk to her about what you had done?

"I tried once," Mary said. "It was soon after she began to visit me. I said, 'What did I do? Why did I do it?' And she said in that hard voice she often had, 'I don't want to know. Don't talk about it. Don't ever talk about it to no one.' And she'd only been there a minute and a half and she got up and, she didn't walk, she ran . . . ran out of the room with her blond wig flying . . . out of the building, and I didn't see her then for months."

And you never tried again? I asked her.

"No," she said. "I just shut . . . She slammed the door and then I shut it [inside myself] tight."

In the spring of 1970, Mary was allowed to visit her father in prison. "And she came," Mary said, "and it was the day it had been arranged for me to go and see my dad. [Mary was almost incapable of referring to her mother as Mum, or Mam, or Betty; even "my mother" was rare. It was almost always "she."] So I says to her, 'Right, I have to go, because I'm going to see my dad,' and she said like I had to choose between him and her. I said all right and that I chose my dad. I don't know if she got a shock when I chose him, but she should have taken that opportunity to cut out. That's what she was looking for all the time. After that I told Mr. Dixon that I didn't want to see my mother again. They wrote and asked her to stop her visits."

It is not clear whether Mary's request was made before her visit to her father or afterwards, as a result of seeing him. The visit, though arranged with the best of intentions, turned out to be ill-advised. In the early hours of the next morning, the special unit's night watchman called the housemaster on duty and told him that Mary was lying on her bed, crying bitterly.

"Old Tom," Mary remembered. "That's what we called the night watchman who made rounds every half hour. There was a night duty roster for staff, and right on top of the stairs was a sleeping-in room where, during his shift at night and our after-lunch rest, the duty officer was on call."

"She was inconsolable," this teacher told me some months afterwards. " 'I saw my dad in that place . . .' she sobbed. 'It isn't a nice place at all . . .' I finally got really worried about her," the teacher said, "and called Mr. Dixon. He came over in his pajamas and sat with her for more than two hours. He finally got her to go back to sleep. She'll do anything for Mr. Dixon."

Of course, your dad had been in prison many times, I said to Mary, but that was the first time you'd ever seen him in there, wasn't it? It must have been a terrible shock.

"He'd lost a lot of weight," she said, sounding desolate even now at the memory. "And when I remarked on it, he joked—as he would, you know, we are very alike in that, we always try to joke. He said it was because he wasn't getting his brown ale. I asked—I don't know

166

why—what do you eat with? And he joked again, and said: "Bloody chopsticks, what do you think?" He was really in there trying to make me feel better, but you know, it was a really old prison, Ribbleton, Preston, an ancient building, and it was all so sad . . ."

It is unlikely that by the time we talked Mary hadn't learned that Billy had committed a more serious offense than his usual small burglaries. But in her enduring affection for him she still tried to embellish it, to make it sound less bad, and to present him as a "protector" of others, and thus a victim, rather than a perpetrator.

"He got eighteen months, I think," she said, "for withholding information. I think he served nine of them."

Red Bank confirmed to me at the time that Mary had asked for her mother not to be allowed to visit her, but this restriction never lasted long. The record shows that, with a few exceptions, Betty saw Mary at least once a month between the summer of 1971 and Christmas 1972. "Altogether I think I asked three times that she shouldn't come," Mary said. "But . . ."—she shrugged—"somehow, a few weeks later, without anything being said, she was back again." It seemed then, and until her mother's death twenty-three years later, that neither of them could ever quite let the other go.

It is impossible to say now how much these visits contributed to the problems Mary began to experience around this time with the onset of puberty. She says that sex instruction was part of the curriculum and that "no great mystery was made of it." Nonetheless, adolescent girls have very different emotional and practical needs than boys. For the nonteaching part of the children's care, the staff was divided into groups. "There was always a female member of staff in each group," Ben G. said. "May related particularly well to the house staff. They had good chats about gutsy things." But Carole saw this differently. "I wouldn't have batted an eyelid talking to a girl, you know, in a contemporary manner, but in fact it was frowned upon," she said. "I honestly don't think anybody specifically talked to May about 'female' things."

Mary doesn't remember, for example, any specific instruction about menstruation. "That's right," Carole said. "It was quite an old-fashioned attitude. You know, Miss Hemmings will have got her Kotex or whatever and put it in her drawer wrapped in brown paper, and even though May doesn't remember it, will probably have told her how to dispose of them. But now that I think about it, the fact of being with the boys all the time may well have affected May in the sense that she didn't ask questions, of me, either, when otherwise she might have."

"In a way," Ben added then, "perhaps because she was more often than not the only girl, there was a permanent underlying awareness of her femininity. By the time I came, which was, of course, after that incident with that housemaster, men didn't ever go into the so-called female wing except in pairs; that was a rule Mr. Dixon made following that incident and also, from that moment on, there were always two duty officers at night."

Not long after Mary's first request to James Dixon to stop her mother's visits in the spring of 1970 a very strange thing happened to me. I received an anonymous letter with a Newcastle postmark enclosing a poem. In the three-line note that accompanied it, the sender claimed that it was a poem Mary had written and sent to her mother and the note ended: "Sister Cath has seen it."

I immediately telephoned Betty's sister, Cath, who confirmed that she had indeed seen the poem and that Betty had told her it was Mary's. But *she* hadn't sent it to me, she said, and she couldn't think who had. As far as she knew, nobody except herself and Betty had seen it.

Although I am certain now that it was Betty who sent the poem, neither I nor anyone else who saw it then had any reason to doubt that Mary had written it. I, as well as the psychiatrists I was in contact with throughout the research for my first book, not only found it an extraordinary poem for a thirteen-year-old but considered it a very important step in Mary's development.

When Mary and I had talked for the first time in 1995, months before we started to work together, she claimed firmly that she didn't know anything about it. When I realized later that she had actually never read all, or even much, of the book, I gave her the poem to read:

MAM
I know that in my heart
From you once was not apart
My love for you grows
More each day.
When you visit me mam
Id weep once, your away
I look into your, eyes. So Blue and
theyre very sad, you try to be very
cheery But I know you think I'm Bad so Bad
though I really dont know. If you
feel the same,
and treat it as a silly game.
A child who has made criminal fame
Please mam put my tiny mind at ease
tell Judge and Jury on your knees
they will LISTEN to your cry of PLEAS
THE GUILTY ONE IS you not me.
I sorry IT HAS TO BE this way
Well both cry and you will go away
to other gates were you are free
locked up in prison cells,
Your famley are wee.
these last words I speak, on behalf
of dad P . . . and me
tell them you are guilty
Please, so then mam, Ill be free, Daughter

                      May*

*See the facsimile in the Appendix.

"No, no, no," she said, sounding distraught even while reading it. "I never . . . My God, I never wrote that. It's hers . . . She will have . . . When she died, you know, there was a lot of stuff in her drawers, rambling poems and letters . . . I read through them . . . well, it did give me an insight into her . . . or what she thought I was feeling, you know. I wondered . . . How did she write these things? What was she trying to write? From me to her, from her to . . . anybody, or to herself . . . what was it? In this one, quite aside from the handwriting, which anybody familiar with hers would recognize right away [although Cath hadn't], there is a sort of . . . Scottishness, isn't there? You know, the word 'wee' for 'small,' I would never use that . . ." And then she added, with a degree of derision, "And—the spelling, and all this rhyming, dadedadeda, same, game, fame, ease, knees, pleas, it's just as rubbishy as all her poems. There was once a letter published in a paper I was supposed to have written and I got to see it, I can't remember how. And my English teacher saw it and laughed out loud: 'That's supposed to be from you?' he said. 'Nonsense.' He would have had my guts for garters if I'd written like that."

It had never occurred to me, I told Mary, that Betty could have written the poem. But what was most important was that if it had not been Mary who had written it but her mother, who had then felt moved to send it to me, then it would have been a huge admission on her mother's part of her guilt, and her own cry for help. Didn't Mary agree with that?

"Well, yes, but it's not what she ever said to me, you know. To me she only said for all those years that what she had to hide from the world was being my mother. That that was what dragged her through the gutter bearing her cross of Calgary [*sic*]. She'd say: 'Jesus was only nailed to the cross, I'm being hammered.' She'd write these strange, strange letters to me. Mr. Dixon would call me in, and rather than just handing them to me as was usually done with post after it had been censored, he read them to me. Later I realized that that was because he found them so disturbing. They were all about 'the Lady of Sorrows will watch over you with St. Jude, the saint for hopeless cases' and that sort of stuff.

"It's pathetic," she said, suddenly sounding angry, "that people would believe that I wrote this. I mean, anything I wrote was censored, and everything I received was censored and signed by the censor. How could I have written this without it being noticed and then discussed with me? Mr. Dixon discussed everything with me. Why wasn't it analyzed? You know, why wasn't the handwriting analyzed?"

I said that as no one except her Aunt Cath had seen it until I published it in my book, it would never have occurred to anybody to doubt that Mary had written it if her mother said she had, unless they were suspicious to start out with.

"Well, isn't that pathetic, too?" she asked. "How? How was it possible," she asked once again, in a mixture of anger and helplessness, "that they . . . you know . . . the social services and all these clever people knew nothing about me . . . about her?"

Within weeks of receiving the copy of this poem, which for the next twenty-six years I believed had been written by Mary, I learned of another disturbing event in her life. On an early evening in the spring of 1970, Mary told her latest counselor, Miss X., whom I was told she particularly liked, that during the weekend just past one of the housemasters had indecently assaulted her.

Today the subject of pedophilia is very familiar to us. We have become shockingly accustomed to hearing or reading about lurid discoveries of children who have been hurt and damaged by members of their families, by teachers, and most particularly by so-called carers in children's homes and institutions. But even as recently as 1970 the phenomenon was not familiar and, where known about, was kept secret.

Mary spoke to me for two whole days about her experience with the housemaster. When I had heard the story in 1970, I hadn't believed every detail, but now, so many years later, when her account was almost identical, I believe that in essence she spoke the truth.

She had barely had anything to do with Mr. Y. when it had all started, she told me.

Had she liked him when she met him?

"I didn't like or dislike him. He seemed OK."

171

It had been shortly after she'd met him, she said, that he had been on after-lunch rest duty and (as the children had to do) she rang the bell to go to the toilet.

"We were not allowed [to stay there] alone. The duty staff had to wait for us," she said. "And I was . . . well, sitting there . . . when I heard him ask from outside whether I'd started my periods. I was . . . really surprised . . . and I said, 'God, no, I don't want to have periods.' And he says, like, 'It won't be very long before you do,' and then he says, 'Have you started growing pubic hair?' Well, I giggled you know, but I became . . . sort of curious . . . I now think I felt that he was . . ." and she went into a long and confused explanation of how a child can recognize what she called "a nonce"—a word she applies to a man who is sexually attracted to children.

Later that afternoon, she and another "lifer," a fifteen-year-old boy, D., were in the greenhouse, planting seeds. "He had killed. I can't remember exactly what had happened, but he was thirteen then and not overly bright. When I knew him, he was nice, you know, mild and inoffensive." She had by then, she said, been quite aware of "boy and boy or boy and girl stuff," and had seen boys "fool around together, kissing and such, you know." But nobody had ever bothered her. "He was totally not interested anyway," she said about D. "I think in girls or boys either."

Were you interested in him that way? I asked, and she laughed. "God, no," she said. "I was just a tomboy. That afternoon I was interested in gardening, and so was he."

Mr. Y. had begun talking to them "in a funny way: 'When you plant the seed trays and you've got your fingers like this,' he said, sticking his finger into the earth, it was, he says to the boy, you know, 'like if you're giving someone a good poke,' and he looked at me and then back at him and said, 'I bet you've never done that to a girl in your life,' and D. blushed and I felt myself blushing too." (As my work over the years has made me unhappily familiar with the manners and vocabulary of pedophiles, Mary's account became eerily authentic here.)

She had stood up then, she said, and Mr. Y. had pushed against her and she could feel he had an erection. How did she know about erections? I asked.

"Well, I was living with all those boys," she said. "I'd seen them and I'd heard them talk about 'hard-ons,' jokingly you know, but we had sex education, too. It wasn't, you know, treated as a great mystery . . ."

When Mr. Y. "rubbed against" you, did you pull away? Did you mind?

She laughed. "No, I didn't. I think I thought it was funny."

The boy D. had been sitting "underneath a trestle and he could see what was happening. Mr. Y. then went out saying, 'I'll leave you alone now for five minutes'—which was special, because we were never supposed to be alone with just one other person [another child]."

And after the housemaster had gone, she said, she'd felt, "I suppose, excited, and I could see D. was too. So I said, 'You've got one on, haven't you?' And I sort of challenged him, you know. I said, 'You show me yours and I'll show you mine,' sort of thing, so he took it out and there was"—she laughed— "a mix of his jeans and my dungarees, which of course I couldn't take off, you know, but there wasn't a hell of a lot we could do because Mr. Y. would be back any moment, but I said he could put his hand down there and he did but it didn't make me feel . . . well, what I thought I ought to feel, so I just helped him to masturbate."

She knew all about masturbating, did she? And she laughed. "God, yes. I was living with twenty-two adolescent boys. What do you think they talked about?

"But then," she continued, "Mr. Y. came back and right away made some scathing remark to me about playing with little boys and, with a wink, what I needed was 'a good stiff telling-off sort of thing.'"

D. had never tried anything again or spoken of it, she said. "We weren't attracted to each other, you know. All the boys were too accessible, I think, and they knew Mr. Dixon would slaughter them if they bothered me in that way."

But later, as she got older, was she never attracted by any of this changing boy population?

"There were some on the other units I liked, you know, boys at the approved school," she said. "I watched them out of the windows. There was one. I thought he looked just like Paul Newman. I fell in love with him. I'd watch him six times a day when he walked past and I died a thousand deaths . . . But you know, it was puppy love, like being in love with Donny Osmond, not really 'sexual.' I felt quite inadequate as a female, even when I got to be sixteen, because I was always just like a boy dressed in baggy trousers and baggy tops. Only on Sundays and when I had visitors I had to wear a dress, you know, 'dress appropriately,' as Mr. Dixon would say."

It was during a rest period the following weekend that Mr. Y. came to her room.

Did he knock on the door? I asked.

"I don't know," she said. "He unlocked it."

But you were a girl. Didn't they ever knock?

"They could see through the observation glass what I was doing, and I had no choice in the matter: if someone was coming in, they were coming in. Some were OK. They'd call out to warn me—'Are you decent?' "

What were you doing when Mr. Y. came in?

"I was reading the *Jackie* magazine. And he took it out of my hands and handed me a book and said, 'You ought to read this instead, it's more interesting.' And he sort of flipped it open, pointed to the pictures, said he'd be back, and then he left. It was just a pornographic book, full of pictures . . . you know what I mean? It was called *Oral Love*. I only read a bit of it, but . . ." She smiled—and that sudden smile which so often preceded or followed a revelation was always a surprise. "I looked at all the pictures. It was very exciting for me then . . . ," she said, and laughed. "It *was* very interesting."

She said he had come back fifteen minutes later. "And then he undid himself and rubbed himself . . . it . . . against my vagina. No, I wasn't fighting it . . . I liked it. He told me to sit on him but he couldn't penetrate because I was too tight. I was sore. I cried and I said it hurt so he stopped. If he had broken my virginity, how the hell would he have explained that? But to my massive frustration he went on rubbing me for a couple of minutes, then he told me to do it to myself and I said, 'But it's not the same,' and then he said, 'Well, we'll have to arrange something,' and he did, twice more that weekend, once in my room and once in the staff sleeping-in room." On both occasions, she said, "it was finally mutual oral sex. He spoke dirty. He said: 'Dirty little whore.' He said it wasn't his fault, it was my fault, because I was there and there to be fucked . . . No, I didn't mind. When he masturbated me, he told me to say what I thought it would feel like if he went in. I couldn't, because I didn't know. And when he ejaculated in my mouth, I got sick and ran to the bathroom and vomited. The night watchman heard me and took me to my room and he gave me some cocoa from a flask he carried.

"I asked Miss X. not to tell anyone," Mary said, almost in tears now. "I suppose it was silly of me: after all, it was her job to report it, but I knew they wouldn't believe me."

Mr. Dixon, doubtless deeply embarrassed by the incident, questioned Mary and gently advised her to tell the truth. Eventually the matter was dropped as Mary's account was considered unreliable. "But it wasn't," she said to me. "It was true."

As we can see from the many cases that are emerging now, some of which date back thirty years, the fact is that twenty-five years ago, any child who made such an allegation would probably have found herself disbelieved, and Mary, who might have confused or even slightly dramatized some details in the telling but who had probably essentially told the truth, fared no better. The system was not geared to accept such unpalatable truths from a child at the expense of an adult. Nonetheless, as Ben G. told me, from then on Mr. Dixon ordered that night duty should always be shared by two staff members.

After this, Mary went through a period of considerable confusion and unhappiness. "I had been so happy, you know," she said. "Red Bank, with Mr. Dixon, had come to mean so much; I knew they were good people."

How soon had she realized they were "good"? (Mary often uses the word "good" to describe people she likes, and it applies as much to the sense of their being nice and kind as to their being strong and disciplined.)

"I don't know . . . I don't remember dates and times, but it was when I couldn't get my own way, when they wouldn't put up with my tantrums, when they were stronger than I was . . .

"There was the odd teacher," she said, "who made me sob. There was a Hungarian I was being particularly abusive to, and he shouted at me: 'You want to get back to the hovel you came from!' And it really upset me, I really cried. And then there was this Miss X., who you thought I liked, didn't you?"

Well, I said, you asked for her to be your counselor.

"Yes," she said, "and I was really wrong there, wasn't I? She tried to get into my head. She would try out this psychodrama crap she knew nothing about. I don't know where the information came from that I liked her. I told her please don't tell, you know, about Mr. Y.; she was the one who brought it all about when I didn't want anyone to know.

"But . . . ," she said, "there were really good times: the interaction with the staff and their families; my friendships with the boys. There were two boys . . . I won't say their names. But when they came they were, I think, about the same age as I was by then, thirteen and fourteen, and they were rather effeminate boys who had both been sexually abused . . ."

They told you this?

"Yes," she said, and repeated, somewhat defensively, "Well, I was also thirteen, fourteen by that time and we had become real friends by then and they probably needed to talk."

Did you tell them anything about yourself?

"No, I didn't."

Remembering

In July 1971, Mary was visited at Red Bank by Dr. David Westbury. "You remember," she said, "he was one of the two psychiatrists who had testified at my trial, and for the first time I was able to talk, not . . . deeply, you know . . . but normally, and I quite liked him."

Dr. Westbury's report to the Home Office says that after "a long talk with her" he had found her "remarkably improved" with "a loss of nearly all of her aggressive tendencies . . . a modification of her inclination to manipulate . . . [and] an improvement in her relations with other people and [in] her capacity to think about the future." He also felt that she had gained insight into her mother's emotional and social instability and added, significantly, that her mother could "hinder her progress" even now. He concluded by suggesting that "one should begin to consider 1975 [when Mary would be eighteen] as a possible release date . . . She will be old enough [then] to stand on her own feet with some support, and, if she progresses as she has, [will] be capable of a life of her own."

Betty used her knowledge of this report for further publicity. In an interview with a Newcastle Sunday paper she said she was determined that when her daughter was released they would change their names and move to another part of the country and make a fresh start together. And she quoted—and showed the newspaper—a letter she said she had received from Mary that morning: "No matter what happens, Mam," it read, "we'll go it together. These past five years have been hard for us and everyone. I can only hope and pray things turn out for the best, Mam. I love you and shall always love you. As long as you are there I'll be OK because I want you and need you . . ."

"That's the letter I was shown," Mary recalled. "I was dumbfounded because I hadn't written it . . ."

Were you angry? I asked.

"I don't remember," she said, sounding tired. "I think I was more fed up than angry, and anyway, Mr. Dixon told me she wouldn't be allowed to visit me anymore."

Had she eventually talked to Mr. Dixon about her childhood, I asked her, either about what had been done to her or about what she had done?

Her reply was indirect, but in the effort to encourage her to speak it was always important to accept her diversions, even if they appeared to lead away from the immediate question. "I remember telling Mrs. R., one of the teachers I liked very much, that I had a twin sister who died and she was called Paula, and I used to cry when I talked about her. Mrs. R. knew of course that I had no twin sister, but she never told me I was talking a load of rubbish—she just listened."

Did you know what made you tell this tale?

"I don't think I knew then why I did it, but I've thought about it since. I think I was inventing a twin who might have done what I really did . . . You know, perhaps, even though I wasn't consciously able to deal with it, it was a way of admitting . . . of testing the temperature of admitting, so to speak."

What do you mean by not being "consciously able to deal with it"? I asked, and she replied, impatiently and almost angrily, that I knew because she'd told me earlier that she had never yet dealt with it . . .

But what do you actually mean by "dealing with it"? I insisted, and she slowly bent forward, burying her face in her hands, her elbows on her knees as if she were having stomach cramps. "I think about it," she said, repeating the words as she did when she was upset, and her voice was muffled with sobs, "but I can't . . . I can't, can't, can't put it into words, not, not what I did . . ."

She invariably lost control of her emotions when trying to talk about the actual killings. In the early weeks of our talks, her distress at these disclosures would be so intense that I sometimes became afraid for her and urged her to lie down and rest or even to go home. But later, too, her unhappiness was such that I often suggested a break, when I would make tea, she would have a cigarette, or, if we were in the country, she sometimes went for a short walk. Her recovery from these terrible bouts of grief, however, was astoundingly quick, and at first these rapid emotional shifts raised doubts in me. After a while, though, I came to realize that they were part of the internal pattern that governs all of her feelings and her conduct. She has an exceptional range of opposing needs, all of which are constantly acute: her needs for disclosure and for hiding, for sociability and isolation, for talking and for silence, for laughing and for crying. Only one thing overrides them all: the discipline she has created inside herself in order to give her daughter a normal life.

She said that one of the most difficult things about working with me was the transition between so intensely being "Mary" with me and then making her way back to her family and being "mum" with her child. She was exhausted after our sessions, she said, and all she wanted was not to think anymore. "I even didn't want to go for walks," she said. "If I walked, I thought. All I wanted was to sleep. So finally, that's what I did. I slept."

As we went further and further toward her most difficult confrontation, she would increasingly associate the existence of her own child with the memory of the tragedies she had caused. Since her own child was born, she said, there was not a single day she hadn't thought about Martin's and Brian's parents (she always refers to the little boys individually, by their first names, as if to emphasize their identity as children and her acceptance of it). "Especially on happy days, there's always something that pulls me up, stops me when I think what I robbed them of . . .

bringing their children up. It never goes. It'll never go away and why should it? I thought about it before, too, but since I've had [my child] it's become oh, so much, much more painful. Before, I would think of it just as an adult, you know, rather than a parent. Then, too, I would feel sad, but not the incredible sadness I feel now. I look at her and I think . . . Oh God . . . of their parents."

There was one occasion at Red Bank, she said, when she did talk or write about what she had done. "It was in an art class, which Mr. P. was supervising, and . . . I don't know what brought it on, except perhaps . . ."

Except perhaps what?

"I can't be sure but I seem to remember it was around the time one of the boys I was telling you about . . . you know, who'd been abused . . . I think it was just about when that boy had been talking to me about that quite a lot."

And you think now that might have got you thinking about yourself?

"That's what I'm thinking. Or else, perhaps I just wanted Mr. P.'s attention or his approval. Anyway, I was sitting at that table in the art room and I was supposed to be working on an art project and stopped and started writing on bits of paper . . ."

What do you mean by bits of paper?

"Well, it wasn't one . . . you know . . . sheet of paper, art paper. I tore bits of paper off used sheets, of rubbish you know, a bit from here and a bit from there and started writing . . ."

And what did you write?

"About Martin and about Brian, and Norma . . . I wrote that I'd killed Martin, and that was the first time I'd said it."

Did you write how you killed Martin? I asked.

She shook her head. "No. Oh no. I said it was an accident."

And did you say that you killed Brian?

She shook her head. "No, I didn't. I said, like at the trial, that Norma did, and I was writing quicker and quicker because, you know, I knew we only had so much time for the period and . . ."—she began to lose the thread—"it was an art class, with everyone around and I wasn't doing what I ought to have been doing in the first place . . ."

And what happened?

"Mr. P. noticed I was writing and he told me to bring over what I'd been doing and I did and he read it and he was very kind . . ." She always defended the actions of the people she liked at Red Bank, however unfortunate their reactions were. "But he said I hadn't written it properly and he would write it out for me as it should be . . ."

Did he mean the look of the writing or the meaning?

"I had written it so fast, it sounded confused. He wanted to elucidate," she said. "And just as he began to write it out on a proper sheet of paper, Mr. Dixon, who'd been away on a conference, came in and asked what we were doing, so Mr. P. told him and handed him my bits saying he was just going to write it out properly for me. Mr. Dixon looked at them"—she suddenly half laughed, half sobbed—"I got the feeling Mr. Dixon was a bit . . . disappointed because it had been dealt with by Mr. P. I just got that feeling, you know, but I don't really know. He just suddenly looked terribly sad and I remember feeling sad, too, and terribly worried that I'd done something wrong when he said I was to come to his room with him."

And what happened in his room?

"Nothing, really," she now sounded puzzled in retrospect. "No, nothing. He just said not to worry and to run along, and he kept the bits."

Does she now think that perhaps Mr. Dixon realized that this was a big step in her development but that it had been mishandled by Mr. P. and now he too didn't quite know what to do about it?

"He was a big man," she said. "He would have been big enough to admit that to himself if that was what he felt, but I don't know whether he did . . . Anyway," she continued, diminishing this singular step in her development, quite clearly in order to avoid any diminishing of Mr. Dixon by me, or by herself, "it was mostly lies, so it didn't matter, did it?"

("Of course, this could have been a considerable shock for Mr.

Dixon," said Ben G. when I told him this story, which he hadn't known about at the time. "We felt he always had doubts of her guilt.")

When do you think was the beginning of this conscious remembering? I asked Mary.

"When I was around fourteen. My mother was coming again, you know, and she told me there was 'that book' now about me—she meant your book—and that it was all lies, and lies about her, her, her, and that she was going into the bookshops and turning it around so people wouldn't see it . . ."

Did you ask her what it said?

"I don't remember, but I don't think I would have dared after she'd said, I don't know how many times, that it was all lies, that it was written by . . . I honestly think she said Marjorie Proops [the famous advice columnist of the *Daily Mirror*] and that I was never to see it, never to look for it . . ."

Shortly before the publication of *The Case of Mary Bell* in 1972 another scandal, quite unforeseen, exploded in the media about Mary. During an "open weekend" at Red Bank, to which parents and officials were invited, Betty Bell and her mother came to see Mary. They went to her room, and in the presence of the supervising teacher—someone sadly lacking in judgment—Betty Bell dressed Mary up in clothes and underclothes she had brought for the weekend and took photographs of her posing—it would be said in the press later—"suggestively" in front of her mirror.

When the book was serialized in a Newcastle Sunday paper, Betty Bell, no doubt in an effort to counteract the effects of it in her hometown, agreed to be interviewed about Mary by the BBC program *Midweek*. The program directors, at first quite sympathetic to her—she could appear very vulnerable and make people feel protective—were staggered, they told me afterwards, when she produced the photographs to prove, as she said, how ordinary and happy a child Mary was now. Not surprisingly, the photographs were shown when the program was screened and caused a storm in the press. I thought the pictures tasteless though not extreme, but allowing them to be taken raised justifiable questions about the conduct of the school. The incident eventually became the subject of questions in the House of Commons during which the minister for social affairs made an ill-advised statement defending the harmlessness of the occasion.

Although Mary realizes the stupidity of this now, she felt bound to defend it, since it called into question not only the good judgment of her beloved grandmother but that of Red Bank. She shrugged. "I dressed up as a gypsy," she said, echoing her mother's explanation on television. "It was just playacting."

It wasn't long after that, she said, that two new boys came to the unit within a short time of each other. "They were really nasty boys and that's when I began to have a sort of . . . inkling, you know, when they . . . each separately . . . called me nasty names. The one who was the worst, he was a really slimy character, was sitting opposite me at dinner soon after he came and he called me a murderer and I grabbed his hair and smashed his face into his dinner. And a bit later there was the second one who said the same and I hit him; they had to pry me off him and the more they tried, the more I held on. The place was in an uproar. Mr. P.—who I was always somehow scared of and whose approval I always longed to have; he could make me feel guilty even if I hadn't done anything at all, just by looking at me—got me by the ear and twisted it, it felt like all the way round, and marched me down the corridor and then Mr. Dixon talked to me. You see, the thing was, for years I hadn't had a clue what I was in for . . . I mean, I probably did, somewhere underneath, which is why I invented that twin, didn't I? And by this time, of course, I had . . ."—she suddenly smiled—"I suppose you would call it 'made another step' by writing that stuff for Mr. P., but even that was, I think, somehow on the surface. Consciously, or with my conscience, I didn't know. I don't know what I expected to happen. But nothing did. Mr. Dixon only said I had been a disturbed little girl, an angry little girl, and now I was growing up and that I was clever and what I could do one day if I let myself grow up and out of the anger and tried to make the rest of my life a good life. You can see, can't you, that Mr. Dixon really tried, but I got very, very unhappy."

At about that time in 1972 Mary told Mr. Dixon that she hated Red Bank and wanted to go somewhere else. "He sort of 'Madam Fusspotted' me," she said. "But I was serious. I felt contained, as if I had a bra on that was too tight. I stopped doing gym and I had periods and couldn't go swimming and, you know, all the boys knew, and oh God, I was getting fat. And then I got into provoking the boys, you know, and there was one time when I stuck something into my bed to look as if I was in it and managed to make my way out and into a boys' dormitory and fooled around with them and then one teacher, Mr. L. . . . saw . . . and I saw his face through the observation window and I ran back down. And then Mr. Dixon came over and I felt terrible and I said to him, oh God, I was a whore, a slut . . . and he just said it was perfectly natural, he was so calm, but I hated myself. I told myself, oh you slut, you prostitute . . ." (She was unable to explain to me how she had managed to get out of her locked bedroom and into the boys' equally locked dormitory.)

There were many manifestations of unhappiness around this time. She took a huge dose of Senakot (a laxative) and was quite sick; there was the "fooling around with boys" she told me about; and finally she found a way of wounding herself when she broke a window and inflicted a large number of cuts on her arm. "This is where Mr. Dixon must have got really alarmed," she said, "because he told me I'd have to see a doctor at Winwick Hospital and he and Mr. P. took me there. I don't think I knew it was a mental hospital till a man who was just standing there got a hold of my wrist and it was like an iron grip and I got into a total panic. Mr. P. got him off me: he wasn't afraid of anybody, Mr. P., but I was. I was terrified."

Mary didn't remember exactly what had happened, but when I asked if she had seen a psychiatrist that day, she said she'd seen a woman psychiatrist and that her mother had been there, too. And that the psychiatrist had asked Betty questions. "She asked her, 'Why do you think your daughter is feeling like this?' And she said, 'What are you trying to do, get inside my head?' She'd just been in North Gate," Mary told me.

"Cath had had her sectioned"—committed to the largest mental hospital in the region.

It seemed strange to me that Betty should have been brought in on this and above all that she would have been present when the psychiatrist talked to Mary. But Mary didn't know how this had come about.

"It's funny, though, isn't it?" she said. "I began to talk to this psychiatrist about the past, and she [Betty] said, 'You don't remember, you're too small.' And I said I remember a man who has three fingers and . . . whiteness. I remember blindman's buff . . ."

What was this about? I asked.

But she wouldn't, or couldn't, explain to me then what she remembered about the man with three fingers and blindman's buff.

"I don't remember the psychiatrist asking, or me saying, anything else. I don't suppose there was anything *to* say, I mean, with my mother sitting there, I mean, about cutting myself. I just . . . I just . . . hated myself, I suppose."

Did she think she had injured herself to get more attention?

"I had all the attention in the world, and I had Mr. Dixon's love," she said, "and yes, I did know that. So it wasn't that. Now, in retrospect, I think that it was because I was totally confused as a growing girl with all these boys, and I suppose I had feelings I didn't know what to do with. And then, of course, with it all, my growing inner awareness that I had done something terribly, terribly bad." This had been, she said, her lowest point. "From then on, I don't really know why, I grew up."

In 1973 James Dixon began to plan for Mary's future. "Sometime before," Mary said, "there had been a boy nicknamed Sooty who'd been a little bit in the same position as I was—he had killed a policeman—but had later done very well at Red Bank. And Mr. Dixon got permission for him to go on to the [approved school] training unit and from there to college. He got an education and also learned a trade and he lived with some other boys in their own flat within the grounds of the approved school. It was really good. They were supervised but they were helped. Mr. Dixon told me that something like this was what he was thinking of for me, if I was really good, and got good O levels." (She passed six O levels, the earliest of three levels of standardized examinations, in the summer of 1973—"I took them in the Town Hall," she said. "I was registered as 'Miss Smith.'")

"That's what I expected to happen. I'd move out of the secure unit into a hostel or a room in the staff quarters of the approved school, but still under Mr. Dixon's supervision and care, and I'd take A levels and go to college and get myself a profession. I was so excited, so happy. I had a future."

Her optimism lasted for about ten months. "Till Wednesday, November 7 [1973], to be exact," she said. "On Wednesday afternoons the staff had their case conferences, so the rule was that we'd have early dinner at eleven-thirty, and then we'd all go to the common room and watch a feature-length film with just one teacher with us. Case conference would go on till 3:00 P.M. As soon as it was over, the staff started coming in and I noticed one of the masters, Mr. Hume, a really tiny chap who used to be in the merchant navy: he was white, his face just white. There was a very strange atmosphere and Miss Hemmings was drying her eyes. I told myself it had to have been a really distressful conference, and nosy as always I whispered to her, 'What's happening? What's wrong?' And right away then Mr. Dixon came and said to me, 'May I have the pleasure of your company, madam?' and he took me out of the unit to his house, which was about fifty yards away.

"And there in the sitting room he said: 'I've never wrapped anything up for you apart from Christmas presents so—you are leaving tomorrow and you are going to prison. *Damn*,' he said, and Mrs. Dixon burst into tears.

"I said no first, sort of laughing, you know? I mean, it just couldn't be. 'No, no.' And then I started crying and I said, 'Why? What have I done?'

"And he really couldn't speak right away, he kept swallowing. And then he told me he had tried his best, had tried for two weeks to change their minds, had told them of his plans for me and what have you, but it just didn't work. He said he had waited to tell the staff until that afternoon because he was fighting for me and until then he'd still hoped he might succeed. 'I can't tell you how astonished I am about that decision and how heartbroken,' he said to me. And then he said: 'You'll get to pick the hymn for tomorrow morning.' That's what people did on their last day."

"We had heard rumors that Jim Dixon was talking with the Home Office about her and changes to be made because she was now sixteen, but nothing definite," Ben G. said to me when we talked. "And to be honest, we couldn't believe they would do such a thing, not when she was doing so well there."

From this point on, Mary's account of these last hours at Red Bank is full of mistaken memories. It is almost as if her trauma was such that she was no longer totally aware of who was there and what they did with her.

"That night," she said, "Mrs. R.—Veronica, as I called her later when we met again—was with me all the time, but everybody dropped in . . ." She listed a series of teachers' names. "We cooked a pot of ratatouille . . . Mr. Dixon kept coming in and he said I was to 'go forth as Red Bank's ambassador.' He said, 'We all know things aren't fair, and they were trying to convince me that you couldn't deal with the task that lay ahead. But I don't believe it.' And they were all giving me presents, they were . . . you know . . . not bricks and mortar, they were people, family, you know . . ."

"Her memory is playing tricks with her there," said Ben G. "Two of the teachers she mentions had long left by then. If she cooked her last meal it would have been with Barbara, the cookery teacher."

"You see, those last months at Red Bank," Carole said, "she had changed quite a lot—I mean in the sense of keeping herself much more apart from the boys. She obviously made a decision not to spend as much time with them as before. We had noticed for some time before that to what extent she was . . . well . . . suppressing her femininity. She had a nice figure but didn't want to show it."

"For a while I bound it tight, you know, like Chinese women do, so that I'd look flat like a boy, and I no longer did PT or athletics or went swimming," Mary told me. "I did quite a bit with the female staff then, cooking and all that . . ."

"She quite obviously didn't like her body," Carole said. "One could see it in the way she touched or didn't touch her body, or the way she walked moving her legs across the floor without lifting them up. It was really sad how this beautiful, beautiful girl was always walking with her head down. But, given the situation, her decision to—in a way—separate herself more from the boys was sensible, wasn't it?"

Did they think, I asked, that the Home Office's decision to transfer her to prison could possibly have been influenced by a feeling that at sixteen she shouldn't go on living in this male environment?

"I don't think 'feeling' had anything to do with it," Ben said. "They were just going along with the system, applying their rules."

I asked Mary if her mother and Billy knew she was being moved.

"I don't know about my mother. I don't think so, because Mr. Dixon would know she'd go to the press with it. That's what she always did, for money, though I didn't know the extent of it until later. But I think my father knew, because he'd been to see me the Saturday before and he had a tear in his eye when he left, and then, you know, I didn't see him again, because he never came to see me in prison.

"There was a young American [at Red Bank] at the time as a volunteer teaching assistant," she said. "He was a friend of Ben G.'s—they traveled through Europe together. But even so, he must have been in the same sort of work in the States, otherwise he wouldn't have been allowed in. I quite fell in love with him. He wasn't what you'd call handsome, you know, he wore little round glasses, he was sort of a cross between John Denver and John Hurt, a hippie . . . a flower-power-type person. He wrote to me for a long time afterwards and I to him, too. Well, he gave me a shirt and a message inside a shell . . ."

"In this whole story about her last day," Ben said, "she seems to be telescoping her memories. My friend Jeff was there in 1972 [a year earlier]. He gave her those presents that Christmas; he left in early '73."

"A lot of the boys came in before they turned in," Mary said, "and they all gave me presents, too. I cried a lot, every time anybody looked at me, because they were all saying incredibly nice things to me.

"I stayed up all night. They tried to get me to rest, but I couldn't. And much later Mr. Dixon and Miss Hemmings came and told me what I was to wear and I said please, no, because I had these really white jeans called 'skinners' I wanted to wear. But he said no way, I was to wear my navy-and-white dress and navy-and-white T-bar shoes. And I said they'll all laugh at me, they'll be there with fags hanging out of their mouths and bleached blond hair and roots showing through . . . And he said, 'What difference does it make to you? Would you rather be covered in tattoos to be accepted? No,' he said, 'you have your standards. You can relate to a dustman or to a duke.' "

So what happened?

She laughed. "I wore the dress . . ."

Carole G. was on duty the afternoon and evening of Mary's last day at Red Bank. Ben was off, "but he came over to say goodbye."

"Yes," Ben said to Carole, "and you were packing all that stuff, her things and her presents, and she said that she needed something to put it all in so I found a brown suitcase for her, with a key. And I told her we'd put it in the storeroom but she'd have the key."

"Miss Hemmings was distraught," Carole remembered. "She couldn't cope with any of it. In fact she was driving us absolutely spare because she kept walking up with the same things, and then seeing May and me she'd walk away with the clothes in her hand and then come back again, to and fro. This packing went on for a long time. And then at one point Jim Dixon came to me with tears in his eyes and he said, out of May's hearing, 'Let her think you are packing them for her to take, but she can't take anything.' She could only take a small bag. So after that I was left with the task of packing this child's life away, five years of her life. Later we went to the cookery room and made cocoa. I got her to go to bed and I put a mattress on the floor next to her and lay down there. But she didn't sleep and I didn't either; we talked. And at one point she talked about prison and she whispered, 'You've no idea what it's like,' and she cried. I think she thought of me as very innocent. Of course, I had a good idea what it would be like, and when we'd heard those rumors [about Mary being transferred] a couple of weeks before, Ben and I had wondered how, after the nurturing for freedom . . . yes . . . freedom she had received at Red Bank, we could prepare her for life in prison. We couldn't think how it could be done, even if there had been time. But anyway, we didn't believe it could come to that."

"In the morning Miss Hemmings made me have a bath," Mary said, "and she packed for me and I came down . . . I don't think I had breakfast. I chose the hymn." She half sang, half recited it for me: ". . . Wondrous cross on which the Prince of Glory died . . ." And then Mr. Dixon sat and gave a very nice talk, praising me, and the loss it meant to have me go. And he told from the beginning about me walking in the door and the things we'd been through together . . . I cracked up and everybody else did, too. And then I was taken to prison."

PART THREE

PRISON

November 1973 to May 1980

Setback

They had left Red Bank midmorning. Mr. and Mrs. Dixon took her, Mary said, and Mr. P. followed in his car. "I looked back as we drove out," she said, "and there were faces at every window, the boys, the staff, and everybody waving to me from behind the glass. My friends."

"It's funny that May remembers it like that—obviously because that's how she *needs* to remember it," Carole G. said, "because actually, and I know that sounds dramatic, but no one was allowed to go and wave her off."

Why would that have been decided? I asked. It seemed normal enough that her friends, with whom she had lived for so long, should wave her goodbye, at least through the closed windows.

"I'm not sure why Jim decided that. Perhaps precisely because for him it *was* such a huge thing to lose her, and yet kids routinely left Red Bank all the time. Perhaps he wanted to avoid her being given the sort of send-off that no one else would have. I don't know, but certainly his big thing was that no one should see her off and everyone should stay inside. That said, perhaps there were some boys who went to the windows anyway and waved and she, turning around in the car, saw it as 'everybody.'"

Mary thought it was about a two-hour trip from Lancashire to Styal prison in Cheshire (but as usual, her timing was way off: it is, in fact, much less). "I really don't remember much about the trip." What was uppermost in her mind, as always, was the fear that she would wet the bed. And when Mr. Dixon said we were getting there—to sort of pre-pare me, you know—I leaned forward and whispered to Mrs. Dixon about it and she says, 'Don't worry, we'll sort it out.'

"Somehow," Mary said, "I didn't sort of believe that we were actually driving to a prison. But suddenly we turned a corner and there was this monstrosity, HM Styal prison, the most godforsaken place on earth—it was like stepping back in time. It was huge, you know, just huge: it isn't one house but four rows of massive old Victorian-type red-brick build-ings. When the gate was opened I could see bars right away on windows and doors, and I saw prison officers, oh God, with keys . . ."

The staff at Red Bank carried keys too, didn't they?

"Oh yes, but not visibly, not sort of demonstrating it, you know. These prison officers carried them round on chains and they rattled with every step they took.

"The guard at the gate, a man, said something, I didn't know what, to Mr. Dixon, and he had to drive round till we got to a . . . oh . . . huge red building in black sort of tiles. I expect it looks different to visitors, but to me it was . . . so forbidding."

Were there gardens?

"Yes, there were, between the blocks, and I did notice that right away. Of course, it was November so it was bare, but in the spring there were flowers, vegetables, and later there were big plastic hothouses . . . I know, because I helped build them. It was a lot more open than Red Bank because it was so big: to go from A to B you had to go out-side the building, even if it was to go on governor's call-up or for a medical."

Mr. Dixon, she said, went to see the deputy governor. "Mr. P. went off to recce the place. In the end I couldn't see either of them to say goodbye. Later I heard they were furious about it and made a row. Mrs. Dixon came into reception with me. What struck me most was how high the ceiling was, the walls painted that horrible institutional green, and then that silence, you know, hollow, sort of echoing, almost.

"They told me to strip off, which I was going to find happened all the time in prison: if they suspect you of owning what you shouldn't own, of having drugs, illegal letters, or even for anything that smacked of disobedience, humiliation is the game. Mrs. Dixon said, 'Is there a real need for that?' and they said, 'This *is* a prison, you know,' and told her to leave while I was searched and weighed and she got quite upset. All I was thinking about was what if Mrs. Dixon didn't have the chance to warn them and I then wet the bed. I barely saw her again either. I think they [the Dixons] were made to feel very uncomfortable and were told to leave."

"They came back very soon," Carole G. remembered. "Styal isn't that far away. I know Jim came in and sat for a while and said, 'Well, that's it.' He was broken up about losing her. He just sat there, looking awful. He died a year and a half afterwards and to be honest we always thought that losing the battle for her affected his health."

There can be little doubt that this transfer was destructive for Mary. The success of her moral re-education at Red Bank was almost entirely due to the love she had felt for and received from Mr. Dixon. In ignoring both his proposed solution and the recommendations of Dr Westbury, whose opinion it had sought, the Home Office brutally interrupted the slow growing-up process that with the help of interested teachers she had just begun. The carefully constructed security and her developing intellectual ambition were replaced by immersion in an all-female penal community where Mary, now the youngest prisoner in a world of iso-lated women, would regress entirely. Not only would she be used emo-tionally as well as sexually as a fresh young girl, but also, and perhaps this was worst of all, she would be treated by her fellow prisoners as a child, not responsible for her crimes.

Although there are exceptions—the best-known experiments are tak-ing place in California and Scandanavia—prisons are rarely benign places. They don't have the time or the staff or the financial means to educate or encourage prisoners. And the prison system on the whole does not promote the consideration of prisoners as individuals. The attitude of individual prisons depends largely on the personality of the governors and wardens, and inmates are there at worst to be punished and at best to be contained as compliantly or (if necessary through medication) as passively as possible for the duration of their sentences. There are, as Mary was to demonstrate time and time again in her account, many kinds of prison officers: some with hardly any specialist training, others (whom she says the inmates may dislike but respect) who have served in the police or the army and have greater under-standing of the problems of communal life and the proper ways of enforcing discipline. But irrespective of where they come from and how they have been trained, it is, as she said repeatedly, the personalities of individual prison officers and how they choose to impose them on the prison community that determine the quality of the inmates' lives.

But there was a strange dichotomy in her reaction to her seven years of prison life. For although she remembered them, and even found a strange enjoyment in recalling them in vivid detail, she seemed to have retained them in her memory as a long string of emotionally linked experiments she provoked or had with other women rather than as a sequence of cumulative experiences that have contributed to the development of her personality and her life as it is now.

By the time we got to Styal we had talked for just over two months, and except for the actual killing of the two children—which she couldn't face until almost the end of our talks—she had managed to lend a totally unexpected degree of shape and form to the telling of each part of her life. She could never remember exact dates, or seasons, or even her own age, but she nearly always knew who was in her life at which point, and almost precisely which experiences followed which. It was as if her memory functioned in a long series of steps, over which it hardly faltered, each one representing a batch of days, weeks, months, even years that she described to me in images, like a collection of photo-graphs, more or less in sequence.

But this did not apply to her account of prison. Given that she had seemed exceptionally positive about talking about it and indeed, weeks before we got there, repeatedly expressed her longing to tell me about it, I was entirely unprepared for the psychological void I found in her about those years. Except for a few graphic descriptions of specific events, her years there were conveyed to me in a stream of consciousness mode without form or chronology. I have twenty tapes about this period, almost two hundred pages of transcript, and much of the time it sounds as if two voices are talking: one in half thoughts and unfinished sentences, jumping back and forth, often angrily, across months and years from impression to impression; the other much more lucid and thoughtful, suddenly describing a hitherto unmentioned occasion, the quotes and personality sketches of the people involved so witty and sharp, so present, that one almost forgets that the occasion has no connection with what went before it or will follow. They are certainly highly emotional memories, but only a few are of deliberate brutality to her, and many are gentle, even loving, with Mary's two best qualities, compassion and humor, running through them. But as the days went by and words upon words rained down without commas, paragraphs, or full stops, what I came to realize was that she reveled in not talking but *chatting* about Styal, as if chat were a verbal reflection of the essential aimlessness of prison life.

(What was easiest for you to talk about? I asked her a few months after our talks ended. And she laughed briefly. "Oh, you know it, prison," she said in that low voice of hers, and repeated it with a note almost of tenderness, "Oh yes, prison.")

"Mrs. Bailey was the reception officer when I arrived," she said. "Later she was my house officer and I called her Ma Bailey—she was an ex-service lady, a northern woman, you know, and the most humane of the lot. I really got to like her. Even that first day she was all right, you know, and I finally told her about the bed-wetting and she said it didn't matter: 'There's a lot of people like that here.' And she looked at me and said, 'I think you'd better have some dinner, lass, you look like you could do with some feeding up . . .' And then—it blew me over—suddenly there was somebody behind me speaking Geordie.

" 'God, I'd recognize you anywhere,' the voice said. 'You're Billy Bell's lass, aren't you? I know yer da well, we drink in the same pub. I'm Betty. Remember me?'

"And I *did* remember her. They used to call her Betty Blue and she was a sort of singer.

" 'I'm doing five years but me time's nearly up now,' she said. 'You're a lifer so you'll be on five block where I am. Don't worry, pet, you'll be all right here, just keep yer nose clean.'

"And Mrs. Bailey said, 'Right, that's enough gabbing, Betty. Off you go,' and she breezed out. But that was such a comfort to me. I had expected everybody to be . . . Oh, I don't know, rough women like I'd seen some of in my life, but here she was, and she was Betty the singer from Newcastle, and she knew my dad.

"Mrs. Bailey told me to get changed. You're allowed to have three sets of clothes, three of everything, underwear and all. I put my jeans on."

Did she put on the white skinny ones she'd wanted to wear before?

"No, I knew they wouldn't suit. I put on my big baggy ones with all the patches, falling to bits. And a top with a peacock on it. When Mrs. Dixon, who had waited outside, saw me, she was horrified. 'What will people think?' she said.

"One of the assistant governors came, a Mrs. Naylor. And I was told to stand in her presence. I found we had to stand for all officers except our house officers. We were up and down 'like a pair of whore's knickers,' I heard one old dear say later. Mrs. Naylor said I would be going to Mellanby House, one of the eleven blocks in the prison, each named for a female prison reformer. Mrs. Bailey had filled out a property list which I had to sign with my name and number—774987. Mrs. Naylor told me to repeat it several times so I wouldn't forget it: whenever an officer addressed you, you had to stand straight and say your name and number."

Then a girl had come with a tray of lunch, she said. "One plate for me, a different lot of food—staff food—for Mrs. Bailey. I didn't want mine and Mrs. Bailey asked whether I wanted hers but I said, 'No, thank you,' and she was absolutely astonished because I said things like please and thank you. I don't know what they were expecting . . .'"

New prisoners were usually taken to see the governor, Molly Morgan. "But not me, no, she didn't deign to meet me, not until days later. She was going to show me right away what was what and that my life was going to be *as* she ordained it, *when* she ordained it."

The Mellanby house officer came to get her and her "bundle": two sheets, two blankets, and a pillowcase. "You know, with one sheet wrapped around the whole thing so that it became a bundle. We walked, it felt like miles, past all these long big blocks with hundreds of barred windows and all of them linked by huge black pipes, heating pipes they were. I later worked on those, too, when I was on 'engineers' party,' cleaning up the sewers.

"And without telling me what it was, she told me I was going to the 'Education Block.' There were quite a few women about, walking from one place to another, and they all turned around and shouted hiya. Later I heard that Betty had run and told everyone that I'd come, and I could hear them shout to each other: 'Isn't she tiny?' I think they meant 'young' with 'tiny' because I heard two of them saying, 'She looks about twelve.' I was really insulted, you know."

Does everybody usually know about new arrivals? I asked.

"Oh yes, they all do, but you normally arrive in shipments and are taken to houses in groups, while I . . . well . . . was brought on my own."

Do you think that made you stand out right away?

"Well, I did anyway, you know. First of all because I was so young— certainly the youngest there. And then . . . well, prisons are floating populations, with many people coming for short periods, months rather than years—I was to find that women get sent to prison for truly ridiculous reasons which men would get a financial slap on the wrist for, that's all. Though of course there are many there for longer. Anybody who gets more than three years is considered an LTI [long-term inmate] and if they have over five years they are usually lifers. There were about five hundred women prisoners there and many of them would have read about me five years before, and . . ."—she smiled, kindly—"what with your book, not to speak of my mother's outpourings in the Newcastle press and on TV, many since."

Given how prisoners are known to feel about co-prisoners who have killed or abused children, was she made to feel that right away?

"No. Later there were some women who had children and who had done atrocious things and some . . . you know . . . wanted to turn things round onto me. But the general consensus of opinion, really throughout my time in prison, was that as I was only ten and eleven, I wasn't a child murderer. There were of course child murderers there and there was talk about them, and I'd be sitting there and somebody who'd been talking would notice I was there and turn around and say, 'Oh, I don't mean you. Why would I think you? You were nothing but a kid yourself.' And that's when I started in a way to realize what was meant when papers write 'child murderer,' and when I saw that I'd say to myself, 'Oh God, no. I wasn't like that.' So you see, people in prison made a distinction which, as I would find out much later when there were headlines again describing me as 'the child murderer,' the media didn't—couldn't make."

What sprang to my mind when she said that was her immediate, instinctive reaction when Mr. Dixon had told her that she was going to prison: "But why? What have I done?" Her perception of herself—unaided by anyone since the terrible events in 1968—simply excluded the reality of her crimes. In these talks, however, it was essential not to contribute to the false security she had been given.

Of course, I said to her, in a literal sense, having killed two children you *were*, in fact, a "child murderer." Nonetheless, you accepted that distinction of being different from "other child murderers" because of your age, did you? You felt that was justified?

"It was a long, long time—years, before I could think about it in terms that would allow me to answer such a question," she said. "At Red Bank I'd just about reached a point when I think I could have begun to face it: I think Mr. Dixon would have helped me."

Helped you in what way?

"It's just what I think, knowing him," she said. "He must have known I needed help. He was biding his time, getting me ready to think, so to speak . . . at least, that's how I see it . . ."

In the course of what by then was already months of talking, during which her feelings of guilt and unhappiness about the two little boys, Martin and Brian, had come up time and again, she had certainly begun to understand and accept that by the time our talks ended and before I could begin to write this book she would have to face the fact of having killed them. Her words here are understandably romanticized. Saying that she now "sees" how Mr. Dixon intended to give her the "help [she] needed" is in a way her gift to this teacher she came to love. She probably knows quite well that Mr. Dixon would never have brought her into this confrontation—he avoided it, as we know, the one time when, writing the notes for Mr. P., she had actually sought it. And the reason, we also now know, appears to be that he did not believe—or could not bring himself to believe—that she had killed the little boys. Knowing now that this is the help she should have had during those five years in Red Bank, she invests James Dixon with the intention of giving it to her — that is her gift. "But then, you see," she went on, "I was taken away from him before I was ready. So it never happened. So what it was . . . still mostly is in my mind . . . is unconnected flashes of horror."

When she was finally taken to Mellanby House—she remembered a yellow back door being unlocked and her being led in—"there was that smell of polish again," she said. "They're all potty about polish . . . there were those big tins, 'Cardinal Red,' it was called, which you lug around and smear on everything." The other, by now predictable smell that pervaded the place was stale cabbage.

"The outer doors of all the houses are locked," she said, "but inside, it's open; they do try, you know. Miss Parker, the house officer, took me to her office, sat me down, and told me the rules. There was a letter sheet for every prisoner, she said—a list of people she intended to write to. "I could write one letter that first day—they called it a 'reception letter'— to tell one person on my letter sheet that I was there. After that, she said, I could write one letter a week and I would only be allowed to receive letters from people I had written to. Any others, whether they were on my letter sheet or not, would be classed as 'nonentitled.' Because I was a 'star' prisoner [she was referring to the asterisk prisons put against the names of first offenders] and also a YP [young prisoner], I'd be allowed two visits a month. Until I was allocated a work detail, probably after one week there, I'd be on housework in Mellanby."

She laughed. "In the end they took me off it quicker because I kept ringing the fire bell—first just by mistake, but then, when that brought all the screws running, I thought it was a great joke and did it a few more times till the girls told me to stop or I'd be put 'on report.' That was the first time I heard that expression and I couldn't have imagined in my worst dreams what it meant till it happened to me later. But that afternoon, Miss Parker took me across the corridor from her office to a dormitory with four beds, told me to make up my bed and put my affairs in the locker, and went. So far I hadn't seen any of the women and I was scared, really scared. I imagined them in uniforms and green aprons and big fat bellies and boobs down to their knees and covered in tattoos and hairy legs. Well. I had a surprise coming. But then, they told me later, they had too: God knows what they thought I'd be like.

"It was four-forty-five or so when they came in from work, in twos and threes. And that's when I found out how and why Mellanby had been designated the 'Education Block.' I realized very quickly it was a real joke. Because I was coming, and at sixteen by law should still have been in full-time education, they'd apparently scurried around the day before and moved anyone who could string a sentence together into this block. What they ended up with were a few who had been there in the first place, nothing to do with being 'educated' or 'educable,' and then about a dozen other girls, mostly in for smoking dope or, I don't know, doing something foolish with a car or something, were moved in. They were all from areas where children are privately educated: St. John's

Wood or Knightsbridge in London, or that something-belt on the Thames where people own those large houses. There were a couple of Lady So-and-sos and other girls with posh voices, some really, really beautiful."

Is that what you mostly remember?

"From that first afternoon, yes, because I had been so frightened and found that there were after all human beings there."

The "posh" girls?

"Well," she said, her voice a little defensive, "I liked it when people spoke properly. I like it still. That's what I learned in Red Bank, you know. It had been ... well ... become my life. It was just ... oh, a relief that afternoon to find they weren't all ... rough. I'm not trying to mislead you. That was just a few of them ... It just helped me, those first hours."

Mary is particularly conscious of, and embarrassed about, her partiality for middle-class language and standards. She is conscious because she was subjected at highly sensitive ages—eleven and sixteen—to a series of extreme social upheavals that, occurring by force and not by choice, increased her recognition of class and social divisions. She is embarrassed because she is both intellectually and emotionally aware of these divisions and therefore not only does not wish to be considered presumptuous by those who naturally belong to this social category but also realizes that her preference for middle-class mores alienates her further from her blood relatives—above all her siblings, to whom, against all odds, she would like to be close.

The next-youngest inmate in Mellanby was twenty-two, she said, and the average age was thirty-plus. "Geriatric for me, though I have to say most of them didn't look it. All the women were referred to, and referred to each other, as 'the girls': 'the girls' in the workroom, 'the girls' on the garden[ing] party, and so on. Women in their sixties and seventies were the 'old girls.' But yes, I'd say the average age was thirtyish: to them I was just a child and I think most of them felt sorry for me. I was offered 'rollies' [homemade cigarettes] and advice and told to keep my nose clean.

"Tea [supper] was served in the kitchen on wooden tables which I was to find had to be scrubbed every day till they were white. People are put on cooking shifts and each block does their own cooking though there was an overseer; at my time it was Mrs. Carr. She was a cordon bleu cook and God only knows why she chose to waste her talent teaching cookery classes in a prison. It was certainly wasted on me when I landed there—for a very short time. It was soon evident to everybody that I was an anti-talent in the kitchen: the porridge I made could have been used to plaster walls; even the boiled eggs sprouted white lumps like fungi. I produced nothing but disasters.

"At nine o'clock we were searched and prepared for bed; lights went out at a quarter to ten. For the first night or two I was in the downstairs dormitory, where there was an officer sitting just outside the room all night because, you see, the doors weren't locked. There were bars, but the inner doors weren't locked. You could get up and go to the loo without asking permission, you know. I didn't wet the bed the first night because I didn't sleep. I had candy-striped pajamas and I lay on my bed staring through the barred windows and up at the sky, thinking of everyone at Red Bank. I had a horrible gutted feeling in my stomach. I thought it couldn't be real, this couldn't be happening. I remember I was crying, with tears rolling down my face, and I couldn't stop and my pillow got all wet and someone whispered, 'You'll be all right.' And then I decided that I wouldn't let it happen. I would tell the governor the next day when I saw her that I couldn't . . . I just couldn't live with all these women and that I wanted to go back to Red Bank.

"I'd heard a lot about the governor already," she said. "Women talk all the time, you know, and there are just three subjects of conversation: the nick [prison] and stuff about other women; the nick and gossip about staff; and a long time after that, and only when you have friends who trust you, home and their private lives.

"About the governor, I'd heard she was a monster, that above all she didn't like 'pretty little things,' that the prisoner was always guilty. I was told she always met new prisoners, but she hadn't met me and it made me very nervous because I didn't know why. It made me very nervous about meeting her."

She wasn't to meet the governor for another three days, but on the Saturday two days after she arrived her mother had come to visit her.

Were you glad she'd come? I asked.

"I can't remember what I felt. In all those years I never felt . . . just one thing about her coming to see me. And I'd seen her a month before in Red Bank. I . . . I always worried how she . . . how she was and how she would be, you know? I was told to go . . . they had a sort of classroom or something in another block and that's where she was waiting for me. And it was embarrassing, you know, really, really embarrassing. 'My baby!' she screamed. 'My baby,' and sobbing, she pulled at me, trying . . . God . . . to get me to sit on her knees. She wasn't really crying, you know, she just sobbed for Mrs. Sissons who supervised the visit, just as she had regularly sobbed for the staff at Red Bank. And Mrs. Sissons got extremely upset at seeing this young mum so upset and she told her that it was all wrong and that I shouldn't be there and then she even said that to me. She meant well, but she didn't know my mother, who then went, of course, and repeated that to everybody in Newcastle. God only knows what other 'grim' tales she told about me in prison. She only stayed for half an hour. That's all she stayed, you know, and I said nothing and she saw nothing and nobody. She no doubt felt she was an authority on Styal after that, or perhaps on all of HM's prisons or whatever. But at least, as far as I knew, that first time she didn't give interviews or go on TV about it. The next time she came she did and that was awful for me, just awful."

Didn't your mother ask you how you were? How you felt?

"No, she didn't. She never did. She just complained about her own life and, worrying me to death, about her health, always her health, but on that day I was just as glad she didn't ask anything because I was very unhappy, just incredibly sad, and I didn't . . . I just didn't want to talk to her.

"Even that first day after I arrived, I began to have this feeling of . . . I don't know how to put it . . . hopelessness? No, it's not the right word. It wasn't that or just that. You see, there were people I knew there . . . of course Betty Blue, who was going around the place saying she'd known me since she was a kid and anyone says anything about me, she'd punch their brains out, you know. And she was telling the screws about my dad and everything. But then, too, there were sisters of some of the boys, you know, at Red Bank . . . it all seemed so . . . so . . . *pat*."

Pat?

"Yes, you know, there were the sisters, and over at Red Bank there were the brothers, and I remembered my dad in that horrible prison, and here was I, and it just seemed that this was where everybody had to end up . . ."

You mean it felt inevitable?

"Yes, yes, as if nothing could have prevented my being there or their being there. And if nothing could have prevented it, what was the use of anything? And I knew nothing about my brother or the girls, nobody told me nothing, God, how were they?

"Those first days in Styal," she said, "I heard more horrors than I thought ever existed. They pointed out an old lady to me and they said it was Mary Scorse, who'd been sentenced to hang for murder when she was twenty-six in the 1940s and was already in the death cell when she was found to have TB, and they came to tell her that the medical officer had found her unfit to swing. By the time I saw her, with her glasses slipping down her nose and gloves on for gardening, she'd done twenty-odd years and somebody says, 'Oh, she is on the murderers' block and you'll be ending up with them,' and then they went on, this one had done this, and that one that, and I got really frightened. Later, of course, I understood that the stories were horrendously out of proportion: anybody who was new got them served up. In fact, all the girls who became my friends were first-time offenders, almost all of them with horrible domestic troubles, with long records of broken jaws and having unborn babies kicked out of them. How some of them ended up in prison I'll never know. They'd taken it all, time and again, but when abusing them was no longer enough for their husbands or whatever and they started on the child or the kids and she hauled out and killed the bastard, she gets life imprisonment. Women's prisons are full—full, I tell you—with women like that and among them many who, rather than have their children grow up with a mother in prison for life for killing their father, they allow the kids they love ... the only thing they love ... to be adopted and give up seeing them and after that there is nothing in their lives."

It was on Sunday afternoon that Mary heard her name and number called out and the order "Governor." "Usually when you are called on report," she said, "you go to her office or you appear before her in the adjudication room, as they call it, at Bleak [the punishment block], and all that was going to happen to me countless times. But on that day she just had me brought to her while she was on her rounds. I had this image of her, you know, of a ghastly ... like a hippo in a dress. Well, to be honest she wasn't like I thought. I mean, well, she was very young, her face was young. The first thing she said to me was: 'What's your number?' Of course I'd been so nervous I had forgotten that rule. 'All right, 774987,' she said, 'you call me Ma'am or Madam.' And then she said, 'I suppose you were expecting a red carpet, the way Mr. Dixon came on in here?' I said, 'How long will I be here? They told me only the governor will know.' And she laughed and said, 'I don't know, come back in four years and ask me the same question.' I said, 'But in four years I'll be twenty,' and she said, 'Yes, positively decrepit.'

"And then she said: 'Get it into your head that your Mr. Dixon doesn't have control any longer over what happens to you. You are in a different place now ... And don't bother to sweep the floor with your eyelashes,' she said, 'it won't work with me.' And that was that. If there was anything I could be sure about, it was that—God knows for what reason—Molly Morgan disliked me intensely and, very unusual for me, and really for no reason at all, I found myself strongly returning that dislike. It was instantaneous and I knew from that moment on that there would be—there was already—a private war between us. In the years that followed she tried her utmost to break me and of course, on the face of it, I was always on the losing side. How could I not be? But I wasn't, really. I think at times this battle between us was the only thing that kept me going. I wasn't going to let her thwarted sense of justice beat me into the ground, so in a way she served a purpose."

Her "battle" with the governor became one of the two focuses of her life, certainly for the first two years, during which rebellion became her only purpose, and resistance to rules her only weapon. The other means by which she could assert her individuality, rather than to allow it to "sink," as she puts it, into the prison quagmire of compliance, was her sexuality. After spending her early adolescence in a male environment, where to all intents and purposes she adapted herself to being as much of a boy as possible, she only discovered how to exert her female sexuality in prison.

Had she hated Styal in those first weeks?

"No," she said, "I didn't hate it. It was just really strange, you know, being with all women. It was just so strange. There was a lot more *noise*. I noticed that women argued rather than being physical when they were angry. You see, boys don't argue, they punch each other. There were tough young characters at Red Bank, and yes, there were outbreaks of violence, but when things were building up, they had to get in the gym with boxing gloves and box the lives out of each other with Queensberry rules. That doesn't mean there weren't times when people threw chairs or whatever, but at the end of the day it was how you yourself felt, and because Mr. Dixon was what he was and the staff were what they were, you felt pretty shitty because it was letting yourself down more than them. And always, always, however you behaved, whatever you did, you were talked *to* and *with*, and never *at*. You knew you were part of something, something you *wanted* to be in step with: grown-up people who cared about you.

"But at Styal, well, the POs [prison officers] certainly were not there to care for you: they were there to contain you. And if you wanted to have a life, you either submitted to the system or you fought it. I learnt very quickly that the more one was in opposition, the better one felt. At least that's how it became for me—and already was for many of the younger women who became my friends. But women's prisons, I'm sure men's too, are full of anger; prisoners are angry people. And in women's prisons, anger, fury, dislike was expressed in words, in shouts, in vulgarity, if you like. The rarest thing—I saw that very quickly—was quiet. And one thing one never did was physically attack another woman. And I had to learn this the hard way.

"Just a few days after I got there, I had an argument with another girl about something absolutely ridiculous, I can't remember what, and she swore at me—which in Red Bank was absolutely taboo—and so I punched her and to my total amazement she burst into tears. I mean I hadn't *hurt* her and I didn't *mean* anything by it. I was just emphasizing that I wasn't to be sworn at.

"She was about twenty, I think, a doctor's daughter. She went flying back on the chair and starts crying and I just sort of laughed, God, and the other ladies looked at me, tut tut tut tut. And I just could not believe it. I could not get my head around it that there was all this disapproval. For me, this was just incredible, I mean, not something I knew how to deal with. What I had been used to was that if you hit out in anger or fury or whatever, well then, that's that. I mean that would be the end of it. I mean it's like a physical reaction instead of finding words to say, 'Don't swear at me, don't call me names.' But if it can't be physical . . . at least that's what I felt . . . then anger remains there however much shouting there is. It's, like, in the air, the atmosphere, and it goes on forever. This was an awful discovery to make."

But was there no other discovery? I asked. You were so young and pretty. Did none of the women want to touch you? Was there no offer of tenderness?

"Yes, there was one girl whose father was something high in the police in London. She was very much part of the seventies crowd, very glam, sort of Carnaby Street girl, really beautiful, about five foot seven inches, with long blond hair, and she'd go on, 'Everything's OK, babe. You'll be all right, babe,' and always stroking my hair, 'Oh you, you're only a baby.' I used to get really embarrassed and say, 'I'm *not* a baby,' which of course made me sound like a baby, right? And she had a friend in another block who really ought to have been a man . . . who looked very much like a young man . . . and I was told that that was a relationship. And of course I saw very soon that there were many such relationships and how important a part they are of life in prison—the only form, you know, of nonaggressive contact. This is especially for women who were used to—not just to a regular sex life but to . . . oh, just *being*—living and sleeping with a partner. Of course such women—and let's face it, that's most women—are going to need and to seek a continuity of life. I understood quite soon that it wasn't just sex. In the case of the older ladies—you know there are some there *really* old—there was a Greek lady there of eighty doing a ten-year sentence—they just needed a cuddle. I mean, feelings, longings, needs don't *die* because you are in prison. In fact, to be honest, they are intensified. I mean there really isn't anything to think about there except . . . well . . . feelings."

You mean sex? I said.

"Yeah, but more . . . more."

You knew all about homosexuality from Red Bank, didn't you?

"Well, yes. But they didn't there, you know, they couldn't. It was just . . . Oh, some of the lads would say about somebody, 'Oh, he's a poof,' or they'd say one to the other"—she put on a campy voice—" '*Ooh*, I *like* the color of that jacket . . . I mean, they'd *talk* it, but the way the system was run there they couldn't *do* it. I mean no two boys were ever even allowed to be alone together; only one boy could go to the toilet at a time, and always with a member of staff nearby. When it was time for showers, they all went and the staff were there all the time." She laughed. "Of course, they masturbated." She laughed again. "All the time, and joked about it; you know, significant remarks, winks, silly words like 'wank-wank.' But with Mr. Dixon there, with his navy experience, nobody weaker could be put in the position of having anything forced upon them as happened in other places. He looked out for them. People were very safe at Red Bank."

Did that mean she felt women in prison were not safe?

"I don't even mean that," she said. "I don't think anybody forced anybody into anything sexual at Styal. It just went on all the time . . . How could it not go on all the time when there were all these . . . well, yes, women, but I really mean adult and sexual human beings together?"

Whether they actively engaged in lesbian sex was very much a matter of age, she said, and the prisoners' hierarchy. "You see, you have the lifers, and in many ways they are at the top of the hierarchy, in the sense of running the workshops. It makes them very important because it means they control what people earn—in the workshops you are not paid by time but by piece. If you get across these old lifers, they can just make you redo a piece indefinitely. It can get very bad. When I came to Styal, most of them lived together in the lifers' block, and they lived like it was . . . well, their home forever, you know. They had privileges, like their own rooms, their own bedspreads, and upholstered furniture. That *is* their life and they really identified more with the prison officers than other prisoners . . ."

Did many prisoners have affairs with prison officers? I asked.

"There was some, but not many at all, basically because women can't keep their mouths shut and that would be fatal for POs. It would end their careers."

Later she heard that while she was in Styal there had been a big write-up in the press about lesbian protection rackets and rapes there. "It's rubbish, utter rubbish," she said. People did what they wanted or needed to do and of course that couldn't be prevented. "And why should it be?" she asked. "I myself can't think that any affection is bad. And in prison? For God's sake, prison staff may not be well trained, lots of things are wrong, but on the whole they are not monsters. Above all, people don't become governors of prisons because they are stupid and anybody with a spark of intelligence knows that the relief of relationships, including sex, is essential for prisoners. Where it becomes dangerous," she said, "and this is outside my personal experience though I've heard a lot about it happening in male prisons and youth offenders' institutions, is when affection plays no part or almost no part, and younger or weaker boys and men are forced into sex that then becomes nothing but a commodity and brutality." Oddly though, she says, this isn't a problem in women's prisons, though of course emotional pressures and drugs are.

"Don't be funny," she said when I ask how much of a drug problem there was in Styal. "*Everybody* smokes dope; prisons are full of it. Hard drugs? Well, it depends what you mean by it. Certainly, a lot of drugs—painkillers, tranquilizers, sleeping pills—are prescribed . . ."

On demand? I asked, and she shrugged.

"What is demand? I don't know that there is a great difference here between demand and apparent need. People are very, very unhappy in prison, and for prison administrators, full-flared unhappiness, whether individual or in a group, is not just hard but nearly impossible to deal with. Yes, they want to keep prisoners healthy; but they also *need* to keep them controlled. So in the end, the handing out of pills becomes not only a question of medical judgment but, let's face it, very often in prison one of necessity, right?"

If, however, I was asking her about drugs such as cocaine, morphine, heroine, or the like, she said they were no doubt available but, except for one time when she had tried heroin and got very sick from it, hard drugs hadn't been part of her prison experience.

She said that in the case of most lifers, sexual activity depended on their age. "I was to learn quite soon that the younger ones among them refused to have any relationship with anybody sentenced to less than five years. It was, as I would find out for myself, too difficult, too painful. But quite a few lifers are older, you know, quite old really. They'd committed one crime in their whole bloody life and were sent down when they were fifty or more when they had grandchildren and everything. To them the idea of sex with a woman is really dreadful, I mean morally awful and physically repugnant."

But certainly, she said, relationships, whether sexual or not, ruled prison life, and she had realized this very quickly, realized, too, the marked distinction in sexual identity. "Between prisoners there was never any name calling, though angry POs might call someone a 'bloody dyke,'" she said. "But it was simply a fact of life that you were either a 'butch' or a 'femme' and that—much more than in ordinary gay life—the 'butch' was always the dominant part of such a relationship."

Was this a frequent subject of conversation? I asked. I mean, did you get the feeling that this was what was uppermost in most women's minds?

"Oh God, yes, yes. Oh yes." It was so pronounced, so conspicuous, she said, that she very quickly became extremely curious about it. "Very soon after I got there, I became aware of this woman on my block, you know, who also really did look like a boy but she'd done something wrong, I never found out what because it had happened just before I came and nobody would tell me. And for punishment she was being made [by the staff] to wear a dress, which to her was total humiliation. So one night, I can't remember when, but I think before the end of my second week, I slipped into bed with her and I asked her: 'What do you do?' And she was quite embarrassed and said, 'I can't . . . no, really . . . I can't say.'

"So I asked her what kind of girls she fancied and did she fancy me. I said that I was sixteen and old enough, didn't she think? Yeah, well, she obliged, you know, but when I wanted to touch her she stopped me. And I said, 'Why?' And she said, 'Because I don't.'

" 'Don't what?' I asked and she said she just didn't like to be touched and later I not only realized that that was the case for most of the 'butch' women but I came to feel this myself very strongly when I went butch."

Was that, I asked her, because they couldn't take tenderness or because they wanted to be and remain the initiator and dominant partner?

"Well, they are all that, you see," she said. "But much more than that, they protect the hiding of their own femininity—at least that's what I found when I asked questions and then felt when I did it myself."

Mary had become both emotionally stirred and sexually active within two weeks of arriving at Styal. There can be no doubt whatever, and no particular surprise, that sexual feelings had been stored up in her during her last year at Red Bank. But one thing that is important to remember is that whatever happened to her in her childhood, and then in early adolescence, she was physically intact when, four days after her arrival in Styal, she was crudely and painfully examined by an inept doctor.

She described her first encounter with the prison medical staff with some of her usual humor, but quite graphically. "I told the medical officer that I was enuretic—which he already knew—but also that I was suffering, as I did every month, from severe period pains. I said that when that happened at Red Bank I was allowed to lie down with a hot-water bottle. Well, he said I wouldn't get any of those creature comforts, but I could have a pill. 'There is a contraceptive pill,' he said, 'which alleviates and regulates.' And he warned me that I might not be regular in the near future because periods sometimes change or cease altogether after traumatic experiences: he meant my move to prison, I suppose. But I said, 'I won't take pills,' and he went off on how much the damned things cost and that they have to be imported from Germany, but I said I wasn't interested. I just wasn't into taking any chemical pills. And then he said I had to see another doctor and have an internal examination. I said, 'For God's sake, I've got my period. And I've come here from a totally secure place. I'm hardly likely to have VD or whatever.' But he said, 'It's procedure,' and he told me to strip and I said no and he said not to be silly, they could make me, so I did and put a dressing gown on and then ran out into the corridor, but they caught me and the MO [medical officer] came back in and told me I was the sorriest person in the world, God only knew what was in my head, and I said, 'I'm a virgin, a virgin,' and then he pushed me through the door into another room where this man . . . yes, in a white coat . . . was sitting with a cup of tea dipping his biscuit disgustingly into the tea while a nurse pushed me down on a bed or something and put my legs up in stirrups. I was never so embarrassed in my life, him with his tea, me with my legs up and everything showing; it was outrageous. And then he ambled over and before I could say anything he pushed this thing into me and it was spring-loaded, you know, and it shut or opened or whatever, but it hurt like mad, and I was screaming that it hurt and the sister [nurse] who was nice, was saying, 'Now, now, now,' and he was telling me to stop being so tense and I'm saying again, 'It's hurting,' and he said he just had to take a swab and my God he pushed it in even further and then snap, I felt this sharp pain and heard this dull thud and he'd been sitting on one of those chairs with wheels on and he went back saying, '*Ahhh* help, Sister?' And it was she who undid it and pulled it out you know, quite slowly and carefully . . ."

They could at least have waited till your period was over, I said. Didn't you suggest that?

"I didn't know what they were going to do. After all, I'd never had that. Anyway, I was already telling the MO I had my period and I was a virgin and begging them to do nothing to me. I wouldn't have known what else to say. Well, anyway, that was that, wasn't it? And I walked around afterwards in a daze—as if I'd just come back from the Korean War and didn't realize that Big Ben was a clock."

But you knew what had happened?

"Well, yes, I suppose so, that horrible thing had snapped shut on me, but you know I just hurt and that's all I could think of and I just went back to Mellanby and was embarrassed because I was crying. And then, really only a few days later, I fell in love."

Rebellion

Many of the experiences Mary would relate to me, mostly in anecdotal terms, about her first weeks and months at Styal, demonstrate the extent to which she had been emotionally and sexually unbalanced by her five years in a peer group made up almost exclusively of adolescent boys.

All her reactions to the ultrafemale environment she suddenly found herself in will be familiar to any ex-boarding-school girl. The crushes, the blushes, the unspoken pursuits of older females, the trembling hands in the proximity of the adored were those of a twelve- or thirteen-year-old just coming into puberty and not the sexual feelings of a sixteen-year-old growing into womanhood. The girl Mary had "fallen in love" with so soon after her arrival was on a different block, a "butch" girl, inevitably years older than she was: "I just loved her to bits and I couldn't, you know . . . I mean she wouldn't have . . . and I told myself if not her then nobody, and it became sort of love from afar."

Did it ever turn into something more than that?

"No, no." She still sounded regretful. "She treated me like a little sister. And I never . . . you know, oh God, told her, 'I love you' . . . I would have died. So I just arranged to be next to her whenever I could and I sort of, but never really, touched her, just sometimes brushed against her, you know, as if by accident. But once, just once, I saw she did like me or something, because one of the male prisoners who used to come and do chores, electric stuff or whatever, he tried to give me a letter and she intercepted it and went berserk. She was a very quiet, deep sort of person but she went totally spare and wouldn't let me have the letter . . ."

But did she tell you why not?

"Yes, she said because it was full of filth, filthy words, filthy stuff, bloody men."

I had always realized that the trauma of Mary's transfer from the male environment of Red Bank to the aggressively female one of Styal had to be deeply engraved into her psyche. But it would be some time before I began to suspect that there might be a different and much wider meaning to the expressions Mary had used when talking, quite easily, about "butch" sexuality. The refusal to be touched and the wish to protect and to hide could equally be interpreted as Mary's own determination to protect herself by not allowing herself to be affected in a lasting way by any sexual—or other—experiences in prison, to "hide" from her emotional memory those basically mindless and therefore destructive seven years of her life.

Clearly, though, from what she began to tell me about her management of her sexuality and other prisoners' management of their own, it was a part of prison life of overriding importance to her. Many of her memories of Styal—and it was these she treasured—were anything but deep, and though she was never vulgar, many of her anecdotes contained a note of broad, at times quite bawdy humor, more often than not directed against herself. "By the time I was romantically reveling in my infatuation with Carol—that was her name—and imagining myself a celibate forever more, I was actually quite eager to have a go, and after that first rather stilted attempt with the reluctant butch, I jumped into bed with another lass where again little happened. What I remember most was her saying, 'You're too young, go away,' which was really more shaming than frustrating. Of course, what I didn't know but found out soon after was that the word was out that if anyone touched me they'd be sorted out."

But who put the word out? I asked.

"I was never sure, but I think it was Betty Blue and her friends." She laughed. "You know, a sort of protective Newcastle-Scotswood mafia: Betty because of my dad, so . . . even though he never knew it, my dad was protecting me as I had felt years and years ago when I was, oh, about eight, that he was protecting—or would protect me if I asked. But anyway, by that time . . . about two weeks into my time there . . . I felt I knew it all, you know, and when my mother came next I told her . . . you know, showing off . . . that I had had a lesbian affair and she went, 'Jesus Christ, what next?' she says. 'You're a murderer and now you're a lesbian.' "

Mary's first work assignment, she said, had been to assist the Mellanby cook, Pat. But that, as she had told me, ended very soon by mutual agreement—"they were quite democratic that way, ha ha," she said— "and I was assigned to the bottom workroom [at the southern end of the prison], where Carol was working, too."

At this point, as had happened before when she described her childhood or emotional moments in Red Bank, she suddenly dropped into broad Geordie, which was almost totally incomprehensible to me. "We w're cooping th'ends offliprs," she said.

You were "cooping" what of what? I asked.

"Cutting," she said patiently, back in her Red Bank English. "We had these big scissors and we were cutting the ends off flippers, honestly, great big black rubber things, I think they were for the police divers. There were little thin bits [of rubber] all over and we had to sort of trim them, get the bits off you know, with sharp scissors. We engineered a sort of sit-down there, because it was freezing and there was no heat, and we hadn't even been given hot drinks and our hands froze with those bloody cold flippers, so we just stopped and sat and refused to work.

The governor came and said did we know that this was called mutiny, and it might have gone bad for us except that even she saw how cold it was and she told us to go to our blocks quickly, and we made ourselves hot drinks and warmed up under blankets and by the next day the heating had been fixed."

What was the actual schedule every day? I asked.

"The same, always the same," she said. "I got up at six, did morning chores like dusting, sweeping, washing floors or toilets or whatever; at seven-thirty had what they laughingly called breakfast—a slice of bread, something grainy they called marmalade, and tea—and went off to the workshop at eight, came back at twelve for lunch, went back to work at one and back to the houses at four-forty-five or so; then tea and that was that."

What about personal cleanliness? I asked. Did people have showers, baths?

"When I was on the gardens and what have you and I was particularly filthy, I would ask someone to keep an eye out and dive in the bath, but that was unofficial. Officially, unless you were working on dirty outside jobs like pipes, or you were on the engineering party, or of course in the kitchens, when you could have a bath every night, it was one bath a week. But anyway, we strip-washed every day."

Did they have their own bath stuff, oils, salts, etc.?

"Only certain types were allowed: no commercial deodorants, facial cleaners, nail polish remover, et cetera, because they contained alcohol. For deodorants there was a powder provided in every house that you could use. There were some people who couldn't take care of themselves and shouldn't have been there in the first place," she said. "But most people were pretty clean."

Over the years, she said, she had done every kind of work available at Styal, inside and outside. "But the first six months it was as I said, first cutting the ruddy flippers, and then it was making football shirts on huge sewing machines and I wasn't much good at that either." She burst out laughing. "The armhole for a football shirt looks very much like the neck hole, doesn't it?" Still laughing, she said, "There was a lot of football shirts out there with three sleeves. Mary Scorse—you remember, I told you about her?—she was in charge of that workshop and everybody was very frightened of her and I really wasn't any good at this. One day she started on me and one of my friends says, 'Here, next time she gives you any hassle, just say to her your name might be Bell but it isn't Madeleine,' and I said, 'Why would I say that?' and she said, 'It'll shut her up.' So show-off that I was, I did—you know, open my big mouth and said: 'I might be Bell but I'm not Madeleine.' And she says, 'You little bastard, come here, what did you say?' And she came up to me holding out some big scissors and I was scared to death but stood my ground and it stopped right there. Later, all the girls were rolling around with laughter. They thought it was hilarious. And I says, 'What was that all about? What did I say?' And they said that Madeleine was the name of the girlfriend she had killed when she had found her in bed with a man, and I said, 'You bitches,' and later I apologized to Mary Scorse. I was really sorry for her. She'd been released and then recalled twice, once when she'd been in a pub brawl and then, after serving another eleven years and after only a short time outside, for allegedly taking an overdose."

I thought people on license could only be recalled if they committed another violent crime, I said.

"Yeah, well," she said bitterly. "I suppose they decided trying to kill yourself was an act of violence meriting recall. She had a pet bird, you know, a blue tit she fed every morning. I watched many times how that little bird would be sort of waiting for her, always in the same place. If anyone came by, she'd pretend to be shooing him away—it doesn't do, you see, to show kindness in prison. I liked her, but I saw her getting more and more confused, so unhappy, wandering around at night in her house. But at least there she had friends, and she knew her way around. So what did our glorious caring system do? They sent her to Durham's top-security wing. I was sick: it made me sick."

In prison, what one was always fighting, she said, was monotony: "As I told you, every weekday was the same and weekends were worse: if you didn't have a visit there was nothing to do, just simply nothing. It was boring, boring, boring, so that horrible as weekdays were you actually longed for Monday to come around because at least you could get out to go to the workshops. I'm not saying they didn't try to make it more bearable, you know, by moving us from working place to working place every three months and even allowing us to change earlier if we applied." But against that, she said, in order to avoid relationships becoming "too close—whatever that means," they also frequently moved people from one house to another.

"There are eleven houses, or blocks, and I was certainly in six of them; they moved me to and fro between them like a yo-yo and certainly every time I was on report. Let's see," she counted them off in her memory and simultaneously on her fingers: "Mellanby, Davies, Righton, Barker, Bleak—that was the punishment block and I was in there, oh, dozens of times . . ."

Dozens? I said skeptically, which she hated. "You don't believe me, you don't trust me . . . How can you still not trust me?" she would cry, and I would explain, as I had done before, that memory is imperfect and, mixed up as it is with wishes, dreams, and imagination, deceptive. And that it was my function to be skeptical, to re-question, to check and then check again. Usually she would reject such explanations and, sometimes quite angrily, insist that my distrust was not of her memory but of her, just her, who had always been accused of manipulating people. But that time she just shrugged and looked dispirited. "It seemed like dozens," she said wearily, carrying on with her list. "And then I was in Fry . . ." She looked distraught. "God, I can't even remember the others, what's the matter with me?"

I said nothing was the matter with her: she was remembering specific things very clearly about each of the houses she had been in, so the probability was that she had not been sent to any of the other five.

She doesn't know whether this moving about had a positive effect for the prison population, helping to prevent monotony, or whether, on the contrary, it destroyed any chance of stability. What nobody could understand who hadn't been in prison with a life sentence, she said, is that for lifers prison is not a set time, a period in or out of their lives, it is all of life, forever. "You fight that realization," she said. "But most lifers can't fight it for long. You remember I told you how depressed I was on my second or third day there, the Saturday my mother came? Afterwards, with all the new faces and stories and experiences, I was able to suppress it for a bit. But after, oh, I don't know, a few months, I began to feel that this was it, that there would never be anything else. And this is what most lifers come to feel and why most of them—specially the older ones—kind of make a nest of their prison life and, in the process, of course, become institutionalized."

She understood perfectly, she said, how difficult and indeed impossible it must be to run prisons such as Styal without enforcing submission. But once the prisoners had submitted—a state she herself deplored and finally fought against for years—they should surely be allowed that nest without the threat of destabilizing them.

Of course, she didn't find prison life monotonous for quite some time. "But that's because, as you know, I'm so hopelessly curious, and in prison"—she suddenly laughed raucously, the words becoming hopelessly entangled as she did—"one has . . . ha ha ha . . . captive victims . . . [renewed guffaws] for one's nosiness." The laughter stopped. "Actually, I realized quite soon that women are very selective in who they will tell things about themselves. It was just at first, I think perhaps because I *was* so young and of course 'new' and . . ." She shrugged. "I suppose it worked both ways—most of them were curious about me, too, so really for the first weeks almost anybody I went up to talked to me. After that, well, it changed. It took quite a while but then I began to have friends, not . . . you know . . . not at all necessarily lesbian friends, though that too, of course, but some were just friends. One learned; it was dreadfully painful to allow oneself to become attached to someone who had a short sentence or was at the end of a longer one. That is the most depressing thing of all about being a lifer: to see people leave.

"I realized very soon—I had no need to ask the governor about it— that there was no way that I could get my ERD [expected release date] before I was twenty-one. I'd been told often enough. If Mr. Dixon's plan had worked out it wouldn't have mattered. Because even if I had to have remained under some restraint—like the hostel situation he was think-ing of for me at Red Bank—I would have been helped meanwhile to prepare for a future. But there was nothing like that now."

Was there no possibility of further schooling for you? I asked.

"I already told you . . ." Her fear, which never quite disappeared, of being distrusted or perhaps being "tricked" by "clever" questions made her—and she is well-mannered—sound almost rude. Certainly, she was very impatient if I appeared to have forgotten something she said or asked a question twice.

So tell me again, I said and explained again, rather more sternly, that I would ask several times over until I was sure I understood the answer. She had told me earlier on, I said, that by law she had to be provided with further education. (In fact this is only until O level; after that it is no longer the prison's obligation to provide further education, though it is still, at least in theory, an option a young prisoner can select.) Didn't they provide educational programs? Was there nothing you could learn?

"Yeah, yeah, yeah, they provided," she said scornfully. "Because I was under eighteen I still had to do a certain amount of ha ha, joke . . . 'studying.'" (Here she became very confused, skipping years and claim-ing not to remember names or activities.) "There was this education officer, that's right, she tried to get me over on the education block where I had to sit . . . a woman . . . I didn't even know her name and I don't know what the hell I was doing there to tell the truth, just discussing things, oh yeah, because the Open University came into it like, didn't it . . ."

Wait a minute, I said. Are we talking about when you were still sixteen?

"No, I was eighteen then, wasn't I? Because they said, 'Oh, aren't you pleased that they made an exception and you can be on it,' and I didn't even ask to go on it, I didn't even want to go on it, and the governor was saying, 'You want to equip and arm yourself with this . . .' Oh my God, it was like I'm going out into a battlefield, you know, and even then, after all, I knew I wasn't going anywhere for years and years . . ."

Let's go back to when you were sixteen, I said. For those first two years, didn't you do anything intellectual or vocational?

"Yeah, I learned how to make gravy from flour," she mocked.

What about books? Did you read?

"Yes, every Sunday the library was on. I used to go and look but it was a crap library, it was rubbish. I don't call what they had 'books.' I mean at Red Bank, you know, there were books, real books, and Mr. Shaw would discuss them with us after we'd read them, and we read Shakespeare and Oscar Wilde, lots and lots of poetry; Mr. Shaw was wild on poetry. But at Styal ... I don't mean to be rude ... but I just wasn't interested in Georgette Heyer and Barbara Cartland, and that's pretty much all there was. I think all the time I was there I must have got about four books out. I did read books prison visitors brought in but the only one I remember is *Papillon*, that was my bible."

There were evening classes, she said, and you could do three a week. "I did learn the guitar. There was an absolutely fantastic, brilliant teacher and I had already played it at Red Bank. But on the whole, well, they said the opportunities were there and that it was up to the individual, etc., etc. Well, maybe, and yes, there were classes, but they were taught by volunteers who, of course, never stayed. I mean, they came and went. What was the point of trying to learn then? And things like music appreciation. I mean, who is interested in listening to *Iolanthe* or other operas? ... I mean, listening to operas, or even any classical music, that too has to be taught, learnt, or maybe, you know, lived with as a child. I mean, as I told you, there are some educated women in prison, but not most of them. You see, what happens is that there are so-called classes in things they find volunteers for and that is usually educated people, so they teach, or play, or show what they enjoy or know. But it isn't what is wanted or needed ..."

What would women in prison want? I asked her. What would they respond to?

"Well, how about first-aid courses? How about classes on kids or on parenting, with films? People really don't know how to be parents. I'm one of the lucky ones: I had Mr. Dixon and what have you and later Pat, my probation officer. But if I hadn't had this help, I don't know how I would have managed.

"And you could offer classes, also with films, on nature and animals. People would sign up for that. I would have. But as it was, one just used classes as a means for meeting up with friends from other blocks."

There *were* vocational training courses and she did ask to join some of those, she said. "But I wasn't allowed to because they took place out-side . . . Oh, just a hundred yards the other side of the gate. Other lifers were allowed to go but not me, of course. My God, it might actually have been something I enjoyed. Molly Morgan wouldn't have that."

Did she really still feel that? I asked. Was that fair? (Fairness, as taught by Mr. Dixon, is to this day a matter of honor to Mary and any suggestion that she might be being unfair is anathema to her.) Wasn't it more likely that everybody in charge of her, from the Home Office on down, was afraid of the media's abnormal interest in her, which, though originating in her crimes as a child, had been stirred up continuously since then by her mother?

"That's true," she said thoughtfully. "She made a living out of being my mother, didn't she?"

By the time Mary was transferred to Styal, Betty Bell was living with her young boyfriend, George, whom she had met in 1968, just before the tragedy in Newcastle, when she was twenty-nine and he was eighteen. It was on her second visit, Mary thinks, that she found her with a heavy cold, in spite of which she had been sent to the workshop every morning of the week just past. ("We were not coddled," Mary said.) Betty, we don't know how, had barged in on the governor and told her it was out-rageous that her sixteen-year-old daughter should be forced to work when she belonged in the infirmary.

"She told the governor she was 'stupid' not to see I was ill," Mary said, "and I never heard the end of it. I was called in to see Molly Morgan the next morning and she was furious. I couldn't blame her; I could well imagine how my mother would have come on to her."

The governor had told her that, given her mother's "immaturity, with a boyfriend in the house," it was unlikely she would ever be released to her. "I was really gob-smacked," Mary said. "I mean, I'd only just arrived . . . what was she talking about? But also, how dare she talk like that about my mother to me?"

Molly Morgan must have been extraordinarily angered by her encounter with Betty to allow herself such a personal and premature remark. It was based not on any real knowledge of Betty's troubles or of Mary's childhood experiences with her but on an entirely conventional disapproval (still prevalent in the early 1970s) of a woman cohabiting outside wedlock.

Whichever authority had supplied her with this information had no idea of the extent to which Betty's circumstances had changed in the five years since Mary's trial. By 1973 George, a hardworking young man with considerable business flair, had stabilized Betty's life. He had got her to take courses in typing and accounting and encouraged her to work with him in building up his business. She had learned to drive, and George would eventually buy her a car.

By the time Molly Morgan made her remarks, Mary, of course, knew all about these changes. "My mother told me endlessly about all she was doing and the nice house George had bought or was buying for them and 'my room' in it. I was so offended when Molly Morgan talked about her like that. Wouldn't you have thought they [the nameless authorities] would know that George was a respectable person and that they were living a respectable life?" (George did in fact marry Betty at some point in the next few years—Mary has forgotten when—and it would be some time before Mary herself became aware of Betty's increasing drinking problem, which George would find himself eventually unable to deal with and which, thirteen years later, Betty by then a full-blown alcoholic, would finally break up their relationship.)

Mary's first real trouble came only a few weeks after her arrival at Styal when two girls asked her to help them escape. They had stolen a wrench from a workshop and needed someone strong to prise the bars open and then straighten them out once they'd gone. "I believed them, stupid me,"

Mary said. "I thought this was great, just like a film. I didn't realize they were just mouth, mouth, mouth, and that nobody could escape, not that way anyway. So I helped them and then I hid the wrench and then of course they were caught and there was a tool count and everybody was called in for questioning, and although one of the girls owned up to stealing the wrench, there was still the question who hid it afterwards, and so there was no way that I could get out of it without grassing anyone else up. So I was put on report and told I'd be taking the eight o'clock walk the next morning." That first punishment award was to be traumatic.

"Yes," she guffawed, "that's what they called it, an 'award.'

"An officer came for me at eight o'clock and we walked to the bottom end of the prison. Eight o'clock is the time of morning they used to hang people and they kept the report walk to the same time. There is something sinister about that to me. I'm sure it's *meant* to invoke the psychological reaction it causes, an unknown fear, a sense of foreboding which is unlike anything else, certainly, I have ever felt. By this time, too, I had heard so many stories about Bleak House—the punishment block—I was really scared.

"My first sight of Bleak was really dismal," she said. "It was a low, grim building, straight out of a Dickens novel, sort of crouching and decaying, surrounded by a metal fence, with bars and wire mesh on the Perspex windows. The screw with me rang a bell and then a kind of door inset within the big doors was unlocked and there was a stench of urine and disinfectant. They searched me and took my shoes off me, and then led me to a cell with a small light high up on the ceiling under a big grille which I later saw was full of dead insects and spiders which had got caught. There was nothing in the cell but a bedspring with a bottle-green rimmed metal frame, a stained plastic chamber pot, and an equally filthy plastic mug. You weren't allowed to have anything of your own. They gave me a toothbrush and soap for ablutions and stuff to roll one cigarette after each meal.

"I couldn't believe it could be as bad as it was," she said, "but it really was. I've often wondered whether they've made any changes to it since then. I almost can't believe they wouldn't have. I mean, how can it be allowed?

"There was supposed to be a Gideon Bible in each cell but there wasn't even that. The screw said they were taken away because people made obscene drawings on them. 'Your kind of art,' she said scornfully. She said I was not to lie down on the bed, which may have been her idea of a joke because there wasn't any blanket or sheet or anything—they brought bed stuff at six in the evening and took it away at six in the morning, so all you had to sit on was the rim of the bed. The walls were full of graffiti, names, sentences, threats to the governor, the staff, but also lines from songs. By the time I left that cell fourteen days later I knew all the names, all the sentences, all the songs and lines from poems, too, by heart . . ."

Couldn't you have requested the Bible? I asked.

"Much later, when I'd been in Bleak several times, I did," she said. "I said I'd read the rule book and that I was *allowed* to have religious scriptures, but they just told me to shut my mouth. It was the younger POs who were the worst, really cruel and using terrible language, real little Hitlers. The principal officer at Bleak was actually quite a nice woman. She was older and had been in the services. She'd taken enough discipline to know how to dish it out. 'Oh God, not you again,' she'd often say later when I was brought in again. 'Why don't you give it a rest?'

"The formalities are always the same. Soon after you get there, the principal officer comes with two others, reads out your number and name and what you are on report for. Then she hands you a paper and a pencil and says that if you wish to reply you can do so by writing on the back of the paper. 'You will have every opportunity to state your case to the governor,' she says and then you sign. Not long afterwards, the MO, accompanied by a nurse, looks in, says, 'Good morning, how are you?' and disappears before you can answer. That *is* a rule: if you are in solitary, a doctor has to see you every day. There was a bell I had been shown for 'emergencies' and after a long while I rang it and a screw looked in through the spy hole and when I asked when I could see the governor she said, 'When she's ready,' and told me not to dare to ring again.

"I think that morning was about the worst I remember. I don't think I have ever felt so deserted in my life, either before or since. I sat on the rim of the bed and cried and wiped my face with my sleeve and couldn't think how I could stand it.

"Hours later they took me to the adjudication room. It's like a court in session, you know, but no defense for you. There is the governor sitting behind a table with the chief officer and a principal officer—I don't know the difference between them—next to her. I had to stand barefoot—I don't know why—on the edge of a mat facing them, with two officers standing in front of me, legs apart and hands behind backs, the same military way I had been told to stand. Another officer read out my number and name and the report."

What sort of offenses got one sent to Bleak? I asked.

"Refusing to work, insolence, caught in the possession of somebody else's things—you know, a sock or something—swapping clothes with somebody, holding hands publicly, shouting out of windows, childish, childish things."

But it sounds so petty, so silly, why would they bother?

"I'm not sure. I sometimes thought it was almost at pre-set times, to demonstrate power when it seemed to be getting too lax."

But it couldn't only have been for such absurd reasons?

"No, of course not. I told you, there is a great deal of repressed anger in prisons, and sometimes something small, like disobeying a direct order because it seems unreasonable, can turn into violence. That is when a PO will ring the aggro bell and the 'heavy mob' comes running: that's up to eight special POs whose job it is to remove prisoners as quickly and, yes, as painlessly as possible. What they do is about two of them get a hold of each limb in such a way so they don't damage or hurt the prisoner and carry them off."

But one *can* imagine this becoming necessary at times, I said to her. Even your stories underline the anger and occasional explosion into violence. No prison administration could allow that, could they?

"That's true. It's only that in some prisons, and Styal at the time was one of them, it happens too often, so that one has to wonder what is wrong with the atmosphere. It had a very bad reputation among prisoners. I've heard women scream to go back to Durham or Holloway. And once you are in Bleak, you really have no out: you just plead guilty, as I did, the first time and every time thereafter. What else could one do?

"That first time I couldn't stop myself from crying. Molly Morgan told me to stop sniveling and to remember that I wasn't in Red Bank now and she gave me the fourteen days 'behind the door' . . . That's what solitary confinement is called.

"Well, that was the first of many times for me in Bleak—many times because I decided that day that I'd never let any of them see me cry again: as far as they were concerned I was going to be hard, hard to the core."

Mary's memory is particularly vague about the "dozens" of detentions she spent in Bleak. It is not the transgressions she has forgotten or her feelings during the detentions but, again, the precise or even approximate dates. All she knows is that the first time was within weeks of her arrival and that after three years, with a few exceptions, her visits to Bleak stopped. "By that time," she said, "I had learned how to play the system. Not by submitting, not that, ever, but to be in charge of myself."

What did that mean? I asked her.

"It meant retaining my anger, but instead of expressing rebellion through childish pranks or by screaming abuse at POs, to keep it within myself, so to speak in reserve."

The pressure of holding her anger "in reserve" may at least partly have been what led to two halfhearted attempts at suicide, for both of which she was punished by detention. "I cut myself so I bled," she said, and laughed—she really did find it funny—"so they sent me to Bleak for damaging government property."

"Very soon after I came out that first time, they sent me to Davies," she said. "It was my second house and that actually happened because the governor decided all LTIs, instead of being spread across the place, were to be housed together in three houses on central row and that was Davies, Fry, and Barker."

That surely was intelligent, I said. Don't you think it showed compassion?

She shrugged indifferently. "Perhaps, considered from outside. But at the time, the girls only felt she was wanting to isolate them even more. Nobody was prepared to assign anything but mean motivations to her.

"So I went to Davies. And Janey Jones—you know, the famous madam?—she was in there. She was *really* nice. She was a character, an entertainer through and through. But she didn't have a malicious bone in her body. She would have us in fits with her stories, but she could laugh at herself too: that's class.

"But . . . Oh God, I was so *stupid*. One Sunday when my mother was coming on a visit, Janey, out of the goodness of her heart, offered to put a bit of makeup on me. It was fun, you know . . . that was before I went butch. And when I went on the visit [to the visitor's room] my mother said, 'You look like a tart. You put much too much on.' Well, it takes one to know one, doesn't it?" Mary's voice was quite vicious when she said this. "And when I said I didn't make myself up, I didn't even know how, Janey Jones, who was in my house, had done it for me, that tore it, she went totally berserk. The truth is, she was deadly afeared of prostitutes, my mother was. It *was* so weird, wasn't it? Here she was, Catholic to the eyeballs, the saints here and the saints there, and sin sin sin and . . . well . . . *you* know what she was . . . True, not anymore then: she was becoming *respectable*, with a *respectable* man and a brand-new house with brand-new furniture she'd endlessly describe to me, a lifer you know, at Styal. She'd tell me about 'my' room in that house . . . *my* room? Oh God, she understood nothing, never anything, never that prison was not a . . . a . . . an *interlude*: it was my life, the place where I would be forever."

Mary had suddenly started to cry and kept shaking her head, her face streaked with tears. "She came all the time, you know, every month, even sometimes twice a month in that first year, and I tried to feel . . . even though I always knew it wasn't so . . . that she must be doing it for me, she must mean well, but there had always been this tension when she came, to Red Bank too . . . But there I felt cared for, both during her visits and always, always after them. In prison, well, you are not an individual, just a number and . . . how can it be otherwise? They know nothing about you except your crime and the sentence of the court, and with a few remarkable exceptions—and there were those—POs don't care. Why should they and how could they? One thing one has to face in prison is that you are not there to be helped, you are there to be punished.

"Like for old Mary Scorse—the time of your crime and the feelings that made you commit it are so far away you may not even remember them. Certainly most people try not to remember. So if you are being punished, it is finally for *being*, not for doing, do you know what I mean? And many, many people, women probably more than men, give in to it and as they won't or can't remember the perhaps one occasion when they wronged, they just come to agree, come to feel, that they are bad. My mother had always told me I was bad, as long as I could remember. Mr. Dixon told me I wasn't, but slowly, or perhaps even not so slowly, that reassurance disappeared. My mother had to be blameless. I understand that now. I couldn't have lived if I thought she wasn't. But I could hardly bear to see her. I didn't know where my head was anymore about her."

But however ambivalent Mary felt, Betty was her only regular visitor at Styal throughout the seven years. "At Red Bank, lots of people came," she said. "Above all, my dad. But he never came to Styal, I suppose because it was prison." From what her family had said to me, it was quite clear: Red Bank was a beautiful school to them, where Mary, as Cath said, was likely to "get a better education than my kids." It was such an attractive setting and the staff they met were so pleasant and educated, there was no sense of embarrassment to them visiting her there; after all, Cath had brought her little boy once and Mary taught him swimming in the pool. But Styal was a very different matter. One cannot doubt that they were deeply shocked at her being there: now she was different. And without deliberately wishing to hurt her, at that point all of them cut themselves loose from her. One has to believe that for Betty this was a victory. Now in a way she had Mary all to herself again, and at Styal no one knew, nor did the system have time to care, that Betty continued to spell disaster for her.

"Anyway," Mary said, "on that Janey Jones occasion, my mother said she was going 'to do something' about it and I thought, Oh God, she's going to go to Molly, like she had done before, so I told her not to be so bloody stupid. I didn't know she was going to go to the papers again," Mary said. "But there it was, the next Sunday, splashed all over the front page of the *News of the World:* 'Take my sixteen-year-old daughter away from Evil Vice Queen' or some such bilge, *God!*

"Janey Jones was livid. Can you blame her? She was going to sue my mother ..." Her voice became cutting. "I wish to God she had. She didn't but she was very upset with me and not only that, a *lot* of people, girls and POs, got really careful of what they said to me. And that Sunday I was put on report, as if it had been my fault. I was really scared I'd be sent back to Bleak," Mary said. "But I wasn't that time. I was just pulled out of Davies and put into Righton. I say just, but you know, that was the worst thing Molly Morgan could have done to me because Righton was the place for what they called 'inadequates'—unfortunate women who were not insane enough to be committed by Mental Health Act standards, but neither were they sane or capable enough to integrate into ordinary prison life.

"It was referred to as a 'nuthouse' and putting me in there was the worst kind of humiliation. It was really for women with special needs. We were never allowed to mix with other prisoners, not even to go to the hospital block to get medicines: they were brought to us. And my mother got onto it; the house officer told me: 'I see your mother's at it again,' and she showed me a newspaper with a story about me being held in a security block. She was so stupid, you see. I'm sure ... even now I'm still sure she didn't *only* do it for the money, not then anymore, anyway. She was married to a good man; they had money; she didn't need it. No, she had these drinking pals who were reporters and in her silliness she thought the stories would help me. Of course, it was just the opposite. I know now that for prison administrators there is nothing quite as difficult as so-called high-profile prisoners and that's what I was, from the beginning to the end, and it was largely my mother's doing."

Was there anyone you could make friends with in Righton?

"No, really not. Oh, there was a girl, in her twenties, I think, and she was a psychic. I had interesting conversations with her. She *was* quite extraordinary ... she knew all about my Alsatians, my dog, you know, I mean about games I played with him, and walks we took. I mean she couldn't know about that, but she did. I honestly think that's the only thing I learned those four months: that there are things beyond ... you know ...."

Beyond what we can know? I asked.

"Yes, I know they thought she was mad. But she wasn't, she was just ... just *more* ... But it's true," she then said. "I was ... oh, not just lonely. I was forlorn in Righton. It was terrible, terrible."

Giving Up

And it was at Righton that Mary herself first experienced violence. "That's certainly how I remember it," she said. "Because I think that what they did to me was an invasion, a total invasion, which was totally unjust and I didn't deserve ... nobody deserves such a thing.

"What happened, not long after I got to Righton, there was an old lady there also called Mary, and I don't know what she'd done, but they were taking her out of the building and she fought, so they dragged her by the hair and I was shouting my mouth off about it and calling them names or whatever. Somehow it was just the last straw, I mean, treating an old lady like that. Well, I went berserk. I was letting out all the anger and frustration, not by doing anything violent you know, as people quite often did, smashing windows, throwing furniture about, or kicking the doors. I just screamed and yelled and I started crying and just couldn't stop. Any good PO could have stopped me, but the screw who was there rang the aggro bell and the mob came running and they carried me into the lockup and sat on me, pinned me down, and a sister was called and she injected me with what was called 'the liquid straitjacket.' I never dreamt for a moment that they would do such a thing to me. I mean, I knew it happened. I'd heard about it and I'd often seen Sister Watson walking around with that big syringe I'd been told about but . . ." She swallowed repeatedly in an effort to control her sudden emotion. "I hadn't done anything that required that kind of treatment . . ." and she began to cry. "I'm sorry . . ."—she hiccuped—"but it was hideous, bloody hideous.

"It's a hypnotic drug, paraldehyde, I think it's called," she said when she had calmed down a little later. "It's a green oily substance, horribly painful when it goes in. I was left in the lockup all night. I can't remember getting downstairs but I remember coming round in the dayroom, sitting up in a chair with the same clothes on. That's all I remember, them sitting on me, the injection in the lockup, how much it hurt, and that awful special smell of it. And then sitting in the dayroom downstairs, and I went to get up and I couldn't, and I went to say something and I couldn't, my mouth felt all heavy and my tongue swollen. And I knew I had to pee, but you are, like, paralyzed. I couldn't move and couldn't say and felt the warm water run down me . . ." Again she cried, this time softly. "Why, why would they have done that to me? Later I tried to think why and you almost hope you find a reason, but all I could ever imagine was that they just decided, 'Now it's your turn, we'll show you, you cocky little bitch.' "

You're still very upset, I said. I haven't seen you so upset about any one thing that happened at Styal, not even Bleak.

"That's true," she said. "I came to terms . . . I made peace with Bleak I was there so often. And I mostly provoked them into it, so, you know . . . I didn't mind the seclusion all that much. I often quite liked it, and I could see or find a humorous side to most of the things that happened there, the awful food, the vulgarity of the POs: in a funny way, because one needs to be in opposition to the system in order to beat it, it was my victory. But this, this . . ." She stopped as if to catch her breath. "I'm not stupid," she said. "I know about tranquilizers—there are lots of them; they gave me an injection of Largactil, much less bad, on another occasion—and I can understand their having to use them when people get out of control, but this, this *poison* they forcibly inject that makes you incapable of moving, speaking. You are awake but totally, totally incapacitated. How dare they? They don't have the right. It can't be a medication that can just be given like that. I'd like to know," she said, "I really would like to know, whether they still do it." (I am told that this heavy drug, widely used in mental hospitals and prisons twenty years ago, is now considered outdated.)

How long did this experience last?

"With the aftereffects of pins and needles, which you have for hours as it wears off, I think almost forty-eight hours."

At this point in her story, she digressed, as she so often did, months and even years away from the event she had just described. By now I knew that trying to force her into accounting sequentially for her years in prison was pointless. It wasn't that she didn't want to; it was that she couldn't. "I just can't think about it that way," she said when, on two occasions, I urged her to try. "I feel bad, I feel I'm letting you down by not telling it in some date order, but I can't. None of it is in my head the way you want it and I have to tell it the way it comes, because when I try to find the order you ask me for, it just stops altogether." The only way she could relate it, I realized, was to relive emotions as they rose up in her, prompted by images or whatever reason, as and when they did.

Paraldehyde was never given to her again, she said, though on one occasion later, she wasn't quite sure when, a halfhearted suicide attempt gave her a second experience of "the mob." "It was when I was very, very depressed," she said. "I can't quite remember whether it was after Mr. Dixon died in the summer of 1975 [one date she would always remember] or later, when Alicia, a girl I was seriously in love with, was released." (It was, I discovered later, on this second occasion, by which time she was twenty one.)

"I was at Fry then. I ran a bath, put the towel over the door, which was a sign to say don't come in, and I had broken a coffee jar and had a thick piece of glass and I went slash . . . It hurt—the first cut is the deepest, you know, and it really hurts, but I carried on, though I couldn't bear slashing my wrists, so I went along my arm and then put the arm in the bath because I had heard that that made the blood flow . . ."

But you weren't really trying to commit suicide, were you?

"No, no, it was just a sort of manifestation of, like . . . Oh, I suppose unhappiness."

Or wanting to be noticed?

She laughed, the laughter a little shrill. "Oh no, I got enough of that, no . . ." The laughter stopped. "Just a few times those years I just . . . couldn't go on. I mean, I think I knew I would go on, so you are right, it wasn't suicide or anything like that . . ." She shrugged. "I don't know what one could call it."

A gesture?

"Yes, yes, but a gesture for me, you know, not really for anybody else. One of my friends at Fry House was Tricia, a beautiful, gentle girl who'd been a nun before she became a prison officer, and then was sent to prison herself for seven years because she tried to help Myra Hindley escape. Tricia had seen bloody water come out from under the door," she said, and alerted the staff. "Next thing I knew I was being sewn up in the hospital block and, as I told you earlier, being escorted to [Bleak] because"—again she laughed that special, unamused "ha ha" laugh—"I had deliberately hurt myself on government property. There, I suppose, because I fought them, they put a straitjacket on me, a real one this time, and forcing my arm under it burst the stitches."

By that time two new high-ranking officers had been appointed to Styal, both of whom managed to establish a relationship with Mary. "Miss Fowler was assistant governor and Miss Kendall principal officer. They were both brilliant in their own way, super," Mary said. "Miss Fowler—we dubbed her 'Filly' because there was something horsy about her—she was a St. Trinian's sort of figure. She was very mannish, with short gray hair, and she wore brogues and big tweed checks and she had that wonderful loud laugh—more often than not about herself. She came when I was at my worst and was put in charge of lifers. She told the governor that if she would let her manage me, she'd get me right. She told me this, straight out, the first time she came to see me: in Bleak of course. That was when I was more in than out of there, long before that cutting-my-arm episode.

"Miss Fowler told me in that loud voice of hers—she was incapable of speaking softly—that she didn't pull any punches with anybody, nothing underhand. 'But it works both ways,' she said. 'If you've got anything to say, come out and say it and then we'll deal with it.' Then she told me that she and I had a very special person in common: Mr. Dixon. She had worked at Red Bank. That blew my mind, you know? Then she said, 'If I get you out of Bleak now, where would you like to go?' Well, that's the kind of trick question I'd heard before. We knew they'd be sure to send you anywhere *but* the house you asked for. So usually you guessed the opposite of the house you wanted and asked for that. At least that gave you a chance to get where you wanted to be. But when *she* asked, something made me say the truth, which was that I wanted to go back to Fry and she said: 'Right. Fry it is. Tomorrow.' And that was it."

Miss Kendall was different, she said. "She was a very wiry sort of person, about forty years old and not very happy, I think, but of course I don't really know. She didn't laugh so much but she cared about people. She'd do anything to avoid putting people on report. 'You behave yourself,' she'd say to me. 'I get nightmares that you'll still be here when I finish my service. I won't have it,' she'd say. 'So pull yourself together.' But then at Christmas, when she'd had a glass or two, she'd say, 'I hope this is going to be your year. It's got to be your year.' Every year she'd say that. It sounds sentimental, but she had real authority: prisoners always know when authority is real. She went on to Holloway later as assistant governor."

And it was Miss Kendall who sat next to her in the cell in Bleak when Sister Watson, using a flat needle, restitched the twenty-seven cuts Mary had made on her arm (she pushed her sleeve up to show me the scars). "She held my hand and she said: 'Squeeze my hand, squeeze as hard as you can.' Somehow she was always there when something was really wrong with me. It happened again later. I can't quite remember when. But it was a period when, contrary to all my intentions, I had accepted to take tranquilizers and I was supposed to come for a dose at nine and one at eleven and somehow they hadn't written it down and when I went again at twelve, I don't know whether because I forgot or just for the hell of it, they gave it to me, and then they couldn't wake me up. When I did finally wake up at seven at night, Miss Kendall was sitting on my bed and took my hand and said, 'Oh, thank God, thank God,' and, you know, I was pretty blurry, but I heard that and it meant something to me. It still does. I wonder how Miss Kendall is."

Mary isn't sure when it was that Mr. Dixon came to see her the first time. "He came three times," she said, but oddly enough she remembered almost nothing about his visits.

When he told you about your transfer to Styal, I said, trying to help her remember, he said you have to be Red Bank's ambassador there. Did that come up when he visited you?

She shrugged. "He said for me to sit up straight."

About a year later, while I was completing this section of the book, I asked her why, given how uniquely important Mr. Dixon had been and indeed still is to her, she had not been able to remember more about his three visits to her in Styal.

"Thinking about it now," she said, "I wonder whether somewhere, in spite of all my love for him, or perhaps because of it, I was angry. To me, you see, he was so powerful. Perhaps I felt that he should have been able to get it right for me. Perhaps I did somehow blame him that he didn't. But then, too, it was very, very difficult to talk to visitors, anyone from 'outside,' even Mr. Dixon. What was there to say? How could one tell anybody except those who shared that life, what this life, which was *all* of life, was like? No, all I could do, and that is what I did for all those years, was to put myself away. Eventually I could write letters, about the weather, about the work I did, about what other people wrote to me. But the things I really saw and really felt could not be put into words to those outside."

"Jim Dixon never talked about visiting May," Carole G. said when I asked her about it. "This is the first time I learn that he did. But he felt so deeply about her, I would imagine that seeing her at Styal was traumatic for him.

"Ben and I went to see her, I think it was six months after she'd gone there. She had written to invite us." (Mary, though speaking fondly of Carole and Ben, does not remember their visiting her at Styal.) "We went to see her twice," Ben said. "First in the spring of 1974, and then about a year later. She came to the visiting room to meet us; it had a stage and tables and chairs."

How had Mary impressed them on that first visit? I asked. "We saw the May we knew," he said. "Obviously older, but still quite herself, quite feminine, you know. She came and gave us a big hug and Carole and she both cried. The only thing was, she wore prison garb, a heavy sort of canvas dress, and we hadn't expected that."

"I guess I didn't tell them: I must have been on punishment," Mary said to me when I told her. "They made you wear that horrible uniform for a while if, for instance, they caught you in somebody else's clothes. Silly, but there you are: we had three lots of everything and that's what we were to wear, nothing else."

"The whole thing must have depressed us, too," Ben said, "because I remember, when we left and got to the car, both of us cried."

The second time Carole and Ben G. went to see her was in the late summer or autumn of 1975, just before they left Red Bank to work in the south of England. "By that time she seemed really changed," Ben said. "She looked so different. She had these deep shadows under her eyes, they were sunken in her face. She collapsed into tears when she saw us, but when we sat with her—and we stayed for several hours—she was just very subdued. All that bubbliness, that vivaciousness had gone. We were very, very worried about her when we left."

By mid-1975, Mary had had a number of letters from Carole and

Ben, the last from a holiday in the United States. On their return they found Mary's reply, written on successive evenings, in which, to their surprise, she asked whether they would do her a great favor if she withdrew some money from her account and sent it to them.* After thanking them for their letter and postcard and telling them how much she longed to travel to increase her knowledge of the world, she tells them that she had begun that night an Open University prep course and already learned a lot within two hours. "And, look," said Carole, showing me the letter, "she asks us there to buy her a battery stereo."

I can't ask mum [Mary writes] because I want to surprise her and show her what a little money-wise daughter she has. Really, you'd be doing me a favour, after all, that's what friends are for. I'm not trying emotional blackmail but let me know how it works out. I shall close for now, we have to be tucked in and lights out so I'll leave this, probably until tomorrow night, because I have work on tomorrow for another eight hours—how do I do it? So I'll get my head down, do my yoga relaxation spiritual and fly to you in my dreams. Wish me a bon voyage, good night, good rest. Your sleepy-head.

It's now eight-thirty Wednesday night [the letter continues] I'm bathed and in bed. I've been to beauty culture tonight, had my eyebrows plucked, had witchhazel purple skin cleanser on my face. It still looks just the same. I expected a miraculous change in two hours: it took nearly an hour for my eyebrows to be plucked properly. [She then asks about some of the Red Bank counselors and Jeff, the G.s' young American friend whom she had been a little in love with.] I hope that if and when I meet him again I shall be strong enough to stop this really weird

---

* Prisoners' earnings were banked for them in an account, which was intended to accrue for their release and from which they were given weekly pocket money. They could ask permission to withdraw larger amounts for presents if they had someone on the outside to buy them for them.

feeling . . . like a mother or an analyst. It's hard to admit that your hero is just another person. I was only 14 I know, but some things take a while to sink in. Although, it would be nice to see him again and see just how I'll react now.

Not much to write about—is there ever? I don't know how I manage four pages. The stars are out now. I really love to lie in bed and look at them all. What do you see, stars or bars? Difficult question in here. I'm afraid I only see the stars and sky etc. Bars I hardly notice, only now and again when I feel down. I must close now, friends, take care until next time.

Mary was kept at Righton for about six months, she thinks. "I suppose until they thought I was civilized enough to join the ranks of other prisoners. I had no idea they were moving me . . . we never had any warning of anything. It was Miss Kendall who came one day and told me she was taking me to Barker's. 'Let's try that,' she said."

Barker, at that time, was the elite block of the prison, home to about a dozen selected lifers. "It was the 'show house,'" Mary said. "That's where they took film crews who came to do documentaries about women in prison. It was really unbelievable, like a mad hatter's world. These women lived there like in an old folk's home, a rest home, you know. They had their own bedspreads, they were allowed to wear watches, and there was knitting all over the place and flowerpots on doilies. All the furniture was covered in chintz. The house screws were treated like guests, you know, brought cups of tea and all. I couldn't believe any of it. They were totally institutionalized, content, you know. Later I found out that nobody had ever, ever been put on report from Barker's." She guffawed. "I changed that in a hurry. That morning when I was taken there, I charged up the stairs to recce the place and Pearl, oh, she was about fifty and she said, in that schoolmarmish tone they all adopted: 'We take our shoes off when we come into the house,' and when I told her that I'd kick her teeth in if she ordered me about, she says, 'Your reputation has preceded you,' and, 'I'll put you over my knee and smack your backside.' So I told her that she was a bloody pervert and that I'd knock her head off if she touched me. Actually we became good friends later, she was all right, old Pearl."

Much later, after Mary had left Styal, I spoke to a former Styal prisoner, a woman in her midthirties, about Mary. "She could be terribly aggressive, terribly rude," she said. "She used terrible language, about the officers and even to them." And what did the officers do about it? I asked. She shrugged. "Nothing. They treated her differently from any of us. She *was* different. She was—like a lady. Compared to me, she *was* a lady." Despite the rudeness? Despite the terrible language? She shrugged again. "If anybody else had behaved like that, they'd be in a cell in minutes. With her . . . they just let her be." Was that resented by other prisoners? I asked. She shook her head in a perplexed sort of way. "I didn't like her when I met her first," she said. "But afterwards—and I was never close to her," she said quickly—"I came to feel she was in the wrong place, just completely in the wrong place. She should have been in a hospital. She was eleven, just *eleven* when she did that awful thing," she said, sounding angry. "Eleven . . . I have two kids and one is eleven. If he did such a thing I'd *know* he was sick. So perhaps the officers thought like I did that she shouldn't have been there and perhaps that's why they treated her as a star prisoner. Resented?" she said then, picking up my previous question. She shook her head. "No. She had *good* friends," she said. "She could be terrible, quite terrible, but she was a good friend to a lot of people."

Margaret Kenyon,* an attractive woman passionately involved in the reform of women's prisons, is a prison governor who, at the beginning of her career, was at Styal when Mary was there.

"I wasn't much involved with her," she said, "but everyone knew about her. She *was* different from most of the other prisoners. She was not just ingenuous, but, contrary to many of the others, she hadn't lived on the streets. Although obviously intelligent, she was curiously naïve and somehow pure; there was a sort of maternal feeling about her, not even so much among the staff but certainly among the prisoners. Particularly the older women wanted to keep her as she was; I think they saw

* Changed name.

her as a surrogate favored daughter. Of course, she was so young—even when she had been there for years, she still seemed so young . . ."

When Mary told me about Barker House she realized that by then she would have been at Styal for over a year. "I was seventeen," she said, "and the wonderful thing was that Diane was there, too, and so was Angie and they were eighteen. For the first time, I was with girls of my own age, and though I didn't like Angie because she was a suckup, Diane became my best friend, the best friend I've ever had."

She was to stay at Barker for nine months, her longest period in one house. "And somehow, between Diane and me, we treated it like being kids in boarding school," she said. "We laughed and cried a lot together, we played jokes on everybody and on each other, silly, silly things like once at night I was just dropping off to sleep when I suddenly felt my pillow move under me. I jumped out of bed in horror, thinking, you know, of mice or rats, and then heard Diane giggling under the covers: she had sewn a thread to the underside of my pillow and was holding the bobbin and pulling. The next night I paid her back when—after lights out, of course—we were playing 'jump,' which meant climbing up on top of the high wardrobe and jumping down onto the beds. When it was Diane's turn, I pulled her bed away and told her she had to sing before I'd put it back and then, as she sang, and sang, and sang, sitting on top of the wardrobe, I pretended to go to sleep. But it was all in good fun, I mean really childish nonsense.

"But above all, there was this wonderful closeness between us. We'd lie in bed at night looking through the bars and talk about freedom. We had a dream, she and I, that one day we'd go to Disneyland, both of us wearing big hats, hers white, mine blue. Disneyland was everything we believed freedom would be, where people were laughing and happy, where life would be perfect. Every New Year's Eve we'd look out and find the brightest star in the sky and we'd make a wish. Even now, each New Year just before twelve, I go off by myself a moment and look for the brightest star and I know Diane is doing it too, to keep our pact lest we ever forget what it was all about and that we did a lot of growing up together."

Did you have a sexual relationship with Diane? I asked.

"Most people thought we had, but no, we didn't, we couldn't. It would have been like incest, you know. We did try it once, but it didn't work—both of us just burst out laughing. Even so"—she sounded puzzled at this memory—"I think both of us were jealous of the relationships each of us had with others. Funny that, isn't it?"

It was during 1975, when Mary was now eighteen years old, that she made many decisions. "I think it all . . . crystallized," she said, "after Mr. Dixon died."

It was a lovely day in June, she said, and she was on a gardening detail in the afternoon, when she began to feel "really down, you know, so down I didn't know what to do. I parked the rake against a tree and I just lay in the grass and went to sleep. And when Mr. Walker, the gardener, found me and woke me up I knew something was wrong. I couldn't think what, but I could hardly bear the feeling. And all I wanted was to be alone.

"They come around in the evening and ask is there anyone wanting to see the MO, Welfare, or the governor. And I asked to see the governor, because I wanted to go down on rule 43 [solitary], because I was fed up, I just wanted time by myself. They said no, I couldn't see the governor for that. So the next morning I just stayed in bed because I knew they'd have to put me on report and that's what happened and they sent me to Bleak. And at four that afternoon I was called into the adjudication room, where Miss Morgan, for the first time, showed her humane side and told me, quite gently, that Mr. Dixon had died at 4:00 P.M. the previous day. And I had known—at four o'clock I knew, didn't I? Something died in me that day and it didn't come back to life until . . ."—she counted—". . . until nine years later when [her baby] was born. She gave life back to me.

"I went back to my cell that day and just sat there. I couldn't cry, not

246

until several days later when I was back at my house and there was a concert on TV and I suddenly found myself sitting there sobbing, unable to stop. And I think when I stopped sobbing I had changed."

This change that she described to me was twofold: on the one hand she decided that openly bucking the system as she had been doing for two years was self-defeating. "If all I did was say no," she said, "I wasn't using my wits. What I had to do was, yes, continue to fight the system, but I had to graduate from being a prisoner to being a con, and that meant that rather than being open and angry, I had to be closed and crafty. In prison the eleventh commandment is: 'Thou shalt not be caught.' And from now on this was the one I would obey."

Her second decision that week—"And believe me, it was quite in line with the first one," she said—"was to become 'butch.'

"As a butch," she said, "you are in charge of your life. You select who to be with. You have an established and dominant position within the microcosm of society which a prison is. This doesn't mean that you only 'take': that things are done for you, your bed is made, things are given to you, cigarettes are rolled for you, people take over duties for you. It also means that you 'give.' Sexually ... I already told you ... you *never* take, you *only* give, but quite aside from that, you are someone people come to ..."

For what?

"Help, advice ..."

Did you have one girlfriend at a time?

"I had a lot of them, lots of black girls. They were so beautiful."

Did that make you sexually happy?

"No, sexually, no. But if you didn't have relationships, though not necessarily sexual ones, you were too lonely and that would have been intolerable."

But how did you manage sexually for yourself?

"By myself," she said matter-of-factly. "But for the rest, I developed a sort of Jack-the-lad attitude. It was so easy for me to be like a boy, because I didn't have to pretend. After all I'd been with boys since I was eleven, I mean I knew boys like nobody else, I knew how they moved, how they sat, how they joked . . . I knew how they felt, too. I could *be* a boy." Over the years, she said, she'd probably had sex with (or provided sexual relief for) two hundred women.

"Well," said Dr. Chamarette, smilingly drawing the word out, "I *think* the figure two hundred may be a bit exaggerated, as is her feeling now that she was more in than out of Bleak House during her first two years at Styal. But she certainly 'knew' a lot of the women, whether"—he smiled again—"biblically or not may not be that important."

Norman Palmer Chamarette, consultant child psychiatrist at Macclesfield Hospital from 1954 to 1968, fondly referred to as "Chammy" by all who know him, is now ninety-three years old: tall, slim, in excellent health, highly articulate, with a remarkable memory. For eleven years, including those of Mary's detention, he held a much sought-after weekly group therapy session at Styal.

"I begged for two years to get into Chammy's group," Mary said, "not because I was changing or 'developing,' but just as a skive—a Thursday afternoon skive, something else, something new, out of the routine. And also because Alicia—you remember, I told you about her—was in the group. Alicia was one of the most beautiful girls I've ever seen, but she was in a different block, so this was a chance to see her. Some people—Puerto Rican Americans—took the group very seriously, as Americans do. I knew I would never take it seriously. But I'd heard a lot about Chammy. They said he listens to all your problems. 'Lovely man he is,' they said, and that if you were in the Chammy group you were given a book and it was totally off limits to screws or even the governor. Nobody could touch it, nobody could read it. Of course I didn't believe that. It would be unnatural for a screw to pass up anything in your possession when you were searched, without opening it. I don't even blame them: it's female nosiness. If I saw something on a desk, I'd look. But I did believe them about his kindness and intelligence: prisoners know when somebody is real." (She had always believed that Chammy, no doubt by association of psychiatrists with Freud, was Austrian and Jewish, and she told me how much she had liked his 'foreign accent.' I had to disabuse her of this idea, for despite his distinguished English origins, Dr. Chamarette has no discernible accent of class or region and is a devout Christian. In the sitting room of his light and airy small house in Lancashire, the Bible was not only close to hand but much in his mind when we talked.)

"But the MO, through whom I had to apply, always said no," Mary continued. "He said what did I want with a psychiatrist? And that he knew all about me and that all I wanted was to drive the group *and* the psychiatrist mad, like I was driving all of them mad, and that there was nothing wrong with me that required a psychiatrist and if there had been I would have asked to see Dr. One-to-One ["an old goat they sent the suicides to," she told me in an aside] and why hadn't I done *that* and the answer was that I was having them on as I had done from the moment I came through the Styal gates." She drew a deep breath. "That's how it went, but finally, after more than two years, he probably got sick of me and said, 'All right then, go on, go and drive him mad.'"

"Yes, I knew she was trying to get in," Chammy said, "and the others canvassed for her. They kept saying, 'Can't you do something to get May in?' But I couldn't. She had to be referred."

Did you consider her to be popular among the inmates? I asked.

"I don't think 'popular' is the word. She was a personality. She was important to people. And no, I don't think it is correct to say that people thought she was 'funny' or even 'fun.' She was not at all a comedian. She was very intelligent, very articulate, markedly superior to most of the female officers, and she could argue people's cases when they got into trouble. The prisoners would tell her things—she was very trustworthy, they knew—and often said that she would never 'grass' on them. They may well have told her their most intimate problems." He laughed. "I think she did see herself as a kind of psychologist. She certainly had great talent for it. I suspect she knew a great deal about the lives of a great many people which she never passed on to anyone else."

What was the routine about somebody joining the group? I asked.

"I'd get a notification from the governor via the MO that so-and-so was going to join, though it did, of course, depend on my having space: I had limited the group to eight, though at times I agreed to go up to twelve, splitting them into two working groups. Yes, of course I accepted her and was interested in her. Not at all because she was particularly high-profile or because of her particular offense: there were many women there who had committed quite horrifying offenses, and, don't forget, I knew nothing about her background. Nor, as I was to find out, did anybody else. I went carefully through her file before she came, but there was nothing in there except the court case, a few pages of police reports, a short reference to her first referral—the five years at Red Bank—but no details about that either and no social reports nor any psychiatric evaluations whatsoever."

(Pat Royston, who has access to Mary's original case file, confirms that there were no social reports on Mary prior to or as a result of her arrest in 1968.)

Was that different from other case files? I asked Dr. Chamarette.

"All I can say about that is that some case files certainly had that kind of background information and I was surprised that hers didn't. But I was much more surprised when, soon after that, I read your first book and saw at least some of the things that had been going on in her childhood: then I couldn't understand at all why her file should have been so ... so limited. How could there have been no social inquiry at all? How could they not have known any of these things?"

Why was Mary prevented for two years from joining your group? I asked.

"I think Styal had no idea of May being amenable to any kind of treatment. They didn't think it cost-effective. Eric, the MO, would have said, 'She'll only be skiving'—which was probably true, but it wouldn't have mattered to me—and that anyway I had my full complement and I couldn't handle more."

So what changed their minds?

"[It was] partly because May went on and on about it, but also, and

May would find this hard to believe, I think Molly Morgan exerted some influence . . ."

So the governor *was* interested in her?

"Oh yes," he said. "I think so. She was a very good governor, you know, came up through the ranks, was young, energetic, very fair. Of course, the prisoners wouldn't have thought that: you had to be a pretty tough character to do that job. But the staff certainly did. I can't tell you how interested she was in May. Probably not as intensely as May thought—there were an awful lot of women there who were very, very difficult to handle. But knowing Molly Morgan, I think she would not have been unaware or unaffected by May's extreme youth when she came. Nobody could have been not interested in her."

"Dr. Chammy was like Heidi's grandfather," Mary said. "His group met in a separate block on Thursday afternoons and I was quite surprised when I went the first time because we were all searched, going in and then again going out. I couldn't really understand why. Did they distrust *him?* I never found out, but I finally decided it was just their usual need to show control.

"There were about ten of us. When I walked in, he took my hand and held on, or wanted to hold on, to it while he said hello, but I pulled it away. It's, you know, a dyke thing, not to hold hands with a man. Anyway, he didn't make a big deal about it or anything, he just said, 'Hello, May, is that how you like to be called?' And then he told a story about a tree, I can't remember what it was, and then he laughed and everyone started laughing and suddenly he banged the table and everyone stopped laughing. I thought that was amazing. It was control, but his kind of control, which the whole group accepted—no, not just accepted, *wanted,* and it was good, very good. I thought I was going to be skeptical of him, like, you know, I was of everybody, but I found I wasn't. I trusted him. And I realized very soon that he knew I was more aware . . . of people . . . It did me a lot of good to see that someone saw me . . . differently. Later I got some wonderful letters from him in which he talked about some of the girls. That, too, was good for me. He reminded me, you know, that it happened, that he knew I . . . understood people, and that he trusted me as I trusted him."

Did Mary talk to you about herself in Styal? I asked Chammy.

"There was very little chance for any one-to-one," he said. "And it wasn't intended to be that: it was group therapy. But of course, talking about themselves is to a large degree what people do in this sort of group work. A lot of things emerge."

Mary's main involvement during the time he knew her there, he said, was with the problems of the other women. "Her way of thinking about them—the way, if you like, she 'analyzed' them [he emphasized the word]—was quite feminine, but her way of *being*, of speaking and how she carried herself, was quite extraordinarily masculine. She went a long way toward persuading her world that she was masculine." She didn't walk like a woman, he said. "She strutted. She told us that she had worked for three months for Burton's the tailor as a man, in men's clothes, and making up as if she had stubble on her face."

But did anybody believe that? I asked. Did *you* believe it? After all, this was an eighteen-year-old who had been under detention since she was eleven.

"Of course I knew she fantasized and probably at least some of the others did too. But it wasn't my function ever to appear to doubt them: the whole point of the exercise is for them to say whatever they like in the way they like. In May's case, this is what she needed to say, both publicly and privately. It supported her Styal persona, because there too she 'dressed up,' if you like. She rolled up stockings in the shape of male genitals and she pointed this out to me in class. I think she wore these all the time, but perhaps not as obviously, not as provocatively in front of the staff, but they saw it, I know they did, and somehow they left her to it."

"What I mainly remember about her," said Margaret Kenyon, "were those very blue eyes and that dark curly hair and that politeness of hers: she really was more like a boarding-school girl than a prisoner. Still, I'd heard all these stories about her, you know, how angry she could be, how hard . . . They said she had eyes like flint. I don't know that I felt that, the only time I really had something to do with her. It was when she was going to be transferred to Askham Grange; when girls were about to go to open prison we'd always outfit them, you know, so I was detailed to take her out shopping for undies, you know, and whatever else she might need. She was OK, polite as ever and again a bit like a child out on the town, until we got to the lingerie section at Marks and Spencers and she said . . . sort of spitting out the words . . . 'What are we doing here?' I said we were going to buy her some knickers.

" 'Knickers?' she said with contempt. 'I don't wear knickers; I wear Y-fronts,' and for the next few minutes railed at me in that sharp and sharply enunciating little voice of hers, with the lady shoppers watching us with their eyes popping out. I'm not sure Marks and Spencers had ever seen anything like it.

" 'Y-fronts,' she dictated, 'or I'll run away.' I'm sure she thought I'd fold up and give in, but she didn't know the half of it. 'Go on,' I said. 'Run.' Of course, I haven't a clue what I would have done if she had— I'm sure she was faster than I; anyway, she looked like it. But she didn't run."

And what did you buy? I asked.

"Knickers," Margaret said, and giggled.

Had Dr. Chamarette ever told Molly Morgan that he thought she needed help?

"I don't think I did," he said, a little sadly. "I had some very serious cases there, one girl, for instance, who had stabbed her husband seventeen times, one woman who killed her five year-old daughter . . . Oh, so many very, very complicated women. By comparison, May's problems, strange as it may seem, were almost minor. You mustn't forget either that by the time I met her she was no longer sixteen—she was almost nineteen. It is outrageous that she was sent there at sixteen—it is outrageous that anyone so young is sent to such a prison at all. And with hindsight, it is true, I would have taken a stronger stand about her needs had I known her earlier and more about her background, but as you know, I didn't. Nobody did."

The women in the group often talked about their crimes and their feelings about them, he said. "And one day one of the girls did ask May about what she had done. And she said that she had picked little Martin up by his ears, just to show her friend Norma how strong she was, and that he slipped out of her hands and fell and that that was how he died. And she added that she had picked Norma up that way, too, and other children."

Had she mentioned the other child, Brian? I asked, and he shook his head. "She never mentioned him and she certainly represented Martin's death as an accident."

Did you believe this? I asked, and he shrugged. "Not really," he said. "But on the other hand, nor did I think that as a ten- or eleven-year-old her intention had been to 'murder' or even to 'kill.'" He shook his head. "It is quite incredible," he said, "that no one tried until now to help her confront herself. It shows how little we value human beings."

Did you ever tell Chammy about what happened to you when you were a small child? I asked Mary.

"Not in so many words, no, I didn't," she said. "Not in the group. He and I came to an agreement, though, about the book . . . you know, the one the screws were not supposed to read but I *knew* they would anyway. So he and I agreed he'd give me two books: in one of them, the one I carried in and out like everybody else in the group, I wrote, so to speak, for the screws . . . sort of nothing, you know, like, 'I hate Mrs. Jones' or whatever. But the second one he gave me, I wrote in during the sessions, thoughts and poetry and what have you, and then gave it to him and he held on to it for me and brought it back every Thursday. And in there I think I did perhaps write some stuff. Maybe he still has it, he could show it to you."

"She has forgotten," Chammy said. "She wrote to me and asked me to send it to the governor of Askham Grange [her last prison]. I wrote back and asked her whether she was sure she wanted me to do that and she said yes, she did, she wanted him to know her, so I sent it off."

Did you write about your mother in that second book? I asked Mary.

"Oh no," she said at once. "Not about my mother. I couldn't have. I told you: she was blameless. She had to be blameless."

"Well, she did actually talk about her mother," Chammy said, "but only basically in the past tense, to say that her mother had been inadequate, drug- or alcohol-addicted, a prostitute, and that she'd always gone to Glasgow."

Had she expressed hate or love for her mother? Or fear?

"I don't recall her doing that," he said. "The one word that remains in my mind is 'inadequate,' and that she said she had had no mothering whatsoever."

He did not remember her mentioning her "dad," Billy, nor did he see his name in her file.

"That's really strange," Mary said, "because one of the few times I did talk to Chammy on my own, just for a few moments, he told me something that upset me a great deal. He asked me who would I like to see most walk through the door. And I said, 'My dad, because he hasn't been to see me even once since I came to Styal.' And he said, 'Which dad?' And I said, 'Well, not Georgie [Betty's second husband], that's my stepdad.' And he said, 'No, I know, but Billy isn't your father, either.' And I just ... well, he hadn't said it to hurt me , . . he thought I knew, you see, he told me the governor knew, and then I thought everyone knew, and I wondered did Mr. Dixon know ... well, then I went a bit funky, you know, confused, angry, up the wall, and much later well, years later, you know, I asked Billy and he says, 'Who says I'm not your father? Of course I'm your bloody father.' And he is, of course he is. But then, also, he isn't ... Not my biological father. But nobody will tell me who is."

Soon afterwards she had asked her mother about it. "When my mother came on her next visit—it wasn't long after, and by that time I'd decided it had to be something, you know, really awful—I said, 'Tell me, just tell me. Look,' I said, 'was it your father? Was it your brother? Is that why I became what I became?'"

And Betty had answered very quietly: "You are the devil's spawn," she said. "That's what you are." And then she had got up, Mary said, and left.

. . .

A long letter Mary wrote to Carole and Ben in 1976 is indicative of the changes being wrought in her at that time.

> At long last a reply to your letter, it cheered me up ... I had some bad news from home. There's been a car crash on the motorway and George is in hospital. Mum is ill which is the cause of the delay in my letter-writing.
>
> Well, not much news. Haven't heard anything about parole yet. I need you so very much lately. I know it's very wrong and weak. I don't like weakness of character but I feel myself falling into depths of despondence and non-identity. I try to talk, to relate, but having built up a barrier around myself for such a long time I guess people think I have an ulterior motive when I try to break it down. I don't know, things just don't seem to be going right at all. I haven't given up hope, just given up hoping. It's strange, because I lie awake at night and try to think, picture faces, to put things in perspective, but nothing comes, just a sort of emptiness. Blackness, like I feel mindless. I'm writing this to you because I know you understand, because you know me so very well.
>
> Also the absolute enormity of my crime has suddenly dawned on me, that I have actually taken a life. I just cannot bear to hardly think of it. I know it was a very long time ago, a lot of tears have been shed, but bitterness has grown too. But I know too in my heart of hearts that I couldn't do such an awful thing on purpose. I can't remember exactly what happened. The other girl who was charged with me, I don't feel bitter towards her, I feel very very sad, because she knows that what happened wasn't meant in my case. I cannot find it in my heart to forgive her, because she has for nine years been walking free while I'm inside.
>
> I just want someone to talk to, I want to be 'me' again, Ben. All this bottling up of emotions doesn't do anyone any good.

But it is very difficult here for a number of reasons. I can't turn to drugs as the doctor doesn't approve. Also I don't want it to get to the Home Office that I cannot go without drugs, so I'm stuck. I'm not feeling sorry for myself, just very frustrated and I suppose lonely. Do you ever get the feeling of being scared and not knowing what to do? That's how I am, frightened but I don't know what of. I want to be alone, but I'm scared of being left alone. Very hard to explain.

I'm trying so hard to be good, for a number of reasons. I have a new AG [assistant governor] and she's been very straight and fair with me: she reminds me of Mr. P. in her way. I'm no angel, not by a long stretch of the imagination, but slowly and surely I think I'm finally learning to believe in people again. It's taken me a long time to reach this point. I just lost all faith in mankind, but I shall eventually be restored. I get into trouble here and there but nothing very serious. At the moment I'm working on the painting party. I enjoy the work painting the hot-houses in the nick and there are only six girls, so I'm not being smothered by people, which I found was happening to me in the workrooms. I was getting really paranoid. And I'm the invincible Mac [she had now altered the spelling of her name to the Scottish "Mae"], the one who could walk through life without being affected by it, who said 'prison won't change me.' It has changed me, but in what way it's hard to say, for better or for worse. Basically it has hardened me, and at the same softened me. I feel harder, in that I can accept knock-backs and let-downs as part of the day, but softer because maybe I have an insight into how others feel, like I really feel . . . getting involved with some people makes one softer.

You know, I got involved with a girl in here . . . she's gone now. To me she was a very beautiful person. The side of herself she let me see was. For a while I was very happy until she went home, that finished it. After all this time of seeing people come and go, one would think it wouldn't be too bad, but it cut me up so much, because I loved her, I really loved ... had a genuine affection for that girl. And now, she's just going to be another memory, at the moment a painful one, for I just can't get used to the idea that I ought to forget. She's done a lot for my mind, she made me want to be alive and happy. I guess I'll get over her in time—it's the in-between stage that hurts so much. I've kept the letters from her to me. Some were just pretty ordinary, but she's such an honest person, so good for me. Something she said to me once almost made me cry. The day before she went home she said 'If there was one thing in this world I could do, I'd give you back your childhood, Mae.' That she could say something like that was just typical of her consideration, her depth of feeling. Usually I can dismiss nick friendships with the vagueness they deserve, but this was so different. It was more than a friendship.

Well, I really must close. Thanks for being you, just standing there and listening. I can't say I feel like a new woman now, but I know you'll receive the feelings I've been trying to portray and write back to me. So my friends, I shall close now. Along with all my love and thoughts, and smile sweetly upon your cactus for they have not seen the sun. Forgive those who torment you, for they have not travelled far in realms of understanding. My friend told me that. Love as always, Mae

Defiance

When Mary arranged for me to see Chammy and the G.s, she said I could tell them anything; she trusted them absolutely, and she'd given me a note for the G.s and one for Chammy, to say that they could tell me anything too and show me any letters or poems of hers they might have.

With the amazing Chammy I talked mostly about Styal and about how an ideal system, capable of recognizing the difference between a seriously disturbed child and an "evil" or "criminal" personality, would have handled a child such as Mary. The very first time I talked to him, on the telephone, he quite rightly corrected me when I told him that Mary was only just beginning to confront the reality of having murdered two children. "Not murder," he said. "She killed. And it is terrible that this eleven-year-old child killed. But for anyone working with May, the difference between these two terms is absolutely essential to always keep in mind."

In the case of a child such as Mary, he said, "The very first thing that should have been done, instead of punitive incarceration, would have been to find someone who could have created a relationship of trust with her. Yes, it would have been a desperately difficult task, which is why all those psychiatrists you spoke to during and after her trial said they wouldn't have been able to take it on: it would have demanded a huge commitment. Because of *course* the answer to her terrible troubles was—perhaps still is—her mother. So do you see what such a therapist would have been asking her to do, a child only just eleven years old? He would have had to ask her to betray her mother, the deepest bond there is. Of course, her mother had broken this bond, almost since the child's birth, but as you are discovering, this is precisely what May, in order to function at all, has had to hide from herself for—what is it now?—more than thirty years. And anyone who treats such a child would have to help her abandon that hiding place.

"When I was starting," he said, "analysis—which meant peeling away the layers—was de rigueur. It is true that this is different now and many of the new methods of therapy work." But the treatment of severely disturbed children, he feels, allows few shortcuts: "The maxim 'the younger the sapling, the easier to train' still applies," he said. "But it is true that this demands enormous energy, enormous faith, and, if it is to be properly done (and as we can see from what was done with May in the surely well-meaning Red Bank, there is no point in *not* doing it properly), enormous resources. I cannot tell you," he said, "how completely I stand behind you in your effort with this book to effect changes in the system both as regards how children who commit crimes are tried and how they are dealt with afterwards."

Unfortunately, he said, the fact that in the long run it is infinitely more cost-effective to find out what has gone wrong in a child's life and put it right before such a child turns into an antisocial adult is only very, very slowly entering the official minds.

"The whole experience of May's life," he said, "proves the crying need of children in trouble for—yes, therapy—but more than that: for the will to believe in them, for the will to believe ..." He stopped, watching my face for signs of skepticism as I noticed his hand lying, as if by chance, on the Bible. "Don't worry," he said, laughing, "I won't preach. The will to believe," he then repeated, "in the capacity of the individual human being, however young, to overcome impossible odds.

The will to believe," he said more quietly, "in the intrinsic goodness of the child."

I spent many rich hours with Carole and Ben G., who have devoted their working lives to helping children such as Mary, but I was surprised to find that it had been fourteen years since they had been in contact with her. "When she phoned us now," Carole said, still sounding surprised, "it was out of the blue."

"How can I explain this?" Ben said. "On the face of it, it seems so wrong not to have kept in touch with her." In his career there have probably by now been some five hundred children with similar problems—between him and Carole, nearer a thousand. "All we can do," he said, "is to give our best while we are with them and hope against hope that whatever they are going on to they will continue to benefit from that."

"You are bringing us up against a moral issue we have pondered together innumerable times," Carole said. "But we have had to consider our self-preservation, our home, our daughter, everything that's vitally important to us."

"It may sound like a cop-out," Ben said, "but it is in fact why we switched away from residential work with such children: the intensity of it became impossible if you were going to have a life of your own, a family. In order to keep your sanity, you have to learn to shut off, to turn the key, to walk away and say: 'Right, that's me, that's us, it is our life, too.'"

"But that letter of May's can make one cry," Carole said. "It's very revealing, though, isn't it? You can almost hear her thinking about her need to be alone and yet not alone; about that beautiful girl, Alicia; about how feeling love is making her softer ... And perhaps as a result of this and because of her very first contact with a *real* psychiatrist, one who obviously remained a human being, her confronting for the first time the enormity of her crime." (What Carole meant by a "real" psychiatrist— contrary to all those perfectly real psychiatrists whose task was to evaluate Mary for the benefit of the Home Office—is one who, like Chammy, even in group therapy sets out to treat people.)

I told them what Mary, in her lucid Red Bank voice, had said to me about Alicia and the curious emotional morality she applied to her relationship with her: that she had loved her so much they lay on a bed together sometimes and cuddled—"We held each other," she said—but she did not have sex with her. "I wanted to, but it wouldn't have been right," she said. "She was going to leave. She was going to have a normal life. I couldn't be . . . I had to *not* be . . . part of it that way, not even as a memory for her." That selfless view seemed to me a kind of victory. However, as I told Carole and Ben, despite her determination not to become institutionalized at Styal, though appearing outwardly to achieve this goal, inwardly—perhaps inevitably—she had succumbed.

"What happened at Styal," she said, "is that every twelve months, or maybe it's eighteen, I hardly know anymore, they review your case and then you go before the LRC—the Local Review Committee—composed of, you know, upstanding members of the community like a magistrate or a retired judge or doctor or what have you. When they see you, they would have looked at the so-called six-monthly progress reports to which all the POs contribute—they write reports on each of us daily, can you imagine it? They used to threaten us with that. And then the governor of governors from the Home Office, Madam Perry it was for me, would ask you inane questions, like did I know the price of bread?—How the hell would I know the price of bread?—[and] what did I intend to do, what was I going to do when I got out? Totally idiotic given that I wasn't being trained to do anything. I wasn't allowed to take vocational courses, and I didn't have a hope in hell to study for anything I might *want* to do, such as be a vet, study biology, chemistry, psychology, because the law says—and I knew it—that anyone released on license is not and will never be allowed to work with *people*. So what's the point?"

But wasn't it possible to *talk* to these people on the review committee? I said to her. Couldn't you explain your interests and *ask* to be allowed to study? God knows, you were articulate enough.

She told me patiently it was the "What's the point?" I didn't understand. If in Red Bank she had learned to be "articulate," as I put it, in Styal she had been virtually forced to unlearn all that. "Red Bank took me out of my environment and replaced it with something I came to accept as better. But Styal put me right back into a four-letter word environment. I'm not saying that's how everybody in Newcastle or Scotswood spoke, but *my* world did and so did what became *my* world at Styal—everything reduced to 'fuck this,' 'fuck that.' You'd have to be incredibly strong—much stronger than I was—to maintain verbal opposition rather than give in and return to what had been, after all, the familiar language of your childhood. Oh, sometimes one or another friend and I agreed to try to stop all the effing and blinding, which meant that every *word* you said contained the fuck addition, for instance, 'hospifuckingtal' ... I mean, can one believe it? But that's what it was and ... [here again she made that strange quick switch from memory to evaluation] ... language does affect behavior rather than the other way round. I see it in people who are now the age I was then, in films, in the streets—they don't speak as they behave, they behave as they speak, one follows the other. And what I came to understand and to accept in Styal was that while I could rebel against the *system* and for a long time take strength from that rebellion, I couldn't remain, or perhaps pretend to be, a socially different person from those around me, who were ... who *had to* become my friends."

Red Bank's acceptance of Mary as an individual, and her adoption of the "difference" in social attitudes as a proper and happier way of life, had given her for the first time a sense of self-worth. Her enforced removal from this new way of life back into the world she had learned to reject led her down a path from what she called honest rebellion to "con" resistance and finally—setting her up, as we will see, for the ultimate kind of prison exploitation as a young, attractive woman by a man in authority—to the weary "What's the point?" of the institutionalized prisoner.

She knew perfectly well—she thought—that there would be no hope of parole for her for years. "So all these review committees were nothing except opportunities for boards to feel important," she said. "And I was sick of it. And I finally decided I wasn't going to any of the LRCs any more. Styal was going to be my life and I didn't want their bloody release. Why?" she repeated my question. "That's like me asking you why don't you want to live on Mars."

And she told me about the day in 1977 when she was on a painting detail and they called her to attend the LRC and she said she was damned if she'd go. "Miss Kendall came and I said, 'No, no, no. I'm not going to eat any carrots. I'm not a donkey . . .' And she took me by the ear and dragged me, paint-covered as I was, to the parole hearing. 'If you think I'm spending the rest of my service here with you,' she said, 'you've got another think coming. In with you,' and she opened the door and pushed me into the room, paint and all."

The system, as we have seen, is concerned, on the face of it, with protecting the public while being humane toward the prisoners. Inevitably, however, given the number of prisoners involved, the extent to which it can be adapted to their individual personalities is limited. By mid-1978, ten years after Mary had committed the crimes for which she was sentenced, the authorities realized a first move had to be made toward her release. What they didn't—indeed, as we can see now, couldn't—know was that her apparent compliance to discipline only thinly covered not only intellectual frustration—which they recognized and rather naïvely hoped to alleviate by moving her from one day to the next into a more stimulating and demanding environment—but profound emotional confusion and resentment.

It was two days after her paint-spattered appearance before the Local Review Committee that the governor called her in and told her she was being sent to Moor Court in Staffordshire the next day. (The reason for not warning Mary of any moves in advance was the authorities' knowledge of her mother's habitual indiscretions to the press.) "Miss

Fowler," said Mary, "who was there too, said that it was a great step forward.

"Oh yes, I knew it was an open prison," she said. "One knows all those things. I can tell you about every prison in the country. I told Miss Fowler I didn't want to go. If they'd said Holloway or Durham I would have been quite happy. But I didn't even have my ERD [expected release date] and I wasn't twenty-one yet, so I knew I couldn't get it. So I didn't want to be in an open prison. It wasn't a 'step forward' as she said. It was pure cruelty. My feeling was that Styal was my life, my way of life, and being sent to an open prison was like being sent to prison, because, you see, you are *more* in prison when it's open."

You mean you were afraid of Moor Court because it was open? I asked.

"It wasn't a question of being afraid," she said quickly; she was not to be thought afraid of anything, ever. "It was an unnecessary process because either way I didn't want to be released; the pressure to run away would be too great. Anyway"—she changed tack—"I didn't want to leave Diane. Well, whatever . . . Of course I had to go. I don't remember the date, but I know I still had my birthday at Styal: I remember because Diane baked me a cake and lots of the girls gave me presents. Before I left, Diane and I wrote together to Madam Perry at the Home Office appealing for permission to write to each other. We didn't think they'd give it, but they did."

She arrived at Moor Court in June 1977. "A seventeenth-century manor house," she said. "Ridiculous for a prison." But she found she knew a lot of the girls there and all of them seemed to know about her—principally about her position as a "butch." But in contrast to Styal, this aspect of her "identity" appears to have been avoided rather than welcomed. "It was a different world," she said. "There were more short-timers than lifers there, and what everybody wanted was their boyfriends, their men."

At Moor Court, she said, lifers and short-timers were not separated.

"It was the first time I was with nineteen-year-olds who talked about nightclubs, boyfriends, dressing up and going out, getting drunk, having a laugh—you know, strobe lights and all kinds of things I'd never seen."

The prison, set in a valley among the hills of Staffordshire, was very pretty, she said, too pretty for its purpose. "It was a beautiful building with winding stairs and lovely views of fields and trees. They had very comfortable dormitories, about a hundred beds, four to a room, with chintzy curtains, nice furniture, sitting rooms with armchairs, a dining room where pretty wooden tables were laid for meals and food prepared by cooks. It's a waste as a prison," she said. "Just think what most of the people there are going back to: high-rise flats, two-up-two-downstairs houses. It's a disgrace to use such beautiful places for people who scar the wood. Prison is prison, you know—I don't mean it in a punitive way, but it ought not to set unrealistic ideals. Red Bank was pleasant enough, with colors on the walls and all that, but even so, it was institutional. Because it was for boys up to eighteen it had a fish tank, but it wasn't artificially homey or cozy and I think that's right. Styal was a horror, and that's right too. Moor Court, you'd have to be a millionaire to live somewhere like that: it sets unrealistic standards, it leaves people with a feeling of discontentment, feeling they are better off in prison than outside."

But if you are in a place like this for years, does it not create different standards in you that you might aspire to, even on a less extreme level? I asked.

"Yes," she said. "But the sad thing is that, unless you have inner resources to meet those standards, all I can see and saw it doing is creating very unhappy people."

Miss Leichner was the governor of Moor Court. "There was nothing wrong with her," Mary said. "She was a nice woman and I liked her and I told her the moment I met her that I didn't want to be there but wanted to stay in Styal, that I didn't want to be released, and that I would run away. It was all I could do, be honest with her, give her fair warning."

What did Miss Leichner say?

"What could she say? She said I should give it a fair try. That at Moor Court 'open' meant open: that my being moved to an open prison meant that my case would be reviewed regularly by the Parole Board and release was now a practical possibility within two or three years. She said it all depended on me, that I had been living in enclosed conditions for ten years and that I now had to find out whether I could withstand the pressure of being put on trust. Because, she said again, 'Open here is open: you can go for walks, you can go and lie in the grass, you can be alone or be with others. The only thing you can't do is go outside the prison perimeters. What we are doing is requiring you to make your own decisions.' Did I understand this?

"Well, I nodded but I didn't understand a thing except that they were asking the impossible of me and I didn't want it. I couldn't do it. How could I suddenly without, you know, any, any . . ."

Bridge? I asked.

"Yes," she said, sounding grateful. "Bridge. How without any bridge could I make my own decisions—and not just any decision, like to be obedient or disobedient, which I had made a hundred times, but the decision whether to be in prison or free, when for years I had been locked in every night of my life?

"Miss Leichner finally said I was to take an office management course, typing and all that, to equip me for a job. Well, I'd already touch-typed since Red Bank. Mr. Dixon put me on a course for that quite early." She sounded angry. "Wouldn't you think they'd have known that? They didn't care, you see: they didn't know anything about *me* because they didn't care about me."

But surely there was something you could accept to learn? Were there no books again, nothing for your mind?

"They had what you'd call 'inspirational books.' I was so desperate I read some of those. I remember there was one called *From Prison to Praise*. So after a few weeks of that I thought, If this guy can do it, so can I. And so I went into the chapel—they had a nice chapel—and threw myself on the floor and said: 'Please let me feel something.' "

And you didn't?

"Nothing," she said. "All I felt was unused, dead, like a double-decker bus could drive through my stomach. All I wanted was to *feel*, just feel . . . Maybe it was the pills," she said.

At Moor Court almost everybody was on medication, she told me, and though in Styal she and the medical officers between them had largely managed to keep her off drugs, at Moor Court she finally gave in to them.

"It wasn't long, a few weeks, I think, I was called in to see Miss Leichner and she said the Parole Board had reviewed my case and at that stage I'd been refused a pre-release date. She said it was normal, that it often happened, but I thought it was quite abnormal. People were leaving every day, every *day*, among them lifers who . . . Oh, I wasn't judging or comparing, but they had been grown-up when they did what they did. I was a child.

"Miss Leichner said my behavior had to improve. I had to finish the typing course and then they'd review me again. But for me it was a kind of end: it was all pointless; I was quite ready to never be released. If I ever was, what was I going to do? Where would I fit in? I couldn't see myself with normal people. I felt I could no longer relate to people who had ordinary lives like Mr. P.'s daughter at Red Bank with whom I'd made friends. I remember thinking, what would I say to her now, even if she asked me a little thing like doing some dressmaking with her, or go out shopping, or have lunch in a restaurant . . . What would I *do*?

"It was after that that I was given the first medication, Hemeneverin, a knockout drug [a very heavy tranquilizer]; they give it to alcoholics, drug addicts. I knew it was just a question of time before I ran off. I knew what the publicity, the repercussions would be if I did, so I asked for this drug—I wanted to be blitzed. I told the MO, 'I'm a lifer, I've been transferred, I hate it, and I'll run away.' So he said, 'You'll have a pint of milk a day and I'll give you something that will help you sleep and calm you down.'" Mary's account of taking the drug was disjointed. "I took it and it knocked me out. I walked away and became ravenously hungry and then I remember I was sitting at the typewriter and listening to music when I should have been listening to somebody's voice, and there were Jerry and Trudi walking me around. As soon as I sat down again I went to sleep. I took it," she said vaguely, "I think for a couple of days."

I would find the same vagueness when I tried to talk to her about her present-day drug consumption. I have no doubt whatever that she was given considerably more drugs in prison than she now wants to admit, no doubt either that this kind of conditioning of prisoners to strong painkillers or tranquilizers is extremely hard to break free from after release.

It was three months after she arrived at Moor Court, in September 1977, that Mary did what she had told the governor on her arrival she would do. "It wasn't very difficult," she said. "We just jumped over a fence and headed off over the fields." A few days before, she had started talking to a girl she hadn't known before. "Her name was Annette and she was just a short-timer—you know, a young girl who had been silly and now wanted to go home. She said she was fed up and I said I hated it and was going to run off. And she said, 'Don't be silly, you don't have very long to go.' But I said I had to get out, and she said, 'OK then, I'll go with you.'"

Mary said that at the time she probably saw herself as a great organizer of escapes: she went around to a few friends and asked whether she could have this or that, a pair of jeans here, some shoes with six-inch platforms there, "just so I wouldn't be seen in my things 'outside.' And I told them as far as they were concerned I stole them. They all told me not to be stupid but I was beyond all that. It would have taken an earthquake to stop me."

They planned the escape for Sunday, when visiting hours started at 1:30 P.M. with lots of people around walking in the grounds and the next head count was not until 6:00 P.M.

"We got to a road very soon," Mary said. "I had like an Afro hairstyle with twigs in my hair. We got a first lift and this fellow gave me a map, and of course I knew nothing about reading maps and was reading it upside down, and he turned around and said, 'I think I'll drop you ladies off at the first junction.' I think he was local and knew what was what."

The next driver who stopped and asked where they wanted to go said he wasn't going there. It was finally three young men who picked them up. "The police never knew there had been three." Mary still whispered when she said it. "The third one must have suspected something because he told the others to stop, he was out of there. I said OK and never mentioned him when I was later questioned and neither did Annette. The other two, Clive and Keith, said they were going to Blackpool to the fair."

The girls had noticed that the boys had a lot of tattoos, and the conversation got around to prison. The girls finally admitted they were on the run and Mary told them she was doing a life sentence. A little later she told them who she was. "Clive said, 'Christ, I've read a book about you,' and my heart sank, and I said, 'So what are you going to do?' But he said, 'Nothing,' and Annette nudged me and said they'd *want* something, but I didn't care—we were going to the fair. Annette whispered again that they wouldn't pay for us for nothing, they'd expect something in return. But I was hyper-high, euphoric, and later when I was on the big dipper and looked down and saw the fair spread out below me and the sea beyond, I thought, I don't care. If I'm lifted now, at least I will have had this."

By then they'd had a couple of drinks. "Except for Babycham it was the first alcohol I'd ever had and I was drunk as a lord right away. I don't know how I was standing up. We went on to a nightclub till very late and I was the only person dancing, still with the twigs in my hair."

Were you attracted to Clive? I asked her.

"You've got to be kidding," she said. "The guys took us to a B&B on the seafront. They were in one room, Annette and I in the other. That I was drunk is not an excuse, it's a fact. Listen, I'm not a puritan or a prude. But would I give myself away like that? Sex was the last thing on my mind, that is, if I could have had anything on my mind. Sex to me . . . well, you know what sex was to me: in Styal the people I was closest to I didn't have sex with. All I remember is I was in bed and then there was Clive in the bed and I got up and there was blood all over the sheets. I didn't feel anything and I hadn't felt anything, so if that was it, it wasn't much. I was absolutely paralytic."

But you hadn't said no?

She laughed. "It was probably over before I could say no. People may say it's rubbish, that it's just convenient for me to say now I can't remember. But no. I can't remember. The second night—we were at his mum's in Derby by then and she was nice [later, to protect Clive's mother, Mary told police she had never met her]—he had a go and I told him to get off and he did."

Annette had left them by then, and in a coffee bar at breakfast the next morning Mary saw that her escape was all over the front pages. "They'd bought me a big sort of sun-hat the day before and I pulled it down over my face and then the boys went and bought me some other clothes and some hair dye and they took me to the house of a friend of Clive's and I dyed my hair ginger in her bathroom. Clive went out. He said he had to see somebody. Later I found out he'd gone to see this social worker he knew to ask her what he should do."

(I had been asked by the *Sunday Times* to look into Mary's escape and met thirty-one-year-old Clive soon afterwards. I also met the social worker whose advice he had sought. She knew him well and spoke kindly of him. Eventually, with the offers of ridiculous sums of money from the tabloids, he succumbed to temptation and thereby—as Mary no doubt felt—betrayed her, sold her just as her mother had been selling her for years. But my impression was that he was a rather vulnerable young man who had been making a real effort to "go straight" when he bumped into Mary and she had touched some nerve in him—of compassion? of love? I don't know. Certainly the relationship was inappropriate at the time or perhaps at any time. Although Mary, oddly ashamed of what happened in those three days or with whom it happened, now claims the alleged letters from her that he sold to the papers were inventions, some of the phrases and indeed sentiments attributed to her sound very familiar to me.)

"The woman was nice," Mary said about Clive's friend. "She gave me coffee, we chatted, and I played with her kid, who had a monkey that could bend its arms. When Clive came back he said there was a barge I could stay on, and I said no, that I was going to London and he said OK, but we could go for a drive first, and they took me to another café, where there were boats.

"We were there in the car and I saw a policeman ride past on his motorbike and he turned his head, probably to look at the car and, I don't know, something clicked and I said, 'Right, I'm going now,' and Clive said, 'Right, I'll give you a lift to the station but we have to buy something on the way,' and then it was like *Hill Street Blues* and Keith murmured to me, 'He's grassed you up,' and a policeman came over and said to wind the window down on my side, and he said, 'Mary.'

"I said, 'I don't know what . . .' and before I could finish the sentence he took my sunglasses off and put handcuffs on me. I said, 'I don't know what you are talking about, I'm only seventeen . . .' And he said, 'All right, we'll go to the station.'

"And there they found identifying marks on me. You know. It was all on record. And I said, 'Oh, God, what's going to happen to me now?' And the police officer said that they'd been told, and it was announced on the news too, that I wasn't dangerous and that really they hadn't searched the country for me but just put out their usual absconder notice and that they only found me because I was turned in. Even so I just hoped and prayed that no crimes of any description had been committed which could be applied to me."

"We were working in Wiltshire then," said Carole G., "and on Sunday night we heard on the six o'clock news that Mary Bell had escaped." "We were just horrified," Ben said.

"We couldn't believe it," Carole went on. "We didn't even know she'd been moved. We'd had a call some weeks or months before, down in Dorset where we were then, to ask whether we would be prepared to have Mary to stay, to live, we didn't quite understand what they meant: on visits, or when she was released, or what? But our first reaction was that we just *couldn't*, you know. We were working, doing research, living on site [on the grounds of a school].

"But then Ben and I kept asking ourselves whether we couldn't somehow manage after all. So actually we wanted to ring up and talk and find out more. But of course you can't just ring up and get whoever you want. And then in the middle of thinking about that, this happened, and in the early evening we had a call from the police up north to say May had been seen catching a lift south and they had found our letters to her with our address and they wanted to tell us she might be heading our way. Well, we listened to all the newscasts and finally went to bed. We actually had a new dog, an Alsatian, and he suddenly started to bark."

Ben said, "Carole was still pulling on her dressing gown when I opened the door and these cops barged in and got a hold of her and we asked what on earth they thought they were doing and it turned out they thought Carole was May. And when they realized she wasn't, they started searching the place. When they saw there wasn't anything they were OK; they apologized and explained."

"The police in Derby were quite nice, really," Mary said. "I told them that I had intended to go to London and get a job and that after a while, two months or so, I would have rung the Home Office or whoever and said, 'Here I am. I just wanted to prove to you that I could do it.'"

Was that true? I asked. Did you really think it out like that?

She laughed. "Well, not really. I just wanted to party, I think—you know, be normal. But then, sitting in the police cells, with the press, so I was told, surrounding the building, I suddenly felt very old and very tired. Before the night was over I'd be in another cell in some prison or other and there wouldn't be any smiling, understanding policemen, only the furious system I had kicked in the face. And then two screws from Moor Court arrived and told me that now I'd torn it. That it would be years before I'd be out of a high-security wing. 'You silly girl,' one of them said, quite sadly I thought, and asked what the hell I had been up to. And when, I don't know why, I told her, she said, 'Christ, I hope you're not pregnant.' It made me sick to my stomach. I'd never thought of *that*. And then they told me that I was going to Risley, Grisly Risley, as it's known, the most appalling, notorious remand center in England. Never did I think I'd end up there."

It was while working on the *Sunday Times* article after Mary's escape that I spoke to a young woman—I will call her Joan—who had committed a minor offense and was a short-term prisoner at Moor Court when Mary had arrived. Joan was twenty when we met, a pretty girl with a pleasant manner who brought along her one-year-old baby. She had only recently been discharged, but she had not been unhappy during her few months at Moor Court. "It was a holiday camp," she said. "Not bad at all. The only thing that's bad, really bad, is if you have a baby like I had and you were separated from it. That was horrible."

Did she feel prison had taught her a lesson? I asked.

"Oh yes," she said fervently. "Never again."

Had the prisoners been told that Mary would be arriving? I asked her.

"Yes, they had," she said.

Did you know who she was?

Joan laughed. "No, not before she came. I was only nineteen [one year younger than Mary at the time]."

But did the other prisoners talk about Mary, about what she had done? I asked.

"Oh yes, they talked a lot." And there was great excitement, she said, at the prospect of Mary's arrival.

Did you meet her soon after she arrived?

"Yes, right away. She was intelligent, a very intelligent girl. She used to go to the library every week and get out four or five books."

But Joan hadn't liked Mary. "She was different. The staff treated her like somebody different." She had talked a lot about the kid she killed, Joan said, "But she said she'd killed only one of them, not two as was said. And that he was eight years old, just *two* years younger than she was at the time, and that she'd been playing with him in a playground and she'd pushed him down a bank or something . . ." Joan said she'd kept away from Mary because she didn't want to hear about this. It frightened her.

Did Mary have friends? I asked her.

"She was always saying she was so alone, but she wouldn't have had to be. There were nice girls there one could make friends with." She added, with sudden wisdom, "I think she wanted to be alone."

"She was always taking pills," Joan said then. There was no psychiatrist at Moor Court, she said, only a doctor once a week and Mary saw him often. "She had stomachaches and headaches. She was on Valium and another tranquilizer three times a day. And she was always saying she wouldn't stay here, that she'd run away; that she'd *show* them."

By the time Mary arrived at Risley, it was 2:00 A.M. "I was reassured because I knew the reception officer, Miss Ogden, from Styal. 'Oh God, it had to be you, didn't it?' she said and told me to strip. And after ascertaining I had no hair or body lice and supervising me having a bath, they put me in the 'box.' It was a narrow cubicle where there was a plank of wood placed a few feet from the floor for sitting on, but I couldn't stretch my arms out, front or sideways. I think it's the only time in my life I had what I later understood was a panic attack, trembling all over with sweat running down my whole body. But thank God, the 'box' only lasted an hour or so, then a matron or sister, I can't remember which, came and took me to a cell. I was so relieved, I just lay down on the cot and fell deeply asleep."

After all that, her three months at Risley turned out to be relatively benign. "I knew the assistant governor there, Miss Harbottle; she was quite a good egg. She told me in the morning that I would have no 'association' [contact with other prisoners] till I had been seen by the VC [visiting court of magistrates] and that I was to write out a statement to explain my behavior. I made three attempts; the first two were returned to me—the governor said it wasn't good enough. Miss Harbottle said it wasn't going to help me just to write that I'd felt like absconding. 'You have to do something to help them understand you,' she said. So then I wrote the statement you've seen . . ."

This statement, which Mary wrote out on a typewriter, describes both the events of her escape and her reasons for it. It begins:

> Since my parole was turned down in July–August 1977 and I haven't been given any release date I felt rather depressed, since I have seen girls come in and out and I have felt so isolated. I wanted to prove to the authorities that I am stabilised and given the opportunity I could lead a normal life just like anyone else. What happened ten years ago, although all the truth didn't come out in court, is something I will have to live with for the rest of my life and no amount of years in prison is going to erase it from my mind. I took a life, but not in the savage way the press made it out to be. At the age of ten I did not realise the meaning of death. What happened to me could have happened to any other child of my age and circumstances . . . Last week by chance I saw in reception [at Moor Court] a Christmas card from my dad which I had never received and also news that my grandma [Bell] had died. All of these things started to build up and I thought I am shut away and I have never experienced any life. I don't even know what the other girls are talking about when they come in because I have never been anywhere or done anything . . .

She then describes her escape with Annette and their meeting Keith and Clive and her subsequent arrest.

> I . . . told the police that Clive and Keith knew nothing about it. I didn't want them to get into trouble because of me. They showed me that I could be normal and enjoy myself and have a nice time [and] mix with people like anybody else. I am sorry for mucking up their lives because they were just trying to help me. I

am grateful to them both. I am asking now that my case circumstances and situation will be reviewed in a different light and I may be given a chance to live a normal life. Because in these three days I know I can cope with outside life and feel at ease with ordinary people. I only hope the press don't start dragging up all the past and try to make me look a horrible person. Perhaps you don't believe I deserve my freedom, specially after running away, but I don't want to spend the rest of my life in prison. I plead for leniency and hope you can understand it from my side. I am sorry I have created a disturbance but I just wanted to be free. Give me a chance to be so.

Transition

Mary had thought it could be weeks before she would see the visiting court, but it turned out to be just two days. "I was to see the magistrates in the afternoon, but my mother came that morning. She slapped me across the face, knocked me off the chair, and shouted, 'You little slut, don't you think you've dragged us through the gutter enough without this!' I said, 'Sorry,' and she screamed, 'Is that all you can say? Sorry? Are you twisted in the head to do such a thing, making me go through hell, with the police coming to our door . . .' And all about how she had to go down to the police station and how she had been looking for me all over—knowing that I'd make my way to her. And when she hauled out to slap me again I said, 'Don't!' more sharply than I'd spoken to her in years and we just sat, staring at each other.

"What could she have been thinking?" Mary said. "That I had run off to have a good time with *her*? She understood nothing. It wasn't that I wouldn't have gone to her because of what she had done to me when I was little—I never thought of that. No, [it was] because I knew she would have handed me in, that's why. It's true that it's bollocks that I planned to hand myself in after two months or whatever, but certainly I didn't run away to get pregnant. That was the story that went around, so everybody told me later, because that Clive, he made all that money telling the papers that I told him I wanted a baby with him. God . . . *never.*"

The visiting court that afternoon, she said, consisted of "a little old lady who looked as though she belonged to every committee there might be in a rural village," and two men. "I was shaking inside but she was quite nice, really. She said she'd show me leniency as I'd only been gone two days. They gave me twenty-eight days' solitary confinement, loss of privileges [association and cigarettes], and loss of pay [for work]. Also, any further consideration of parole was put off by six months."

She was so depressed and so tired, she said, she hardly minded the solitary confinement, only that the light was kept on all night. "I couldn't sleep and applied to see the SMO [senior medical officer]. That's how I met Dr. Lawson."

She had seen him once, shortly after her arrival at Risley, when he had reassured her about her fears of pregnancy. "He was a fair man and took time to listen. I liked him," she said. But Dr. Lawson said he wouldn't give her sleeping pills or any other drug. He had seen her medical records and was shocked at the number of drugs she'd been given. " 'What do you want to be, girl?' he said. 'A cabbage?' "

"I'd done a lot of thinking by then, specially about what had happened with Clive and what had then appeared in the press, and I told Dr. Lawson that I was a transvestite and would he help me toward a sex change?"

What? I looked at her. Were you mad?

"Well, no and yes. I mean, in reality it was nonsense, but it was something to think about, a road I could follow in my head, you know: the idea of not being me. I knew I wasn't and didn't want to be a man. On the other hand, I didn't want to be me, either. It was just exploring things, using Dr. Lawson as a sounding board. He just listened. I could say all kinds of things to him. I didn't think for a moment I was conning him and I know he didn't think I was trying to manipulate him—it would have been impossible even if I had wanted to. He just let me get it out of my system, which was so kind of him. And then he said that with my prattle about sex change and all that, I was going to the ridiculous, that my brain, with nothing to focus on, was obviously just meandering. 'I salute your intelligence,' he said, 'but what do you want from me?'

"After this stint out and the terrifying fear that I could be pregnant, I said I needed something to aim for, not so much my ERD, which I knew was now far removed, but what I desperately wanted, I said, was to get back to Styal. And he said, 'Right, we'll see what we can do.' And much later I learned that he had written a letter to the Home Office and told them that I was a catastrophe ready to happen, and if they didn't want that, they'd better get me released, the quicker the better."

In fact, three months after her escape, in December 1977, she was told—"to my joy," she said—that she was going back to Styal. "In the next shipment, the governor said, and two days later I found myself in a van on the road back to Cheshire and after a few hours I was back with all my friends."

Given the many weeks Mary talked to me about her seven years in prison, she had virtually nothing to say about the next nine months at Styal. "It was peaceful," she said. "It was home. I was with Diane and I had other good friends. I was quite prepared to stay there, for however long."

Her last letter to Carole and Ben, written in the summer of 1978, shows her state of mind.

> We've had beautiful sunshine up here, it's been tropical. I was on the grass yesterday splashing myself with ice water. When it's like this, it always reminds me of Rimington Park [where Carole and Ben had taken her on an outing from Red Bank five years earlier]. I'd like to return there one day, it'll be like walking back in time . . .

(Years later, she was to take that "walk back in time." "Somebody drove me to Red Bank," she said. "But when we got there, I couldn't even get out of the car. I just looked across at what had been such an important part of my life, by then more than fifteen years before, remembered myself, four foot and some inches high, arriving, remembered Mr. Dixon, and then couldn't stand it. 'Please let's go,' I said, 'please.' " And she never got to Rimington Park.)

The next lines are a sad reminder of what happens to many boys despite benefiting from the comparative excellence of a place such as Red Bank and the influence of a James Dixon:

> I've got some news from abroad. Remember Derek C? I had a letter off him about three weeks ago, he's in Freemantle State Prison serving a ten-year sentence for armed robbery. I nearly fell through the floor. He said on visits they have glass screens and machine guns, and I don't think they have a parole system over there. Also Tommy C. has got five years for snatching wages from the docks. And Ray C. has just got out; he's had an accident and is paralysed from the neck down.

> It is now 9 pm. I got called over to the MO before I could finish writing this. I've been feeling a bit rundown and had a couple of headaches, so have been on a tonic for a couple of days. We had a dance last night; I did my 'John Travolta' a bit . . . exhibitionist to this very day, eh? The deputy governor and a few girls made a fantastic float, a huge papier-mache show, the old woman who had lived in a shoe. The staff kiddies were inside watching from various windows. It won first prize. Well, I've given you the newsy bits.

> I have some not-good news which mounted up to my running away. My granny Bell died, and my dad hasn't been seen in over a year now. I think our P. [Mary's brother, whom she had not seen since she was eleven and he was ten years old] knows where he is but won't say. My old nana McC. is deteriorating in her geriatric home, which really cuts me up. She doesn't remember anyone and lives in a world of her own.

"I phoned my Nana," she told me, "and she didn't recognize me. She thought I was someone else. I said, 'No, no, I'm Mae.' But it meant nothing to her. That was the first time I talked to her in—what is it? Five, six years? And of course, she didn't remember me. It made me feel I didn't exist."

> I feel so helpless not being able to do anything except hope that she feels happy in her own little way. To be honest, it's my da I'm really pining for. I haven't heard from him in years, not a birthday card or anything, and you know how much I love him. Still, worrying won't make anything better. He's well capable of looking after himself.

Except for the Christmas card she was never given and only saw by accident at Moor Court shortly before she ran away, Billy Bell had never communicated with her or been to see her at Styal. Did you ask him why after you were released? I asked. And she shook her head. "I didn't. I hardly saw him. What is there to say after what was, after all, a lifetime?"

> Even though we haven't written for a while I want you both to know that you're never far away from my thoughts. I often think of you and wonder how life is treating you. It is now Thursday. I went to the hairdresser today and had my hair streaked. It looks okay. This afternoon I have been to group therapy so all-in-all it hasn't been a bad day. It's been very warm again today, although we've had some thunder and lightning rain. Probably scorching hot tomorrow. I'm on the garden next week so I'll be in the fresh air, thank God. I hate indoors work, yuck. So monotonous and moronic. Well, I have to go, as I have things to do believe it or not, some washing and ironing waiting for me down there. We're certainly not molly-coddled—I guess we have everything but shoe parade and rifle inspection ha ha. Well, I really have to sign off now, hope to hear from you soon and

until then remain just okay so tara for now, love as always, Mae. Just received your address card, over the moon to hear you're having a baby!

It was nine months after her return to Styal that at 1:00 P.M. on a midweek day— "I'll never forget it," she says—she was called to the governor's office. "When I went in, Miss Fowler and Miss Starr, the two AGs, were there too and Miss Morgan had this big sheet of paper in front of her. She said, 'I think you'd better sit down.' Well, I'd only sat down in her presence once in six years so I said I'd rather stand.

"So she started in that formal voice of hers in which she had adjudicated me a hundred times or whatever: 'The Parole Board have recommended to the Home Secretary that you be—' and then she broke off. 'Oh, the hell with it,' she said. 'You've got your parole: you are going to be released in May next year.' And when I just stood there, stiff as a board, she said: 'Well, you could look a little more pleased. Most people are ecstatic.' And I said—and I know now that was less than gracious because I think she *was* pleased for me, and not only because she was at last getting rid of me— 'Well, it wasn't you who gave it to me, was it?' Nasty, wasn't I?

"I was sent out then and I started to do cartwheels and then I put my wellies back on"—it was about September, she thinks—"and ran as fast as I could to tell Diane, who was in the kitchen of her block. I suddenly felt awful. Here was my best friend and she didn't have her release date and I had. I was looking through the door; I was white. She said, 'What's the matter, have you seen a ghost?' I said, 'I've got my release, next year.' She burst into tears and we stood there, with our arms around each other, and she said, 'We can't cry. You'll be taking me with you. Part of me will be with you, and you'll be here with me.' "

Mary has only once dared to offend against the strict ruling that forbids communication between ex-prisoners. After Diane was released, she once talked to her for an hour on the telephone. "She and I had promised each other that one day we would meet up again. We made a date at Marble Arch on a certain day of the year. But finally I didn't dare.

I think they very much wanted to keep us apart and I couldn't bear to harm her by risking anything."

How would it be if you simply and honestly asked for permission to see her? I asked.

"I've thought of it," she said, "but what if they say no?"

Are you a bit afraid that perhaps *Diane* wants to forget that time, wants not to be remembered?

"No"—again a quick reply—"I'm not, I'm not," and then in a tone of voice that brooked no further discussion: "We are *friends*. I'll never not be her friend; she'll never not be mine."

A lifer's last period of imprisonment before release is quite carefully and thoughtfully worked out. During the final nine months or so at an open prison, lifers first work inside and then outside the grounds. Already they will have had regular contact with a probation officer, but they will also be allocated a prison visitor whose function is to help introduce them back into society. When Mary was moved to Askham Grange, an open prison, she was assigned such a visitor. "In my case it was an Asian girl called Pam," Mary said. "She was a student of sociology, whose boyfriend, Mark, was a male nurse. She was real nice, introduced me to a circle of their friends, took me to Bonfire Night [on Guy Fawkes Day]."

What did she know about you? I asked.

"She knew my name, but we never spoke about anything."

Did you think that was a good system?

"It is in a way, if you get on with your prison visitor; there were others I saw and heard about, well-meaning people but with whom I couldn't have managed."

Didn't you think it was thoughtful of them to give you a young visitor? I asked.

"Yes," she said at once, "it was. I had my difficulties with Pam, too, because I was being forced in a way to slip in and out of character, but then, I probably would have had with anybody. I always felt I had to be respectable with Pam—she was very well-spoken and gentle, very much like the people I had known at Red Bank. And why not? If she hadn't been, she probably wouldn't have offered to do the job. It wasn't the effing and blinding crowd, however kind and familiar with the kind of people who end up in prison they might be, who were going to offer to be, or be accepted as, prison visitors. But it was disconcerting. It was unreal."

Askham Grange was another beautiful old building set on large grounds, she said: "Lots of character, a huge library, real books this time, a big ballroom, several dining rooms, and a mother-and-baby wing. It's one of the few prisons in the country—Holloway is another now, too—where mothers can keep their new babies for a while. Also the food was really good. For breakfast we had cereal, beans on toast, tea, good jam; for lunch, curries, rice, spaghetti, and fruit; then for tea there were salads or pigs in blankets [bread wrapped around sausages], meat pies, or that sort of thing; and later at night we had supper—poached eggs on toast, sandwiches, cocoa. It was all very, very different from the other places. People were nice to each other, you know. I was given things like shampoo and all kinds of nice smelling stuff. And you could do sort of interesting things aside from the obvious cleaning: there was an archaeological dig, there was a duck pond to clean, gardening, helping in the library, but it was all sort of relaxed.

"The governor was known as a 'clean-up governor.' Typically for the place, when I got there I wasn't taken to him, you know, like in handcuffs or whatever. No, he came to the small dining room I'd been taken to to be given a cup of tea and he said, in his Liverpool sort of voice, homey, you know, 'Hello, I hope you'll enjoy your stay,' and he told me I was quite free to go for walks in the grounds whenever I liked outside working hours. 'Just don't go beyond the gate; and be there for the head count at 8:00 p.m.' "

So, did you think again about running away?

"It wasn't that I didn't think, but it was different thinking . . . sort of playing with the idea in my mind. And very soon I realized I no longer imagined, as I had done before, that I was the kind of prisoner, like POWs, you know, who have an obligation to escape. Nor did I feel the *need* to run that I'd had at Moor Court. Perhaps it was simply because I now had my ERD, but though it must have played a part, I don't think that was all of it. It was because the place, the atmosphere, was different: I was ready . . . ready to be me again, you know?" She laughed, half embarrassed. "Like Mr. Dixon had said, to go forth and be the ambassador of Red Bank. Slowly, off came the jeans, on went a skirt . . . it was for myself: I felt that though I didn't seem to have learned anything practical that would be useful for my life, in eleven years of it I had established the fact—for myself quite aside from for others—that I couldn't be pushed around. There was a girl there I got very quickly friendly with called Phoebe, a very educated woman who was in prison for tax evasion, and she said: 'Why do you insist on swearing, speaking the way you do?' She said she could see there was an intelligent person underneath just putting on a front of aggression. 'Why bother?' she said. And though she wasn't quite right, because it was more complicated than she understood to keep the various strands of 'me' apart and going, it was true enough, I had no need to be aggressive anymore."

The prisoners' move from the main part of the prison to a hostel depends not only on their behavior but on when a hostel place becomes available. The move is always combined with the beginning of outside employment in nearby villages or towns. In Mary's case, it happened after she had been at Askham Grange for three months.

"The hostels are a number of bungalows in the grounds," she said. "By comparison to the main house, they are sparsely furnished, you know, more like doctors' waiting rooms, but you do have your own room." The women made breakfast for themselves and in each hostel there was a set evening meal. The prison is dependent upon local employers offering jobs to inmates, "and there aren't that many who are willing," Mary said. "Most girls worked as cleaners in a nearby mental hospital. One souvenir shop did take a few as salesgirls, but mostly it was cleaning and waitressing. That's the job I got, waitressing at St. William's College restaurant. And I had a friend at my hostel, Jane, and we used to meet either during our lunch breaks or after we could get evening passes, which happens after a few weeks if your behavior and work is OK—then you can stay out till 10:00 P.M.—and we'd go to pubs and come back dead drunk. I can't even believe how we managed to stagger in."

What about drugs? I asked.

"Well, as I've said before, everybody smoked hash, in all the prisons I knew. And yes, there were drugs; by comparison to high-security places like Styal where you can see hard drugs have to be rare because prisoners look so healthy, open prisons are notoriously easy to get drugs and drink in. At Askham Grange—and Moor Court, of course—I saw heroin, and certainly people smuggled in bottles. But I didn't see crack or coke and angel dust and all that muck, but then I didn't go in for it and that was known. Even so, I think the papers, at least then, exaggerated their reports of drug use, certainly in women's prisons. Most of the drugs I saw in Askham Grange, and before that in Moor Court, were medicinal—things like Largactil, Librium, Hemeneverin, Halcion, and Nembutal. You could always get those off the doctors, though only short-term." She shrugged. "Of course, that's relative, isn't it? Short term prescriptions over years spell addiction. Still, believe me, you don't think of that if they make life bearable, and they did.

"For me though," she said, "as time went on, my nightmare was the press. I never could understand what they wanted from me."

The media had always been exceptionally aware of Mary, thanks in large part to her mother's initiatives while she was in Red Bank and Styal. But her escape from Moor Court somehow created a determination in the British tabloids and in some foreign magazines, such as the German weekly *Stern*—for a long time the most persistent—to "get" her, not, one must believe, because they were really interested in the more serious aspects of her life but because of whatever sensation, presumably about prison life, she could provide. "It made me very wary of people," she said. "From the time I was allowed outside, people pointed me out to each other and reporters waylaid me. I never knew how and why. On one occasion, one lot pulled my friend Jane into a car, mistaking her for me, and she led them on till she was sure I was safe. Later, some time after my release, I was helped to change identity. But even so, some people found me, and others kept looking."

Was there any supervision in the hostels? I wondered.

"Absolutely. There were sleeping-in officers; they were OK, they were good to me, never got me into trouble even when I was trouble. And when I was *in* trouble, with the press stalking me once they found out I was there and on outside work, they quite often came to my aid by driving me to the job or getting me from there."

There is no doubt that over her years in detention Mary had given way to outbursts of anger, and there was one such incident at Askham Grange. "Something bad happened one day," she said. "There was a girl who was in for child abuse and she started in on me when I jumped a queue in the dining room—all lifers jumped queues; it was accepted, you know, nobody ever said anything. But she did and I suppose I'd just been waiting for a pretext, so I went and beat her up. I broke her thumb and smashed some ribs and she was taken to the hospital wing. Some friends of mine had got me out in the kerfuffle and when the police came we were sitting in the library reading newspapers. But the governor called me to his office and he said that he knew it was me who'd done it and, if he got proof, I was looking at another five to seven years. The girl finally said she didn't know who'd beat her up."

When it came to telling me about the most important or the most difficult thing that happened to her during her time in Askham Grange, Mary was very much of two minds, not about telling me—which she obviously felt a need to do—but about seeing this part of her experience appear in print. I too feel reluctant, and yet the consequence of it at the end of her twelve years of imprisonment for having killed two little boys at eleven was so appalling, I can't see how, in a story of this young woman's life, a mention of it, however brief, can be avoided.

It would appear that while she was at Askham Grange, a respected married man in the community fell in love with her. She was living a somewhat freer life, working days outside the prison in preparation for her approaching release. After various meetings and conversations, her first home leave was being prepared. "When you get close to your release," she said, "they give you some home leaves so you can find out where you want to be. So I applied to go to my mother. I mean there wasn't anywhere else." (Interestingly enough, Veronica, one of Mary's counselors at Red Bank, had written to the Home Office and offered to have her stay but was rejected, probably because, like Mr. Dixon, she was known not to have believed that Mary had killed the boys.)

For this first home leave she was given a pass for three nights. But before she left, the man suggested that she should stay for only two nights with her mother. "He said for me to take a train after that and he would pick me up at Darlington."

You knew what he wanted, I said. Did you want it?

She sat for a bit, saying nothing. "You see, there was the home leave first of all and . . . you know . . . I went under another name, and it was all a thing of shame, you know. My mother made it into shame, blame, guilt, more guilt. She told me right away not to tell anyone, anyone ever, who I was. And at the pub the first night she told her pals that I was her cousin and that my parents were dead, and that's really how it went, both days. She had all these pills, sleeping tablets, Nembutal capsules, and she always gave me those when I couldn't sleep. She fed me drink—as a cure-all for colds and whatever, not to harm me, I think.

"Apparently that first time I had a cold and I got drunk as well, and she and George said I screamed in my sleep . . . Well, no one who has shared a dorm with me has ever heard me scream. I never woke up screaming, and, you know, I didn't believe it. But I remember getting drunk."

I'm surprised George would allow you to get drunk on your home leave, I said to her.

"He was always saying about going easy, always 'Go easy,' but my mother would be slipping me . . . putting more stuff in the drink. Yes, it was whisky and orange."

Why did she do that?

"I don't know, but I got up early in the morning and the first thing I was given was a drink. A whisky. To stop me sniveling. My nose was running and I was shaking. That was the cure."

For her?

"Yes, that's it. She said, 'This will stop it.' Because I was going, 'Tea, tea, I want some tea. I want some milk, I want something. Why is my mouth like this?' No matter what I drank I still felt thirsty. And she said, 'Just hold your nose and drink it.' So you know, I was just so glad when the two days were over and I could leave."

And then were you looking forward to seeing him? Were you excited?

"He had said we were going to a little town on Teesside where there was a nice hotel and I did sort of feel . . . anticipation."

You knew what would happen at this hotel?

"I knew I wasn't going for coffee," she said dryly.

But did you want what was going to happen? I repeated.

"I was . . . sort of . . . in a way excited."

Was he attractive to you?

"I wasn't unwilling. He said he was determined to show me I wasn't a lesbian. It . . . it was a power thing, you know. He knew it, I knew it, and he even said it, that it was . . . that I was like an animal that needed to be trained. He . . . talked a lot."

Oh, Mary, I said. Did you need that? Did you want that?

"I don't know. I don't know now. But, it was different . . . I felt different."

It doesn't sound as if it was a good experience for you.

"Well, it was an experience." She stopped. "I was immature, you know, very immature. It was hard for me not to think of sex as dirty . . ."

Did you think sex dirty with the girls?

"No, that wasn't sex."

Well, it was a kind of sex, wasn't it?

"No, it wasn't, it wasn't. That was different. But men ... it must have been because of my ... what must have been my memories and associations ..."

Did you ever say no to him?

"Oh, that wasn't in it ... And he was nice to me. He was OK. He wasn't bad to me, he was always concerned, protective. Basically he is a good person. You know, people always think of women having problems at a certain age, but they overlook that men go through crises, too, and I think that's what happened to him.

"I think he did love me, or at least fell a bit in love with me. On a second home leave he took me on a trip and we stayed in a hotel in Finchley for four days. But not long afterwards he told his wife and I met her. She was so nice, so honest with me. I couldn't ... you know, I couldn't see him ruin his life and his marriage."

And was that the end of it?

"Yes, he came to say goodbye to me when I was going to be released and he gave me a golden ring."

Unfortunately however, it was not quite the end. Months before this, at the beginning of her pre-release scheme, the senior medical officer at Askham Grange had suggested she should go on the pill. "But I thought that was quite offensive," she said. "I said, 'What are you inferring? That I'm going to go on a rampage, jump on every male I see?' And he said no, that they just offered it to women on pre-release, so that our bodies would get used to it. Well, I thought that was really invading my privacy; also, I was scared of these pills. I'd read of the possible side effects and, you know, I wasn't *planning* anything. And then, when this happened with this man [which was her first contact with a man except for her brief fumble with Clive more than a year and a half before], well, he was in total control and he seemed to know what he was doing. I didn't question ... I didn't think.

"Anyway, then I realized I was pregnant. I had to talk to somebody, so I told the Askham Grange probation officer, who was particularly nice. I lied of course about who it was. And she said I had to think about what I wanted to do, and I had to talk to . . . the man. So I told him. He took me out to lunch at a restaurant and I told him I didn't want to get an abortion, I said I wanted to be pregnant. And he said it was my decision, entirely my decision. He held my hand, sort of stroking it, and he told me not to be worried, that it was entirely up to me . . . He said that if I had the baby of course it would be very difficult . . . but it didn't matter, we would find a means of . . . a way of living.

"Well, you know, it was impossible, wasn't it? So I had the abortion. But if I think that almost the first thing I did after twelve years in prison for killing two babes was to kill the baby in me . . ." Mary was crying now. "But, I mean, it was the only thing to do . . . wasn't it?"

PART FOUR

AFTER PRISON

1980 to 1984

A Try at Life

Mary's accounts of her last nine months at Styal and just under a year at Askham Grange had become strangely quiet, tidy, and sometimes quite gay. The relationship with an adult man, however much some aspects of it upset her now in retrospect and whatever we may think of the ethical aspects of it, was curiously useful for her. "He'd say, 'I love you whatever you've done,' " she said, " 'for all your bad points and your good points.' It was amazing for me." It is certainly significant that it was in the course of this relationship that, for the first time since she was four or five, she ceased to be enuretic. "I couldn't believe it had stopped," she said. "It had been with me forever it seemed, and suddenly it was gone. I was . . . clean."

The inevitable break with this man, her pregnancy, and her release all contributed to what, under any circumstances, would have been a traumatic transition. When she left prison in May 1980, half of her was in a state of euphoria at the idea of freedom, half of her was entirely incapable of looking ahead. "Where was I going? What was I going to do? What . . . what would I do without my friends?" In prison Mary had created a kind of life for herself and, oddly enough, because of her talent for friendship, a sort of feeling of self-value. "It all went," she said.

"Went, I think, as I passed through the gates. Outside I felt . . . I was . . . as in a void."

She had not had a home outside prison; she had not had a friend who was not a prisoner; she had essentially no family, although there were many relatives, good and kind people. "I had been to my Auntie Cath's on my home leave, and they were kind, you know. It wasn't that they didn't welcome me. Uncle Jackie was brilliant, as if I'd just been to the corner shop and come back. But, realistically, I didn't think it was on. I'm different from my family. I had a different life. They were OK with me, but they wouldn't want me around their doorstep. I'm an embarrassment."

It was four weeks before the abortion could take place, and that month, with its painful doubts and realizations, was the beginning for Mary of what would be, with two significant exceptions, almost two years of a floating existence without purpose. It was not only the result but an exacerbation of the destructiveness of prison life.

The usual routine for long-term prisoners with families is to be released to them. Years before, Molly Morgan had told Mary that it was highly unlikely she would ever be allowed to live with her mother, but the precedent had been established by her home leaves and Mary says she expected to be released to Betty. It is entirely consistent with Mary's ambivalent reaction toward anything to do with her mother that she did not remember that both she and Betty had requested she should not be sent there. All she remembers is having "mixed feelings" when the deputy governor of Askham Grange, who was dealing with her release formalities, told her that the decision had been made against returning her to the Northeast, and that as yet they didn't know where she was to go.

In fact, the authorities were looking for the best solution for her: we have Carole and Ben G.'s testimony that they were asked quite early on whether Mary could live with them. One of the many reasons why the Home Office had such difficulties in placing—or lodging—Mary was that she had always been a high-profile prisoner. Her mother had continued to fan this media interest: on Mary's second home leave, Betty introduced her to an old drinking pal who was a reporter for the *News of the World*, she said, and suggested in a conspiratorial whisper that he would be the right person with whom Mary could "write a book." "And you can imagine the arrangement she had in mind when she suggested *that*," Mary told me. "When I did get out he was one of the people who always seemed to know where I could be found." But even without that—and also discounting my book, which doubtless added to the public interest—Mary's notoriety had endured, above all, in the north of England, and there was every reason to fear that her release from prison would reactivate both the trauma for the victims' families and the media's pursuit of Mary.

In the end it was only just before her release, on May 14, 1980, that she was told of her first destination. "There wasn't anything I could have done for myself," Mary said. "What did I know? Who did I know? What could I do? My friends in prison were appalled that nothing was prepared for me, and one of them even tried to get her family to have me to stay. They were a nice mining family in Yorkshire, and they said they would gladly, but of course it was disapproved."

One of the most important things that had to be done before Mary was released was to establish a new identity for her. It was the governor who had suggested a new first name. "He said that if he had had a daughter, that is the name he would have given her and it made me feel he cared," Mary said. With help from the deputy governor she then decided on a new surname, and someone came from the social services in York to give her her social security and national insurance numbers made out in her new names. She took them, but she understood nothing. "You know, that woman handed me some papers, I said thank you. But I didn't have a clue. About P45s, National Insurance, National Health, taxes. . . ? Don't make me laugh. Oh, the girls chatted endlessly about this and that, but that was all about how to con the system, not how to obey it: half the people in open prisons are there because of tax evasion, for God's sake. And the new name? God, I was Mary. How was I going to be somebody else? How could I remember that I was? It was like being an alien."

The name—or the lack of one—only resurrected the identity crisis she had gone through in 1977, when she found out in Styal that Billy Bell was not her biological father. It was to be a long time before she could respond to her new identity, and it was never real to her. Indeed the new name is not helpful: it neither looks nor feels like her, and although, slightly altered, it eventually became her statutory name, she has used many others since—every time a newspaper seemed close to finding her, and as pseudonyms on various documents. Like many of us, she has a pet name used by her family and friends, which suits her, and it is what I too call her now. But it was a huge step toward her commitment to the process of self-examination necessary for this book when she suddenly said, about a month into our talks, "I want you to call me Mary while we talk. That's who I am, aren't I?"

Late in the afternoon of May 13, twelve hours before her release, she was told that early the next morning the hostel officer and the officer's husband would drive her to Cambridge, where a senior probation officer who was a friend of the governor would be waiting to take her for ten days to a small village in East Anglia. "There was no reason for me to go there, except that this was where that probation officer had a house. She usually worked at a nearby prison but she took the ten days I was there off. What it felt like was that they didn't know what to do with me, so they did this until the next place I was due to go to was available or whatever. That was a Quaker family back in Yorkshire, just ten miles from Askham Grange, who, you know, took people in who needed a roof over their heads, prisoners or whatever."

The village in Suffolk was tiny, Mary said. "It sure wasn't anything zippedydooda, you know, like Blackpool, which I suppose I must have been hoping for. I just met two people there, an old lady who knitted, a very Dickensian character, and a bearded chap who used to be a monk and became the village butcher; he wore shorts under his apron and sandals, very hippyish." But she didn't really talk to them much. "The probation officer was nice, you know, but not somebody one could talk with. I think she was sort of at a loss herself what to do with me."

So what did you do for those ten days?

"I went for some walks, but mostly I slept. I ate a lot of macaroons and cheese. Brie, she had lots of Brie, I don't know why. I felt lonely, incredibly lonely. I didn't know one could feel as lonely. I was very preoccupied with the coming abortion."

Did you have doubts about your decision?

"Not doubts," she said. "Just many thoughts. Given what happened to me as a child, I felt that *I* ought to have been aborted. Had there been common sense and an iota of responsibility in my sixteen-year-old mother's family, surely I would have been. That is why I had no doubt. I wouldn't bring a child into this world that I wasn't ready for and would—or might—ultimately resent. Nine months out of prison: what kind of a mother would I have been? And anyway, I wouldn't have been allowed to keep it and it would have been emotionally as deprived as I. Had I not committed murder as a child, I think the moral argument about abortion would not have occupied me as much as it did. It was terrible that the first responsible decision I had to make was one so gravely . . ."—she paused—". . . linked."

When you decided to have the abortion, was it your own childhood that was uppermost in your mind, or was it Martin and Brian? I asked her.

"It was both," she said. "I was thinking very mixed . . ."

She was trying to say—and it was the first time she had ever expressed it, I believe even to herself—that her childhood and the murders she had committed were not divisible. "It was just totally impossible," she said. "I talked . . . apologized to the baby in me in my own way: 'Next time round,' I said."

Ann Sexton was the third of many probation officers she would have— "I seemed to go through them like they were going out of fashion," she quipped—"Ann took receipt of me again in Cambridge—"

I interrupted. Took receipt?

"Well, that's what these handovers feel like," she said. "I don't mean it critically, not at all, but you know, it's a routine for them. They have so many clients . . . that's what probation officers, and social workers too, call their charges, and that *is* meaningful, isn't it? It means we are a kind of transaction, doesn't it? Anyway, Ann was young and very nice but she was a very shy person. I sort of felt perhaps I should get her to talk to me rather than me to her, you know what I mean? She was very religious. She told me she'd applied for a Winston Churchill pass to go to South Africa to be a probation kind of missionary, but she had been rejected. The Quaker family she took me to were friends of hers."

Geoffrey and Elizabeth Henderson* had two daughters, one married, the other Mary's age, working in an art gallery in London, and two sons, David, who was in his first year of university, and fourteen-year-old Tim, in boarding school. "Tim was the only one who didn't know who I was," Mary said. "All the others knew. They were really good people. Dr. Henderson, Geoff, was a strict sort of man—he held Bible classes every Thursday. But they were truly good. Liz was rather timid, probably because he was so strong, but really nice, nice to me, too."

Mary said she had gone into the hospital for the abortion three days after arriving at her new home, but in fact the abortion was just over a month after her release.

Her new hosts thought she had some female trouble and asked no questions. "I was very tired when it was over," Mary said. "I felt awfully weepy. I just couldn't stop crying. I remember I went to the hairdresser's and I just burst into tears . . . I spent a lot of time in my room on my own and Liz and Geoff were good, you know; they left me to it. Liz wasn't the kind of person to intrude, and anyway, I think they thought above all I was disorientated: first the change of identity, which they knew about, then the hospital. After that, all I wanted was to get a job," she said. "I just wanted to work, you know, I didn't care at what and I knew it would be hard with no job record, no references, so I just walked around and applied where I saw vacancies advertised."

Her very first job, which she got, she thinks, not more than a week or ten days after coming out of the hospital, was in the local nursery, or

*Changed names.

preschool. "But of course I had to tell the probation office and they said no, absolutely not."

Well, to be fair, I said, a nursery of all things . . . ?

"I know," she said. "But you see, I didn't associate . . ." She stopped.

The primary rule for prisoners released on license is that they are not allowed to work "with people." It wasn't, however, that she didn't associate a job at a nursery with the rule but that she didn't make the association between a nursery and the crime for which she had been convicted, though the Probation Service and without doubt the media and the public would have made it at once. "So I went and handed in my notice and then I sort of says to myself: 'Well, enough. I'm going back.' And I walked back, back, you know, to Askham Grange. And two hundred yards or so from the prison there was this prison officer who stopped me and asked me what I was doing. And I said, 'I don't like it out there.' And she—she was nice, you know, but of course she said I couldn't come back, that it was hard but I had to stick with it 'out there.'"

Then she went to work for a painter and decorator. "I'd liked painting at Styal, so I helped paint the town hall and then the inside of some houses." (It was evident from her account that the Probation Service neither prepared the ground for her when she came out nor helped her later to find jobs.) "And then I had some other jobs, a few days at this, a few days at that, and somehow the months passed.

"And then one day Geoff took me along on a business trip in the direction of Newcastle and I asked whether we could go by my mother, whom I hadn't seen for months. He drove through Scotswood and along Whitehouse Road, and he asked whether I wanted him to stop the car anywhere there but I said no, no. I wanted to get away because driving along there reminded me of a dream I used to have quite a lot and it was about my dad and K. [her sister, five years younger]. The dream was me at the back of Whitehouse Road . . . It was windy, very windy, and I would be outside looking through the window of the bedroom. I'd be shouting, calling out, 'Dad, it's me, it's me, can I come in?' And there would be just blank faces at the windows and no response." (And there is another dream she told me she has had time and again over the years. In this one the faces at the window are those of both her little sisters, and K. asks Billy, "Who's that?" And Billy says, "No one we know.")

"Geoff drove me to my mother's then . . . I don't remember anything about it except that he stayed in the car—I don't even remember whether she was there, only that he took me to a restaurant for dinner on the way back and I told him about the abortion, but of course not whose baby it had been."

How did that come up? I asked. What made you suddenly tell him, months later?

"It was a quiet place where we ate and . . . Oh, everything came together, you know." She meant Scotswood, the dream, seeing or not seeing her mother. "And he looked at me, you know, *me*, and said I looked tired and . . . It just . . . well, nobody ever looked at me like that and noticed . . . And you see, I *was* tired, I was awfully tired, and I suppose it was still uppermost in my mind and so I told him, and I said it had happened three months before and that's all I said and he didn't ask no questions."

Mary hadn't seen or talked to her mother for months when, very shortly before Christmas, she was "wandering about not far from the Hendersons' house" and realized there was a car "sort of following" her. She thought it was a reporter and that they'd found her again. "I finally thought, 'Sod this,' and stopped. And then the car stopped and out got my stepfather, Georgie.

"Georgie is the most honest person I know," Mary said. "I really admired the way he'd worked his way up in life and—you know, the way he loved, or anyway stuck to, my mother, warts and all. And that day in that street, Christmas and all, yes, I was glad to see him. He said, and these were his very words: 'Your mother wants you to give her another chance to be a mother to you. She wants you to come home.' And my mother was in the car and we went back to the house and Geoff was there and he was not pleased at all. He said that of course I could go out with them the next day if I wanted but that if I returned north with them I would no longer be welcome at his house. I wouldn't be able to live there again because, he said, if I went back to my mother, 'It totally defeats the object.' "

Did you understand what he meant?

"No, I didn't. And really, I was quite offended, you know. And he seemed so cross, like, 'That's all there is to be said about it' . . . It was like an ultimatum, you know."

Mary's presentation of her reaction to this ultimatum was somewhat disingenuous, for I have seen her anger when she feels she is being dictated to or when she thinks her privacy is being invaded. She becomes inaccessible then to argument or persuasion from those she thinks have offended her. There are two things that are likely to happen when she is angry: one is that she drives the anger inward, goes out, walks for hours, and when she finally comes home goes to sleep but retains that inner anger for quite a while, days and even weeks during which, unusual for her, she is cold and withdrawn toward the person whom she feels attacked or offended by. Her second reaction, rather than withdrawal, is verbal attack: her tone then, berating the offender, becomes very sharp—not the terms she uses, for she is never vulgar—but her voice, the timbre of which is usually both low and hesitant, rises an octave higher and the words become suddenly very precise, sharply articulated and defined. "I am fu-ri-ous," she will say, "ab-so-lu-tely fu-ri-ous." And the angrier she gets, the more middle class she sounds and the less there is of that soft Newcastle lilt.

I could have predicted her reaction that day in Yorkshire, for certainly Dr. Henderson, for all the right reasons, *was* dictating to her. Her mother and Georgie went to a B&B, she said. She had stayed home but had not spoken to Dr. Henderson that evening and she spent the next day with her mother and George. "We drove to a nearby town and it was market day, when the pubs were open—all day, I think. Anyway, there was a bookshop and I said I wanted to rummage about there and my mother followed me in. But she said what did I want with all these books and let's go to the pub, so I went along and they just . . . oh . . . sort of got settled in there and I remember saying, 'God, how can you sit in here when it's a really nice day outside?' It was cold but sunny—there was a lot of music, you know like there is everywhere around Christmas; it was really pretty. And she started out how I was living in a dream world, that it was unrealistic for me to be where I was. I didn't belong with 'these people,' she said, meaning Liz and Geoff, and the life I was living wasn't a life for somebody like me. And I listened, you know, and I felt just the contrary: I felt how different a person I was and that I didn't, that I couldn't belong to . . . their . . . to my mother's scene.

"But then, when she said, 'It's Christmas, come home with us for Christmas,' I just couldn't say no. I know now . . . Of course I know now that I could have handled the situation much better with Geoff . . ."

Were you still angry with him?

She didn't answer. "I liked them so much, you know; the kids were all coming home. Some were there already. I know I could have struck some sort of compromise with him, but I didn't. I just went north that night to where they lived in the Whitley Bay area."

So Betty, who had always known how to press Mary's buttons, had succeeded once again. No doubt counting on the festive spirit, she had appeared on the scene just before Christmas and used the nice young stepfather, whom she knew Mary liked, to wave that magic "mother" wand—which had always worked. In the pub on market day, Mary had seen clearly for a moment and might have wavered. But by then Dr. Henderson, the strong father figure of a Quaker family, had not only exerted his authority—which to Mary was like a red rag to a bull—but in challenging her loyalty to her mother had given her an ultimatum that she considered offensive, as much to her mother as to herself. And on this pre-holiday day, with the four Henderson children home for Christmas, it had been made clear to her—or so she thought—that the Hendersons' house was intended not to be home for her but merely a refuge from which she could be evicted if she disobeyed. However much she liked them, however prepared she might even have been to love them, the link was fragile. "I think of them now," she said sixteen years later, "as a distant family."

As *your* distant family? I asked.

"As a distant family for me," she specified carefully. "I mean, it's highly unlikely that they'd ever need me. But if pigs ever fly, you know, and they, or any of them, would need me, well, I'd be there for them."

They had, in fact, been there for her when she needed just what they offered. And even though Dr. Henderson clearly knew that the authorities wanted to curtail Mary's contact with her mother, he had been ready enough to accede to Mary's wish to drop in on Betty when they were in her vicinity. It was when Betty had forced renewed contact on Mary months later, without warning, that—as unaware of the complexity of that relationship as of Mary's incapacity to give in to coercion—he had presumably seen no alternative to presenting her with his ultimatum.

Christmas, Mary said, passed in an alcoholic blur. "Between Christmas and New Year, I don't think I was sober from morning to night. It all happened in her pub and I just drank along with everybody. But then I must have come to. I suddenly saw again that anything that had my mother in it wasn't and couldn't be 'home' for me. It was like another home leave I shouldn't have gone on. And on January fourth I left and went to York, to the probation office."

Ann Sexton was away, she said, but the probation officer on duty told her that she definitely could not go back to the Hendersons and must not communicate with them except through Ann when Ann returned. "She was a very kind lady, the wife of a milkman," Mary said, "and that first night I stayed with them. And then they found me a room with a schoolteacher out in the country but there were no jobs there, nothing to do. So after two weeks they moved me twenty miles away to Harrogate, where they said it would be easier. But it wasn't and for months after that it became bashing-the-head-on-the-wall time."

This was a period when, going from job to job, mostly waitressing, Mary lived on social security in bed and breakfast places paid for by the social services. "I had to be out by nine and wasn't allowed back till four. There are always waitressing jobs, wherever you are, but they never last: you do well, you like the job, and then you are sacked, from one meal to the next, and you don't know why." It was only last year, after she had once again been let go by a restaurant and I phoned the manager to find out why, that Mary and I both discovered that it is only by employing mostly temporary workers, who can be let go before the employers' social security contributions become due, that many small restaurants can survive. "It was a very depressing, very lonely time," Mary said. "It's no wonder, is it, that so many people reoffend?"

Mary's state of mind about any period and the subject she was talking about was always reflected in her manner of presenting it. It is not only that both her body and her face mirror all her feelings but that, rather than her mind being in charge of the subject she is discussing, the subject appears to regulate or, as it were, deregulate her mind.

Thus the depression that was the dominating factor of those bed and breakfast months, of what she called the "bashing-the-head-on-the-wall time," overcame her to such a degree during the two full days she talked about these mind-numbing weeks that I was left with almost empty pages in my notebook despite several three-hour tapes full of ums, pauses, sighs, embarrassed unmerry laughs, and sorrys. When I played them—or parts of them—for my husband later, all we could do was look at each other in incomprehension. "What can they be thinking about?" he said. "A girl who's been detained since she was eleven—they release her into a world of strangers, no trade, no education, with handouts for subsistence? She's right," he said. "It *is* no wonder that so many people reoffend."

Finally Mary got a room in a house belonging to the owner of a school for English as a foreign language and here her luck turned. "He said it was ridiculous for me to be living in this void and he got me into college." Altogether she spent six months (two terms) then at a College of Higher Education in West Yorkshire—the "uni," as she calls it—studying psychology, philosophy, and English literature. The first term was probably the most carefree time she remembers. She was living "in hall" with no financial worries, a grant covering both her tuition and living expenses. "I had more fun than I'd ever had, than I ever knew one could have," she said. "At the uni, you know, I wasn't Mary Bell. No one sort of knew . . . I really felt I was [her new name], that I was a different person, but I was able to be me, the me that Mr. Dixon would have been proud of, that he knew I was. I loved the lectures, I loved the library. I had a nice room, a study bedroom, you know, all to myself, and there was lots going on, lots of people I liked."

I was to find her curiously restrained about the details of these happy first months. It was as if too much had happened in a very short time, all of it happy but none of it adding up to experiences of any depth to make them worth remembering or relating one by one.

Did you go out with anybody? I asked.

"I didn't want any involvement . . . We went swimming, to football games, car racing, yeah, dancing too."

Was there any drug taking?

"I had tried LSD while I was still bumming around in Yorkshire. It sort of locked my jaw and I went into fits of laughter, and then all those intensely colored lights . . . But I ended up feeling very tired, so I wasn't very keen to do that too often. And when I had some amphetamines at uni like everybody else did, it didn't do anything for me it was supposed to do; you know, it didn't pep me up or anything, it also just made me tired. I don't think I'm an addictive personality."

Hmm, I said. What about all the drugs in prison? What about the cigarettes you can't give up?

She shrugged. "What else is there to do in prison?" And she added defensively, "Cigarettes? I only smoke when I'm alone or out of doors."

Did people at college ask you about your parents, your home?

"I . . . I didn't *lie*, you know, I sort of omitted," she explained. "I said that Dr. and Mrs. Henderson were my aunt and uncle. I mean, it wasn't a misrepresentation that was going to harm anyone."

And about your parents?

"I said I didn't get on very well with my mother and that she and my father were estranged, and that was really it."

How did your mother feel about you being in college?

"As if it was her achievement."

Did you see her?

"Yes, I went to see her a couple of times. She told people I was her cousin from Liverpool, 'the one at university.' And that Christmas [1981] I stayed with her but I really spent all my time with college friends."

She had begun to think of herself either as a teacher or as a budding therapist. "Dreaming, more like it," she said. "You know, of pioneering methods or whatever. But then, just after I came back for the new term, my probation officer, who apparently hadn't realized until then what I was studying or planning, told me that I'd never be allowed to work in either of those fields, that these were prohibited professions for me. So I wrote a letter to the college board asking to transfer me to a beautician's course, and they wrote back saying no. And the principal, who had been told by the Probation Service who I was before I started, invited me to dinner with his wife at their home but I said no, you know; I felt uncomfortable at the idea because nobody else I knew had been asked to dinner there, so I thought . . . Oh, you know . . . like . . . like . . ."

You felt like a showpiece?

"Yes," she said. "Something like that. So then I was called to his office and he said he was concerned at my trying to move out of the academic field. He thought I should stick with the kind of like-minded people I now knew and that was where my talents would develop and I would eventually find my way into something I both wanted to do and could do. He meant well, I knew that. So after that . . . well, I returned to studying rather halfheartedly, but finally I just couldn't see where I was going, what I was doing, I couldn't think of an academic area I could fit into and, you know, do something with in the future. I was trying to balance an unknown future with what my mother called 'real life.'"

By this time, too, she had got herself into a financial mess, with a large overdraft that the bank said had to be paid off. "I'd just bought clothes and clothes and clothes—no point to it, just angry, just restless, just stupid." George paid off the overdraft and at Easter Betty had again talked to her about facing reality. "She told me which reality to live in—with 'my kind,' she said. So finally I thought, 'She's probably right,' and I asked George to drive me back to pick up my stuff and then I went back to stay with them."

. . .

Two people she was to meet over the next months were to be decisively important to her. The first was a young man (we will call him Rob), at eighteen almost still a boy, whom she met at a party in September and only saw occasionally for several weeks. Did you sleep with him? I asked. "Of course not," she said, sounding indignant. "Not for the first month. The Northeast wasn't like London, you know. Not then, anyway." Eventually Rob would become the father of her child.

The other person was Pat Royston, who took over as her probation officer in October 1982. By this time Mary had been working for six months, the longest period she has ever sustained a job, again in a geriatric home, as she had done before, but by now hoping that she could work toward some sort of qualification in geriatric nursing.

"Pat told me right away that though she appreciated I liked the work, I would have to give it up. I wouldn't be allowed to qualify, however good I was at it," Mary said. "She said I should imagine that I had a relative in the hospital and found out that the nurse in charge had served a life sentence for murder, how would I feel? Well," she said pugnaciously, but then sounding resigned, "I'd feel that it depended on the circumstances and on what that person had become. But there wasn't any point in saying that, even if I'd known her better; she has to follow rules, too. And anyway, I understood what she was saying. It was quite true, there would always be people who would object to me doing such work, perhaps even more if I had a qualification and was put in responsible positions."

I asked Pat Royston why neither of the two other probation officers who preceded her in Mary's supervision after she had returned to the Northeast had objected to her working in the geriatric home, and she shrugged and said only that the first one had been too young for the assignment. The second one, an older man who she thought had been appointed in the hope that he would become a sort of father figure for Mary, was probably too protective of Mary and, finally, collusive with her mother: rare for any of Mary's probation officers, he had formed a friendly relationship with Betty, and her mother wanted Mary at home, in a job "fitting her station." "It's hard to say no to people who are needy," Pat said by way of further explanation. "And both mother and daughter were very needy."

What Pat did not say, because there is a limit to what she can disclose to outsiders, and what the probation officer who preceded her certainly didn't know was that while this neediness arose from very different roots—Mary's starving for love from her mother, Betty's wish to control her daughter—the result was that each almost compulsively sought out the other.

Pat said she had read the reports on Mary very carefully before taking over. "There was a good deal about the trial, of course—the crimes, the defense, the judge, the sentence—but except for the fact that she had always been enuretic, had a disturbed childhood, the mother a prostitute, there was nothing at all about the child: Mary* as a person. Once she was away from home, there was quite a bit about her tantrums at Red Bank, her various acts of rebellion in prison, the worrying circumstances, implied more than described, of her abortion, and the many difficulties my predecessors had experienced with her since her release. And here there were a number of observations about her personality, such as that she tended to exaggerate or dramatize in describing events in prison and afterwards. 'She is a drama queen,' one of my colleagues wrote.

"But what emerged very clearly from this fourteen-year record was what I would be able to confirm for myself very quickly when I met her. Which was that Mary was emotionally very screwed up, with a near-catastrophic self-image, and despite evidence of considerable intelligence had enormous difficulty sustaining any intellectual effort or job. The three-year course she had been accepted for at the college—a tremendous chance for her, and they wouldn't have given her a place if they hadn't considered her able—was a telling example: when, after just one term, she found out she wouldn't be allowed to teach or practice, she

---

*Neither Pat nor Sam, Mary's probation officer between 1988 and 1993, ever address Mary by her past name or as May; both use her pet name, which, for my purpose, I have replaced throughout with Mary.

immediately abandoned the academic side without considering other possible careers. And when she then applied for a health and beauty course and was told there were a lot of applications but that she had a good chance of getting in from a waiting list, she immediately declined. Basically she doesn't believe she can succeed in anything. So she pre-empted what she was certain would be failure, gave up her grant, and left to go to the one place where I very soon realized she should never be: her mother's house."

Pat started working with Mary immediately, seeing her once, and often twice, a week for several hours. "I'd go and see her at the Whitley Bay probation office," Mary said, "a depressing old building with creaking floorboards, where we'd sit in a dark, dusty office with green chairs and a defunct fireplace, or we'd go for drives."

"When we began," Pat said, "she was very confused. She talked without stopping. Her mind seemed to lack any direction and she resisted structuring. It was almost as if she was exploding with the need to get words out, never mind what they meant. She gave me a feeling of someone horribly repressed, emotionally isolated."

Had she felt right away that Pat was someone she could really talk to? I asked Mary.

"I felt that she was responsible, not in the sense of responsible for me as a probation officer, but as a human being. I felt that this was going to be long term, that she was on my side."

Pat said, "I had told Betty I wanted to meet her so that we could get to know each other but that anyway I had to see the home environment, as Mary was living there. Still, it took some time before she agreed. I have to say that her home was very unexpected. Outside it was a beautifully painted end-of-terrace house that had obviously been extended. Inside it was a real *House Beautiful* creation, as Betty would imagine it. I'll never forget it: the living-room carpet was turquoise blue, a really deep pile that showed every footstep. I'd noticed right away that, incongruously, there was a garden rake standing up against the wall inside the room, near the door. Just as soon as I had crossed the room and sat down, she picked it up and raked the carpet where my footsteps showed. I almost felt embarrassed . . . perhaps I should have taken my shoes off.

But she said, quite nicely, sort of apologetically, that it was one of her quirks. It was really, well, weird, given what Mary later told me about her housekeeping when she was a child. And after George finally left her in 1987, the flat she rented and where she died was just as immaculate, even though she became a near-total alcoholic.

"We talked for a while but it was very, very difficult. That first visit was in the same week that French television, heaven only knows why just then, had been trying to locate Mary—perhaps that, too, had something to do with Betty's sudden agreement to see me. Betty, I think, was terrified of it being found out that she was leading reporters to her, either for money, under the influence of alcohol, or for some other psychologically complicated reason nobody could ever have understood. Of course I didn't let on that I suspected or knew that. I impressed on her and George, who was there too, not to speak to anybody from the media, but I didn't have much hope about Betty: she had already spoken to so many of them." (And then Pat told me again about one magazine's £250,000 offer for Mary's story and about the letter on record confirming the offer, and of the magazine's now long-retired London correspondent's many approaches, both to Pat and to Mary's solicitor.)

"George was not at all how I had imagined him," she went on. "He was very quiet, well-spoken, tall, slim, and nice-looking: really just a nice person, with a friendly face. But she, oh dear, she was a very strange lady, thin, gaunt, and . . . cold, just cold, no warmth emanating from her at all. It was, I don't know, almost eerie. She was very well dressed; I would notice that every time I went to see her. Later, when she was not expecting me and wouldn't let me in, she was always obviously at home, too— well put together, you know, careful makeup, good clothes. But talking with her was almost impossible. One was reduced to chatting—very much like one report from Red Bank describes her and Mary's meetings, that they talked 'about nothing.'

"I was there for some time that first visit. They offered me a drink. But the only thing of any significance she said, suddenly, apropos of nothing—significant because it confirmed what Mary had told me— was that she preferred to think of Mary as her sister or cousin. But when

I tried to use that as a starting point for some sort of real conversation, she clammed up."

Very shortly after Pat's first visit, Betty threw Mary out. "She said it was because I stayed out late and worrying about me kept her awake," Mary said. "But firstly, I was twenty-five years old, and secondly, she didn't stay awake, she was drunk every night. But maybe anyway none of this was the reason. Perhaps it was because she met Pat and was afraid of what I might say to her. Anyway, it was OK with me. I got myself a job as a receptionist at a hotel and moved in with Rob."

"I tried to see Betty repeatedly after that but only managed twice," Pat said. "Every other time she would either open the chained door and then slam it in my face or else not answer the bell but look out from behind the curtain; I could see it flick. On the second occasion I actually managed to get across the threshold, she immediately began to yell at me, blaming me for Mary not coming to see her and blaming her for all her ills. When I then tried to question her, about the bed-wetting and other things, I was met with stony silence. Finally she opened the door for me, telling me to get out. "I don't have to talk to you," she said. "I'm not your client." And the only other time I got in she screeched at me like a banshee because I told her that I wanted Mary to see a psychiatrist."

I asked Pat whether during that first visit Betty had mentioned Mary's boyfriend, Rob.

"I don't know whether she did on that occasion or the other time, but certainly she totally disapproved of him: his age, his fairly middle-class background, and even the work he'd chosen to do [in wholesale food]. As it later turned out, Rob *was* too young and immature for Mary. But of course that was neither here nor there: I came to understand when Mary really started to talk to me that Betty would try to stop any relationship Mary might develop which could lead to her 'talking.' With Rob, she had made it her business to meet him and not only told him 'who' Mary was but lied to him, saying that Mary had been sterilized and couldn't have children."

"I was absolutely gob-smacked when Rob told me that," Mary said.

"Not about the Mary Bell thing; I was used to her telling everybody and I would have told him myself, maybe I already had. He had a really nice younger sister who I became real friends with; I think I told her. But the other thing? I know she'd been railing against him ever since I started going out with him, but to say *that*. Why would she do such a thing?"

Rob bought a nice house by the seaside and when Mary moved in with him gave her an engagement ring. "It all went terribly wrong in the end." She laughed with that little hoarse laugh I often heard when she was about to admit to something embarrassing or sad. "I was probably too much for him to cope with," she said. "I'd given him credit for more maturity than he had. And why should he have had it? He was only a boy. But I thought he was an innately good person and at the end of the day I still think he was, despite everything that happened."

"Mary told me of her wish to have a baby very soon after I began to work with her," Pat said.

"It wasn't because of what my mother told Rob," Mary said. "I mean it wasn't that I wanted to become pregnant to prove my mother wrong. It had been in the back of my mind ever since the abortion. That is not the kind of birth control that lies easy on the conscience."

The lives of released Schedule One offenders are subject to a host of regulations and precautions, and the safety of an unborn child ranks high among them. Pat Royston told Mary that if she and Rob were planning on a baby, she should arrange for her to have a psychological evaluation. "I knew she would have problems with the social services about it and such a report might pre-empt their possible objections," Pat told me. "She agreed to that immediately, which was interesting, because I knew by then about her always having gone along with her mother's mania against psychiatrists. Making this decision now showed her strength of feeling about having a child. What was strange, however, was that almost in the same breath as talking about having a baby, she began to talk of her feelings about Martin and Brian, whom she had not yet mentioned at all. It was as if her wish for a child was inseparable from her awareness of the loss she caused to two families of their children.

"She told me that she hadn't admitted to herself for several years that she had killed. She said she wondered why the remorse had taken so long to come out. When she talked about it, it was clear that she had frozen all the emotions completely, with Betty—who she kept bringing up— always in the background saying, 'Don't talk to anyone about anything that happened or you'll be in trouble.'

"Mary told me it had only been at that significant eighteen-year point that she could think of the parents of the two boys and what it must have been like for them. And the moment she mentioned the parents she began to cry. 'It will never be over for them; it will never be over for me.' She has always brought Martin and Brian up, and always in connection with her own child, not so much the details of what she did to the two little boys—she never told me those—but rather her sadness for the parents and her despair about herself."

Had Pat ever thought, I asked—as I had considered when I first talked to Mary—that this remorse was put on for her benefit, that Mary might be manipulating her?

"I certainly asked myself this at the beginning. I knew, of course, that some people in Red Bank, and many more later in the prisons, talked a lot about her being so manipulative. And she no doubt *was* manipulative about all her relationships there. But the situation now was different and it was new for her. I was actually trying to work with her, in a therapeutic sense, and she was responding to it. I think when her mother finally agreed to see me—and don't forget, this was while Mary was still living with them—it was at least partly because Betty realized I was getting closer to Mary and was panicked by this. I saw this very quickly. She really was terribly afraid of me. This was, after all, what she had tried to prevent all these years. It was her nightmare. And the evidence she gave me of hostility, anger, and, yes, obvious fear of what I might discover was striking.

"So my answer to your question is that after my various experiences of Betty, even though I knew none of the details I would learn later from Mary and then from you [Pat had not read my book], I became certain that the acts Mary committed in 1968 could only be understood in the context of whatever acts her mother had committed in Mary's early childhood. And associating this certainty with the despair I witnessed in Mary, yes, I was entirely sure that her remorse was real and true."

On April 28, 1983, Pat took Mary up to London, where she was seen by a psychiatrist, Dr. Arthur Hyatt-Williams, and a consultant psychologist, Paul Upson. "I felt I had nothing to hide from them," Mary said. "If there was something wrong with me when I was a child, there wasn't now. I felt that if they could X-ray me inside, they could see that anything broken had been fixed."

Dr. Hyatt-Williams saw her in his consulting rooms at home and, understandably enough, conflict arose at once.

"Do you know what the first thing was he said?" Mary asked. "He said, 'What big hands you have. What do you feel when you look at your hands?' I mean, can you imagine a doctor saying such a thing?"

He was trying to provoke you, I said. And he obviously succeeded.

"I cried. And then he said that I was upset because his remark reminded me of using these hands to kill the children."

Having very limited time to evaluate your emotions, I said, getting you to manifest them was exactly what he aimed for.

"Perhaps. But all I was aware of feeling was anger that he should have said something so personal and so unkind about my hands. And then he said, didn't I think it was strange that I had chosen to fall in love with a man who was exactly the age Martin would have been?"

Do you remember what you answered?

"Well, no," she said. "I mean, that had just never occurred to me. I just liked Rob, you know, and although I was aware he was younger than I—after all my mother never stopped telling me—I didn't feel older. I felt pretty young.

"Then he told me that I had been 'in denial,' and I knew what that meant—I'd read about it—and I thought he was wrong, that I was doing something different, even though I didn't know what it was called."

It's a pity you didn't discuss your feelings with him, I said. That is precisely how a good psychiatrist would want to help you.

"I don't think he wanted that," she said. "He just wanted . . . I suppose, as you said, he was just seeing me this once to write a report, so he just said things—provocative things—to see how I'd react. Like he said that if I became aware at fourteen of what I had done, it was because I was in puberty, had my periods and all that—but it wasn't just that, was it, either? I mean, a lot of things happened to me at that time, didn't they, and it was those things that made me think. It's all just clichés how they put things, isn't it?

"I was shown the reports later. He said something like that my 'murderous manifestations' would never 'explode' but only 'implode,' whatever that was meant to mean, and then he went on there, too, about Rob being seven years younger and that it meant I was looking for 'atonement' or whatever. More important, though, he said I was a danger to no one, so I was grateful for that. And the other chap—the psychologist—he was a lot easier to be with and it was quite interesting. He flashed a lot of cards in front of me and I had to say what I thought of them or felt about them. Anyway, he also wrote I was OK."

Although it took the two experts six months to write their reports, both did eventually say that it was entirely safe for Mary to have a child.

"Rob had asked me after I came back from London whether I still wanted to have a baby and we decided to have a real think about it," she said, "what it would mean, and how we were doing financially and how his family would feel about it. His father was dead and his mother had just remarried but she was OK with me."

Did his mother know your real identity?

"She did. Everybody seemed to know. I was never quite sure how—my mother, pub talk. Much later, when things went so wrong, it was Rob himself who told people, but that early on, it was really all right. He was happy, working hard. We had this nice house. He had these wonderful paternal grandparents who were so glad he was settling down and that I was so sensible—they said—and his sister was pleased, too, at the idea of a baby, so it was good, really good."

The two reports came through in October 1983. "I told Rob. We threw my pills down the toilet." She giggled. "I knew two weeks later that I was pregnant and told Pat."

"I couldn't just let Mary go ahead and have her baby," Pat said. "Schedule One offenders are only rarely allowed to keep their children and additionally in her case there was always this problem of Mary's high profile, which dominated so many of my dealings. We had to ensure that the information about her pregnancy and all the decisions that would be made remained secure. This is why, when I called a case conference in January 1984, the heads of departments—health, police, social services, legal, and probation—all attended."

At the conference, the authorities had been given all the information that was on hand about Mary's life. Her mother was described as mentally unbalanced, Billy Bell was irresponsible, with many criminal convictions. About Mary herself, it was said that she was emotionally and physically battered as a baby, that the battering continued through to 1968, by which time Betty and Billy were living apart and divorce was pending. There were old psychiatric reports from Drs. Westbury, Rowbotham, and Cuthbert, which spoke of bed-wetting, including daytime incontinence, but of otherwise "normal development" (Cuthbert), and the new reports, which declared her safe for motherhood. "It was agreed nothing would go on a computer," Pat said. "All reports then and afterwards would go through me and remain in my office. The question on the table was basically who should have care and control over the child once it was born, the parents or the social services. But underneath this there was another danger: that Mary could be considered unfit to keep her child.

"My own feeling was, and had been for months," Pat said, "that while the child should and no doubt would be made a ward of court, and everybody in fact agreed on that, not only must Mary be allowed to keep her child, but the parents—Mary and Rob—should have care and control. Health and legal supported my point of view; the police were on middle ground until instructed by the social services, who finally came around to agreeing that Mary could keep the child."

Two or three days after the baby's birth, the first of three ex parte hearings was held at the High Court Family Division. "[Mary's solicitor] represented the parents and I gave evidence," said Pat. "We had tried to keep as much of the details away from Mary as we could." At this first hearing, the child was made a ward of court and an interim order was issued giving care and control to the parents until the full hearing, several weeks away. But at the second hearing, ten days later, the social services contested this order, and the judge asked Pat Royston into his chamber to find out more about Mary's previous psychiatric evaluation. A week later, at the full hearing, the social services applied for care and control with a view to moving Mary, Rob, and the child into a family center for observation—this would have meant up to six months in a residential unit, with several other families, miles away from where they lived and under close supervision from morning to night.

"There was no justification for that, none at all, and it could have been destructive for their relationship," Pat said. "Mary's solicitor and I fought this proposal all day, and by the end of the hearing the court awarded care and control to the parents with a supervision order for the child."*

---

*The supervision order was lifted in 1992, which meant that the parents were considered capable of looking after the child, then eight.

"The last weeks before the baby was born I felt—oh, just warm within myself," Mary said. "Content. Even though Rob handed in his notice on May 10, and I came to understand later how bad that was, for him and for us, it didn't bother me then. He was involved with me and the baby, that's all I cared about then. We were all ready: Beatrix Potter wallpaper, stripped-pine chest, pictures on the wall, an ABC mobile. I got the date wrong, of course. She came before we expected her. But it was all right. I remember more laughter than anything else, Rob coming in with a mask. I laughed and laughed, and they said, 'That's good, keep on laughing.' And Rob kept saying, 'Come on, you can do it,' like a horse race, and that made me laugh some more. And then they said, 'It's a little girl. You've got a little girl,' and I burst into tears and I held her and they said they had to take her away to clean her up and I said, 'No, I want her here,' and they took her anyway and brought me some tea and toast. And then they brought her back all swaddled and I held her to me and there she was, so tiny, with a sort of orange-colored lick of hair that just came up and went phut and I said, or I thought, 'Hello, I've been waiting a long time to see you,' and then she was in a cot next to me. Sometimes she woke up in the night and I would pick her up and nurse her and the nurses said I shouldn't, but I felt it was right."

She suddenly stopped, giggled, and then whispered to me as if telling a secret: "I woke her up sometimes so that I had reason to hold her." She laughed. "And she would wake the others, and then she would go back to sleep and so would they.

"No," she said, when I asked her about her mother. "I never thought of her. I hadn't seen her, oh, for a year or so."

Do you think that was the moment you were freest of her?

She looked at me. "It never occurred . . . [I had] no thoughts of her; it was my time, my baby's time."

PART FIVE

RETURN TO CHILDHOOD

1957 to 1968

"Take the Thing Away from Me"

As I had discovered that first day in 1996 when Mary and I met to talk about the possibility of this book, she had not read my earlier writing about her until, at the age of twenty-four, she finally opposed her mother and read—as she put it—"little bits of it." Betty had always told Mary that my book was all lies, that the family had never met me, that Mary was never to read it or speak to me.

In 1969 and 1970, when I was preparing that book, her aunts and uncles and her maternal grandmother, horrified by what had happened, hoped that if people knew more about Mary's life they might be kind to her in the following years. So they told me as much as they knew, or perhaps could bear to say, about her earliest childhood. I think Mary understood from the moment we started our talks in 1996 that what had happened to her as a child, and then the deaths of the two boys, would have to be central to the story that she would tell me and that I would write.

On the first two days we spent together—as I said at the beginning of the book—she talked only about her child and, by extension, about herself as a mother. It was on the third day that I told her we needed to talk about her own childhood now, as far back as she could possibly remember. How much did she know, I asked, about what her family had told me about her mother?

Did I know, she asked, countering my question without a pause, that her mother was hidden away in a convent when she was pregnant with her?

No, I said, I hadn't known that. Who had told her that?

"She did," she said. "One night when she was . . . oh, drunk, I suppose, to show me how hard it was on her, how hard the nuns were, how hard she had to work, just like it was in old times for Catholic girls who had an illegitimate child . . ."

She said then that she knew I had written about some of the things her mother had done to her very early on, but now she wanted to know whatever I knew. "Then," she said with a curiously abrupt shake of her head, "I'll tell *you*."

I told her that her aunt Cath and her grandmother couldn't understand why the first thing Betty had said when they tried to put the baby in her arms was, " 'Take the thing away from me.' Cath said you were the bonniest baby."

"Well," Mary said, her voice hard, "that's when they should have taken me away from her forever, shouldn't they?"

There was never any possibility of Billy Bell's being Mary's biological father. Betty had only met him a few months after Mary was born in 1957. She married him in March 1958, and P., her second child, Billy's son, would be born that autumn. They were living with her mother and her younger sister, Isa, in a pleasant flat in Gateshead, just across the river from Scotswood. Betty's mother, Mrs. McC., despite suffering from migraines and tension, for which she took medication, had always been good at making a comfortable home. She was very careful about where she kept her pills, as she would tell me in 1970: "specially when there were kids about." She kept the bottle in the back of the used-needle compartment of an old gramophone that stood on top of a small chest and kept the knitting needle she used to extricate the bottle from its hiding place in a drawer.

Despite these precautions, one-year-old Mary somehow got hold of these pills and ate them. To achieve this, the baby would have had to find the knitting needle, climb up to where the gramophone stood, reach to the back of it with the knitting needle to dig out the bottle, unscrew its top, and eat enough of the unpleasant-tasting pills to almost kill her. As it happened, her grandmother found her in time; she was rushed to the hospital, her stomach was pumped, and she recovered.

A year and a half later, in November 1959, when Betty and Billy and the children had moved away from Mrs. McC., and Cath, Betty's older sister, received a letter from her saying that things were bad for her. She had "given May to the [D.s]," friends of Cath and her husband, Jack, who lived in a nearby market town and had always shown interest in Mary and repeatedly asked to adopt her. Cath rushed to the D.s and Mary was returned to her mother.

Six months later, when Mary was almost three, Cath came to visit her sister and brought two bags of candy, one for Mary and one for her brother P., who was now eighteen months old. The sisters went into the kitchen to make tea and when Cath came back she found the two children sitting on the floor munching sweets that had spilled onto the floor. To her horror, she saw among them a number of little blue pills that she recognized as Drinamyls (amphetamines) and the children said yes, they'd eaten some of them. Betty said the kids must have taken the bottle out of her handbag. Cath rushed to get a glass of hot water with salt in it. Both children were sick in the sink and were then taken to the hospital, but the doctors said everything had come out.

A few weeks after this, Cath and Jack, by now seriously concerned for Mary's safety, wrote to Betty and Billy, as they had done twice before, and asked to be allowed to keep Mary—"not to adopt," they specified, to make it easier for her, but until she finished school. Betty said no.

Three months later, in the summer of 1960, Betty and Mary were visiting her mother in Glasgow. Because her flat was on the third floor and the lavatories on the ground floor, the family was in the habit of letting the little children "wet in the kitchen sink."

One day while Betty's mother was at her receptionist's job at a nearby hospital, Betty's brother Philip and younger sister Isa were sitting on the settee about six feet from the sink. Next to the sink was a window that was wide open. Suddenly Philip saw Mary, whom Betty had been holding straddling the sink, falling out the window. He lunged across the room and somehow managed to grab her by the ankles and pull her in. "He was off work for three weeks after that because he hurt his back catching her," his sisters told me later.

Mary has a vague memory of scratches or bruises on her legs and angry voices associated with them on that occasion. She also remembers part of what happened next. Betty's family had now become anxious, and Isa was instructed by her mother not to let Betty and Mary out of her sight. A few days after the window incident, Isa followed Betty as she took Mary into an adoption agency. A woman had come out of the interview room crying and said they would not give her a baby because of her age and because she was emigrating to Australia. "I brought this one in to be adopted. You have her," Betty said, pushing the little girl toward the stranger, and walked out.

Isa, who later told me the story, followed the woman and Mary and after noting the address where she was taken raced to the hospital (where Mrs. McC. worked) to tell her mother. They rushed home and Mrs. McC. apparently told Betty that if the child was not back inside two hours she would notify the police. Mary was fetched, with some dresses the woman had already bought her and allowed her to keep. "That is what I remember," Mary said. "A nice house, and lots of new clothes, and Isa, I think, coming and taking me away. Why did they do that?" she asked me, her voice childlike, as it was to be repeatedly throughout the next days. "Why didn't they leave me with that lady who wanted a child?" She suddenly sounded more thoughtful. "That would have been a chance for her as well. It would have stopped her, stopped whatever it was. She is not to blame," she said then. "You must say she is not to blame. I don't want her to come out like, 'Oh, what a bitch, what a horror,' 'cause she wasn't, she wasn't."

What do you think it was in her? I asked, and she shook her head.

"I don't know. I just don't know."

Mary's worst "accident" happened about six months later, when she was almost four. The register at Newcastle General Hospital states:

"Mary Flora Bell, 28 Elswick Road, Newcastle/Tyne 6/3/61 to 9/3/61: under care of consultant Dr. Cooper."

Cath had rushed into Newcastle after a policeman came to tell her (she had no phone) that Mary was in the hospital. By the time she arrived, Mary had had her stomach pumped and had regained consciousness. Betty was standing outside the ward. "Don't believe her," she implored her sister, crying. "She says I gave her those pills."

This time Mary had apparently swallowed a number of her mother's iron pills. When she woke up she said to the doctor, "Me mam gave me the Smarties," and kept saying this on and off for twenty-four hours. And here there had been a witness, a little girl of five, Mary's best friend. Cath met her in the street a few days later and she said, "May's mam gave her the Smarties in the backyard."

After this incident there were bitter words between Betty and her family. "Once is an accident, even twice it just might be," Cath remembered saying to her, "but three and now even four times is impossible." Shortly afterwards, Mrs. McC. and her other daughters received letters from Betty—Cath later showed me hers—saying she never wanted to see them again and they did not see her for more than a year. In 1970, when I was conducting my research for *The Case of Mary Bell*, I believed that the family's concern had achieved the desired effect, for this, I understood, was to be the last of Mary's accidents at home. But I was terribly wrong.

I do not think for a minute that any of Betty's family knew of the dreadful use Mary's mother made of her from a point some time soon after she stopped seeing them. However reluctant they might have been in the first four years of Mary's life to let anyone outside their family know of Betty's pathological feelings toward her first child, had they had any idea about what happened next, and would carry on happening over the next four years, they would, I am sure, have acted to save her.

Mary remembered both the hospital and being given the pills. "I remember I was on a tricycle. I'm sure they were in a Smartie tube and, you know, Smarties, the color comes off, I remember that, and I remember getting sick and feeling 'glassy.' And I remember a white bed and people in white standing around me. And I remember one of the doctors saying, 'Look at those eyes.'

"Then I remember, not long after that, I walked in on her with the landlord: I suppose she was paying the rent," she said grimly. "She hit me and the landlord was trying to get past me doing his trousers up at the same time. She dragged me by the hair and threw me into the scullery. Westmoreland Road, where we lived, had a sort of living room where my parents and K. [her baby sister] slept, but mostly Billy was away and K. was with my Auntie Audrey. And that room was full of crucifixes and hanging rosaries—they were everywhere, when you were on the bed, they touched you. Then there was the kitchen-scullery and a room in the back, formerly a sort of coal bunker, where P. and I slept. Billy made a hutch for my rabbit. There were other rooms in the house: Harry Bury, Billy's friend, lived on top, and his brother had a room, too, and a woman called Frizzy, who had a baby. Everything was all right when my dad was there. But he wasn't often."

The story sounds as if it were all one memory, told in one breath, but it wasn't like that at all. I was, I must admit, at first so skeptical about the details that she remembered, and so concerned at the horrific nature of them, that I made her tell me three times over the months.

The first time was two weeks after we began to talk, in July 1996. The last time was at the beginning of December. In July it took her four days to get it out, sometimes in a monotonous voice but more often in deep distress, her face growing paler and paler, breaking into a sweat, and finally, she would speak through desperate sobs, reverting at times, as she had done before under emotional pressure, to the present tense.

She couldn't remember how old she was, but she thought four or five. "I wasn't yet in school," she said. She remembered being made to sit in the living room and that there was a man on the bed with her mother. "What I remember, this man's penis is all white, that's what I remember, really white and when he ... er ... *you* know, stuff comes, I just couldn't understand it, where it came from, you know, or what it was." She moved her nose as if she was smelling something nasty. "There was this smell, horrible, nasty like . . . But it was horrible, and then I was on the bed, and then . . . they turned on me."

As she answered my questions, one memory went into another. "I had these little white socks on and just a little top and, um, a nappy, a nappy-type thing . . . and my mother"—she sighed deeply (my notes say, "letting her breath out bit by bit")—"my mother would hold me, one hand pulling my head back, by my hair, the other holding my arms back of me, my neck back like, and . . . and . . . they'd put their penis in my mouth and when . . . when, you know, they . . . ejaculated, I'd vomit.

"Sometimes she would blindfold me—she called it 'playing blind-man's buff.' And she would tie a stocking around my eyes and lift me up and twirl me around, laughing. And then she'd put a thing . . . a silky thing around my face to . . . to keep my mouth open and it was so dread-ful, with the rosaries you know, bumping into me, you know, I felt so bad, so bad."

You told me that when your dad was around, you always felt safe, I said. So why didn't you tell him then? Why didn't you ask him for help?

"I was so frightened because before it, or later, she says if I ever told anything I would be taken away and locked up. You know I told you about the sentry box on the Tyne Bridge? That's where she said I would go. And she said nobody would believe me. And anyway, I think I must have thought it was my fault. I had done wrong and was being punished. I . . . I . . ." She cried and cried. It was one of the very worst moments of our time together. "I felt so . . . so dirty."

How often did this happen? I asked.

"I don't know. Not that often perhaps, or maybe quite a few times. I don't know." What is clear is that both the image of the white penises and the obscene blindman's buff her mother subjected her to had been in her unconscious memory all along. For the "game" had come up unexpectedly and out of context in Mary's visit, at age fourteen, to a psychiatric hospital where her mother was present. And in 1983 she spoke to Pat Royston about memories of white penises and people being beaten, without detailing the rest of the abuse.

I knew that a medical examination before she went to Red Bank had shown her to be intact. Did the men touch you, below? I asked. It was very, very difficult for her to find the words for the answer. "Yes, but . . . and I don't mean . . . Not, you know, I don't think it was there with their penis, I don't think . . . I don't . . . I mean I was held down on my stomach. It hurt like hell, it hurt . . . it really, really hurt. I was gagged but I screamed, 'It hurts, it hurts.' And she said to me, softly you know, 'It won't be long now, it won't hurt for long.' But it did. I was sore. For going to the toilet, I was sore, and I had marks, scratch marks on my legs and marks where I had things stuck into me."

Things? What sort of things?

"They were . . . sort of bullets, like a shotgun kind of bullet, with a brass thing, a suppository-type of thing . . . I used to have them twirled into me."

Where into you?

"My . . . bottom . . . Up on my legs." She pulled up the skirt of the long dress she was wearing and showed me some curious round scars.

Did you ever wonder why they did that?

She shook her head. "Perhaps to make me cry? But I didn't. I wouldn't cry."

You are crying now; you are crying here.

"I wouldn't cry then," she repeated.

Did your mother give you things afterwards?

"Yes, sweeties, and she was nice to me, and she laughed. I can remember times when I had these games, I felt afterwards she loved me. I had a bag of chips and I wouldn't get hit. I remember her then as very pretty and she didn't call me names, and even taught me to knit. But then she ripped all the stitches off and threw the stuff at me."

It is of some significance that when Pat Royston and I talked she had never yet read my first book. "Mary told me not to read it," she said. "So I didn't. It is how we work in the Probation Service: if I had read it I would have had to tell her and could have lost her trust. Her early childhood memories," Pat said, "seemed entirely focused on punishment, whether it was with beatings, or being given away to strangers, or being made to do other awful things she didn't specify but which felt bad, hurt, tasted bad, smelled bad, or whatever, all of these terrible memories dominated by her recollection of her mother directing this hate-filled look toward her—of her mother looking at her with hate. She told me about these constant beatings at home, but also whippings, with a whip, I understood in the presence of men who she recalled having erect penises. It was an incredibly emotional account. I remember feeling that I had to sit down to record it all at once, but I felt totally exhausted by her despair. I remember coming home that night and my partner, Martin, just had to hold me, I was so distraught."

How long did this horror go on for? I asked Mary.

"At Westmoreland Road," she said. "And also in another room nearby, in Elswick Road, which I think belonged to her friend Elsie. I think while I was small, you know, really small, four, five, six. After that, she or Elsie would take me to rooms where old men lived and leave me."

And what would happen?

She shrugged. "Not that much. They'd touch me. They'd masturbate. I didn't care."

A Decision

Of course, Mary did care. And she demonstrated this in an extraordinary way when she was about seven going on eight, she thinks. "I told you about Dad's friend, Harry Bury, the rag-and-bone man who lived upstairs in Westmoreland Road? He was brilliant. He called me his lucky mascot. And one day I went up to his room and he'd probably had a drink and was asleep lying on his back. And I went up and fiddled with his trousers . . . You know . . . I opened his buttons or zip or whatever and took it out."

You took his penis out? Why?

"I wanted to see whether he'd be like all the others. And he shot up and he was absolutely disgusted and said, 'What the hell are you doing?' But then, almost right away, he was like, 'It's all right, it's all right. Let's go and have a cuppa tea and feed the cat.' And after that I was OK, you know. The next time it came up, I told my mother I wouldn't do it no more."

In 1970 I'd talked briefly with Harry Bury. How did he think it happened—whatever it was that happened to Mary? "When she was very small," he said quickly, "that was when it started, like . . ."

· · ·

After Mary's decision to say no to her mother and her extraordinary experiment—the "test" of Harry Bury's character—she spent a lot of time, she said, trailing around after him, helping with his rag-and-bone collecting, and in some ineffectual way Harry Bury probably appointed himself her protector. He would no doubt have been aware of Betty's profession—the fact that women were prostitutes and had their "specialities" was not rare in that part of the city—but I am sure he had not known how she used her child.

What Harry Bury could not protect Mary from was the anger that was emerging in her and that, after her decision to resist her mother, began to show itself in her behavior. Even at this late point, when she began, unconsciously but with deliberation, to make herself extremely conspicuous, if somebody with judgment and compassion had taken notice the terrible things that were about to happen might never have happened.

One has to imagine the chaos of those lives. Betty and Billy, Betty and six-and-a-half-year-old P., Betty and eight-year-old Mary, all in mutually destructive relationships, each seeking his or her own way out: Betty's prostitution; Billy involved in more and more small crimes, repeatedly in trouble with the police; P. up to his own capers, for which he was now beaten with increasing severity by his mother; Mary, beginning to take her revenge by using, rather than being used by, men: "I'd get pennies for watching the old guys masturbate," she said.

Just over a year later, when they moved to Whitehouse Road in 1966, she would graduate to provoking men in cars: "I'd go up to the window and they'd ask me in. They'd expose themselves; some asked me to touch them and masturbate them. I used to hate them, threaten them, point at someone and say, 'That's my uncle over there, he knows I'm in this car.'" (By this time, of course, Betty had told the children they had to call Billy Bell "uncle" so she could claim social security as a single mother.) "They'd tell me to get out of the car," Mary continued. "But I'd take my time until they were really scared. They made me feel dirty, but I kept on doing it. And then they'd offer me sweets, and I said, 'You've got to be kidding,' and then they'd give me half a crown and I'd laugh, and I remember the black marks down my legs, dirt and sperm . . ."

And your mother didn't know this?

She laughed scornfully. "She'd have asked me for the money."

Did you do this often?

"I did it for about a year and a half," she said, now sounding tired. "I think maybe only four or five times."

But what about Billy, your dad? Couldn't you have told him?

"He would have murdered them," she said at once, then added impatiently, "But I told you, he was never there when she was there and she was always there when she wasn't in Glasgow."

After the move to Whitehouse Road, Betty began to live a double life. The new house, on a much better street, right across the road from her sister-in-law, was her respectability, and from this point she transferred her "business" to Glasgow, disappearing for days at a time. The two youngest girls now lived almost permanently with their Aunt Audrey in her spotless house. "Audrey was immaculate," said Mary. "I was ashamed to go over there . . . Denise, her daughter, was always well turned out, you know, her hair was always plaited. I always thought Audrey was bothered that I would get lice on Denise; [before we moved] the whole family used to trail up there from Westmoreland Road for a bath.

"P. and I were alone for days, weeks, it seems to me," Mary said. "He was all over the place; he had lots of sidelines. He was much more of an entrepreneur than I. He knew when the bakery opened and we could swipe sweets and rolls and stuff—he could do things without confrontation or violence, in and out, that was him. I'd hold him up. I had to pay to be with him. He paid me for going away. I'd say, 'I'll give you sixpence to play with me'; he gave me sixpence not to . . .

"Sometimes when she [Betty] went, my dad came, but not otherwise. And when he was there, he and Harry brought things to eat, and he cooked and we ate together. When my mother was there, it was pies and sausage rolls and fish and chips I was sent to get, and she never ate with us and there were constant screams and beatings. She hurt P. too. She was horrible to him, called him all kinds of names like 'spastic bastard,' 'thick bastard.' He hated her."

Did your mother ever beat the little girls? I asked.

"No, she didn't," Mary answered. "We wouldn't have let her. She only beat P. and me. I loved my little sisters. We wouldn't have let her touch them."

Did Billy ever beat you? I asked.

"Never," she said firmly. "He couldn't beat any of us. I remember my mother telling him to give me a beating one day, and he took me upstairs and told me to jump up and down on my bed and make a noise so that it would sound as if he was beating me, but he never did, not P. either, ever."

But though she was "always away," Betty always returned to Scotswood. It was as if she could not bear to be parted from the object of her love and hate. Perhaps, under the pressure of the life she had created, she became more violent toward both children and, because of Mary's ever more obvious rebellion against her, particularly savage toward her.

"It was a Sunday and she was out or away, so I thought I'd draw myself a bath," Mary said. "But she came back when I was in the water, and I had used all the hot water and she went berserk and made me fill it full of cold and then she pushed my head under and held it down and I found . . . from somewhere . . . found . . ." Strength? I asked her, but she went on, disjointedly, without hearing me. "Perhaps from the lack of oxygen, I held my breath and I put my hands up and tried to grab something and was hit on the back with something and I tried to jump up and she pushed me back down. But then I managed to jump out and put my foot in a hole on the floor and ran outside and sat on the back step with no clothes on and then P. came and we went in together and she started on him and me too, with a dog chain. The police came that night. By this time I was wearing an old brown baby-doll thing of hers, torn and ripped, but she just said it was nothing and they just went . . ."

The Breaking Point

By 1968, Mary had become best friends with her new next-door neighbor, Norma Bell, and was now approaching the weeks before that first incident which would bring her and Norma to the attention of the police: the pushing of little John Best down the "embankment" near the Delaval Arms.

After the murders, in the hysteria they created, people in Scotswood came forward claiming to have seen Mary committing all kinds of violent acts—strangling a bird, killing a cat, putting her hands round the throat of a baby—none of them proved, all of them rejected by the court.

All Mary remembers is an enormous buildup of tension in her during those weeks. We know from neighbors' accounts that she came at that time to the attention of a lot of people who, however, ascribed her behavior to her usual naughty ways and ignored it.

But, rightly or wrongly, she has come to associate "the day of Martin Brown," as she described it, with a specific fight with her mother.

"She'd sent me to the shop that morning for a brush. And when I got there, I didn't know if it was a brush head or a [whole] brush, and I was too frightened to go back and ask, and I thought it was a broom she wanted, so I came back with that and she pulled the long bit that goes into the brush out and beat me with it and I ran upstairs into P.'s room to hide under the bed and she was poking me with it. And I grabbed it and she dragged me out hanging on to it. And I says, *"You whore!"* and punched her in the stomach and she hit at me and hit at me while I raced down the stairs and then I was out. That was the first time ever I'd stood up to her, the first time I called her a name or hit her back."

She must have thought it was safe to go back at dinnertime, however, because, according to both her own and Norma Bell's story to the police, after her dinner Betty had sent her once more to the shop, this time for dog meat and pease pudding. But then her memories of that month and that day, and of everything involving what she did to Martin Brown, are broken up and confused—not, I think, because she was lying, on this or any of the other occasions when she tried to talk to me about what she had done, but because the trauma was unexplored and unresolved. "I didn't even remember until you told me that it happened the day before my birthday," she said in a small voice.

In the intervening years she had presented several versions of Martin Brown's death. In two of them, at Red Bank and at Styal, aged fourteen and eighteen, she described it as an accident. In one, to Pat Royston in 1983, she described it as an act committed together with Norma (who was not present). In 1985, in the draft for a book she wrote at the urging of her ex-husband, she said she did it quite simply "in anger."

Eleven years later, with terrible difficulty, she would give me four different versions, the last of which I have decided is probably as close to the truth as her memory could manage. I have quoted from some of these in previous chapters but must now present them in context. Each of the following accounts was interspersed with other memories— of Norma, of seeing the coffin of a baby in Westmoreland Road, of crying her eyes out reading her mother's book, of Betty's poem to her father, "In Memoriam." "Can you believe it," Mary said again, in the same disgusted tone as before, "a love poem like that to your father?"

In the first account she admitted immediately that she was on her own. She had gone to the derelict house in St. Margaret's Road, where she found Martin Brown, whom she knew, playing in the yard. He had followed her inside, where Mary had climbed "like a monkey" along "the beams above a room without a floor" and told him not to follow her. "It is ironic," she said. "I told him to be careful, but he came anyway, so I got hold of his hand and we both fell."

The second version was a fuller account and by this time she was sobbing. "Martin was already in the yard, but I thought of, you know, play dead . . ."

A game? I asked.

"No, I didn't think it was a game. I just thought, I'm not really hurting you. I'll lie down with you. And I did. I didn't drag him. There was no shouting and screaming—everyone would have heard it. I said, 'I'm not going to hurt you, not really.' I said, 'We will go to heaven . . .' I told him to put his hands on my throat and I put my hands on his and . . . we fell through the beams. I don't know whether he landed on me or I on him . . . There was junk on the floor, the sort of thing you find in derelict houses . . . I had been picked up by my throat lots of times, by my mother, by some of the clients. When my mother used to pull my head back, with the throat stretched, she used to say, 'It won't hurt . . .' and when I'd lose consciousness and then wake up I'd hear her or them say, 'It'll be all right . . .' "

Have you always associated what happened to you with what you did to Martin on that day?

"Not until much later . . . a few years . . . a few months ago," she said.

So why didn't you say this, to Pat, for example, or later on to me?

"I didn't ever want to say it. Not today either . . . It sounds too much . . . too much like . . ."

I waited. She couldn't, wouldn't say the word.

338

"Nothing can justify what I did," she finally said. "Nothing."

In the third description, which was almost identical to the second, she quoted her partner, Jim, asking her how she had known how to strangle someone and her reply that she hadn't really known. Years ago she allegedly told Norma she had seen it in a Bond film. "But I knew he was unconscious," she said. "I recognized that state of not moving, not wanting to move. So I lay down next to him and covered myself with bricks."

Of all the fantasies or associations I had heard from her, this was one of the strangest. Very early on, in her descriptions first of her mother's sexual abuse of her and then of the killings of the two children, I had asked her how much she had read about sexual child abuse or about the murder of children. And she had assured me she had read almost nothing and "never read the papers." I knew very soon this was not true. In Styal a number of women had talked to her about Myra Hindley, including the former nun, Tricia, who had been an intimate friend of Hindley's, and all of them would have spoken about the terrible child murders Ian Brady and Hindley committed. I knew, too, that Pat Royston, once she had realized that Betty Bell had sexually abused Mary, had lent her books on child abuse, though Pat was sure that none of them contained descriptions such as those Mary had given both of us. Like me she thought Mary's memories of her own abuse were too detailed, too specific, and indeed too strange, to allow any doubt. Nonetheless, she had not told the full truth about the two things, and it was something I knew we had to discuss.

I had realized from the start that her stories of Martin's death, those she told to others and the early versions she told to me, had been either wholly or partly invented. This was very clearly a matter not of exaggerating or fantasizing but of an incapacity to face the truth. This description of "covering" herself with bricks—not true either— appeared to me to be something more. Despite her statement that she never read the papers, she might well have added to the confused images in her mind the reports that the two boys who had killed James Bulger in 1993 had covered his body with bricks, but I suspected there

were other and possibly significant meanings to the association of brick-
ing, or walling in, that I was not equipped to interpret. When I asked her
again, she still said she'd resisted reading anything about the Bulger
killing.

"I stayed, it seemed for hours," she continued. "So long, I don't
know, I might have fallen asleep, but still no one came . . . I don't remember any voices."

Do you remember coming back to yourself?

"No. No. I only remember being on the outside [*sic*]. It wasn't long
before there was a lot of commotion. I remember thinking, If I'd stayed
a little longer, they would have found me . . . and Martin, and I would
have come alive . . . and would at last have been taken away, and everyone
would have understood."

But you knew *you* weren't really dead. Did you know Martin
was dead?

"Not dead, not really dead; just unconscious, unconscious like I had
been unconscious . . . I didn't understand the concept of death *forever* . . .
I think to me it was, 'You'll come round in time for tea.' "

It is extremely difficult to describe the extent of her distress during the
ten to twelve days in the early part of our talks when she spoke first
about the abuse she suffered and then about the killing of the two little
boys. For the first week of it, when she was staying with us in London, I
was sure almost every evening that she could not possibly go on with it
the next morning. During the second week, when she lived at home and
my husband and I stayed nearby, I doubted every day that she would
turn up, because I didn't think she could put herself through any more
of it. Although I knew that much of what she said was fantasy and evasion, I had still carefully limited my expressions of doubt and formu-
lated my questions as unaggressively as I could. However, about five
months later, as we were nearing the end of our talks, facing her with the
reality of Martin's killing had become inevitable.

I told her that I thought that there had been some truth in everything she had said to me about the killing of Martin, but that the evidence produced at the trial showed that most of what she said could not have happened. You cannot bear to remember it as it really was, I told her. But you must try. You must make another, final effort to tell it honestly. In the final analysis, I told her, only the truth would serve the purpose of this book, which was, on the one hand, to tell her story as completely as it could be told, but also to use what had happened to her, and the reactions of others, as an example and a warning.

"I don't know how to do it," she said. "I don't know if I can."

I had known this, of course, for months and, in trying to get Mary to face up to her most difficult memory and tell the truth, had discussed with the few people who knew about the book whether or not I should continue trying. Among them were two psychiatrist friends, Dr. Virginia Wilking in America and Professor Dan Bar-On in Israel. Dr. Wilking, who has worked for many years in Harlem and with children as severely traumatized as Mary, bluntly advised me to give up on the effort altogether: she was concerned over the unrelenting intensity of these sessions, which would normally, under therapeutic treatment conditions, have probably stretched over a period of years. Professor Bar-On did not agree. "The main reason [to continue]," he said, "is because she urgently needs to say it."

And so, a few weeks before Christmas, I told Mary I was going to ask her one more time about the day she killed Martin Brown and that she must concentrate as never before. I had turned off the telephone, the window was closed, and the curtains were half-drawn—not to make the atmosphere overly dramatic but to underline to Mary, who finds concentrating so difficult, the need to search back in her memory about this day and relate what had happened as far as it was possible in a sequence of events.

She sat with her eyes closed and her hands clasped in her lap, and again, everything came out very slowly, with long pauses between the words and crying, and once again, as the phrases jerked out, she slipped into the present tense.

As she had said before, she was in the yard of the derelict house.

"Martin is there," she said. "I climb in to look around the ground floor, and he follows me."

She paused. Go on, I said. "I says, 'Go home.' He won't . . . He won't . . . I take his hand and pull him after me up them stairs . . . broken stairs . . . He is crying. 'I don't want to,' he says, 'I want to go down . . . down . . . down' . . . He stops on a half-broken step which wiggles." Then. "Stop crying—" she said, quite sharply, and I interrupted her. Mary, I said, this is not happening now, you are only seeing it in your mind. She stopped for a long moment and I thought perhaps that was all she would say. But then, keeping her eyes closed, she nodded twice and then spoke again, this time in the past tense.

"He wouldn't stop crying . . . ," she said. Then stopped again. "When we got to the top . . . his crying had become hiccups . . . He had snot on his nose. 'I want to go down,' he said. I don't know why I took him up," she said. "I said, 'It's all right, I'll take you down' . . . But I can't carry him . . . I knew I couldn't get him down those broken stairs. There was a hole in what had been the upstairs floor, the ceiling of the room below, a small hole but big enough. I said to him, 'See that hole?' He stopped crying then. 'I'll let you down through that hole; hold on to my hand, I won't drop you.' And I did. I lay down on my stomach, held one of his hands, and let him down through that hole as far as I could stretch my arm and then he dropped to the floor. But it wasn't far. He fell but he didn't hurt himself. And I run down the stairs . . ."

Her concentration broke. "He could have run from me then," she said in a much louder voice, for the first time sounding defensive. "There was an opening where there had been a window, too; he could have shouted . . . called, but he didn't, he didn't. He wasn't frightened of me."

What happened then? I said. Close your eyes again.

She began again, the strain showing in her face. "He is in the corner, near the window, standing up with his back against the wall. I don't know how he got there."

Is he crying?

"No, no. I'm kneeling in front of him. I think I'm kneeling on a brick. I say . . ." She began to cry. " 'Put your hands around my throat,' and he does and . . . I put my hands around his throat [her hands are lying open in her lap] and I press, I press, I press . . ." She had leaned forward until she was bent double, her face down on her knees, her body trembling.

Do you know why you did it, Mary? I asked her. Were you angry? Can you try to tell me what you felt when you pressed Martin's throat?

"Angry?" Her voice was muffled, talking into her lap. "I'm not angry. It isn't a feeling . . . it is a void that comes . . . happens . . . opens . . . it's an abyss . . . it's beyond rage, beyond pain, it's black cotton wool . . ." She paused; the crying, too, had stopped.

Is it a sort of excitement?

"No, no, it's not, it's a draining of feeling."

Is there an urge?

"It's like a light being switched off without your knowing it's been on. It's like a train behind you and you have to walk, you have to keep walking but there's no noise, not even your own heartbeat . . . Sometimes if you are frightened, as I had been before, you feel your heartbeat very strongly, but not even that . . . muddy waters . . . ," she said, incomprehensibly. She was sitting up again now, leaning back again. Her voice had become monotonous. "Once I jumped into a pool and almost drowned, but it was different now, because then there was light—I remember looking up and I could see light [and] because I didn't know I was drowning I didn't have apprehension or fear. Though it was different with Martin, it was somewhat the same, but I can only equate it up to a certain point, because there was no light, no physical pull, no sensation . . ." She paused.

Was there no sense of feeling "I must stop"?

"No," she said. "There is a point where that walking ahead of the train gets more suffocating in your head."

What is it that suffocates?

"I'm trying . . . trying . . ." (At times I felt as if she was saying, "I'm trying for you.") "But it's black cotton wool, one has to get through it . . . One would die [if one didn't] . . . I'm saying that now. Now I'm . . . you

343

know, looking back, I feel an element of pain in me which wasn't there but which as an adult I imagine to be there."

You think now there had to have been panic. But what *was* there? What did you feel?

"Quiet," she said. "It was very quiet, very still, I wasn't aware of noises anywhere, in my head, outside, not from anybody. Martin . . . he . . . it was so . . . so quiet." She stopped.

She was motionless for what seemed a long time before she looked up, her eyes seeing me now, not—as she had put it earlier—looking at the past as through a curtain.

"Dr. Godfrey at Styal told me I would never understand until I had a child of my own and he was right. I didn't, but I do now." And now her voice sounded tired but unusually clear. "I didn't want . . . didn't intend to hurt Martin; why should I have? He was just a wee boy who belonged to a family around the corner . . ."

From the very beginning of our talks about the two killings, there had been a vast difference in the way she spoke about the death of Martin and that of Brian and it would take a long time before I understood the reason. From the moment she was arrested, throughout her trial, her imprisonment, and the fifteen years that followed—twenty-eight years in all—she had denied having killed Martin Brown, but she had admitted first a passive part in the killing of Brian Howe, then the inoffensive small part of covering him with flowers. The reason, now that I think I understand it, is that killing Martin was her own decision, or her need. She was alone when she felt it, alone when she did it, and she has been alone ever since with having done it. And even though she had hidden it from herself, just as she had hidden the memory of that dreadful abuse, the growing child knew somewhere inside that she had done something terribly wrong and that only one person could explain to her what and why—her mother.

She had tried once, at Red Bank. And she had been rebuffed with a finality—"Don't ever talk about it to no one"—that had stopped her ever asking again.

Killing Brian was different in many ways. Not only or not so much because she was not alone—whatever part Norma played or didn't play, she was *present*—but because where she had had no conscious wish or need to kill Martin Brown, she said, or to leave her "mark" on him, nine weeks later—whether it was because no one had paid attention to what she had done or because no one had understood—there had been an urge to manifest the doing of it.

I had pointed out to Mary time and again that in the case of Brian she could no longer persuade herself that death did not mean forever. It was a question I put to her over and over: if she understood that she had murdered Martin Brown, why had she continued with Brian Howe? And she would not, I had to conclude could not, answer it.

Her descriptions of Brian's death, both at the trial but also to me, were almost entirely about Norma. She pays lip service to not feeling angry with or bitter about Norma, but it is not, nor can it be expected to be, true. Whatever that young girl did or did not do that July day of 1968, her very presence was a reassurance and confirmation of purpose for Mary.

I know you try to deny this, I said to her, but however much I condemn what the court did with Norma, I have always been certain that you were the stronger and therefore had to have a part in the killing of Brian.

"Yes, I accept that," Mary said. "Though when one *is* the stronger and the other weaker, the weaker makes the other stronger by being weak . . ."

We will probably never know exactly what happened on that summer afternoon, except for two things that Mary finally told me. It was just after she had described what I firmly believe to be entirely true—how Norma, seeing the child lying there, had begun to scream. "I touched his face [she touched her own face as she spoke], his eyes weren't open, he wasn't getting up. And so I used one hand and closed his throat."

So it was actually you who killed him? I said.

She didn't answer. She had said it, and she would not, could not say it again.

"And then," she said, "Norma began laughing hysterically . . . and

there were weeds and tall flowers . . . I covered him over with the bul-
rushes . . ." And then she told how they had come back later, with a razor
blade and scissors.

So you would have cut his hair? I asked her. (In their statements,
Norma had said one thing and Mary had said another, and we probably
never will know who cut little Brian's hair or drew the letter N altered to
M into the skin of his stomach.)

"Yes, and . . ."

This is after you came back?

"Yes . . . and . . . to cut, trying, trying to cut . . . to cut his . . . penis."

Who wanted to cut his penis? I said, startled. She did or you did?

"Me."

But this didn't happen, did it?

"No, I wasn't successful."

Do you have any thoughts on this? I asked her.

"As an adult I do have," she said. "I can see all the reasons, all the
pointers, all the . . . the . . . Everything, you know, yes, what had happened to me and blah, blah, blah. But maybe it was just . . . I think it was
just because . . . It wasn't for a trophy, you know. It was . . . I can speak
now but not for then, I can use words now which I didn't know then: you
know, sort of symbolically castrating, taking away the offending organ."

And then weeks later, when I asked her to tell me once again what
happened with Brian, just as I had with Martin, she told the whole story
exactly as she had done before, repeating that it was she who had "closed
his throat," but she did not mention the scissors.

When you told me about this before, I pointed out, you said you
tried to cut his penis.

"I didn't say that."

Yes, you did.

"No, no, no, she . . . I . . . the razor blade and the marks on his tummy
and my initials, you know . . ."

But you always said it was Norma who put that—

"Yes, yes, yes, yes."

Then I asked you what you did with the scissors and after long hesitation you said: "I tried to cut his penis but I wasn't successful." Do you remember that?

"No," she said. "No, I don't, I don't, I don't."

I'll show it to you, I said.

"When, when did I say this?"

Weeks ago now; it's on the tape. It must have happened, otherwise you wouldn't have said it.

And a little later—a cigarette later—she said, "No, that's right, I wouldn't have invented, God, no. I must have . . ."

You were very upset.

"I mean, to remember . . . to sit here and say, yes, I said that. I'm so shocked because why would I forget saying something so horrid as that, so horrid to *me*."

But, I said, horrid as it is, in connection to what had happened to you years before, it is actually an explanation of your state of mind.

Still obviously in a state of shock, she asked whether she could phone Jim, her partner. "He knows everything. If I said that, he will know."

After a long telephone conversation with Jim, she came back, looking drained. "Yes," she said, her voice almost without tone. "He says that's right. I did."

PART SIX

BEGINNINGS
OF A FUTURE

1984 to 1996

Faltering Steps

I don't think that Mary sees the first eleven years of her child's life as being governed by her unconscious desire to keep as much distance as she could between her mother and the child. But the fact is that while from shortly after her prison release until her pregnancy she could not resist her need for her mother, nor Betty's for her; by the summer of 1985 she had not seen her for almost two years and Betty had not seen the baby. "I didn't want her [the child] to feel the vibes of her [Betty]," she said.

In 1985, Mary had a hysterectomy because of suspected cancer, and three weeks later, as Pat Royston told me, she had to go back to the hospital with an infection. "It was the day Mary returned home," Pat said, "that Betty suddenly appeared at their house, extraordinarily enough wearing purple satiny trousers. Extraordinary," she added, "because it was the sort of getup she would have worn years before but none of us had ever seen her in since she had lived respectably with George."

"I was sitting holding the baby," Mary said. "I couldn't believe she [my mother] had just come like that, uninvited, you know. I mean, this was *my* home; I didn't want her there. I didn't even want her to see me with the baby, so I said nothing, just left my face in the baby's hair. Pat said to my mother, 'What do you think of your granddaughter? Isn't she gorgeous?' 'I don't have to speak to you,' my mother answered, and walked out."

Didn't you give her the baby to hold? I asked.

"God forbid," she said in a heartfelt tone of voice, but by now almost with wry humor rather than anger.

It was also at this time that Mary's marriage showed the first cracks. Rob, she told me, and Pat confirmed it, was too young to understand the physical and emotional effects of a hysterectomy on a young woman. "I heard that he was making jokes about me to his friends," Mary said. "And he told everybody I was frigid."

He did more than that, however. He began to exist on Mary's notoriety. ("Really, like my mother had always done," Mary said.) He increasingly talked about her past, not only to friends but to strangers. "When we'd first become friends," Mary said, "I'd made the fatal mistake of telling him about that offer for my story from the German magazine, and I now realized that had stayed in his head ever since. When he packed his job in, he'd said he wanted to spend time with the baby, and he did that—it was true, he loved the baby—but he had other plans, too."

At some point later that year, urged by Rob, Mary spent a week (seventy-two hours in one go, she told me) writing down some of her story—nothing about her childhood, nothing about her mother, a repeat performance of her statements in court about her crimes, but a lot about her years of detention.

"Prison was easy to write the truth about," she said, and shrugged. "But the rest was mostly lies." She shrugged again. "Sensation—I thought that was what people wanted."

It was to be many years before she developed enough moral judgment to understand that "sensation" was precisely what people would reject coming from her, as indeed the agency that agreed to handle her draft demonstrated when it stipulated that 50 percent of whatever such a book would earn be given to the National Society for the Prevention of Cruelty to Children. "I thought it was entirely hypocritical," Mary said. "It was sycophantic, tasteless, and tacky. It felt as if I would be saying,

'Please like me, I *am* a nice person, because I'm giving to charity and to a children's charity at that.' Ugh, it was sick. And I didn't think [that] to decent people that would make me into or prove that I was a nice person. So I told them to fuck off."

A year or so later, when her own relationship was near the breaking point, George came to see Mary and said he had left her mother. "He said she had put all her miseries, her lies, and her guilt on him for twenty-one years and he couldn't take it any longer. He said he would see that she would always be financially OK, and for me, he'd always be my friend, but that was it.

"Well, I was sorry for her then. I rushed over and she was sitting there like a dying duck and she pleaded with me to get him back to her. But that was impossible. He'd found somebody else very nice, and I knew that would be his life from then on."

But Mary's life, too, was about to change. For several months, while Rob was increasingly "out on the tiles" as she put it, she had got to know, at a rock club she occasionally went to with friends, a young man called Jim whom she liked. "I didn't think about him seriously, you know," she said. "But because the relationship I was in was really, really rocky, I fantasized. But I never dreamed that he—Jim—was thinking about me in the same way. I would never have dared . . ." They had become friends, and when, a few months later, in early May 1988, a really major fight (about Rob's going around talking about Mary as if she were "some sort of a freak show") finally put an end to the marriage, it was to Jim she went. "You understand, I *had* to get out," Mary said. "For twelve years it had been drummed into me that I must control myself and I did: I not only learned it, I felt it. But that evening, after a girlfriend had told me what Rob was saying about me, that control broke. I hit him and punched him and then I stopped myself and rushed out . . . I knew he loved [the child, who was then almost four] and was more than capable of looking after her for a night, and I *had* to go."

"I'd been watching their relationship those four years," Pat Royston said, "and I had realized quite soon that Rob was just too immature.

Mary is, of course, a very, very complex person, and he couldn't cope. In his frustration he had repeatedly been violent to her and she had taken it. But when it finally got too much for her, she found herself responding violently to him and, quite rightly I thought, walked out when she realized she was losing control."

The next day there was a meeting in the probation office and Pat brought the child to Mary. Four days later, Jim, Mary, and the little girl moved south. It had been their intention to settle there, and Jim quickly found a job making precision tools. But only six weeks later he walked off his job in protest of a fellow worker fired—fired, Jim was convinced, simply because he was black. "Jim just won't take that," Mary said, "but we had no money saved, so we just had to go back where he had his parents and I had Pat."

Pat had worked for years on building up Mary's fragile self-esteem and had helped in emergencies. "But the next one was really catastrophic," she said.

The three of them had settled down in a little village. "Wherever Mary (or any released lifer) goes to live," Pat said, "her probation officer has to inform the chief constable of the region, and he in turn must tell the local police. In this instance, a policeman in the village, on learning who she was, told his wife." Together with other villagers she got up a petition and soon people were parading through the street with banners saying "Murderer Out." "Of course, I had to move them at once," Pat said. "Mary was distraught, really totally distraught. She said thank God the child couldn't yet read, but how could she live putting her at such risk? It was terrible. And they said they wanted to go back south and never come back to the Northeast. Well, I felt this was a legitimate reaction, and we then helped them move into an area in the south of England where she could have the support of an experienced probation officer.

Samantha Connolly, who became Mary's probation officer from October 1988, is one of the warmest and most attractive people I would meet while I worked with Mary. Now retired, she worked in the Probation Service for thirty years and, except for Pat Royston, became Mary's wisest counselor.

"I first met Mary on a late autumn day, in the early afternoon," she said. "They had managed very quickly to get themselves sensibly established on an estate farm, where the owners had given them a really nice cottage rent-free, against Mary helping in the manor for twelve hours a week and Jim working one full day in the grounds. For the remainder of the week, he had got himself a job as a carpenter and he loved this and worked hard."

Sam was impressed by the reception she was given by the little family. "Mary had been very friendly, very polite when I phoned her," she said, "and she had laid out a nicely prepared tea when I came. It's not what I'm necessarily used to when I visit clients." She laughed. "There's quite often a cup of coffee or tea, but a carefully prepared little feast isn't somehow the way they usually react. You see, she wasn't making up to me or anything; she was a house-proud young woman and she was shy and warm . . . all quite unexpected. I was impressed, too, by how tactful they were: the child was not there when I arrived—she had been taken to play with new friends—and Jim excused himself after a cup of tea, saying he would go and get her, but it was clearly because he realized I would want to speak to Mary on her own.

"Pat had of course briefed me to some extent and I had carefully read the file she had sent me. I learned a lot from Pat, but very little from the pre-release part of the file, which after all was supposed to cover twenty-three years of Mary's life. I was surprised.

"But it was clear from what Pat had told me that Mary had talked to her about her childhood and I had decided not to touch upon her past unless it happened on her initiative. It seemed to me that my role was to keep an eye on how things were going, with their jobs, with their relationship, and of course in relation to the child . . ." For the next five years, Sam would not only supervise and counsel Mary but (as Pat had done from the start) also keep an eye on the child, who remained a ward of court.

Sam has both humor and a sharp eye for what is behind the front people often put on, and she was to take a considerable liking to Jim. "I felt from the beginning a kind of inner strength in him which I came to understand is absolutely crucial to Mary," she said. "I watched that little girl over five years; I don't know how Mary does this, but she is an entirely secure and happy child."

"In some way," Sam said, echoing my own feelings about Mary, "Mary has made herself into two people for her own sake. There is the consistent Mary, capable of what I can only say is excellent gentle discipline for the child and very clear principles mixed with a lot of gaiety. And then there is the other Mary, who has a mind that ranges helter-skelter over countless things, unable to hang on to one subject for more than a moment, particularly when she is depressed, and her depression is always about her own guilt. In talking to her then, you couldn't catch hold of a subject she brought up before it had disappeared in a welter of other thoughts and ideas. And if you wanted to get back to it on another day, *that* Mary couldn't do it. But the other Mary—the little girl's mum—was totally consistent not only in what she did but also in her thoughts and ideas which she communicated to the child."

Sam felt that we cannot begin to understand how, given the family model of Mary's own childhood, together with the fact that her late childhood, adolescence, and young adulthood were totally institutional, she has learned to mother a child.

"I watched her for years," Sam said. "It was my job, but finally it was also my pleasure. It was extremely interesting to me how she, who can stick to nothing for any length of time—jobs, courses, even ideas—was able to create lots of opportunities for the child. It is almost as if she can transfer—if you like—that buried ability in herself to the child. She is very, very loving. Quite tactile, but not overly so; not satisfying her own needs. It is a mixture of allowing the child quite a lot of freedom to do things on her own and with friends and, on the other hand, this very protective side. When she went to school, either Jim or Mary always took her and fetched her. And they did a lot of things with her, sports, games, bicycling when she was able. But with all that, Mary was quite a disciplinarian—you know, bedtime was bedtime. If she went out to play, there were places she couldn't go to. If she wanted to go beyond an established distance, she had to come and ask, and if Mary said no and the child sulked and said, 'You are a horrible mother,' as children do, Mary appeared to be able to accept it with the kind of equanimity that helps a child get over the sulks. If the child asked a question, her mother gave her an answer; there was no fudging the issue. You see, as far as the child is concerned, Mary thinks only healthy. I remember the second time I visited her, I was having tea with her and the little girl suddenly said, 'I have two daddies, haven't I?' And Mary hugged her and said, 'Yes, aren't you lucky?' "

Having said all this, Sam explained she didn't want to give me a false impression. Mary, though one of the most interesting "clients" she'd had, was certainly also one of the most difficult and draining. "After a while, Mary did talk to me about her past," she said. "Quite often just in little dollops. I believe that people can only handle so much at one time. I always responded to what she wanted to bring me. There were many good times, but the bad ones could be very bad, very intense, and I remember days when, coming home, I just had to lie down I was so exhausted with it and I often thought, How does Jim stand it? because surely it all had to come down on him."

She had not found Mary to be what she called a "crying" person. "She only cried when she was very low, when she was overwhelmed with her feelings of guilt. But then it could become storms of unstoppable sobs. You see, you can't take the guilt away from her. It's there. It's a fact. And basically, of course, it has to be. It's only—how can one help her to live with it?"

Sam had found the responsibility of supervising Mary particularly lonely. "Our departments are very small. Everyone carries large case-loads, and though most clients are probably not as complex or as much at risk from this bugbear of publicity as Mary is, they are still difficult. [In Mary's case] first of all there was her hidden identity, about which there had already been that dreadful trouble up north; then there was her high profile and your responsibility for keeping the child safe, away from it all. And when you are dealing with a human being in such terrible pain, you become very concerned about whether, even with all you have learned, you know enough. When there is a crisis, you can't exchange opinions with anyone. You have to carry the anxiety whether you are doing the right thing around with you alone, and that's hard." At least she and Pat could communicate by phone, she said, and settle a number of Mary's urgent practical problems together.

Within weeks of Mary's arrival in the South there had been a report of a thirteen-year-old boy who had killed a two-year-old girl. "The press went mad," Sam said. "Pat rang to say they were searching everywhere for Mary. She'd had calls from TV and press and I don't know who else and she said for heaven's sake to warn Mary. I went round like a headless chicken trying to contact her; she was out on a hike with a group of children. I finally raced around to be there when she got back and told her. Oddly enough, she was totally calm."

Mary remembered the occasion but said it was only one of several and that it seemed the press would chase her whenever there was any crime involving children, as perpetrators or victims. "That day," she said, "all I was glad about was that I hadn't given my mother my address; if I had, they'd have been all over me already. As it was, I felt we were safe."

Sam said yes, Mary had finally quite often talked about her mother, in turmoil about the need in her to belong to her and at the same time the rage against her.

"The rage was not only for what her mother had done to her in the past," Sam said, "but for continuing to make her feel guilty and worthless, isolating her from the rest of the family and squeezing her dry emotionally. And then of course there is the question of who her natural father was, which seemed to torture her." Finally—Sam thought it was in 1992—Mary had told her she wanted to go and have it out with her mother on her own.

"All three of us were going north in May, but I went earlier, for Mother's Day," Mary told me. "I hadn't been in touch with her at all.

And as soon as I came into the house, she said, 'It doesn't make any difference to me whether you come or not; you could live in the same street and I'd never see you.' But I asked her point-blank, as I had done once before, you remember, after Chammy told me, and she just walked out on my question. This time I asked her much quieter, you know, and she did tell me a name, a man who was a friend of my Uncle Jackie's. So a few days later, Jim and I went to see Uncle Jackie and I said, 'Will you tell me the truth, because my mother has given me a name?' And he said, 'I will if I can.' And I said, 'Is L.D. my real dad?' And he looked . . . well, his face just showed total surprise . . . so surprised that both Jim and I had to believe it wasn't him. After that I went to see George and asked him once more and he just said like he'd said before, 'It's best for you not to know.' "

And the next day, when they were staying with Jim's parents, Mary and Jim's mother were sitting in the living room in the evening, talking about Jim's family, "and I was telling her about my granny McC., who'd died [in April 1981], and how my mother hadn't allowed me to go to the funeral, because she said my Auntie Isa wouldn't want to see me because she still blamed me for the death of her little John. I told Jim's mother how terrible I had felt not to be there when I'd so loved my granny, and suddenly she said, 'Do you mind if I ask you something? I'm not being morbid and I don't want to upset you, but it's on my mind, so I want to ask it.' I said OK, and she said, just like that, 'Did your mother sexually abuse you?' She said she'd read your book and she felt there had to be a reason for the way I was when I was ten; that something even more must have happened than was in your book. So you know, I told her, and she said she loved me like a daughter, and to forgive her, but she could honestly kill my mother. But I said, 'She's sick. She's always been sick.' "

"That's what she told me when she came back," Sam said. "She also said she'd have to let go of the question of who her real dad was. She was sure her mother would never tell her, that whatever it was, it was too terrible to tell. And she said that she had wanted so much, had tried so hard to be closer to her mother and that she didn't think her mother consciously wanted to hurt her, or do what she did, or make her feel as she did. She sounded very together that day, but she wasn't. She was in a terrible state and it got worse all the time."

In January 1993 Mary phoned Chammy and told him she wanted to see him before he died: she couldn't cope with the guilt about what she had done.

"Yes, I did," Mary told me. "That was a time when it all came at me, I couldn't stand it. Martin and Brian were on my mind every day, any day, any ordinary day, something would just trigger it off, anything: the sun, a beautiful evening, the word Gillette, my feeling about being a mother and what about their parents, what had they felt because of me, oh God . . ." She began to cry. "It will never be enough, it will never change . . . the weight of it. I'm sorry, I'm sorry . . . sorry . . . But it's words . . . isn't it? Just words . . ."

"That's how it went for weeks, for months," Sam said. "She got terrible migraines she'd had repeatedly before, ear infections, abscesses in her mouth, colds, flu. The doctor prescribed painkillers and Jim was very worried about her. And yet, even though the pain was obviously there, she could push it aside when the child came in . . . But of course then," Sam said, "came the nightmare of the Bulger case."

"It *was* a nightmare," Mary said. "I felt *raw.*" She said that she knew none of the details of how little James Bulger met his death, that she did not *want* to find out by reading articles or listening to the unending news reports about it. "But I wondered whether all of the nightmare would be repeated, whether it would all happen again as it did to me. That they would find one guilty and acquit the other. And I felt so . . . terrible . . . for that small boy's parents. But you see, for the other parents, too, I felt disgusted, absolutely disgusted with the circus that was made out of it and which I knew would inevitably become even worse when they were put on trial as I had been, with their names disclosed and the public allowed in . . . queuing for hours, I heard somebody say, to gawk at them."

Once, she said, she'd been at the house of a neighbor who had the

TV on "and the boys were being taken out of court and there were people, adult people, screaming, beating, pounding on the van they were in as if they wanted to kill them. And then—my blood ran cold—the TV announcer commented on this and he mentioned me: it was like a thunderbolt. Martin's and Brian's parents were on my mind all the time anyway, but when this happened it became worse . . . Just think what it must have done to them to hear this; it was bad enough without making comparisons . . .

"And everybody, just everybody talked about it," she said. "My friends, too, why wouldn't they? I can't tell you what it was like to hear 'Mary Bell' time and time again, countless times, and there were some lies. Once I turned on the radio and happened on some chat-show host who said I had phoned him. I thought I'd faint. I never phoned anybody. I never talked to anybody, after a while no longer even to friends. I was terrified somebody might find me out, recognize me from the old photos which suddenly reappeared in the papers. There was a phone-in a friend told me about, where they asked people what they thought about having a curfew for children. And one woman called in who said that she remembered a day when she didn't come in when her mother called her, and when she did her mother shook her and said, 'If you don't come in when you are called, Mary Bell will get you.'

"It just seemed as if I couldn't get away from the name. I finally couldn't think about anything else, couldn't eat, couldn't sleep. I knew from Sam the papers were looking for me, and she told me frankly she was concerned about the local police. She was afraid one of them would give me away as I had been given away before. I thought it was only a question of time before they would find me and I was frantic about it. I don't know now which I thought about more: what had been done to the little boy and what would happen to the little boys who did it or my awful apprehension about people connecting it with my past and chasing me.

"Yes," she said, "I was frightened not only of the press but also just of people attacking me if they found out who I was. And it was so difficult for Jim and I did know that he was dreadfully concerned with my reaction, the way I connected that case with myself and the pain I felt and my panic. It was just that keeping it all away from [her child] was as much control as I could manage. It helped me a little to have to do that; it somehow forced me to take a breather, but outside of that, like during the day when she was at school or at night when she was asleep, I felt I was falling apart."

It was Pat Royston who finally decided the only safe thing was to bring them back to the Northeast and establish them in an area where she knew the chief constable and could trust the local police. "I had to advise them to go," Sam said. "Jim didn't mind that much. True, there was a recession in the North, but by now it had hit us too and he'd been made redundant and they had been on social security for eight months. Mary hated to go. She didn't want to bring the little girl up in the Northeast. Above all, she didn't want her—or herself—anywhere near her mother. But I agreed with Pat that Pat's resources for keeping them safe were better than mine. They had to go."

Although Mary and Jim occasionally worked over the next two years, they mainly lived on social security. "I just hated, hated to be there," Mary said. "I hardly saw my mother. I'd become angrier about her after my granny McC.'s death. She had no right, did she, to alienate me . . . from everybody? The whole family went to my granny's funeral. Only I didn't. What must they have thought? That I didn't care? I didn't know any of them. How could they know *how* much I cared?

"And she did something even worse when my Aunt Cath died. I was actually at her [Betty's] house, and I said I was going to pop in to see Auntie Cathleen, and she didn't tell me she was dead. The funeral had been two weeks before. And there I popped in like the angel of death, asking for Auntie Cath, and they looked at me as if I was mad, as well they might have. I went next door to where her oldest boy lived, my cousin R., and that's where I went berserk. He had a terrible time calming me down. Then we went back and looked at photos with my Uncle Jackie.

"But all that was in me . . . It had gone on for so long, and I was just so weary of it, of her."

But then two things happened almost simultaneously. First, about three weeks before Christmas 1994, Betty contacted Mary and asked to see her and Jim. "She sounded . . . somehow small," Mary said, "and Jim said we'd meet her at a pub and she asked what we were doing for Christmas, and Jim, on an impulse I think, said why didn't she come and spend Christmas with us. And then I did talk to her about [the child]. She'd only seen her once, as a baby, and I showed her photographs and suggested she should meet her before she came for Christmas. 'You *are* her granny,' I said. 'There's no way we can have any of that my being your cousin crap,' and she nodded, you know, compliant-like, as I'd never seen her."

Mary had always told her little girl that her granny was sick and that was why she wasn't around. "So that night when I told her we'd have a day out with her granny at the Metro Centre [a large shopping center in Gateshead] before Christmas, she said, 'Oh, good. Is she better, then?' And I suddenly thought, and Jim did too, that I didn't really have any more right to withhold her granny from my child than my mother had to alienate my family from me."

The date was for a week before Christmas. "We went along there and there were hundreds of people and [the child] was looking about and she asked what color Granny's hair would be and I joked and said orange, but of course it wasn't. I saw her sitting near the fountain; she didn't have a wig on and her hair was very thin, just a bit of it, sort of permed and gray . . . she wasn't old, you know, just fifty-six, but she looked like a terribly thin little old lady. [The child] ran up to her, nearly ran her down with all that energy she has, and called out 'Hiya, Granny!' and over the next four hours while we shopped and ate and walked, she absolutely wore her out, basically just by talking. She was such a chatterbox, my girl. But it was a good day, a really good day. I was happy, my mother was happy as well, and later [the child] asked what was the matter with her. 'She *seems* OK,' she said. And so I told her that her granny had a drinking problem and she said, 'Can't she stop?' And I explained that if one had that problem one could only stop if one wanted to very badly and that I didn't think she wanted to. I had to tell her: Jim and I always try to tell her the truth as far as we think she can cope with it.

"We had two really good days when she came for Christmas," Mary said. "Perhaps it was because it was short enough that we didn't get on each other's nerves but long enough for her to get to know [the child] and yet for me to be calm because I knew it wouldn't be long enough for her to have any influence on her."

She felt the child was in no danger from her mother, firstly because she wasn't her mother's responsibility but also because the child was so secure. "And she could make her granny laugh . . . To hear her laughing, really laughing, was just amazing."

Betty had left them in a taxi on the morning of December 27. Mary had phoned her that night and there was no answer. "I phoned her next on Hogmanay [New Year's Eve] and there was again no answer. I thought she was at the pub or with her friend Maggie . . ."

It is not known exactly when Betty died. "The neighbors saw her on New Year's Eve," Pat Royston said. "They raised the alarm on January third." When the police broke in they found her nude in a chair very close to the gas fire, which had been on and which had burned one side of her. The postmortem and inquest concluded she'd had peritonitis, but they gave pneumonia as the cause of death. She'd obviously had some sort of attack, had managed to get up, clear the sheets off the bed, and leave them and her nightdress in a pile on the bathroom floor. It appeared that she'd then had a bath or sponged herself clean and sat down in her chair.

"I know Mary thinks she wanted to die," Pat said. "The telephone was more or less within reach, and she had this good friend downstairs. Had she shouted, she would have been heard. There *were* neighbors— but she didn't shout. Still, the police didn't think it was suicide. There were potatoes and vegetables cleaned and ready to cook in a pot of water on the stove.

"George rang to tell me she was dead and that he was going to see

Mary to tell her," Pat said. "Mary phoned me after he left and both she and the little girl cried on the phone. By the next day, when I took her and Jim to Betty's flat, she showed a mixture of upset, relief, and anger. When we got there, the flat was full of the family, all looking through her things, looking for the will. It was that 'book' they were looking for. That's where they thought she would have put the will. But they never found the book and they never found a will."

Did you think that asking to come and stay with you for Christmas was your mother's way of saying goodbye? I asked Mary.

"Yes, yes . . . ," she said, tentatively.

It's good that you and Jim and your little girl gave her these two days, isn't it? I said.

"She gave them to me, sort of," she said. "At the funeral, I was at the front with Jim and Auntie Isa . . . All the family was there, except the girls and P.; he was in some trouble. But I saw him later and it was good, good. I'll always love him, whether I see him or not. And I think he feels something for me. Something from long ago.

"After the funeral, the greatest surprise to me was Isa's boy D. He's a great big bloke, a professional footballer, and he came up to me and, you know, I expected he was just going to shake my hand, which was the most anybody else had done, but he sort of pulled me to him and said, 'Let's have a hug,' and he gave me a big bear hug. That was wonderful, just wonderful.

"But even afterwards, I never got any closer to my family. I did finally go and see my sisters. They were polite, you know, but I knew they didn't—they couldn't—want me in their lives. What was there between us? Our lives had been too different. I think I can understand theirs, but they cannot possibly understand mine. They have their families, their children. Too much time has gone by and we are strangers. I do wish it wasn't so, but it is.

"A week after my mother's death, I went to her flat on my own. I sat there, waiting, I don't know what for. Not a visitation, not voices . . . I just sat, looked around, it was empty, there was just the chair; I think

I was hoping, waiting for an imaginary pat on the head ... something like a 'well done,' but nothing came ... I was hoping, oh, I just wanted ..."
—she put her hand on her stomach—"... to *feel* and then I thought, 'Oh, shit. You come to me. You came into my home, played at grandma, and then you go away and die the first time you had been a normal person around me ...

"And then Jim rang and said come home, and I nodded, 'Yes, I will.' "

It was because Betty's "book" had disappeared that Mary thought her mother had killed herself—or perhaps just let herself die. "She was never, never without that book," Mary said. "Everybody scavenged about but it wasn't there. And if it wasn't there, she had destroyed it. And she wouldn't have destroyed it if she was going to go on living."

While everybody had been looking for it, the day after Betty's death, Mary had opened one of her mother's drawers. "And it was full of letters from me to her," she said. "They began 'Dear mam,' and 'Dear dear mam,' and I had written none of them."

Conclusion

I believe Mary Bell's childhood experiences, as you have read about them here, to be the key to the tragedy that happened in Scotswood in 1968. I believe too that, if properly investigated, comparable childhood traumas will be found in the background to most similar cases wherever they have occurred, in Britain, in Europe, or in America. I further believe that children below twelve years of age do not necessarily have the same understanding as adults of good and bad, of truth or untruth, and certainly of death. I think that the primary responsibility for the behavior and the actions of young children lies with their parents, their carers, and, to a degree, their teachers. This is not meant to provide an excuse or an out for children who commit violent crimes: even if they really don't know the degree of the wrong they have done, *they always know that they have done wrong*. And so, while they need to be helped at once to understand this "degree," they also need quite quickly to be punished, for cause and effect is the way of the world and they have to learn it. If I write this, it is not because I am either indulgent or tough, but because—as is so often forgotten—we are speaking of children, not of miniature adults.

I believe, with many other people in the UK and other countries, that in a civilized society children under fourteen should be dealt with by a formal authority if they commit crimes but cannot be held *criminally* responsible and most certainly should not be tried in an adult court or by a jury.

As I said in my preface, my purpose in undertaking this book was manifold. Although Mary Bell's story, with its many tragic elements, can justify a book, my purpose went beyond that. It was as I said, to *use* Mary and her life.

It was to show how such a terrible story comes about, with all the many flaws it uncovers—primarily within the family but also within the community: from the fact that relatives, closing ranks against outsiders, tend to protect their own, unmindful or unaware of the consequences; that neighbors close their ears to manifestly serious troubles next door; that overextended police officers underrate the potential dangers in conflicts between parent and child and almost invariably side with the parent against the child (unless children, on the rare occasions that they do so, complain of sexual abuse); that social workers protect their relationship with parents at the expense of children; and that overworked primary-school teachers are seriously undertrained in the detection of disturbance in their charges. In the Anglo-Saxon world, we are not just discreet, we make a fetish of privacy. We do not look carefully at our neighbors' children. Above all, we do not listen to them; we do not—forgive me for repeating it yet again—hear their cries.

Fundamental to my determination to write this book was the interest I conceived in that small girl I watched in that Newcastle courtroom thirty years ago and my unease about her then and in the years that followed. It was the first time that I had seen children being tried in an adult court and I found it shocking. And, while horrified for the parents of the two little victims, I found shocking too the blind anger, the irrational fear, and the curiously mindless revulsion about her I sensed both in the court and outside it. As I have said in the preceding pages, I was not unfamiliar with evil: I had seen its effect in children I cared for in DP camps in Germany at the end of World War II and had met it head-on when watching, and listening to, the accused in war crimes trials there twenty-two years later—a year before sitting in that court in Newcastle.

There, in that small girl, I sensed not evil but some kind of deep and hidden distress. But the ceremonial court, with its red-robed judge and bewigged advocates, was not equipped, capable, or required to deal with a child who, above all else, had to protect her mother's awful secrets.

In Britain, we have repeatedly put children through this process of adult courts in the past thirty years. Since the trial of Mary Bell, there have been four others of children who killed children (whose names were not made public) and two more where the names were disclosed. There was also the appalling recent case of an eleven-year-old and three ten-year-old boys accused of raping a nine-year-old girl in their school lavatory, who were tried (and then acquitted) at the Old Bailey—a shaming experience for all who attended, whichever way one looks at it.

But although Britain has an ever-increasing number of cases of serious crime committed by children and, as we have seen, is particularly bad at dealing with them, the British are not alone in this. As I have pointed out, juvenile crime in America, including many cases of rape and murder, has become an epidemic and American states cannot, as is the case for local, that is, county authorities in Britain, call on assistance from neighboring states with better resources. The result is that in the majority of cases where juvenile care facilities do not exist, children and adolescents who are found guilty of having committed serious offenses are sent to jail. But western European countries with the most progressive child care systems, such as Holland, Sweden, Norway, Germany, and France, are also experiencing an unprecedented number of crimes committed by children, among them a number of young children who have killed other children.

There is, of course, a difference between the meteoric rise in Britain, America, and the rest of Europe of serious juvenile crimes, such as rape and robbery with force, and the still comparatively rare instances of young children committing murder. There is also a difference between young children who kill and may not know what they are doing and older teenagers who manifestly do. There is another important difference between the not-infrequent act of children killing a sibling, a parent, or a familiar adult because of anger, jealousy, or fear and those rarest and most baffling cases of a child of any age killing a stranger, worst of all, a younger child.

As Mary's story so graphically demonstrates, these latter cases are almost certainly due to a long buildup of pressures that finally brings the child to a breaking point. But their increased frequency may not be unconnected to developments in society.

The uncertainties of our moral and—yes—spiritual values have caused a fracture in the bulwark of security with which earlier generations protected children from growing up prematurely. Far too few parents now accept the necessity for children to grow up slowly, nor do they realize their own pivotal importance to the development, which only they can nurture, of the child's self-image. It is, I think—and the story you have read illustrates this clearly—the interference with the creation or, worse still, the corruption or destruction of this self-image in the early years of childhood that plants the seeds of serious troubles.

But there is more for us to ponder: the ruthless competitiveness of our time drives most of us adults to discipline ourselves into ever-increasing efforts, but we do not discipline our children. We are afraid of them. Their apparent self-assurance (more often than not only a cover for their needs) baffles us. To compensate for the resultant gap in understanding, we surround them with material advantages, but we cannot give them, and do not have the energy to offer them, much more of ourselves than our occasional half-comatose presence in an armchair in front of the television.

I do not wish to join the chorus of condemnation of television, which for all of us has become a part of life. But what should concern us is that in millions of homes for millions of children it has come to represent not just the only acceptable food for their minds but also the only occasion for family "togetherness." Much more than the disturbing numbing reaction produced by a surfeit of visual violence, a radical change such as this in family life is bound to affect all children, even if only subconsciously. Arguably, it could even be this isolation from their closest adults that drives so many of the young to seek ideals within groups and gangs, and elation and bravery through drugs.

The expansion in juvenile crime is such that in many American states cases of serious crimes committed by children as young as thirteen are now automatically transferred to adult courts and children are sent to prison at younger and younger ages. In the United States the age of criminal responsibility varies (between states) from eleven to fourteen; in some American states juveniles can be and are sentenced to death at sixteen. Even the most welfare-minded countries in Europe are considering the retrograde step of lowering the age of criminal responsibility. Only the Scandinavian countries have so far held to fifteen as the age at which criminal responsibility begins; in Germany it is fourteen, in France thirteen, and in Holland twelve, though in all these countries children are as yet primarily dealt with by youth authorities and rarely end up in adult courts. In Ontario, where the law is particularly punitive toward juveniles, children become criminally responsible at twelve and are widely dealt with as adults.

This is not an appropriate place to analyze further the causes of this global increase in juvenile crime, but it is appalling to think that other countries are tempted to adopt the three worst aspects of British justice, which has otherwise been an example to the rest of the world: criminal responsibility in England as of the age of ten (in Scotland as of eight); children who commit serious crimes tried in adult courts; and juveniles, certainly as of sixteen (but lately in some cases of girls, for whom there are no other provisions, at fifteen), sent to prison. In the administration of justice for children it is in Britain that children have fared worst, and it is Britain that now stands so accused before the European Commission for Human Rights. What are we to do?

I would urge the adoption in Britain, Europe, and the US of what might be called a new children's charter. It should begin with the long-delayed appointment of a minister or secretary for children and the establishment of departments in every local authority devoted solely to children. But this is of course not enough: funds need to be made available and facilities set up for intensive training or retraining in child psychology and the pathology of parent-child relationships both for social workers wishing to specialize in children and for teachers in elementary and junior high schools.

The government, through this newly appointed minister for

children, needs to encourage and support increased discipline in schools and find new ways of dealing with truancy. Here again, different approaches have to be used for different age groups. For example, however difficult it is and whatever measures might be required to enforce it, parents *must* continue to be held responsible for the regular attendance of their children at elementary and secondary schools (as indeed, following European examples, they are already being made responsible if their children commit misdemeanors). But it is unreasonable to hope that juveniles over fifteen who are habitual truants would now suddenly accept parental control. Quite different ways have to be found, not primarily to control but to provide educational or training alternatives for young people who, perhaps even as of fourteen, simply do not want to be in school.

What it all comes down to is that individual responsibility needs to be imposed on adults and nurtured in the young. The principal way to accomplish this is to give the individual child or young person a say in his or her life, an awareness that we are going to treat children as individuals rather than as thorns in the flesh of teachers and social workers. Instead of presuming that children or young persons who conspicuously misbehave want to be bad, we need first to confront them with the question "Why?" and work with them until it is answered. As we can see in Mary Bell's story, none of this happened then, nor is indeed happening now: none of these questions are asked, the parents are automatically believed, and the child is brushed aside. These measures and many others arising out of them *can* bring about changes, if not in this generation of older adolescents, certainly in the younger ones.

I would suggest, in fact, that in our world now, young men and women between eighteen and twenty-one who can vote and marry, no longer consider themselves emotionally and psychologically as juveniles and neither should we—or the courts. So while I suggest long-overdue changes in the legal system as it addresses serious crime committed by children from ten to fourteen and fourteen to sixteen, I am harder on the older groups: I think that juveniles of seventeen and eighteen and young adults from eighteen to twenty-one who commit serious crimes *at those ages* should be judged and punished as adults. For this purpose, their cases would continue to be heard in adult courts. The young offenders' institutions—there is still a serious deficiency in such provisions for girls—should be reserved for juveniles between sixteen and eighteen in order to distance them from the influence of older offenders. Anyone above eighteen should go to prison, and anyone below fifteen must be considered, tried, judged, and sentenced as a child.

The cases I have quoted here have caused many people in the legal, medical, and penal communities to rethink the way our present system deals with children who kill or commit serious crimes. In the UK in 1996, a working party of six experts, members of the legal reform group Justice, produced a report entitled "Children and Homicide" on procedures for juveniles in murder and manslaughter cases, which included among its recommendations that the age of criminal responsibility be re-examined with a view to raising it (possibly to fourteen); that children under the age of fourteen not be liable to public trial in adult courts; that their cases be heard before a specially convened panel of a judge and two magistrates with relevant experience and training, without a jury; that the mandatory sentence of detention for ten- to eighteen-year-olds convicted of murder be abolished; that children found guilty of homicide be detained in a secure unit or young offenders' institution and not then automatically moved to an adult prison.

These recommendations very much echo my own views. However, I have additional proposals.

In Britain, defendants aged ten to seventeen who are tried in youth courts are provided with considerable protection: proceedings are not open to the public, defendants' names cannot be disclosed, and reporting is restricted. These courts do not deal, though, with cases of serious crime or homicide. It is with regard to this group—whose cases under the present system are judged in adult courts—that I propose the setting up, in conjunction with the existing youth courts, of a new kind of Children's Criminal Court. For the bench of this court (very much like the specially convened panel suggested by the authors of the Justice report) the Lord Chancellor would appoint a senior judge and two to five magistrates with special knowledge and training.

Under the existing system in Britain and in most American states, childhood experiences and possible explanations for the crime are not considered relevant in a trial. But I suggest that the function of this Children's Criminal Court should be to ascertain not only whether or not the child committed the act but if so *why*. It is fundamental to this understanding that the court should be fully informed of young defendants' childhood experiences and their entire family dynamics before a trial begins.

I therefore propose that as soon as a child is arrested and charged, the magistrates of this new court would immediately order a thorough investigation by the social services into the child's background (as is normal procedure in all the European countries I have mentioned) and would recommend the child be placed for the period of remand into a psychiatrically oriented children's facility where he or she could be observed and the reports submitted to the court. Such a provision does not exist at present, not in Britain or the US, because anything except the most cursory psychiatric examination of an accused child is considered to carry a risk of adulterating the evidence. There is the additional fear that young defendants who talk to a psychiatrist for any purpose other than his or her opinion as to their ability to differentiate right from wrong might lose their already much-disputed right to silence; moreover, as psychiatrists and therapists in these instances are not protected by confidentiality as lawyers are and might be called as witnesses by the prosecution, children might incriminate themselves before being tried in court.

Although I am aware of these risks, my experience with Mary and other children has convinced me that putting such children into a quasi-punitive facility during many months of remand is prejudicial and that it is essential for the court—if it is to render informed judgment, to have comprehensive social and psychiatric reports at its disposal before trial.

Contrary, however, to the informality that has been adopted by most

European juvenile courts, the Children's Criminal Court I propose should retain a considerable element of formality. I am making a special point of this because I think it is important for children that the appearance of the court underline the gravity of the occasion. Experience in France has shown that too much informality risks minimizing the crime and society's condemnation of it in the child's mind. "I think," said Marcel Lelong, a French juvenile magistrate, "judges should wear their black robes and the advocates, too, should be formally attired. It emphasizes for the child the solemnity of the occasion."

At the time of the trial, the usual judicial procedure would be followed, with a prosecutor to present the case and the accused child defended by a lawyer. But the procedure in Children's Criminal Court would be different in two major respects: first, the accused child would have the support of a new officer of the court, a children's advocate who, particularly interested in this aspect of working both with the courts and with children, would be recruited from either the social or the legal services and trained in child psychology and legal procedure. Providing the child with what one might call a friend in court, he or she would remain in contact with the child throughout the trial, supplying the child with explanations and giving support when necessary, and could be called upon to speak on the child's behalf.

Second, as in the inquisitorial system of continental Europe, children would not be cross-examined and, making the process both easier and more comprehensible to them, would be addressed and questioned only by the judge. The adversarial system would be maintained by the prosecutor and the defense counsel arguing the case between each other and with the judge. With regard to detention, I would add that any special unit such children would be sent to—which should ideally adopt many of the best qualities of Red Bank—would be "special" not only in its provision of security but in the training of its staff, in its therapeutic orientation, and in the ready availability of psychiatric consultation and, when necessary, treatment for the children. What is also an essential part of any treatment children receive, however, is that their parents are worked with simultaneously.

The denial of the importance of childhood experiences in the management of severely disturbed children (as was officially stated prior to Mary Bell's arrival at Red Bank) is not only unintelligent but represents an ideological rather than a protective or compassionate attitude. And to leave children who have gone through the trauma of committing serious and often horrific crimes without the opportunity to confront what they have done seems to me synonymous with "cruel and unusual" punishment.

It might seem that in all of this discussion I have forgotten the families of the victims of these crimes. It is not so. As I have said repeatedly throughout the book, they have been constantly on my mind. I know that their deep wish must have been never to have to relive the memory of those dreadful days, indeed never to hear the name of Mary Bell again. But while I have been writing, I have kept wondering whether somehow, superhumanly, these families who saw themselves so appallingly robbed of their children could come to understand my purpose and find some crumb of solace in that understanding. I think most of us now accept that Mary Bell was not a "murderer"; she was a severely damaged child whom no one helped. No evil was felt, no evil intended: only a child's ultimate despair led to this tragedy.

Mary knows her guilt is permanent. Nothing can remove it, nothing can allay her sadness for what she has done. But her dream—a modest one, I feel—is to work, to study, to live in peace with her family, to be allowed, as she puts it, "to be normal." As I have said, she allows herself no mitigation, and in her despair for an answer has repeatedly said, "There are many unhappy, very disturbed kids out there who don't end up robbing families of their children."

This is of course true. It is true, too, however, that we still do not understand the determining stimulus for the "breaking point" in children who kill or commit serious crimes, and which for Mary came one day before her eleventh birthday. What we do know now, what Mary's agonizing recollections have shown us, is that once that breaking point is reached, the child has no way of suppressing it.

There are many people in our society who dismiss children such as Mary as "evil" and with that both condemn them and absolve themselves of any responsibility for their fate. But if Mary's story is to serve any purpose, it must help us to change that attitude, must help us to change the future—for the sake of all our children.

Postscript

S ince those terrible months in 1968 when, nine weeks apart, the two little boys died at Mary's hand, she has committed no offense nor any violent act for which she would be liable under the law. And although living for many years now in a state of devastating and, she knows, inexpiable remorse, she has managed to sustain a long and stable relationship with a caring man and bring up an exceptionally well balanced and happy child. But all these positive aspects of Mary Bell's horrendous life, as it turned out, counted for nothing with the British media, which—even the best of them being increasingly populist—have long been engaged in an ever more bitter circulation war.

As a rule, children sentenced to detention in Britain (and indeed the US) are intended to disappear into anonymity: care or prison personnel are under obligation not to discuss them with outsiders or divulge their whereabouts. This excellent rule, although it certainly applied to Mary Bell, never worked in her case because, as we have seen, her mother used every opportunity to sell sensationalist stories to the local and national press. The result was not only that Mary's difficult imprisonment was immeasurably worsened, but that the tabloids and popular magazines, both British and foreign, were continuously kept aware of her.

The media pursuit began in earnest in 1979, when journalists learned of Mary's transfer to an open prison and her assignment to the outside-prison work program. Over the next sixteen years, however, she not only rejected every one of the many monetary offers for her story—some of them in six figures—but moved house, time and again, even to other areas of the country, in an effort to protect the anonymity of her small family, above all her child. Consistently supported by sympathetic probation officers and unprecedentedly strong injunctions against media interference with her family's anonymity issued by the Official Solicitor, who held the guardianship over Mary's child since her birth, the protection in fact worked until April 1998.

On April 19, three weeks before the British publication of *Cries Unheard* and before anyone had read the book, two of Britain's most reputable newspapers, *The Observer* and *The Guardian*, without disclosing their source or checking their facts with either the publishers or me, broke the informal embargo that had thus far been respected by all the media and revealed the subject of the book. They also reported that Mary Bell had received money from me. As I wrote earlier, the book could not have been written without Mary—she was thus entirely entitled to a share in the author's rewards. This was a morally decisive point for me, and legally we were in the clear. For while a Proceeds of Crime Act in Britain makes it illegal for criminals to profit from their crimes (by writing or collaborating in writings about them), this applies only to offenses committed within six years prior to publication. In any case, surely no one, I had thought, could think of that eleven-year-old child as a criminal in the accepted sense of the term, as an adult child-killer. Not only had Mary been convicted not of murder but of manslaughter because of diminished reponsibility, and not only was this book about her whole life and the consequences rather than the acts of her crimes, but also thirty years had gone by since those two terrible days. It turned out that I had thought wrongly. The book's subject and the issue of payment unleashed an unprecedented paroxysm of tabloid wrath against Mary, me, and the unknown book, which by June 2, when the hysteria began to subside, had produced 181 front-page and editorial articles, many of them pages long. An unfortunate comment by Prime Minister Tony Blair, visibly caught unawares by a TV reporter (that he "couldn't think it could be right" for people who had committed serious crimes to receive money for a story about their crimes), was reported in headlines, as was an equally off-the-cuff reaction by the home secretary Jack Straw, who then, as a result of tabloid pressure, announced he would hold an inquiry into the origins of the book.

Thus began a competition of tabloid vilification of Mary Bell, with daily screaming headlines about the "child killer" and "evil monster" who was being paid "for her collaboration" on the "story of her crimes" and a no less acrimonious debate about my methods and motives. By the end of the first week my house was under siege by the media and faxes and telephone calls began to come in from family and friends in America, Sweden, Austria, and the UK saying they were receiving calls from strangers in London asking what they knew about Mary Bell and what their connection was with me. Thus I learned that my telephone records had been bought by the tabloids, no doubt in an effort to discover Mary's whereabouts.

On April 29, ten days into the scandal, they found her. At ten-thirty that night dozens of reporters and photographers surrounded the small house Mary and her family had moved into only a week earlier. She had made the down payment with the money I had given her; she would use the rest of it, she'd told me, to buy furniture and curtains. It would take time to set the house up; her partner, Jim, who by then had a good job, would build whatever bookshelves, tables, and closets they needed. ("We already bought the wood, nice wood," she said.) By August, she thought, it would all be ready. "By that time the book, you know," she said, always slightly stammering when she mentioned the book's publication, which by now she feared, "it'll all be over by then, won't it?" When she gave me the new address on April 17 she said, "I'm just so excited, so happy . . . At last, you know, a home."

On that awful evening of April 29, reporters, knocking on doors along the street, asked the residents, none of whom had even met their new neighbors, whether they knew that a killer had moved in next door.

"Did you know that when your children go to school they pass the house of a monster?" people reported being asked. Mary and Jim had the child's room fully furnished and their new three-piece living-room set, but as yet there were no lamps or curtains. When the banging on the front door began and gesticulating hands and faces were pressed against the windows with photographers' strobe lights flashing across the living room, Mary pulled the child into the kitchen, where they huddled on the floor. Mary had desperately wished to protect her little girl until she was mature enough to deal with the knowledge of her mother's past (mistakenly, I thought, as I had told Mary before we started working together), and so the child knew nothing. Mary tried to pretend it was all a mistake. She even laughed, she told me later, and—an almost unimaginable thought—sent Jim out for pizza.

But four hours later, with the media mob still in place and raging, the pretense had to stop. Police and probation officers, covering Mary and the little girl with blankets, removed them from their home and drove them to a place of safety. "What was it all about, Mum?" the little girl asked in the car, and the probation officer said that now Mary had to tell her, so, crying and near collapse, she did. "I knew there was a secret," the child said. "But Mum, why didn't you tell me? You were just a kid, younger than I am now." And they hugged each other. Out of the mouths of babes.

Following the furor, the Official Solicitor issued a further injunction, unique in British legal history, forbidding anyone to approach or from any distance photograph or film Mary's family, friends, neighbors, carers, or the child's school, and Mary and the child have been given mobile alarm units that will bring the police to their side within minutes.

The tabloids justify their sensationalist treatment of serious issues by claiming that they are merely reflecting their readers' opinions and feelings. But as we can clearly see from this case, this is not true. The popular British media's prediction was that Mary's child's life would be ruined by the manner in which she found out about her mother's past, and that the very existence of *Cries Unheard* and the public's reaction to it would drive the family into hiding.

The truth is very different: the child is relieved that there is no longer any secret. Moreover, at fourteen she understood at once that the acts of a small child, however terrible they were, can only be seen in the context of childhood: she, after all, has known her mother as an adult for fourteen years, and she knows the difference between Mary, the child, and her mother, the adult.

As for the public, Mary and her family have over the past year benefited from both the decency of the people entrusted with their care—the police, the probation service, and the child's school—and the compassion of their neighbors. They have not heard one cruel or angry word in the area where they have settled and chosen to stay. Offered the option by the authorities of a new identity and a move to any place they liked in the United Kingdom, Mary didn't hesitate one moment. "I'm not letting anybody drive us out," she told me later. "It's time for us to face reality and live with it."

The media assault on Mary could have ended in tragedy: a breakup of the family; the mother's emotional collapse; the child's psychological breakdown. If none of this happened, it was primarily because of Mary's character and the strength of the bonds she has created. But that would not have been enough had it not been for the kindness of the authorities in charge and the public. They have proved right this book's core premise that human beings are essentially born good.

MARY BELL: DOCUMENTS

"We murder" notes (see page 79)
"I murder SO That I may come back"

fuch of we murder watch out Fanny and FAggot

"*fuch of we murder watch out Fanny and FAggot*"

"WE did murder Martain brown, fuckof you BAstArd"

"YOU ArE micey y BecuaSe we murderd Martain GO Brown
you BEttER Look out THErE arE MurdErs aBout
By FANNYAND and auld Faggot you srcews"

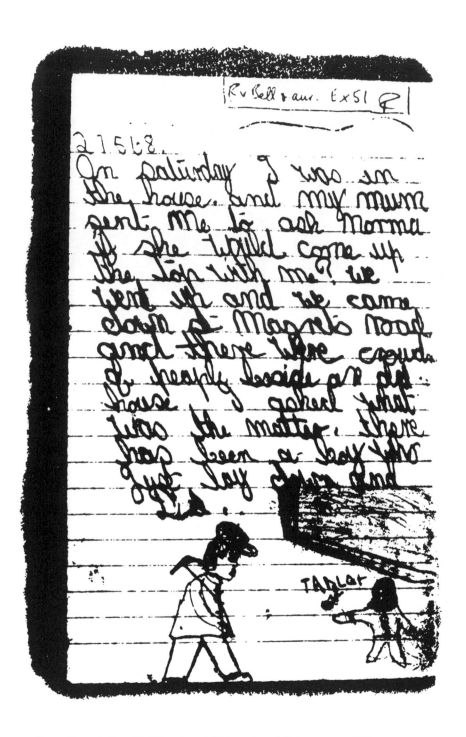

Page from Mary Bell's school "Newsbook" (see page 73)

On saturday I was in
the house and my mum
sent me to ask Norma
if she would come up
the top with me? we
went up and we came
down ot Magrets road
and there were crowds
of people beside an old
house   I asked what
was the matter. there
has been a boy who
just lay down and
Died.

Mysterious letter believed until now to have been from Mary Bell to her mother, spring 1970, but now known to have been written by her mother to herself (see page 172)

MAM
I know that in my heart
From you once was not apart
My love for you grows
More each day.
When you visit me mam
Id weep once, your away
I look into your, eyes. So Blue and
theyre very sad, you try to be very
cheery But I know you think Im Bad so Bad
though I really dont know. If you
feel the same,
and treat it as a silly game.
A child who has made criminal fame
Please mam put my tiny mind at ease
tell Judge and Jury on your knees
they will LISTEN to your cry of PLEAS
THE GUILTY ONE IS you not me.
I sorry IT HAS TO BE this way
Well both cry and you will go away
to other gates were you are free
locked up in prison cells,
Your famley are wee.
these last words I speak, on behalf
of dad P . . . and me
tell them you are guilty
Please, so then mam, Ill be free, Daughter

                                    May